PALMYRA
VILLAGE

GANARGUA CREEK

CANAL STREET

ERIE CANAL

REET

VIENNA ROAD

CHURCH STREET

MARKET STREET

PALMYRA
TOWNSHIP

BEAR
HILL

WAYNE CO.

OLD
HARP

ONTARIO CO.

E
FARM

MINERS
HILL

CANANDAIGUA RO

ARMINGTON ROAD

MANCHESTER
TOWNSHIP

GOLD BIBLE
HILL

THE
WORK
AND THE
GLORY
Pillar of Light

Main Street, Palmyra Village

VOLUME 1

THE

WORK
AND THE
GLORY

Pillar of Light
A HISTORICAL NOVEL

Gerald N. Lund

BOOKCRAFT
Salt Lake City, Utah

THE WORK AND THE GLORY

Volume 1: Pillar of Light
Volume 2: Like a Fire Is Burning
Volume 3: Truth Will Prevail
Volume 4: Thy Gold to Refine
Volume 5: A Season of Joy
Volume 6: Praise to the Man
Volume 7: No Unhallowed Hand
Volume 8: So Great a Cause
Volume 9: All Is Well

First printing in hardbound 1990
First printing in trade paperbound 2001
First printing in paperbound 2004

Visit us at deseretbook.com

Library of Congress Catalog Card Number: 90-83215

ISBN-10 0-88494-770-X (hardbound)
ISBN-13 978-0-88494-770-7 (hardbound)
ISBN 1-57345-870-8 (trade paperbound)
ISBN 1-59038-363-X (paperbound)

Printed in the United States of America
Edwards Brothers Inc., Ann Arbor, MI

30   29   28   27

For behold, this is my work and my glory—to bring to pass the immortality and eternal life of man.

—Moses 1:39

Preface

While Caesar Augustus strutted briefly across the stage of history, thinking that it was somehow he who ruled the world, a humble carpenter named Joseph from Nazareth and a virgin named Mary made their way to a quiet village nestled in the limestone hills of Judea. No royal trumpeters heralded the event which followed. There were no purple robes or crown jewels, no messengers sent racing through the night to announce the coming of the King of kings. Shepherds were told of the Lord's advent, as were the Magi from the East, but for the most part the world slumbered on, oblivious to the fact that on this night the whole of all eternity was being changed.

In similar fashion, eighteen centuries later, events that would leave the world forever altered began to quietly unfold, unnoticed by the millions across the world who toiled on or slept. After all, what was there to note? A young boy, living in an obscure township in upstate New York, simply walked into a grove of trees. But in that grove, soon to be called sacred, God the Father appeared with his Beloved Son.

Latter-day Saints believe this event constituted the opening of the times which would prepare the world for the return of the Savior. It began in the spring of 1820. Soon would follow a succession of heavenly messengers and revelations. But for all its significance, this new age was not launched with pomp and governmental splendor. It began simply, with a young boy, not yet fifteen years of age, who walked across the fields next to his house hoping to find out which of all the churches was right.

Pillar of Light (volume 1 of *The Work and the Glory*) tells the story of the Restoration; but it does more than that. Hundreds of carefully researched and well-written books tell the history of the Church. *Pillar of Light* sets about to tell another story.

In Judea, shepherds were the first to know of the birth of the Savior—not the rich, not the famous, not the great to whom the world paid homage, just simple shepherds. In America, the Restoration followed a similar pattern. The story was first told in one-room cabins and along country roads, not in presidential palaces or the halls of Congress. It was farmers and their frontier wives who first heard of Joseph's vision and picked up the challenge to accept it and carry its message forth to the world.

How did these simple, honest people react? What did they think? How did they feel? The answers to these questions are not easy. Joseph Smith was like a great stone in a river, splitting the waters that come against it. Some who came in contact with him burned with testimony, others burned with fury. Some were so moved that they forsook all—families, farms, and, in some cases, their lives. Others were so moved to scorn and hatred that in some instances they resorted to murder. It is this story—the story of individuals and families pushed up against a man and his claims to heavenly revelation—that this novel tells.

Many modern Latter-day Saints are second- and third- and, in some cases, sixth- and seventh-generation Mormons. Belief in the Restoration is as natural to them as speaking their native language. But many have quietly wondered, "If I had been living back then, how would I have reacted? What would I have done? Would I have believed?" *Pillar of Light* is an attempt to help them explore those questions in their hearts.

And there are many non-Mormons who wonder at us. They know little more than that Mormons once practiced plural marriage and that we engender considerable animosity from some of the mainstream Christian churches of the day. What is it that Latter-day Saints believe? Why do they hold Joseph Smith in such high esteem? Are they Christian or not? Why do they speak of prophets and Apostles and continuing revelation? *Pillar of Light* is an attempt to answer those questions without seeking to proselyte or defend. It simply tells the story from the point of view of one who believes Joseph Smith was all that he claimed to be.

Pillar of Light is a fictional work. The medium of fiction was chosen so that the personal dimension—the individual impact of the Restoration on people—could be explored. But in another sense, it is *not* fictional. It tells, as accurately as possible, the story of Joseph Smith and the rise of The Church of Jesus Christ of Latter-day Saints.

This dual nature of the work has presented some interesting challenges in the writing process. The Steed family is completely fictional, though they are patterned after real people of those times. In the novel they intermingle and interact with real people and are placed in real events, and the reader may thus wonder from time to time, How much is historical and how much is fictional? Without burdening the book down with innumerable footnotes, that is not an easy question to answer. But perhaps the following explanation will be helpful.

As far as the people in the novel are concerned, the character description sheet (pages xiii–xiv) indicates which are fictional characters and which are not. When it comes to the events, every effort has been made to portray the historical setting and circumstances as accurately as possible. Sometimes fictional license had to be used, not to change events, but to have the fictional family participate in those events. Furthermore, sometimes there is simply not enough detail given in the historical sources to sustain the story line of a novel. Here some embellishment was required, but again, maintaining harmony with the historical records has been a compelling concern.

An example may help to illustrate how these problems were dealt with: In his description of the events surrounding the organization of the Church on 6 April 1830, Joseph Smith gave considerable detail about what took place in the Peter Whitmer cabin. We know he and Oliver presided and that Joseph conducted. The sacrament was passed, and there was a baptismal service afterwards at which Joseph's parents, Martin Harris, and others were baptized. As much as possible, the novel follows those events exactly as Joseph described them. Obviously, having the Steeds present to participate in those events is an example of literary license. Also, when it came to actually describing who offered the sacramental prayers, Joseph gave no information. To skip that detail in the novel would have broken the flow of the narration. Since Joseph and Oliver were presiding at the meeting, it seemed the best guess that they offered the prayers.

No list of sources used in writing the novel is provided herein. For those who wish to read more on the history of the Church, I recommend *Church History in the Fulness of Times*, prepared by the Church Educational System of The Church of Jesus Christ of Latter-day Saints and available at LDS distribution centers or LDS bookstores. It is a highly readable and well-researched one-volume history of the Church, and has more than adequate bibliographic references for those who wish a more in-depth study.

Pillar of Light is the first volume in a series titled *The Work and the Glory*. In future volumes readers will follow the Steed family as the Church moves to Ohio and Missouri, as they are driven to Illinois and eventually to the Rocky Mountains. Zion's Camp, the Kirtland apostasy, the horrors of the Missouri persecutions, and the move to Nauvoo will all have a continuing impact on the family. New generations of Steeds will face the exodus across the plains to the Great Basin, the colonization period, and the plural marriage years. Benjamin and Mary Ann's grandchildren and great-grandchildren will continue right up to the last decade of the twentieth century, entering a new era for the Church and facing new challenges as Latter-day Saints.

Today over seven million Latter-day Saints are found throughout the world. Each has to decide for himself how he will respond to the legacy of Joseph Smith that is part of Church membership. Each year an army of some forty thousand missionaries in nearly a hundred countries tells and retells the story of Joseph Smith to hundreds of thousands of nonmembers. *Pillar of Light* begins the story of the Steed family, who—through a chance decision to move to Palmyra, New

York, in the fall of 1826—encounter Joseph Smith and the events of the Restoration. While the Steeds are fictional, the choices they faced, the emotions and conflicts generated by that encounter with Joseph are not fictional—not for them, and not for their children and their children's children.

In the spring of 1820, Joseph Smith went into a grove of trees and emerged bearing witness that he had seen, in a pillar of light, the Father and the Son. To everyone who hears that story, whether at mother's knee or sitting across the table from two young men with short haircuts and missionary name tags, the question is essentially the same as that faced by the Steeds in 1827: *What will be my response to Joseph Smith and his story of a pillar of light?*

Clearly a project of this size and scope involves the talents and efforts of many people, and it is appropriate that they receive recognition, though that recognition can never be commensurate with the significance of their individual contributions.

Foremost, thanks belong to Kenneth Ingalls Moe and his wife, Jane. It was "Kim" who first fired me with his dream of telling the story of the Restoration in fictional form so that readers could feel more intensely its reality and the personal drama that comes with it. His commitment to the project has never lagged. His support—financial, emotional, and spiritual—has been unfailing. His suggestions have been thoughtful, full of insight, and have brought a dimension to the project that would have otherwise been lacking and sorely missed. It can honestly be said that were it not for Kim and Jane, there would be no *Pillar of Light* today. How can one offer adequate thanks for that kind of contribution?

My wife, Lynn, has been now, for almost three decades, not only my eternal companion but also "an help meet" in the fullest sense of that expression. She is always the first to read the manuscript, and I have tremendous confidence in her sense of when it is working and what needs to be done to improve it.

Along with Kim, her vision of this project and its potential has been one of the sustaining forces in bringing it to fruition.

To the numerous others also go my deepest thanks: To Deena Nay, for her invaluable help in setting up files, indexing, cataloging, and computerizing the manuscript. For Frederick "Rick" Huchel, who provided a unique combination of editing and research talents; his meticulous and impeccable research is felt throughout the book. Calvin Stephens, whom I consider to be one of the finest historians in the Church, read the final manuscript and corrected several important details. The staff at Bookcraft were a pleasure to work with, for they were as excited and enthusiastic about the project as was the author: Russell Orton and Cory Maxwell gave their immediate and total commitment to the series; Garry Garff struck that difficult balance which always faces editors—adjusting and polishing the work without imposing his own style or preferences upon it; Jana Erickson is responsible for the overall design and feel of the book, a final but lasting contribution to the finished work.

Finally, while we recognize that the Lord needs no recognition, both Kim and I have felt his continuing presence and help in this project. If there be any praise or honor due, let it be to the Father and the Son, for when all is said and done, it is their work and their glory that is described herein. Our hope is that they find it an acceptable offering of thanks to them.

GERALD N. LUND

Bountiful, Utah
July 1990

Characters of Note in the Novel

The Steed Family

Benjamin, the father.
Mary Ann Morgan, the mother.
Joshua, the oldest son; about twenty as the novel begins.
Nathan, two years younger than Joshua.
Melissa, oldest surviving daughter; sixteen.
Rebecca, "Becca" to the family; age nine.
Matthew, youngest child; six as the story opens.

The McBrides

Josiah, Lydia's father and owner of a dry goods store.
Hannah Lovina Hurlburt, Lydia's mother.
Lydia, eighteen and the only child of her parents.
Bea Johnson, Lydia's favorite aunt.

The Smiths

*Joseph, Sr., the father.
*Lucy Mack, the mother.
*Hyrum, the oldest surviving son; age twenty-seven as the book begins.
*Joseph, Jr., age twenty-one as the novel opens.
*Emma Hale, Joseph's wife.
*Samuel Harrison, about nineteen as the story opens.
*The other Smith children—Sophronia, William, Catherine, Don Carlos, and Lucy—are mentioned but play no major role in this volume.

*Designates actual people from Church history.

Others

Mark Cooper, cousin to the Murdocks.

*Oliver Cowdery, associate of Joseph Smith's; local school master.

*Martin Harris, gentleman farmer from Palmyra.

*Joseph Knight, well-to-do farmer from the Colesville New York, area.

Will Murdock, rowdy from Palmyra.

David Murdock, Will's brother.

Jessica Roundy, saloon keeper's daughter in Indepen dence, Missouri.

*Josiah Stowell ("Stoal" in some historical sources), well to-do farmer from the Colesville, New York, area.

*David Whitmer, friend of Oliver Cowdery's from Fayette, New York.

*Peter Whitmer, Sr., and other members of the Whitmer family are mentioned but play no major role in this volume.

*Designates actual people from Church history.

The Benjamin Steed Family

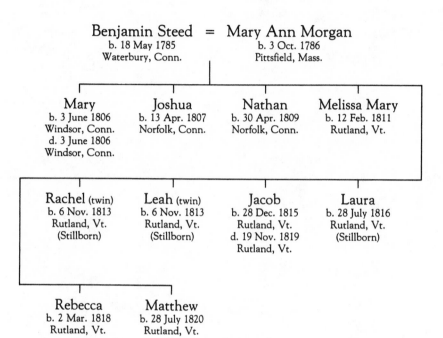

Benjamin Steed = Mary Ann Morgan
b. 18 May 1785   b. 3 Oct. 1786
Waterbury, Conn.   Pittsfield, Mass.

Mary
b. 3 June 1806
Windsor, Conn.
d. 3 June 1806
Windsor, Conn.

Joshua
b. 13 Apr. 1807
Norfolk, Conn.

Nathan
b. 30 Apr. 1809
Norfolk, Conn.

Melissa Mary
b. 12 Feb. 1811
Rutland, Vt.

Rachel (twin)
b. 6 Nov. 1813
Rutland, Vt.
(Stillborn)

Leah (twin)
b. 6 Nov. 1813
Rutland, Vt.
(Stillborn)

Jacob
b. 28 Dec. 1815
Rutland, Vt.
d. 19 Nov. 1819
Rutland, Vt.

Laura
b. 28 July 1816
Rutland, Vt.
(Stillborn)

Rebecca
b. 2 Mar. 1818
Rutland, Vt.

Matthew
b. 28 July 1820
Rutland, Vt.

Pillar *of* Light

Just at this moment . . . I saw a pillar of light exactly over my head, above the brightness of the sun, which descended gradually until it fell upon me. It no sooner appeared than I found myself delivered from the enemy which held me bound.

—Joseph Smith–History 1:16–17

It was a frosty morning this early March day in 1827, and Matthew Steed could feel the chill permeating the cabin. His father, up half an hour earlier, had laid a new fire in the great stone fireplace below—he could hear the faint crackling of the logs and smell the wood smoke—but it would be another hour before the heat penetrated through the cabin and up into the attic loft.

Matthew burrowed more deeply into the "quilt tent" he had made to trap the warmth of his body and breath. The room was mostly dark, but the first light of morning was coming through the four glass panes mounted in the eastern wall of the cabin. At six, Matthew didn't yet fully appreciate the value of having a "glass window." The glass industry was still in its infancy, and glass was rare enough that a house with more than ten glass panes was levied a special tax. Most cabin owners, especially out on the frontier, covered their windows with inexpensive oil paper, or occasionally with glass bottles cemented side by side to form a glass wall. Though the bottle windows were strong enough to withstand arrows or even a bullet, the dark green bottles let in little light. These four panes had been a gift from Grandpa Morgan to Matthew's mother on the day she had married Benjamin Steed. Such a valued possession was not left behind when a family changed homes, and when the Steed family moved from Vermont to western New York the previous fall, the panes came with them.

The hand-poured squares were filled with waves and bubbles of varied sizes and shapes which distorted the light in the most wondrous ways. It didn't take much for a six-year-old's imagination to transform the wavy images into living things. Now, for instance, the swaying branches outside—still without their leaves—became a circle of Indians in a frenzied war dance. Then almost instantly they transformed themselves into serpents of every imaginable shape, raising up to stand on their tails, all the better to strike at the closest victim.

With a little shudder, Matthew pulled the "tent" over his head, hiding the towhead of hair and the beetle-bright eyes. He stretched out his toes, reaching for the square block of soapstone his father had taken from the fire the previous night. Each family member had his own block which was wrapped in cloth and put at the foot of his bed under the covers. But that had been almost twelve hours ago, and the soapstone was nearly cold. For a moment he was tempted to drift off to sleep again, but he knew he'd be foolish to do that. His father had already called up to him once. If it happened again, Matthew would get an extra chore.

A noise below him caused his eyes to fly open. The Steed cabin, built hastily the previous fall before cold weather set in, consisted of one large, open room on the main floor. This served as kitchen, eating area, parlor, and as the main living space for the family. One corner contained a large brass bed. This was screened off at night and served as a bedroom for his parents. Near the west wall, stairs led to a second floor. This contained two bedrooms, only partially separated by a partition, where Matthew's brothers and sisters slept. A notched log ladder just in front of the partition led up to the small attic loft which belonged solely to Matthew.

He pulled the covers back, peeking out, then instantly groaned. Rebecca, his nine-year-old sister, was clambering out of her bed, clothes clutched under one arm, tugging her nightshirt down with the other hand.

"Becca! I get to dress first."

She looked up, startled for a moment, then shook her head, tousled hair bobbing, and darted for the stairs.

"Becca!"

But she was gone, and he knew he had lost his chance to beat her to the fireplace. During the cold months, no one wanted to change clothes in the chill of his bedroom, so a small fabric screen was placed in front of the fireplace to provide some privacy for dressing. Not only did it trap a little of the heat from the fire but it also allowed one to stand on the hearthstone, still warm from the previous day's fire, and feel the heat through the heavy woolen socks. He sank back. He would wait until Becca was finished.

Below him, Matthew heard the cabin door open. "Matthew, are you up yet?"

He sat bolt upright. "Yes, Mama. I'm coming."

The door shut again. With a sigh worthy of a grown man, Matthew groped under the covers at the foot of his bed. The night before he had neatly folded his cotton shirt and homespun trousers and placed them near his feet so they would be warm come morning. He jammed them under his nightshirt, then found his high-topped shoes and tucked them under one arm. Taking a quick breath, steeling himself, he exploded from his "tent." Down the log ladder, past the partition, down the stairs, and out of the cabin door. He ran as fast as his short, six-year-old legs could move, determined to do as Pa always said, "Run so fast the cold can't catch you."

He bounded across the frozen dirt, little puffs of breath trailing behind him. Inside the barn, he paused only for a moment to assess the situation. The mules were already gone, but Old Boss, the milk cow, was lying in her stall, lazily chewing her cud.

"Come on, Bossie," he shouted, darting in to grab at her halter. "Move!" With a low moo of protest, she lumbered to her feet. Leaning against the softness of her chest, Matthew pushed her backward. "Move, Old Boss!"

Good naturedly she backed out of the stall. Careful of where he stepped, Matthew moved instantly to stand on the matted straw where she had been lying. The results were immediate. The warmth from the big body seeped through his socks and spread across the bottoms of his feet. It also filled the air around him. With a little shiver of relief, Matthew shucked off his nightshirt and began to dress.

Melissa Mary Steed, oldest surviving daughter of Benjamin and Mary Ann Morgan Steed, smiled as she watched her youngest brother dash across the yard and into the barn. It was she who had first taught Matthew where to find a warm dressing place on a cold morning. She had learned it from her mother, who had in turn learned it from her grandfather. And so the generations went on. A sudden wave of sadness swept over her. The generations went on, but no longer in Vermont. She had loved the hill country and rich mountain valleys south of Rutland. In summer the green was rich enough to hurt your eyes, and in fall the blaze of reds, yellows, and oranges almost took the breath away.

The Steed homestead had been one of the finest farms around. There had been a fine frame home with a dining room, parlor, and spacious kitchen. Her father had even run a pipe in from the spring so they could lift a sluice gate and have the water come right into the large slate sink. The village was less than half a mile away, and with the prosperous circumstances the Steeds were in, Melissa and her mother had been regular customers in the several dry goods stores which the village boasted. There had also been more than one young man around, watching this fifteen-year-old girl who had suddenly blossomed into womanhood.

Then all had changed. Reports of the rich wheat land of western New York had touched some wanderlust in her father. Almost before the children were aware, the homestead was sold, and her father was off in midsummer to look for land in some township called Palmyra. A month later, with nineteen-year-old Joshua and seventeen-year-old Nathan acting as the men of the family, the Steeds packed up their belongings and headed west to join their father.

Melissa sighed, looking around. She could still remember the sick feeling that hit her as she looked out on the stand of virgin forest and heard her father's pronouncement that this would be their new home. The surrounding farms were rich and prosperous looking, but the acres of trees, with only an occasional clearing or small meadow, which constituted their property seemed formidable beyond belief.

Grudgingly she admitted they had made significant progress since then. They had chosen a small meadow area near the creek with a small spring. Additional trees had been cleared, a cabin-raising with all the neighbors held. Next had come a small barn and a forge. Palmyra Village, only about a mile or so south of their new home, had three fine blacksmith shops, but like many other farmers who had been raised in the colonial era, Benjamin Steed made and repaired most of his own tools, and so a small forge on the homestead was a must.

Last had come the icehouse, with its double-thick walls of stone and mud. With the essentials completed, everything else was held in abeyance as the main task of clearing the land began. Clearing forest to make farmland was serious, back-breaking work, and Melissa understood its urgency. Come this planting season, if they didn't have enough acreage cleared, there would be serious consequences the following winter.

But what it meant for Melissa was no time off, and no trips to the village. Actually, Palmyra was considerably larger than Rutland, with more than a dozen general stores, four dress shops, and even two hat shops. Her father or one of her older brothers went in occasionally for supplies, but there was too much to be done at the farm for the family to go too. Berries had to be picked and dried, venison cut into strips and smoked, the huge blocks of ice—cut from Lake Canandaigua and hauled in by the teamsters—laid beneath thick layers of straw so they would last through the next summer. There was wood to be cut and stacked for winter. The dirt floor of the cabin needed to be smoothed, rolled, and tamped with logs, making it hard enough to see them through until winter snows stopped the field work and time could be devoted to cutting the wood planks.

Sighing once again, Melissa turned back to the quern. Here was another source of frustration for her. In Vermont her father had built a waterwheel on the creek and they had their own gristmill. Her parents kept assuring her a gristmill was part of their plans for the future, but in the meantime they didn't want to spend what surplus cash they had saved from the sale of the farm to purchase cornmeal and wheat flour from town. So grinding meal at the quern became Melissa's daily morning task.

The quern was a simple device. A hollow barrel, about three feet high and two feet across, provided the base of the quern. The first, or lower, millstone was attached permanently on the top of the barrel. The upper millstone was placed upon it and left free to turn. To make it functional, the upper stone had two holes cut into the rock. The first, near the outer perimeter, was only deep enough to provide a place for the quern stick, or handle, for turning the stone. A larger hole, in the exact center of the stone, was cut clear through. Here the corn was poured. As the upper stone was turned around and around, the corn was pulled between the two stones and ground into meal. The circular motion would also push the meal outward so it would fall into the barrel. The barrel had a hole on one side near the bottom so the meal could be collected.

The thing which made the quern different from a simple hand mill held between the legs was that the quern stick was about five feet long and inserted into an overhead beam that projected outward from the side of the barn. This not only allowed the person to stand while grinding the grain, but with the quern stick inserted into the overhead beam it also provided a swivel, greatly increasing the leverage and therefore simplifying the work.

But Melissa was aware of none of those refinements. All she knew was she hated her time at the quern. It seemed the perfect representation of her life. Round and round, grinding, grating. Just three weeks ago she had had her sixteenth birthday. Some girls she knew were married and had their first child by the time they were sixteen. And yet here she sat. The young men who had showed interest were now several hundred miles to the east. And with the demands of forging a homestead from the wilderness she had been allowed a trip into the village only twice in the six months since their arrival in western New York. Twice!

She gave the quern stick a hard twist, sending the stone flying even faster. She knew time was still on her side, but at the rate things were progressing here, she would be nineteen or twenty before she could turn around, and then . . . She shuddered slightly, unable to bring herself to say the horrible words. What girl in America was not filled with foreboding and dread at the thoughts of perpetual maidenhood?

Glumly she reached down for the leather pouch and poured more corn into the hole of the upper millstone. Pull. Pull. Pull. The kernels were sucked between the heavy stones. The grating sound dropped in pitch. And the shapeless mass of cornmeal fell into the barrel.

As a girl, Mary Ann Morgan had always hated the prospects of making soap. She had never quite mastered the knack of collecting the wood ashes and pouring hot water over them to get the necessary potash without getting herself and her clothes filthy black and reeking of smoke in the process. And the smell of the animal fats, melting in the large kettle over the fire, always left her feeling faintly sick. The resulting soap—strong, harsh, reeking of the rancid smell of lard—no longer seemed worth the effort it took. Not now that ready-made soap was available.

By 1805, when she had become the young bride of Benjamin Steed, soap manufacturing was getting its first hold in America. Budding entrepreneurs would collect the animal fats from the various farms, then after making it into soap, pour it into large wooden frames and let it harden. They would then cut it into bars and peddle it from door to door. That had ended Mary Ann's soap making career right then and there.

She smiled fondly, remembering when a Yankee peddler named B. T. Babbitt had started to make soap cakes of uniform size and wrap them in paper. It had been an electrifying development, and Mary Ann had been one of the first in the township to buy them. The other women had at first refused, thinking they were paying extra for the paper. Finally Babbitt had started printing the word *coupon* on each paper and then redeemed them for other merchandise. But Mary Ann had no such reservations. Somehow he had managed to make a milder soap without the strong odor of animal fat. Even if it meant paying a premium, it was worth it to her.

The smile faded. Then Benjamin had announced he was selling the farm and they were moving west. Though there had been a cash surplus, it had to be carefully hoarded to see them through until the first crops could be sold. And for the first time in twenty years or so, Mary Ann was back to making her own soap. Like her daughter, Mary Ann had also felt dismay at Benjamin's announcement they were leaving Vermont. In spite of its harsh winters, she loved the area, and she had made many friends up and down the valley. It also meant leaving a farm which represented years of toil. The stories of fantastically fertile ground and wheat crops of staggering yields had taken less than a week to turn Benjamin's heart. Within a month the farm was sold and her husband was on his way to scout for land in the western part of the state of New York. She sighed, and turned back to the fire.

Benjamin had built her a rack—two forked sticks with a stout hickory branch between the two—to hold the heavy black kettle now filled with potash water and the fat from the pig they had butchered the previous day. The water had a thin skim of ice over it, and there were crystals on the lard as well. She had hoped leaving the sticky mass out in the cold air over-night might take away some of its smell, but the moment she had laid the fire and got it going well the odor had started to rise again. She was only grateful she had chosen a spot down-wind of the house. Holding her nose, she took the wooden paddle and pushed the fat deeper into the water.

Matthew exited from the barn, still tucking one end of his shirt into his pants. He saw her and changed directions. "Good morning, Mama."

"Mornin', Matthew. How are you this morning?"

He shivered a little. "Still cold."

"You should be. Out here without a coat. You'd better get back in the house."

He peered into the kettle. "Can I do that, Mama?"

"You don't have a coat."

"If I get one, can I stir the soap?"

She looked at him closely, then smiled. He wasn't really daft; he just had the bubbling exuberance and poor sense of smell common to most six-year-olds. With a nod, she smiled again. "Get your coat. I need to start breakfast anyway."

By ten o'clock the overcast had burnt off and the sun was starting to dissipate the ground mist, leaving the air softly dif-fused and muting the starkness of the leafless trees and under-growth. Off to the left, somewhere nearby, the raucous chatter of a gray squirrel carried clearly through the woodland. A raven answered with his impudent cawing.

But Benjamin Steed had neither eyes for the beauty of the morning nor ears for its sounds. He made one final adjustment to the logging chain wound twice round the thickness of the hickory stump. Satisfied it would bite deep into the bark and not jerk free, he stepped back, then clambered out of the three-foot trench they had dug around the stump. Joshua, his oldest son, watched from the edge of the hole.

Benjamin turned to Nathan, his second son, who was standing at the head of the two mules, waiting for the signal. He nodded. "Go."

"Hee yaw!" Nathan cried, yanking the halters forward sharply. "Giddyap, mules!"

The well-matched team hit the end of the traces at precisely the same instant, and the singletrees cracked like the slap of thunder across the rolling hills. For a century or more the old hickory tree had sent its roots deep into the soil of western New York. The previous fall its towering mass had finally succumbed to the ax and saw as the Steeds had cut it down for lumber and firewood—one cord of hickory produced as much heat as three cords of maple or four cords of white pine. But the stump was not about to surrender so easily. It barely quivered as the chain gouged into the bark. The mules snorted with the strain, hooves carving great scars in the moist ground, the veins standing out on the sleek dampness of their necks.

Benjamin leaped into the hole and threw his shoulder into the stump. Joshua was instantly by his side, clawing his fingers into the muddy dirt beneath one of the thick roots and heaving upward. There was a soft screech of tortured metal. Joshua jerked up. A few inches in front of his nose, one of the heavy links of the chain was pulling open.

"Watch out!"

He hurled himself at his father, knocking him aside. There was a sharp snap, then a lightning blur. Almost too quick for the brain to register, Benjamin felt a whistle of air pass his ear and a hard tug at his shirt. There was another loud crack. A young birch tree at the edge of the hole toppled slowly and fell to the ground, its three-inch trunk shattered as if from a blow from some mighty sledgehammer.

With the snap of the chain, suddenly there was nothing holding the mules back. They plunged forward, the off animal going down to its knees and nearly dragging the other one down with it. Nathan was jerked violently, and almost went under the flashing hooves, but he hung on, backpedaling furiously to stay clear. "Ho, mules!" he screamed. "Ho!"

The mules pulled up, forelegs trembling, eyes rolling, clouds of steam exploding from their flaring nostrils.

In the hole, Benjamin pulled himself to his feet slowly, holding his ribs where Joshua's body had slammed into him. He stared at the stump. It hadn't budged so much as an inch. Then he lifted his eyes to gaze at the shattered trunk of the birch tree. The chain now lay alongside it, unmoving, belying the deadly force which had driven it only moments before.

He turned to Joshua. His oldest son was staring at his father's shirttail. Slowly, eyes wide, he reached out and touched it. Benjamin looked down and felt a sudden lurch in his stomach. A fist-sized hole had been torn from the shirt. The fabric was cut as cleanly as though done with a tailor's shears.

Benjamin gaped at the shirt, then once more at the stub of the birch tree. *If I had been two inches closer . . .* He leaned back against the soft dirt and took a deep breath.

"You all right, Pa?" Nathan stood looking down at them, still breathing hard from his own near miss with the mules.

Benjamin nodded slowly, finally letting his shirttail drop. "Yes." He dropped to his knees, staring at the white slash where the chain had barked the stump before it snapped, trying not to think about how close he had come to disaster. Finally he turned to Joshua. "Thanks, son."

In spite of the coolness of the air, Joshua was now perspiring heavily, the sweat running in tiny rivulets from the heavy thatch of dark hair that poked out here and there from beneath his flannel cap. He stared at his father for several moments, then just nodded, looking away.

Above them, Nathan was moving slowly around the hole, sizing up the stump. "We're gonna have to go deeper, cut more of the roots."

Benjamin looked up, faintly pleased. In typical fashion, and in contrast to his older brother, Nathan always moved on quickly, looking for solutions instead of dwelling on the problems. No one was hurt, and so Nathan had already focused again on the task at hand.

Benjamin stood, brushing the dirt from the back of his pants. "Ain't nothin' gonna happen without a good logging chain." He looked down at his oldest son. "Josh, take the mules back to the barn, then saddle one up and take the chain into the blacksmith. That will be faster than trying to fire up the forge and do it ourselves. Nathan and I will try to get under this thing and see what's holding her down."

Joshua didn't turn.

Benjamin leaned forward a little. "You hear me, son?"

Still he didn't move, but Benjamin could see his son's lips had compressed into a tight line. Then he understood. "You got somethin' to say, boy?" he said quietly.

Now Joshua turned to face him. "Yeah, I got somethin' to say. We've spent more than half a day on this stump. All of yesterday afternoon, now this morning. It ain't budged one inch. I say we leave it and get on with clearing the land."

Benjamin's jaw tightened a little. True, most farmers did just that. They cut down the trees and undergrowth, dragged the resulting brush into piles, and left them until they were dry enough to burn. Smaller stumps were taken out, but the big ones were simply left in place and the land plowed around them until they rotted away. But Benjamin Steed was not just another farmer. Born in 1785 to a revolutionary war veteran, Benjamin had been deeply infused with the idea that the new struggle—and one in which Benjamin's generation could participate—was the struggle to tame the newly won land. And land pockmarked with stumps was not part of Benjamin's vision of the new America.

He took a quick breath, determined to hold his temper in check. "We've been over this already, Joshua. The stump comes out. Now go get the chain fixed."

Joshua reached out and flipped the torn shirttail. "You was nearly killed, Pa," he said quietly. "I say it stays."

Benjamin straightened slowly, but Joshua stood his ground, glaring back at him. Nathan hopped down into the hole, stepping between them, facing his brother. "Look, Josh," he said, keeping his voice easy. "Ain't gonna do no good to argue about this one. The hole is already dug. It's got to come out. Pa and I will have it ready by the time you get back from the village."

For a moment Joshua glared at his brother, then finally shook his head, muttering in disgust. Without looking at his father, he climbed out of the hole. He drug the heavy chain back over and hooked it up behind the mules, his face still twisted with anger. He snapped the reins and moved off behind them.

If Benjamin saw, he gave no sign. He just stared across the field at Joshua's receding figure. Finally, with a bitter sigh, he turned, picked up the shovel, and confronted the stump once more. Nathan fell to work beside him.

Benjamin Steed was tall, almost six feet, and solidly built, but most people did not think of him as a particularly big man. His bone structure was lean, and the few pounds he had put on over the winter had quickly melted away once they had started clearing the forest again. His features were finely cut, albeit with a nose slightly out of proportion to his mouth. His eyes were pale blue, almost lighter than the sky when he smiled, but darkening quickly when he was angry. That was not often, for Benjamin was fourth generation New England stock and had been born and bred to hold his emotions in check. That was what infuriated him most about his deteriorating relationship with Joshua. Normally he was slow to anger, deliberate in his choice of words, taciturn sometimes to a fault. But lately Joshua had a gift for overturning his father's determination to stay in control.

He stopped, leaning on his shovel, letting his eyes run across the land that was now his. The soil where they had recently cleared the underbrush lay dark and rich, waiting for the seed they would soon plow into it. He estimated they now had nearly thirty acres cleared—more than his entire farm in Vermont—with that much again and more yet to go. He loved it and reveled in the pleasure it gave him to be taming it.

This was the Finger Lakes region of New York, so named by the Seneca Indians, who just fifty years previously had been part of the mighty Iroquois confederation of nations. Lakes Canandaigua, Keuka, Seneca, Cayuga, Owasco, Skaneateles, Oneida—all were set in long, narrow valleys, as though the Great Spirit had dug his fingers into the soft earth and gouged out places for the clear blue water to fill. It was wonderful country, rich with promise. And from the moment Benjamin had laid eyes on this place, he had known it was to be his. Now with six months of work into his particular corner of it, those feelings had only deepened. In a few years their farm in Vermont would pale in comparison, and then his family would understand why he had come.

Fifteen minutes later a shout from across a small meadow brought Benjamin's and Nathan's heads up together. Benjamin took off his hat and mopped at his brow with a rag from his back pocket. His face softened, the eyes crinkling around the corners. His youngest son was coming on the dead run, the big, rawboned, half-breed dog loping alongside him, tongue lolling crazily out one side of his mouth. Further behind, he could see the figure of his wife, following in the track Matthew and the dog had made across the brown grass, wet now from where the frost had melted. She was carrying a pitcher and two tin cups.

He tossed the shovel out and climbed out of the hole, knowing what had brought about this unexpected visit to the fields. His wife would have seen Joshua come in, and whether or not she had talked with him, she would know there had been trouble between him and his father again. This was her way of assessing the damage, seeing if there was anything to be done to repair it. "Looks like it's time to take a break," Benjamin said.

"Mama always knows when it's time," Nathan said with a grin. He likewise tossed his shovel out, taking his father's outstretched hand for a pull up.

"Pa! Did you get it out yet?" Matthew was calling to them even before he was close enough to see the stump still in place. He pulled up with a frown as his father shook his head. The dog stopped alongside Matthew, took a quick disinterested look into the hole, sniffed briefly at the shovels, then bolted into the trees to see what might be waiting to be stirred up.

Looking very much like a miniature Nathan, Matthew walked around the periphery of the hole, soberly sizing up the situation. "Looks like you've got the biggest roots, Pa," he said soberly. Then nodding, sure of his assessment, he added, "Can I chop that root there, Pa?"

Mary Ann came up in time to hear the question, and shot her husband a sharp look. But Benjamin was already shaking his head. "Not quite ready for that yet, Matthew."

Nathan looked at his father. "There's a lot more dirt to come out of the hole before we can chop the root," he said, his face grave. "But I'm too tuckered to do any more right now."

Benjamin nodded, equally sober. "Me too. I'm plumb bushed."

"I'll do it," yelled Matthew. He grinned up at his father, knowing he was being teased, but not caring. Benjamin smiled again, his eyes clearly reflecting the pride he felt for his youngest offspring, then pointed to the shovel. With a whoop Matthew was into the pit and stabbing awkwardly at the soil around the roots of the hickory stump, barely able to manipulate the length of the shovel in the confined space.

"Still haven't got it out?" Mary Ann stopped next to her husband and peered down at what was left of the huge old hickory tree.

Benjamin wiped at his forehead with his sleeve and shook his head. "It's hangin' on to the earth like a baby possum to its mama's belly."

Mary Ann just nodded, biting back a comment. She had loved the giant old tree and had suggested way back last fall that they just clear around it and leave it be. But Benjamin had grumbled about nothing growing in its shade and having to plow around it all the time, and the issue was eventually dropped.

She lifted the pitcher. "I brought some cold buttermilk."

Without waiting for an answer, she set the cups on a nearby log and poured, then stepped back as husband and son picked them up and began to drink. She smiled, her eyes softening with affection. Benjamin drank his steadily, the pale blue eyes shaded by heavy dark brows, completely lost in thought as he surveyed the land over the top of his cup. Mary Ann wasn't even sure he tasted the sweetness of the buttermilk. For a moment she compared him to Joshua. Her oldest son, now almost twenty, was so like her husband in the lean hardness of his body, the angular features, the mouth perpetually set in what appeared to others as grim determination. If he were here, she knew without doubt he would down the milk in three gulps, his prominent Adam's apple bobbing up and down with each swallow. Then with what would almost be a groan of pleasure he would hold out his cup for a refill.

This mental image dramatized the differences between her husband and son as well as any words could have done. Though strikingly similar in physical appearance, their temperaments couldn't have been much further apart. Joshua went at life like it was some kind of contest of pulling sticks or leg wrestling. He hurled himself at it with frightening intensity, battering at it, trying to pull it off balance enough so he could make it his. On the other hand, Benjamin Steed viewed any overt show of emotion as though it were indicative of some inner flaw. His approach to life was more like that of a careful builder. You selected your materials with care, then simply put things in their proper order, moving methodically from one task to another until the structure was complete.

Mary Ann's eyes narrowed slightly. The clashes between the father and son were happening with increasing frequency. Joshua would no longer back down from his father's unbending will. In fact, it seemed almost like he sought opportunity to butt heads, relishing the chance to validate something deep within himself.

Mary Ann sighed. If they had stayed in Vermont, Joshua would almost have certainly gone on to marry the Mendenhall girl and start his own household. She knew instinctively it would have solved the problem between Joshua and his father. But Faith Mendenhall had been just one of the other things they had left behind in Vermont.

The lines of concern pulling at the corners of her mouth and eyes slowly disappeared as Mary Ann turned to watch Nathan. He was sipping at his cup, holding it with both hands, savoring the cool sweetness of the buttermilk as he savored most experiences in life. As lean as his brother, but with a softer cut to him, Nathan was more the product of Mary Ann's side of the family. Sometimes when she looked at him, tears came to her eyes. She knew this must be very close to what her own father must have looked like at almost eighteen years of age. And Nathan had the same gentle temperament as her father, the same quick smile, the same sensitivity to people.

Benjamin straightened and handed the cup to his wife, pulling her out of her thoughts. "All right, Matthew, that really helped. Let Nathan and me get back in there."

With a sigh, half of disappointment, half of relief, Matthew leaned the shovel against the stump and climbed out of the hole. But as he straightened he suddenly cried out, pointing across the field toward the house. "Look, Pa, somebody's comin'."

They all turned to peer toward the cabin. There was a buckboard out front. A man was returning to it from the house, accompanied by Melissa and Rebecca. The man stopped for a moment to see that the horse was tied securely, then started across the fields toward them.

"I think it's Martin Harris, Pa." Nathan had lifted one arm to shade his eyes.

Benjamin nodded, recognizing the well-dressed figure and the purposeful stride. They waited, not speaking, as their nearest neighbor moved toward them. The acreage purchased by Benjamin Steed lay directly northwest of the Martin Harris farm, or more accurately, one of the Martin Harris farms. He actually owned four different farms of eighty acres each. When Benjamin first came to Palmyra and heard about the acreage north of town, he stopped at the Harris home to inquire about it. He had been impressed. It was a clapboard home of generous proportions with a well-kept yard and farm buildings. Benjamin had liked the man immediately. Evidently the feeling was reciprocal, for Harris had gone out of his way to assist Benjamin with the details of the sale.

As he strode up, Harris swept off his hat and bowed slightly to Mary Ann. "Mornin', Mrs. Steed." As was customary for him, he was well dressed in a long jacket with tails, linen shirt, vest, and trousers. The hat was beaver skin and well made. He wore a gold ring on one finger, and a watch chain dangled from the pocket of his vest. In his mid-forties, he was not a particularly tall man, only about five feet eight inches. But he was of medium build and of a narrow face, and this, coupled with the long, tailored coat, made him seem taller than he was. He wore a neatly trimmed beard, Greek style, running from sideburn to sideburn underneath the chin, but leaving the face and the front of his chin completely clean shaven. He had clear blue eyes, high cheekbones, and a sharply defined nose, straight and pointed. At first impression he seemed to be stern and cheerless, but the impression was quickly dispelled once he started to converse, for he was of a pleasant and affable nature.

Mary Ann nodded and smiled in return to his greeting. He put the hat back on and shook hands firmly with Nathan. "Mornin', Nate." With soberness he did the same with Matthew. "And how is young Master Steed?"

Matthew beamed. "I'm fine, Mr. Harris. Thank you for askin'."

Finally Harris turned to Benjamin and gripped his hand. "Good morning, Ben."

"Hello, Martin."

Harris turned back to Mary Ann. "Mrs. Harris sent over a jar of blackberry preserves. I left it at the house."

"Well, how nice of her. Please give her our thanks."

"I will." He turned back to Benjamin. "I stopped by to see if there was any provisions you or your wife might be needing from town. I've got some wheat being ground at the mill."

Mary Ann looked at her husband as he started to shake his head. She spoke up. "There are a few things I'd be needin', Ben."

Harris nodded. "Just tell me what you need."

"Thank you for thinking of us." Collecting the cups and pitcher, she took Matthew's hand. "Come, Matthew. Let's go to the house and make a list."

"I could use some help getting the grain on the wagon," Harris said to Benjamin with half a smile. "If Matthew here and the girls wanted to come with me, I'd be obliged."

Matthew whipped around, his eyes wide. "Oh, could we, Pa? Could we?"

Benjamin hesitated. Mary Ann watched him, then softly said, "It would be good for the girls, Ben."

For a moment their eyes held, then he nodded. Matthew let out a whoop.

Martin Harris laughed softly. "You go along to the house with your mama, Matthew. Tell your sisters to get ready. I'll be along in a few minutes."

The boy was off like a shot, with Mary Ann following after him. For a minute the men stood, watching them go. Then Harris turned and surveyed the stump. "Hickory, huh?"

"Yeah, and not about to let go, either."

Harris nodded. "I can remember with my pa. I thought we was never gonna get the land cleared."

"You'd never tell it now," Nathan said. "You've got some of the finest land in this part of the country."

"Wasn't always so. My father came in '94. Bought six hundred acres for fifty cents an acre. But his problem was he loved huntin' and fishin' too much. Sometimes the farm got neglected."

"Is it true what they say?" Nathan asked. "That he shot the last wolf in the area?"

There was a soft laugh, and Martin nodded. "Everybody used to call him the Nimrod of Palmyra Township." His eyes got a faraway look as he let his mind go back. "They also called him 'Trout Harris.' Back then the land teemed with ducks and geese, deer, elk, wolves, bear. And the fish, ah . . ." He sighed with pleasure. "People talk about the good fishing now, but back then you could almost walk across the creeks on their backs—trout, whitefish, smallmouth bass, even a few Atlantic salmon in Mud Creek."

They all stood quietly for a moment, savoring the memory of better times. Then finally Benjamin looked up at the sky. "Well, living off the land nowadays ain't what it used to be. We don't get enough wheat and corn in this season, it's gonna be a lean winter."

Harris nodded again, then pulled at his lower lip as he looked at Benjamin. "Ever thought about hiring help?"

Benjamin looked surprised.

"Spring's coming hard on us now. You'll be wanting to plant within the month." He stopped, watching Benjamin for a reaction.

He nodded gravely, keenly aware of the implications of what Harris was saying.

"You had some money left over from the sale of the farm, Pa," Nathan said. "I know we've been saving it, but we do need to get more land cleared."

"Know a family a mile or so south of town," Harris went on. "Name of Smith. They've got two boys who hire out doing farm work. I've used them before. Been right pleased with their work."

Benjamin leaned down and plucked off the stem of a dried weed. For several moments he chewed on it silently, looking once again out across the small area they had cleared, then at the stands of trees and brush yet waiting for them. Finally, he turned. "Maybe you're right, Martin. Tell me how to find these boys. I'll go on down there tomorrow and have a talk with them."

$\mathbf{B}$y the second decade of the nineteenth century, Palmyra Village, lying near the western edge of Palmyra Township about twenty miles south of Lake Ontario, had grown from a primitive frontier outpost to a prosperous, bustling town of nearly three thousand people. Much of the growth could be directly attributed to the Erie Canal. Governor DeWitt Clinton's "big ditch"—considered to be America's greatest engineering feat—ran just two blocks north of Main Street and paralleled the entire length of the village. The full three hundred sixty-three miles of the canal had finally been opened just eighteen months before the Steeds had arrived in Palmyra Township. Twenty-eight feet wide at the bottom, forty at the waterline, and carrying four feet of water, the canal represented a project as prodigious as any Egyptian pyramid. But with its completion one could travel from Lake Erie to the Atlantic Ocean without leaving the waterway. The time it took to transport goods from Buffalo to New York City was reduced from twenty days to six, and the cost dropped from a hundred dollars a ton to eight.

Joshua Steed loved the dock area along the canal. So instead of going on to Main Street, he would always turn left just after crossing the waterway and drive along Canal Street. It was a world of its own, sharply separated in many ways from the village life which lay just one block south. There was a constant stream of barges moving both upstream and down. The mule and horse teams plodding slowly along the canal banks kept the boats moving at a steady pace of four miles per hour—as good as any stagecoach on the rough, muddy roads of the time. Surprisingly, the barges were a splash of color meant to assault the eye. Most carried passengers as well as freight, and their captains painted the topsides with the gaudiest shades of reds, greens, and yellows imaginable to attract business.

Most villagers looked down on the canal boatmen, or "canawlers," as they were called, with the utmost disdain and not a little fear. Smoking a tobacco strong enough to choke a goat, driving their animals with language not even found in the barrooms of America, unashamedly fraternizing with the sluttish, hard-looking women who slept with them as part of their jobs as "cooks" on the barges, they would send the genteel women of Palmyra scurrying just at the sight of them.

"Low bridge! Everybody down." The bawling cry of a canawler brought Joshua around. A large boat, hold filled with potash and salt pork, was approaching the bridge he had just crossed. The deck was already lined with the passengers, anxious to be off the boat for a time. This one, coming from the west, was almost certainly from Buffalo, which meant the women and their businessmen-husbands were headed for a visit to Philadelphia or on to New York City. Dressed in their finery, hooped skirts swishing, the women would come mincing down the gangplank, tippy-toeing so as not to step in any of the droppings along the wharf, holding their noses against the smell of the mule, horse, and ox teams backed up with their wagons to either load or unload freight.

Joshua pulled on the reins lightly, turning the mules and the small wagon he was driving to move out of the way of one of the great Conestogas moving toward him, its canvas top looking like a ship's sail. He let his eyes sweep the busy scene. Stevedores, in their sweaty shirts and smoking foul-smelling cigars, manhandled bales of cotton, sacks of grain, and boxes of dry goods on and off the barges. Young boys from the village darted here and there, bringing messages from businessmen in the city, carrying jugs of rum for the dockworkers, or just generally making pests of themselves. It was a constant bedlam of sounds—donkeys braying, dockworkers cursing, heavily laden wagons creaking across the planks, dogs snarling over some discarded scrap of food, wheat brokers shouting at each other for a better price.

Joshua loved it. He loved being in the city, for that's how he thought of Palmyra Village. He knew it was nothing compared to New York or Boston, but he had never been to those cities, and after the quiet hill country of Vermont, Palmyra seemed wonderful enough.

Then, glancing up at the sun, Joshua snapped the reins, moving the mules into a little faster walk. If he was to meet the Smith boys by ten o'clock, he'd better get moving. He had one more stop to make, and there was no way he was going to miss that.

Once on to Main Street, Joshua let his eyes scan both sides of the street, savoring the differences between this part of the village and Canal Street. For the most part, the log huts of earlier times were gone now. One- and two-story frame homes lined the street, with picket fences surrounding neatly tended yards and tall poplars shading the residential properties. In the heart of the village, business thrived. There were now thirteen dry goods stores, three apothecaries, the three-story Eagle Hotel and two other inns, two tailor shops, several saddler and harness shops, a law office, three blacksmith shops, and the print shop and bookstore where the *Wayne Sentinel* was printed each week. Local elementary schools around Palmyra and surrounding townships contributed students to the well-kept grammar school within the village itself. And the Baptists, Presbyterians, and Methodists all had churches in town, as well as the Roman Catholics, who had been one of the first to come west with the settlers.

Joshua stopped in front of a two-story frame building. Over the door was a neatly lettered sign which read, "General Dry Goods Store—Josiah McBride, Proprietor." He swung down, tied the mules to the hitching rail, then stopped. With one sweep of his hand, he took off his cap and jammed it in his back pocket, smoothing his hair back as best he could. With a final tuck of his shirt into his trousers and a quick intake of breath, he went inside. A bell nailed to the inside of the door tinkled softly.

Even though the day was overcast and cold, coming out of its brightness into the dimness of the store left him momentarily blinded, and he stopped next to a large keg filled with nails. He absently ran his fingers through the nails, feeling the sharpness of their points against his flesh. He marveled for a moment. As a young boy he had helped his father make nails in the forge behind their house. Now the large foundries in Boston and New York churned them out by the thousands.

"Good morning. Mr. Steed, isn't it?"

Startled, and with a quick stab of disappointment, Joshua turned around. A short, balding man in a leather apron was peering at him. "Good morning, Mr. McBride. Yes, I'm Joshua Steed."

"What can I do for you?"

"Well . . ." Joshua's mind was racing, trying to find a way to stall. "I've got a list of things, but I need to look over some of your tools first."

McBride nodded. "Help yourself. Tools are on the back wall. When you're ready, let me know."

As he started to turn, Joshua thought of something. "Oh, Mr. McBride."

"Yes."

"Do you happen to know the Smiths that live down on Stafford Road?"

Josiah McBride turned back around very slowly, peering over the top of his glasses at Joshua. "Why do you ask?"

Joshua fumbled a little, surprised at the sudden coldness in the storekeeper's voice. "I . . . uh, my father has hired two of the sons, Hyrum and Joseph. I'm supposed to meet them across the street at ten o'clock. I've never met them before . . ." His voice trailed off, stopped by the look in McBride's eyes.

"Your family's new here." It was not a question, just a blunt declaration.

"Yes." Joshua was wary now.

"That would explain it."

"Explain what?"

But just then the bell tinkled as a woman entered the store. McBride suddenly became all business. "It's none of my affair, but you may want to tell your pa to think about that." With that he spun on his heel and went to greet the woman.

Joshua stood there, bewildered and a little bit angry. What had brought that on? Finally he shrugged it off, moving to the back of the store. He studied the rows of tools hanging from wooden pegs hammered into the wall, moving slowly, taking his time. He felt foolish and awkward, noting the curious looks McBride kept shooting his way from time to time.

Just as he was ready to give it up and bolt for the door, the bell on the door rang softly again. A woman and a young girl entered and exchanged greetings with McBride. The storekeeper turned and called up the stairs. "Mother! Lydia! I need some help down here."

Joshua felt his hopes leap. There was the sound of two sets of footsteps coming down the stairs from the living quarters above the store. The first was heavier, measured and determined, followed almost immediately by a lighter, happier set. He fought the temptation to turn around, feeling a surge of excitement. He took a finely honed ax down and began to examine it closely, hoping against hope.

A woman's voice floated back to him. "Hello, Mrs. Carlton. Hello, Miss Amy. What can I help you with?" Joshua felt his heart beat faster. McBride's wife had taken the new customers.

Joshua ran his finger along the edge of the ax blade, keenly aware of the sound of Lydia's footsteps coming up behind him, then of the soft fragrance of her perfume. Still he didn't turn.

"Why, Mr. Steed."

He set the ax back in its place and turned slowly, unable to suppress the smile of pleasure at seeing her. "Hello, Miss Lydia."

She was considerably shorter than Joshua, and this differ-ence was heightened now because her head was cocked slightly to one side, the dark brown eyes sparkling up at him mischie-vously. She was dressed in a white and blue pinafore dress with puffy sleeves and a shiny black belt which drew the eye to her waist — a waist Joshua could easily surround with his hands and touch fingertip to fingertip. Her ebony hair was pulled back away from her face and fell softly across her shoulders. Her skin glowed like translucent porcelain in the filtered sunlight coming through the store window. People said Lydia McBride was the prettiest girl in the whole of the Finger Lakes region of New York. Joshua had met few single women in the months they had been here, but he had no reason to doubt that judgment.

"How may I help you, Mr. Steed?" It was said with gravity, even as her eyes teased him.

He always felt like a tongue-tied schoolboy in her presence, and now was no different. He fumbled quickly in his pants pocket and drew out the torn piece of foolscap. "Ma has some things she's listed." He thrust it at her. She stood motionless for a moment, leaving him standing there with his hand held out awkwardly toward her. Then finally she took the paper with a soft, husky laugh, letting her fingers brush briefly against his. "Of course," she murmured. "It's always a pleasure to help" — she paused, and looked up again, her eyes demure — "your mother."

Joshua flushed, knowing she was toying with him, but sensing she found pleasure in him or she wouldn't be doing it. Somehow the knowledge emboldened him. "You look right pretty today," he blurted, darting a look to where her father stood behind the counter. He lowered his voice quickly. "Right pretty," he said again.

To his surprise it caught her off guard. She dropped her chin, her cheeks suddenly touched with pink. "Why, thank you, Joshua." She too shot a quick glance at her father, who was now looking at them sharply. Louder now and all business-like, she went on quickly, "If you could get a basket and follow me, Mr. Steed, I'll get these things together for you."

Ten minutes later Joshua came out of the store, a sack of wheat over one shoulder and a jug of maple syrup tucked under his arm. Lydia followed him, carrying a box with the lighter things. He put the stuff in the wagon, then took Lydia's load and put it in as well. "You shouldn't carry that. I would have come back in for it."

She tossed her head impatiently. "I do this all the time." Then she smiled at him. "But thank you anyway."

Joshua took his cap from his back pocket and jammed it on his head, feeling fumble-tongued and awkward again. Suddenly he remembered his primary purpose for coming to town. He swung around to look across the street. Sure enough, a few doors down in front of the Eagle Hotel stood two men. They had turned to watch him and Lydia.

"Do you know those two men over there?" Joshua asked.

Lydia turned to look. There was a soft intake of breath, a quick downturn of her mouth. "Why do you ask?"

"Would it be Hyrum and Joseph Smith?"

"Yes. What do you want with *them?*"

Joshua gave her a sharp look. The last word was spat out with coldness and contempt. It was the same instant reaction he had gotten from her father. A little puzzled, he answered, "Pa has hired them to help us clear the land. I'm supposed to take them out to our place."

"Oh." She dropped her eyes.

He peered at her, but she wouldn't look up at him. Finally, baffled, he turned and raised an arm, calling, "Ho! Hyrum, Joseph. I'm Joshua Steed."

There was a nod, and the two strode quickly across the street toward them. Joshua stepped off the boardwalk and met them halfway. Both were tall men, dressed in working clothes with wide-brim hats. It took no effort to see the two were brothers. One was obviously older—though they were both in their twenties—and a little taller than the other, but both had the same general features, the same light brown hair.

The older one reached Joshua first and stuck out his hand. "Hyrum Smith, Joshua. This is my brother Joseph."

His grip was firm, his smile quick. Joseph stepped forward and also shook his hand. He was more muscular, broader through the shoulders, and two inches shorter than Hyrum. He had the most piercing blue eyes Joshua had ever seen.

"It's good to meet you." Joshua turned and they walked back to his wagon together. Lydia was rearranging the supplies in the back of the wagon. She looked up as Joshua stepped up. "Joseph, Hyrum, this is Miss Lydia McBride. She works here at the store. Lydia, this is Joseph and—"

"We've met," she said, her voice cool. If Joseph noticed her reaction, he gave no sign. He touched his hat and smiled broadly. "Mornin', Miss McBride."

Hyrum nodded, touching the brim of his hat as well. "Miss Lydia. Good to see you again."

Seeming to sense Joshua's probing look, Lydia softened a little, forcing a brief smile. Then she turned back to him. "Well, I must be getting back inside. Good day, Mr. Steed." Finally there was the ghost of a real smile again. "Hope to see you again." She curtsied slightly, then swept back inside the store.

He turned to the Smith brothers. "Well, let's get started. We got trees and brush waiting for us."

"Becca, you're to be helping your sister with the dishes."

Nathan Steed watched his youngest sister with a half smile. At nine, it was easy to be smitten, and Rebecca—Becca to the family—was smitten with the two Smith brothers who had come to work with the Steeds earlier that day. She hung on every word Joseph Smith was saying. The command from her father brought an instant look of dismay and then pleading.

He shook his head firmly. "You too, Matthew. Get the table cleared."

Matthew was sitting next to Joseph, his hand lying comfortably on his new friend's arm. Nathan's mother laughed softly at the sudden pain that appeared on her youngest's face. "Come on, you two. Joseph and Hyrum will be staying the night. There'll be plenty of time to visit."

Joseph gave Matthew a nudge. "You hurry and help your sisters, then maybe we'll go do a stick pull."

Matthew's eyes widened. "Really?"

Joseph nodded soberly. "You look pretty strong to me, but I think maybe, just maybe, I might be able to pull you up." In moments, Matthew was clearing off the dishes with considerable alacrity.

When Benjamin Steed had contracted with the Smiths for day labor, it was for twenty-five cents a day plus the midday and evening meals. Had they lived further away, it would also have included overnight board, for that was the way on the frontier. But the Smith farm was only about a mile south of Palmyra Village, or about two miles from the Steed homestead, so they had opted to go home each night. But with the morning lost in meeting them and getting them to the farm, they had gotten in only half a day's work. Benjamin suggested they stay over and get an early start tomorrow; then he'd pay them a full day's wages for both days. So for this night, at least, they would sleep in the barn.

Nathan smiled to himself as he looked around the room. Visitors were always a welcome diversion in rural areas, and in just one afternoon the Smiths had become a comfortable addition to the family. Part of it lay in Joseph's quick smile and wry sense of humor, and in his warmth with the children. Hyrum was equally likeable, but more quiet, content to let Joseph lead out.

But it was more than just their personalities that won them ready acceptance around the family's hearth. Nathan's father had been pleased with his new help. There was no loafing on the part of these two. Hyrum and Joshua had worked the big two-man saw, felling one tree after another, while Joseph, Nathan, and Benjamin had worked with the axes, trimming the branches off the fallen trees and dragging them into piles for eventual burning. Even though there had been a light, misty rain, they had finished another full acre.

Most surprising was the change in his mother's attitude. When her husband had told her of his decision to hire day labor, she had balked at first. Mary Ann Morgan's father had had eight children—all sons, except for seven daughters! For a man who built turnpikes for a living, it was a bitter disappointment, but he had made the best of it, and quickly his daughters had learned to do men's work. Nathan's mother had grown up with hard work. She had also had more than a little experience with day laborers, not much of it positive. For the most part they were riffraff, foul of mouth and personal habit, and quick to steal. But she had found the two Smith brothers pleasant and intelligent, clean of habit and language. When she learned that both had married in the last few months, any reservations concerning them completely vanished.

"I'm done, Joseph." Matthew had halved the time it normally took him to clear the rough-hewn table. "Can we pull sticks now?"

Mary Ann was at the wooden chest which held the quilt blocks she had been cutting during the afternoon. She turned. "Matthew, you let Joseph and Hyrum be. They've worked hard today."

"It's all right, Mrs. Steed," Joseph said, standing. He ruffled Matthew's hair. "The ground's kind of wet outside. Where we gonna do this?"

Nathan had been waiting for this opportunity. At the earlier mention of stick pulling, he'd sized up the broadness of Joseph's shoulders and the size of his arms. Joseph had him by a good two inches in height and probably outweighed him by twenty or thirty pounds. But that had been sucker's bait before. He smiled innocently. "The barn floor is dry."

Joshua picked up on it instantly. "We could spread a little straw out," he suggested. "There's plenty of room in there." Nathan gave him a quick look, then smiled. Though Joshua could take his younger brother in many things, he had never bested him in stick pulling, and Nathan saw he was only helping him set up Joseph for a contest.

Mary Ann shook her head ruefully. "Joseph, I think someone besides Matthew might be thinking of having a go with you."

Joseph grinned, sizing him up with mock solemnity. "Nathan? Why, I've been pulling brush with him. After an hour he was so tuckered out that I ended up doing most of the work." As Nathan hooted, Joseph became suddenly grave, and looked at Nathan. "You could have a shot at Matthew when I'm done if you'd like."

Nathan snorted. "Ah, so the man's head is swollen, is it? What say, Matthew? Shall we teach these Smiths a little humility?"

Hyrum's hands shot up. "Not me," he laughed. "I know better than to get in on this. Joseph's the champion stick puller of Manchester Township."

"And Nathan bested all comers in the annual harvest fair back in Vermont," Benjamin said, rubbing his hands together. "Let's go to the barn."

"I'm first," Matthew cried, realizing he was about to be supplanted.

"That's right," Joseph said. "Let's get the tough ones out of the way first; then we'll be ready for Nathan."

"Wait for us," Becca cried. She and Melissa were at the narrow table next to the window, which held a large pan filled with dishes. Melissa was pouring steaming water from the fireplace kettle over the dishes.

"Leave the dishes," Benjamin said firmly, taking down his hat from a peg near the door. "Let them soak for a time."

Even Mary Ann's mouth dropped a little. Nothing was

allowed to interfere with chores. She set the quilt blocks down and motioned to her daughters. "You heard your father. Let's go see which of these two big talkers can really deliver."

The rain had stopped and the clouds had cleared, leaving the air crisp and clear. The first of the evening stars winked down at them as they trooped across the yard to the barn, leaving clouds of steam in the air. Benjamin hung the lantern on a nail as Joshua quickly spread a forkful of straw across the floor.

Joshua selected a stout piece of ax handle and handed it to Joseph. "All right, let's start with Matthew."

In a stick pull, the two opponents sit flat on the floor facing each other. The stick is held directly between the two where both can get a good hold on it. The knees are pulled up enough so the soles of both feet can be placed flat against those of the opponent. On a given signal, both contestants begin to pull, the objective being to pull one's opponent to his feet, to pull him out of his original position, or to make him break contact with either hands or feet. With Joseph and Matthew, it was almost comical to watch them line up. Matthew was deadly serious as he stretched his little legs out to their full length. Joseph had to pull his knees up tight under his chin in order to even let Matthew reach the stick. He held on with only one hand.

Joshua stepped forward, trying not to smile. "Ready?"

Matthew was already gritting his teeth in preparation, and merely nodded.

"Ready," Joseph said gravely.

"Pull!" Joshua shouted.

Matthew grunted, and instantly blood rushed to his face as he strained to pull back.

"Oh!" Joseph cried, rocking forward a little. Then he pulled back slightly, lifting Matthew about an inch off his seat. Nathan could see the thin legs start to tremble. But once again Joseph let himself be pulled forward. He moaned and rolled his eyes, as though in pain, but Matthew's eyes had now squeezed shut with the intensity of his effort.

"You're not really trying!" Becca called. Joseph laughed, and then with one steady pull, he leaned back. Matthew came straight up, halfway to a standing position before his grip gave way and he crashed back down. Joseph rolled backwards, ending up on his back as well.

Instantly he swung around to face Matthew as the others applauded. "Whew! You nearly took me there, young man."

Matthew was puffing like a blown horse, but he was also grinning broadly. Joseph punched him softly on the shoulder. "Remind me not to be around when you're about ten years older."

"I'm next," Becca cried, stepping in front of Matthew.

The results were the same, except she started to giggle even as Joshua said ready, and Joseph pulled her right up and over to collapse on top of him. The giggles gave way to squeals for mercy as Joseph grabbed her and began to tickle her under the arms.

Joseph rolled over and sat up, letting her finally escape to her mother. He looked up. "How about you, Melissa?"

At sixteen, Melissa was beyond children's games. She just shook her head, blushing faintly.

Joseph sighed, then shrugged. "I guess that finishes it, then."

He started to rise, but Joshua merely grunted, pushing him back down again. "Not quite," he said. "Let's see how you and Nathan do." He stuck out his other hand. Two pieces of straw were held between the fingers. In stick pulling, the man with his hands on the outside of the stick was thought to have the advantage, so it was customary to draw for hand position.

Joseph shook his head, a mischievous grin pulling at the corners of his mouth. "Why don't we just let Nathan take the outside position. I wouldn't want him left with any excuse when he loses."

"Do it, Nathan," Matthew warned solemnly. "He's really strong."

"Draw your straw, Mister," Nathan said easily. He always loved the confident ones. It was so sweet to make them eat crow.

Joseph reached over and pulled the outside straw. Joshua

swung around and Nathan drew the second one. Nathan's was half an inch shorter. He laughed, a short bark of derision. "I'll take the inside position," he said, sitting down to face Smith. "I wouldn't want to leave you with an excuse, should you lose."

Joseph just chuckled and held out the stick, keeping his hands wide. Nathan put his hands just inside of Joseph's.

Now the bantering stopped. Both men were concentrating on their grip, fingers curling and uncurling. Joshua stepped forward. "Best of three. Ready?"

Their fingers stopped moving, knuckles suddenly tightening down, whitening the flesh. Matthew and Becca inched closer, eyes wide. First Joseph nodded, then Nathan.

"Pull!"

Nathan gasped. For a moment he thought his arms had been yanked out of their sockets, and only when it registered they had not did he also realize his feet had flown free and he had been yanked around to where he sat at a right angle to Joseph.

Joseph laughed softly. "That's one."

The family was hushed. Joshua's mouth had dropped open. Matthew looked shocked. Becca was torn between sorrow for Nathan and joy that Joseph had performed as expected. Melissa and Mary Ann were shaking their heads. It had happened so fast. Benjamin leaned forward. "Come on, Nathan. Watch your grip."

Nathan crawled back around in position, still a little dazed. He spat on his hands, wiped them on his pants, then sat down again. Much more carefully now, he placed his feet against Joseph's, then took the stick. By the unwritten rules of the game, the hand position changed each round, so he took the wide position now.

More subdued now, Joshua again stepped forward. "Ready?"

This time Nathan was ready, but the power of Joseph's initial pull still shocked him, and he felt himself lifted off the ground slightly. He locked his knees, using the tremendous thrust of Joseph's boots against his feet as leverage for his upper torso. The muscles along his jaw stood out like cords, and his biceps pushed at the sleeves of his shirt. It gave him a quick burst of satisfaction to hear Joseph grunt in surprise and rise an inch or two off the ground himself.

"Pull, Nathan! Pull!" Through the pounding of the blood in his head, Nathan wasn't sure who was shouting at him. Matthew certainly. Perhaps his father. Maybe even his mother. His legs started to quiver with the strain, and his arms felt like they were about to snap. He opened his eyes for a moment. Joseph's face was a brilliant scarlet, his teeth were clenched, the muscles along his neck like those of a draft horse.

Nathan grunted, inwardly screaming at his body to give him one more thrust of effort. Then suddenly he felt the stick give a little, coming toward him a fraction of an inch. Joseph's grip was slipping! With an inward cry of triumph he took a quick breath, thirsting for the kill. And in that split second of lost concentration, Joseph yanked back hard. Nathan literally flew upward, almost crashing down on Joseph's legs. His hands ripped free from the stick as Joseph jerked it upward, clear and free.

They lay there for several seconds, both men gulping in huge draughts of air, bodies trembling, sweat pouring down their faces. The Steeds stood silently, staring down in disbelief. Finally, Joseph rolled over, turning just enough so his face looked across at Nathan's. "That's two," he gasped. And he reached out to grasp Nathan's shaking hand.

Benjamin walked over and, taking each one by the hand, pulled them both up. He slapped Nathan on the shoulder, then turned and gave Joseph an appraising look. "Next time we've got one of them hickory stumps to come out, I think we'll just hook you up and spare the mules."

"That's as close as I've come to losing in a long time," Joseph managed between breaths.

Nathan shook his head. "If that's supposed to make me feel better, it ain't working."

Joseph put his arm around him, trying to laugh between his gasping. "Next time, I think I'll stop at Matthew."

J oshua pulled the mules up, stopping the wagon across the street from McBride's dry goods store. He handed the reins to Nathan. "Look, we could save some time if I go in and get the supplies Ma needs while you and Joseph go on down and get the seed."

Nathan guffawed. "Since when were you worried about saving time while you were in town?"

Joseph Smith, who sat on the wagon seat between the two brothers, looked at the younger Steed soberly. "I don't know, Nathan. I understand this Lydia McBride girl is real slow when it comes to waiting on certain customers."

Joshua, who had jumped down from the wagon, looked up sharply, but he couldn't hold it and a sheepish grin stole across his face. "Well, there's no sense all of us going in."

Nathan had gone as serious as Joseph. "Don't know 'bout that. What if Lydia's mother comes out to help you? You might need someone in there to keep her occupied."

Joshua frowned. That hit closer to the truth than he wished. There was always the chance Lydia's father or mother would be working behind the counter. And Lydia's mother was as sour as cider left too long in the cellar, particularly when one Joshua Steed hovered too long around her daughter.

"Tell you what, Nathan," Joseph said, making as if to get down. "I'll take her pa and keep him busy. You hog-tie her mother down. That way Joshua'll get to at least say hello to that young lady he fancies."

Joshua flushed, and waved them off. "I'll get by," he growled.

He shook his head as they laughed and Nathan clucked at the mules. Was his eagerness to see Lydia so transparent? Not that it would change things much if it was. It had been almost three weeks since the day he had come in to get supplies and to meet Joseph and Hyrum and bring them back to the farm. Twice in that time his father had come to the village, leaving the boys to work in the fields. Both times Joshua had volunteered to go in his stead, hinting as broadly as he dared, but as usual his father paid no attention and went himself. But today there was a wagonload of wheat seed to get, and a light rain that morning had left the fields too wet to work. So Hyrum Smith had gone home to work at the Smith farm, and Joshua, Nathan, and Joseph were sent for seed while Benjamin cut planking for the new smokehouse.

Now, as Joshua watched Nathan and Joseph drive off, he shook his head again. Good thing his father didn't know about his real motives for coming to town. Being a New Englander through and through, Benjamin Steed had a farmer's basic mistrust of highbred city folk, and somehow Joshua knew his father would not approve of his burning interest in Lydia McBride.

Taking a quick breath, Joshua turned and went inside. But his anticipation was quickly dashed. The only person in the store was Lydia's mother. A prim woman with a pinched mouth and tiny, fluttering hands, she was polite but cool.

There was nothing Joshua could do but give her the list of the items his mother had requested. He was back out on the steps in less than five minutes, keenly disappointed. It was mid-April, and with the weather warming fast now, that meant plowing and planting time. It would likely be another two or three weeks before he got a chance to come in again.

Glumly he walked to the edge of the boardwalk, set the box of supplies down, and settled in to wait for Joseph and Nathan.

"Why, Mr. Steed, I didn't know you were in town."

Joshua stumbled to his feet with a sudden leap of joy. Lydia was coming down the walk in company with two other young girls of the same age. They were all dressed in Sunday best, their bustle skirts rustling as they walked, parasols twirling merrily.

Joshua swept off his hat, nodding quickly. "Afternoon, Miss Lydia." He bobbed his head at the others, barely taking his eyes off Lydia's face. "Good afternoon."

The girls curtsied, suppressing giggles behind the lowered lashes.

"Joshua Steed, these are my best girlfriends. Miss Elizabeth Ann Rowley and Miss Mary Beth Beesley."

"How do you do, Mr. Steed?" Joshua felt his face flushing again as they held out their hands, appraising him with unabashed openness. Then with knowing smiles they excused themselves and hurried away, glancing back over their shoulders and tittering as they went.

Lydia watched them for a moment, half embarrassed, half amused, then turned up her head and smiled at him, a dazzling smile that revealed the even whiteness of her teeth. "I'm pleased to see you again, Joshua."

"Me too." He stopped, aware of how foolish he must look and sound. He looked down at the box. "We had to come in for some seed and things," he finished lamely.

Just then the sound of a wagon caught his attention. He turned around, frowning. It was Nathan and Joseph already returning, the wagon creaking heavily under the weight of two dozen bags of wheat seed. Trying to hide his disappointment, he turned back. "Well . . . uh . . . I guess we'll see you again next time we get to town."

She watched the approaching wagon for a moment, then spoke quickly. "Will you be coming to the barn raising Saturday afternoon?"

Joshua's head came up, suddenly eager. "Hadn't heard there was one."

"Yes. Calvin Rupert's adding on to his livery stable down on the east end of Main Street. All the men folk will pitch in and help. The women will be fixing supper. There will be games for the children."

"I'll tell Pa. Mr. Rupert helped with our cabin last fall." And, he suddenly decided, if Pa was too busy getting stumps out, then Joshua would come in alone.

"Good." She smiled shyly up at him. "I'll watch for you."

She looked up as Nathan pulled the wagon up to the hitching rail.

Taking the box of supplies he had bought, Joshua walked to the wagon and swung them over the back gate, jamming them down between two of the bulging sacks of grain. Nathan had swung down to help, but seeing Joshua had it done he turned around and came face-to-face with Lydia.

He stopped, his mouth dropping slightly. Joshua stepped to him and poked him with his elbow. "Miss Lydia, this here's Nathan, my younger brother. Nathan, meet Miss Lydia McBride."

Nathan jumped a little, his face coloring. He stuck out his hand, suddenly shy and awkward. "I'm right pleased to meet you, Miss Lydia," he managed to say.

She took his hand briefly, smiling. "Yes," she said, "I could have guessed you were a Steed. You look very much like your mother."

"Afternoon, Miss Lydia."

She looked up to where Joseph was sitting. He had taken off his hat and was smiling pleasantly at her.

"Hello, Mr. Smith." Joshua started a little. There it was again. The instant coolness swept the smile from her face as it had the last time she had spoken to Joseph.

As before, Joseph gave no sign of having noticed. "Hope things are well with you and yours."

"They are, thank you kindly." She quickly turned to Nathan. "Pleased to meet you, Nathan." Then to Joshua, "Well, my family is expecting me. I'd better go in."

He nodded. "We've got to get back too. Good-bye."

"Hope you can help with the barn raising."

Joshua nodded eagerly. "I'll—we'll be there."

Nathan swung up on the wagon seat. "A pleasure to meet you, Miss—"

A raucous cry cut him off in midsentence. "Why, there's ol' Joe Smith."

They all swung around. Across the street three men were stopped. One was pointing towards them.

"Why, it is, it is!" crowed another. "It's ol' Joe Smith." He grabbed the arm of his nearest companion. "Let's go pay our respects."

The three locked arms in mock solemnity and started across toward them. Joshua shot a sideways glance up at Joseph. The smile was gone now and he looked straight ahead. Lydia, her intent to go inside forgotten, turned back to await the trio.

The three came round the wagon and hopped up on the sidewalk to face Joshua and Lydia. The one who had first called swept off his hat and bowed with exaggerated courtesy. "Afternoon, Miss Lydia."

He was about the same age as Joshua and of the same height but much more solidly built. A flannel shirt was hanging out of baggy, worn pants held up by filthy suspenders. His hair was thick and black and greasy, his beard a rough, three-day growth of whiskers. The two with him were younger and slightly smaller; but other than that, there was little difference between the three.

Surprisingly, Lydia responded to them quite amiably. "Good afternoon, Will. Afternoon, David. Hello, Mark."

The other two spoke as one. "Hello, Miss Lydia."

The one called Will shot a quick look up to where Joseph Smith sat on the wagon seat, then back to Lydia. "Miss Lydia, you out here learnin' more about them there angels, are you?"

Lydia laughed lightly, studiously not looking up at Joseph. "No. I was just coming from the piano recital over at Miss Carrie's boardinghouse." She turned a little. "This is Joshua Steed. His father bought some acreage next to the Harris farm north of town."

The leader stuck out a hand, heavily calloused and with dirt under the fingernails. "Will Murdock," he said.

Joshua took it, not surprised that the grip was weak, almost flabby.

"Heard a new family had come in." Then, remembering his manners, he jerked his head slightly toward his companions. "This here's my brother, David. And this is my cousin Mark Cooper."

Joshua shook hands with both of the others, trying not to show his distaste. He then motioned toward Nathan. "This is my brother Nathan. And Joseph you seem to know."

"Oh yes," Will said gravely, "we know Joe Smith, don't we boys?" He looked up at Joseph, his face as innocent as a baby's, as the other two hooted. "And how are you today, sir?"

"I'm fine, Will." Joseph answered easily and with a half smile. "I see you've been warming the stools down at Phelps's tavern again."

Will's mouth tightened and his eyes got suddenly ugly. "You got the gold Bible yet?" he sneered.

There was no response from Joseph, but the question certainly got a reaction from the Steeds. Both Nathan and Joshua jerked around to stare first at Will, then at Joseph.

"What?" Will chortled. "Ain't ol' Joe here told you about his gold Bible yet?" He looked up. "Why, for shame, Joe. People just love that story, especially the part 'bout them angels flying round your house."

Joseph remained calm and unruffled, as though bearing with considerable patience the mindless pattering of a child. He just looked at Will Murdock steadily, the clear blue eyes not wavering. Will tried to match his gaze, then started to squirm and finally turned away.

When it became obvious there would be no further response from Joseph, Joshua turned to Lydia, the look on his face clearly asking for an explanation. She just shook her head slightly. Then, as an afterthought, she looked up and said, "I heard tell, Mr. Smith, the waiting time is up this fall. Is that true?"

Joseph turned slowly and looked at her. Once more it was a steady gaze, without malice, but probing, searching. Will Murdock had looked away under the intensity of Joseph's look, but Lydia's chin only came up a fraction of an inch higher. "Well? Is it true? Will you be paying for your supplies in gold from now on?"

He shook his head, his eyes amused. "No. I think we'll be buying our things same as other folks. You can count on that."

Will's brother, David, stepped forward, chin jutting out, chest expanded. "Hey, Joe, tell us what an angel looks like? Was it a boy angel or a girl angel?" He started to laugh. It was a jarring sound, like the barking of a dog trying to clear a bone caught in its throat.

"Yeah," echoed Mark Cooper. He openly sneered. "Why don't ya send one of them angels to tell *us* how to find some buried treasure?"

Lydia laughed aloud, tossing her head in contempt. Again Joshua was taken aback by her reaction. What was it that she and her pa had against the Smiths? He lifted one eyebrow, silently questioning her, but she refused to meet his probing look. He turned back to Joseph, curious now. "What are they talking about, Joseph?"

But at that moment the door to the store opened and Lydia's father stepped out. "Lydia!"

It brought them all around. Josiah McBride was not a tall man; in fact he was an inch or two shorter than his wife. But he was one of Palmyra's leading citizens, an elder in the Presbyterian church with his own family pew, and a member of the recently elected town council. He was short, but no one in Palmyra thought of him as a little man. And now he was drawn up to his full height, the anger obvious on his face.

"Yes, Father?" Her voice had turned instantly contrite.

"There's better things to do than sit in the street and pass on idle gossip."

"Yes, Father." She turned, lowering her voice as she passed Joshua. "Saturday afternoon. I'll see you there."

Joshua nodded with a quick flush of pleasure.

As Lydia brushed by her father and entered the store, McBride turned to Will Murdock. His voice went suddenly hard. "Unless you boys are planning to buy something, why don't you move on somewhere else."

Will swept off his hat and bowed low, but his eyes were burning with resentment. "Why, sure, Mr. McBride," he said sarcastically. "Ain't nothin' in your store we need." Then to his two companions, but loudly enough for the storekeeper to hear, he added, "Not at your prices, anyway."

With a laugh he turned and started jauntily away, the other two falling in step beside him. Without slowing he called back over his shoulder, "We'll be waitin' for you when you get them gold plates, Joe. You can count on that!"

The storekeeper's dark eyes swung around to bore into Joshua. Jumping as though he had been burned, Joshua hopped into the back of the wagon as Nathan picked up the reins. "Thank you for the supplies, Mr. McBride," he said politely.

The balding man merely nodded, then turned and went inside.

They drove in silence, moving west along Main Street until

they came to the road that led north across the bridge over the Erie Canal. Finally Joshua could stand it no more. He climbed up to the wagon seat, squeezing in between Joseph and Nathan. He was barely settled before he turned to Joseph. "All right. What's all this talk about angels and a gold Bible?"

Joseph had picked up a small piece of straw from beneath his feet. Now he pulled it apart slowly, letting the shredded pieces blow away in the breeze. Finally, he turned. He seemed to be choosing his words very carefully. "Joshua, do you really think angels go around showing people where to find buried treasure?"

Joshua snorted in derision. "Of course not."

"Good. I don't believe angels do that either."

"But they were talking about a gold Bible."

Joseph flipped the straw away, then leaned back, chuckling softly. "When you hear a donkey braying in the barnyard," he said, his voice suddenly wry, "it's one thing to listen; it's something else to assume the donkey's saying somethin' important."

Nathan laughed right out loud. "Well said, Joseph. Well said."

Joshua shot him a withering look. But it quickly became evident Joseph was not going to say any more. He parried two or three of Joshua's further questions, then changed the subject and began talking with Nathan.

Joshua sat back, watching out of the corner of his eye the young man who had come to work for them. The Murdocks were clearly less than the salt of the earth, but Joseph had not denied anything they said, just neatly sidestepped Joshua's questions. Maybe Joseph thought it was over, but Joshua's curiosity had been piqued. There would be another time with Lydia, and then he would get to the bottom of this.

Joshua, working in tandem with Joseph Smith, snaked the chain under the end of the log and snugged it tight. As Joseph jammed the hook through one of the links, Nathan let the log settle back into its place. He turned to his father. "All right, take her away."

Benjamin Steed was at the head of the mule team. Hyrum Smith, standing nearby, moved back. "Ho, mules," Benjamin shouted. "Go!"

The animals lunged forward, hitting the traces. The chain snapped tight, bit into the bark of the log, and the log began to move. Snorting heavily, the mules clawed at the ground. Faster now the trunk slid along the black earth. "Giddyap, mules!" Benjamin called, slapping the near one on the rump.

"I'll go help him unhook it," Joseph said, breaking into a trot to follow them.

Hyrum watched them go, then cupped his hand to his mouth. "Watch out for hornets." Joseph raised one hand briefly without turning. It was an unnecessary warning, for hornets were the bane of the frontier farmer. It was still a little early for them to be fully out of their dormancy, but it had been warm enough the past few days to make one be on alert. In a week or two, as the plowing got fully underway, they would have to constantly watch the ground ahead. Particularly in virgin fields like these, one could hit a nest of yellow jackets every second or third furrow, unleashing a deadly cloud of fury that could leave a farmer and his team half-dead.

Joshua stepped to where three shirts hung from a bush. On the ground next to the bush was a water jug and several rags. He took one of the rags and mopped at his forehead. Nathan and Hyrum moved to join him. The rain and overcast from the day before had gone, and while the temperature was pleasant enough, the humidity was still high, and they had removed their shirts. But the first swarms of mosquitoes were out now, and they didn't allow one to sit around with bare back for long without regretting it.

Hyrum pulled his shirt over his head and tucked it into his trousers, then grabbed the water jug and drank deeply. He handed it to Nathan, then picked up a rag of his own and began to wipe at the sweat across the back of his neck. Joshua watched him for a moment, then cleared his throat. "Hyrum?"

"Yes."

Joshua tossed the rag aside. "We were in town yesterday," he continued.

Hyrum looked up. "Yes."

Nathan, sensing suddenly what was coming, shot his brother a warning look, but if Joshua saw it, he ignored it. "Some men stopped to talk to Joseph."

Wary now, Hyrum waited.

"They said Joseph has some kind of gold Bible."

There was no change of expression, and no outward signs of response, but there was a sudden, unmistakable coolness in the air. Finally, he spoke. "The Murdocks, you mean?" He pronounced the name with great disdain.

"Yeah. Will Murdock and his brother. And a cousin."

Hyrum gave a soft snort of disgust.

Joshua went on more slowly now, but still determined. "He also said somethin' about angels."

"Joshua!" Nathan broke in sharply. "It ain't our place to pry."

Joshua glared at him, but he wasn't about to back down. "Well?" he pressed.

Hyrum lifted his head, his eyes searching across the field. About a hundred rods away, Joseph and Benjamin were unhooking the log and getting ready to start back. Hyrum stood up abruptly and brushed off his pants. "You'll have to ask Joseph about that," he said shortly.

It was just barely sundown. The spring air was cooling quickly now, leaving a misty haze across the fields and meadows. The songbirds seemed muted and still. The smoke from the cabin's chimney rose in lazy, gentle eddies. Nathan hurried through unhitching the mules, then forked some hay into the manger. He had left the others cleaning up the last of the brush, but he knew Joseph and Hyrum would soon be leaving for home and if he didn't hurry he would miss them.

As he came out of the barn, he saw with relief that the Smith brothers were just saying good-bye to Matthew and Becca near the front porch of the cabin. His mother was there too, wiping her hands on her apron, then waving to them as they moved off.

Nathan hurried over to his mother. "I think I'll walk a ways with Joseph and Hyrum," he said. "I'll be back in time for supper."

She looked a little surprised, then shrugged. "All right. We'll be eating in about an hour."

"I'll be back." He hurried off to join the two figures starting down the lane toward the main road.

Joseph and Hyrum seemed glad for the company, and for the first few minutes as they walked they chatted idly about the day's work, the warming weather, the prospects of this year's crops. But as they turned onto the road leading to Palmyra Village and passed the Martin Harris farm, they lapsed into a companionable silence, enjoying the pleasantness of the evening.

But Nathan had not come for idle chat. Since earlier that day when Hyrum had neatly sidestepped Joshua's questions about the things Will Murdock had said in town, Nathan had been bursting with questions of his own. Being like his mother, he was too polite to broach the subject head-on like Joshua had. But if there was any way to find out more, he was determined to do it.

Clearing his throat, he decided to break the silence. "Is your wife from around here, Hyrum?"

"Yes. Jerusha's from the Barden family, down near Canandaigua."

"And yours, Joseph?"

He shook his head. "No, Emma's from Harmony, Pennsylvania."

That surprised Nathan a little. "Harmony? Where's that?"

"About a hundred twenty miles south of here. Just across the state line."

"My," Nathan smiled, "you must have roamed far afield in your courting days."

Joseph laughed. "A couple of years ago a man by the name of Stowell came into Palmyra to buy wheat. He was from down near the Colesville and South Bainbridge area, which is about fifteen miles this side of the Pennsylvania line. Somehow Mr. Stowell had gotten an old document which was supposed to show the location of a cave where the Spaniards had hidden a considerable treasure. I was needing work right then, so my father and I hired on to help him dig for it."

He shook his head slowly, as if remembering. "We dug in the area around Harmony, which is about twenty-five miles south of the Stowell farm, so while I was there I boarded with a man by the name of Isaac Hale." Again a quiet smile stole across his face. Nathan was learning this was characteristic of Joseph. "He had a daughter . . ."

Nathan laughed. "I understand."

"Actually, Mr. Hale wasn't so fond of the idea of me court-ing Emma. I mean he barely knew me, and I was not at that time employed in what folks viewed as a promising occupation. I finally convinced Stowell that looking for treasure was a waste of time. I stayed on in the Colesville area for a time, working for a family named Knight. They were kind enough to lend me a sleigh and a horse to go south and visit Emma. Finally, this last January we got married."

"She's a fine woman," Hyrum said.

"As is Jerusha," Joseph agreed.

"I hope to meet them both sometime."

They walked along in silence for several moments. Nathan's mind was racing. An old Spanish map. Was that what had trig-gered the stories of gold Bibles? Finally, he glanced up out of the corner of his eye. "Joseph?"

"Yes?"

Nathan suddenly changed his mind. His reticence to pry overcame his curiosity. He just shook his head.

Joseph was looking at him. "What?" he asked again.
"Nothing."

One of Joseph's eyebrows came up slowly.

Nathan just shook his head. "Nothing," he repeated. "It ain't none of my affair."

They walked on for several steps in silence. Then Hyrum spoke. "It's about what Joshua was sayin' earlier today, isn't it?"

For a moment Nathan didn't respond, then finally shrugged.

"Do you ask this for yourself?" Joseph asked quietly.

The question caught Nathan by surprise.

"Do you really want to know, or is this just because of the things you've heard?"

"The only thing I've heard is what Will Murdock and his brother said to you in town."

There was an answering laugh, not of amusement but one filled with derision. "You mean you haven't heard Joe Smith is a lazy, no-account loafer, a drunkard who is immoral and untrustworthy?"

"And of limited mental capacity," Hyrum added bitterly. "Don't forget that."

"Yes, that too."

The exchange took Nathan aback.

"That's what people are saying about Joseph," Hyrum went on. "You'll probably hear stories about our family as well— about us being grave robbers, devil worshippers, who knows what else."

Nathan was flabbergasted. He looked first at Hyrum, then at Joseph. "You've only worked with our family for a short time, but I know you pretty well by now. I wouldn't believe them kind of stories for a minute. And neither would anyone else in my family."

Joseph stopped, looking at him closely. Then he reached out and grasped his arm. "Thank you," he said, obviously touched.

"Why would anyone want to say them kind of things about you?"

Joseph let out a long sigh, filled with weariness. But he

didn't speak, just started to walk again, more slowly now. Nathan and Hyrum watched him for a moment, then fell in step beside him. Finally, Joseph looked over at Hyrum, a questioning look on his face. Their eyes locked for several seconds, something passed between them, then Hyrum finally nodded.

Joseph glanced up at the sky, now darkening quickly. Pink and gold tinged the clouds in the west. They were just a short distance from Palmyra Village now, and soon Nathan would have to turn back. "If we stop and talk for a spell," Joseph said slowly, "it will make you late for supper."

"No, Ma said it would be at least an hour." Actually the "at least" was Nathan's addition, but there was no way he was going to cut off Joseph's willingness to talk now.

Joseph gestured to a grassy spot alongside a small stream just on the other side of a rail fence. "Then let's sit for a while."

They crossed over the rail fence and sat down. A cool breeze had sprung up now, and the chill of night would soon be on them. The wind tousled a lock of Joseph's light brown hair. For several moments he toyed with new blades of grass sprouting beneath him, smoothing them with his fingertips, lost in his thoughts. When he looked up, his eyes—those light blue eyes which were always arresting in their intensity—were a curious mixture of . . . what? Nathan wasn't sure. Sorrow? Exultation? Weariness? Joy?

"I'll not ask you to believe what I'm about to tell you, Nathan," Joseph began slowly. "But I would appreciate it if you would hear me through to the end."

"All right."

Hyrum settled back, content to let Joseph take the lead now. Joseph's eyes narrowed thoughtfully, as if trying to choose each word with great care. "Did you ever go to a camp meeting, Nathan?"

"You mean a religious camp meeting?"

Joseph nodded.

"No. Heard a lot about them, but Pa always had strong feelings 'bout them being kinda organized madness, so we never went."

"They're kind of dying out again now, but along about ten years ago they were real popular in these parts. In fact, there were so many circuit-riding preachers and so many people 'getting on fire' with the Holy Spirit, this part of New York came to be called 'the Burned-Over District.' "

"A full-blown camp meeting is somethin' to behold," Hyrum put in. "There was a real big one in this part of the state just last year."

"Word was sent ahead from village to village," Joseph said. "Families came from everywhere, riding two and three days sometimes, bringing tents and provisions. Platforms were built in open spaces and the people camped all around them. There were probably twenty, maybe thirty, ministers come to preach."

"Sounds like quite an experience," Nathan said.

"Yes," agreed Joseph. "My parents had never belonged to any church. Not that they're not God-fearing folk. We've read the Bible in our family from the time we were small."

"That's exactly how our family is," Nathan said.

"So," Joseph continued, "when the preachers started coming into the area, calling on people to join up with this church or that, our family started thinking about it. This was almost ten years ago, I'd say, so I was about twelve or thirteen."

"I finally joined the Presbyterian church," Hyrum volunteered. "So did Mother and two of the other children. Joseph was kind of leaning to the Methodists."

"But you didn't join?" Nathan asked.

There was a slow shake of the head. He broke off a stem of a weed and began to chew on it thoughtfully. "At first I was quite excited by it all. But then somethin' really started troubling me."

"Like what?"

"Well, at first all the ministers kept saying it didn't matter which church you followed, as long as you were really sincere and got 'converted,' as they called it. But even young as I was, I noticed it was mostly just talk. As soon as people started choosing one church or another, all the good feelings kinda disappeared. Ministers would argue with ministers over who had the truth. 'Converts' to one church would tell 'converts' to another church that they had made a terrible mistake and had put their eternal salvation at risk. One thing was clear to me in all this: 'Love your neighbor' and Christian charity quickly went out the window.

"This went on for more than a year. Before long I was so confused, I didn't know what to do. All around me was confusion. What was I to do? What if I made the wrong choice? To my young mind this was a decision of eternal consequence, and I didn't want to do something that wasn't right."

Nathan was engrossed now in Joseph's account. "So what *did* you do?"

"I started to read the Bible. My mother taught us the scriptures were God's word. So I decided maybe I could find the answer there."

He stopped, his eyes gazing out across the field where they sat. Nathan watched him closely, tempted to press, but knowing it was better to let Joseph take it at his own pace.

"One day I happened to be reading in the Epistle of Saint James. I came to the first chapter and the fifth verse." He swung around and looked directly at Nathan, his eyes suddenly piercing in their intensity.

"Tell him what it says, Joseph," Hyrum urged.

Joseph nodded, his voice now soft, almost reverent. "It says: 'If any of you lack wisdom, let him ask of God, that giveth to all men liberally, and upbraideth not; and it shall be given him.' "

"Hmmm," Nathan murmured. "That's a wonderful promise."

Joseph nodded. "Never had any passage of scripture come with such power to my mind. It entered with great force into every feeling of my heart. I reflected on it again and again. Finally, I decided that if there was ever anyone who lacked wisdom, it was me. I decided right then and there I would do exactly as James said. I would ask God which church I should join." He exhaled slowly, leaning back, lost in his thoughts.

"And?" Nathan pressed.

"By now it was early in the spring of 1820. I knew of a quiet place in the woods near our home. I had decided this would be the place where I would go and pray. It was a beautiful clear morning. I went into the woods, and making sure I was alone, I immediately knelt down to pray."

A sudden shadow passed across Joseph's face. He shook his head slightly as if trying to brush it aside. He was staring down at the ground as unconsciously he began to tear off the blades of grass and drop them into a little pile. When he spoke, his voice was low. "To my amazement, I found I couldn't utter a word. It was as though my tongue was swollen in my head."

Nathan blinked. This was not what he had expected to hear.

"Suddenly I thought I heard footsteps behind me, someone walking towards me in the dry leaves. I was startled. I whipped around." Now at last he looked up, directly into Nathan's eyes. "No one was there."

Nathan felt a sudden chill run up and down his spine.

"I turned back, thinking it was my imagination. Remember, I was only a fourteen-year-old boy at this time." He bowed his head, as though reliving those moments. His lips were compressed into a tight line, and he shook his head. "But again, I couldn't utter a word. And then I heard someone behind me again, only louder this time. I jumped to my feet and whirled around, determined to catch whoever it was." Once more there was a long, breathless pause. "There was no one there. Nothing!"

He stopped and took a breath. "Remember, Nathan. This wasn't nighttime. It was full daylight on a bright spring morning."

Nathan nodded, transfixed by the power in Joseph's eyes.

"At that very instant, I was seized by some powerful force which bound me tight." He reached out and gripped Nathan's arm. "I'm not talking about some imaginary force, Nathan. I was in the grip of a being from the unseen world, a being more powerful than anything I had ever experienced. The power was astonishing. I was completely bound. I could not even cry out in my terror."

Nathan's mind flashed to his contest with Joseph in pulling sticks. He knew personally of Joseph's tremendous strength. The power had bound Joseph completely? He shivered involuntarily.

"Thick darkness began to gather around me. I was terrified, for I was certain I was doomed to utter destruction."

"What happened? What was it?"

His eyes grave, Joseph replied, "I exerted all my powers to call upon God for deliverance from this enemy which had seized me. Then . . ." He paused, the line of his jaw softening. "At the very moment of my deepest despair, as I was about to abandon myself to destruction, at that precise moment, I saw a pillar of light."

Nathan's head snapped up.

Joseph went on steadily now, speaking slowly but with great earnestness. "It was exactly over my head. It was far brighter than the sun at noonday. The light was so intense I thought the very leaves would burst into flame. It descended gradually until it fell upon me. Instantly, the moment the light touched me, I was delivered from the enemy which held me bound.

"When the light rested upon me, I saw two personages—" He stopped, noting the expression on Nathan's face. "I saw two personages," he continued firmly, "whose glory and brightness defy all description. They were standing above me in the air."

Now it was Nathan who involuntarily passed a hand across his eyes. A pillar of light? Two personages?

"The one spoke," Joseph continued, softly now, and more slowly, as though giving Nathan time to digest the words. "He called me by name. 'Joseph,' he said, 'this is My Beloved Son. Hear Him!' "

He stopped, watching Nathan closely.

Nathan's mind was reeling. "Are you saying . . ." He faltered, overwhelmed. "You mean you saw . . ." He could not bring himself to say it.

Joseph nodded with the utmost solemnity. "I saw God and I saw his Son, Jesus Christ." He sighed, suddenly weary. "I know how that must sound to you. But I say again, Nathan, and I say it with all the power of my soul: I saw the Father and I saw his Son."

He took a deep breath, then let it out slowly. "Remember, Nathan, you promised to hear me out."

Nathan leaned back, totally astonished. He could only nod.

"When I finally gathered my senses—and you can imagine my feelings; this was not what I had expected to happen." He gave a short laugh of derision at his own understatement. "Not what I expected? Who would ever—could ever!—have dreamed such a thing would happen?" He shook his head. "But anyway, when I finally gathered my senses about me, the only thing I could think of to say was to ask my original question. I had come to the grove to find out which church was right. And so I asked him—"

"What did they look like?" Nathan burst out, not having heard Joseph's last words.

Joseph smiled briefly. "They were glorious beyond description. They were dressed in robes of exquisite whiteness—"

"What did God look like?" Nathan's voice was barely a whisper. "I mean, was he a—" He stopped, groping for an adequate word.

"A person?"

"Yes."

"Yes, Nathan. Most assuredly yes, though a personage of glory and majesty beyond belief. But yes, Nathan, God is a person. When he said he created man in his own image, I know now what he meant. He looks like us—" He shook it off. "No, *we look like him!* He is a person. He is our Father."

Hyrum was nodding soberly, but didn't speak. Joseph, too, fell silent, letting Nathan ponder that for a moment.

Finally Joseph went on, more calmly now. "As I told you, God pointed to his Son and told me to hear him. So I addressed my question to him. I asked the Savior which of all the churches was right."

In spite of himself, Nathan leaned forward. "And what was the answer?"

"He said I was to join none of them, they were all wrong. He said their creeds were an abomination in his sight; they taught for doctrine the commandments of men. He also said they drew near to him with their lips, but their hearts were far from him; they had a form of godliness but denied the power thereof."

He paused, but Nathan did not respond, so he went quickly on. "The Savior again forbade me to join any of the churches."

He stopped. In the distance a meadowlark was calling out its last evening song. The breeze was picking up now, making a soft rustling noise as it danced across the meadow. The stream gurgled cheerfully as it ran past them. But Nathan was aware of none of this. His mind was a wild tumble of thoughts and emotions.

Joseph turned to look at him. "When the light was gone, I found myself on my back. The experience had drained the strength out of me." His eyes were like blue fire as he searched Nathan's face. "But I'll never forget those feelings, Nathan. Never have I been filled with so much joy. It was like I was on fire with the knowledge I had just received, but at the same time my heart was calm, my soul was at perfect peace.

"When I finally returned home, Mother seemed to know immediately that something had happened to me. She asked me what was wrong." He laughed softly. "I told her I had found out for myself that the church she had joined was not true."

Hyrum cleared his throat. "Joseph is my brother," he said quietly. "I have known him from birth. I have never known him to lie or to be dishonest. From the moment he first told us this experience, no one in the family has ever doubted it. We believed him, Nathan. You need to know that. Those who knew him best, believed him."

Nathan turned away. A few minutes earlier he had expressed a similar confidence in Joseph's integrity. He had been incensed to hear that others thought Joseph to be mad or a fraud. Now suddenly he understood.

Yet? He searched inwardly. As Joseph had spoken, something had burned inside Nathan's heart. He had been almost inflamed with the power of what Joseph had said. But another part of him was recoiling. Thick darkness? Some evil power? And God the Father? A person?

He shook his head. It was too fantastic. Too absolutely incredible. This was not one of the world's great religious leaders. Maybe if it had even happened to a parson or a priest. But to a fourteen-year-old farm boy? It staggered all credibility.

He was pulled out of his thoughts as Joseph began to speak again. He was speaking so softly Nathan had to lean closer to hear. "Many times I have felt exactly as Paul the Apostle must have felt. When he told others about what had happened to him on the road to Damascus, they mocked him. And who could blame them? This was the Paul who persecuted the Church. This was the man who threw men, women, and children into prison for believing in Christ. But the doubts and the mocking meant nothing to Paul. He had seen a light and heard a voice. People said he was mad or that he lied, but none of that could change the reality of his vision."

Joseph reached out and laid a hand on Nathan's arm. "And so it is with me, Nathan. The world would have me deny what I have seen. From the moment I first told others of this experience, they have mocked me and ridiculed me. It has never ceased to amaze me that I, an obscure farm boy, should cause such a reaction in others."

He straightened slowly, his shoulders coming back, his chin coming up. Once again those penetrating blue eyes seemed to bore into the very heart of Nathan's being. "But none of that matters. I saw a light, and within that light I saw two personages. Those two personages did in all reality speak to me. Who am I that I can withstand God? I know I have seen a vision. And I know God knows I have seen a vision. If I were to deny it, I would put myself under his condemnation."

He smiled, sadly, wistfully. "That I cannot do. Let the Will Murdocks of the world laugh and sneer. Let the townspeople call me mad or possessed. It doesn't change what happened."

But then he brightened perceptibly. "But oh, Nathan, how can I complain? I went into that grove of trees in darkness and confusion. I came out filled with peace. I went in wondering which church I should join. I came out having seen God. It is enough for me, and I shall forever shout praises to my God for his mercy and grace."

For several moments, they all sat there. Nathan was in too much turmoil to speak. He wouldn't have known what to say if he could have spoken. Finally, he got to his feet, not directly meeting either Hyrum's or Joseph's eyes. "I'd better get back."

Hyrum stood up quickly and faced him. Gently he touched Nathan's shoulder. "We know how you must feel now, Nathan. We know. But listen to your heart, Nathan. Just trust your heart."

He met Hyrum's solemn gaze for a moment, then finally looked away. "I'll have to think about it," was all he could think of to say.

Steed Homestead, Palmyra Township

"O uch!" Melissa Mary Steed grabbed her foot, hopping to keep her balance. A tiny sliver of wood stuck out from the tip of the little toe of her right foot, and blood was already starting to ooze out from around it.

"Joshua!" She shook her fist in the general direction of the window where she had seen him pass a minute or two before. "Darn you!" She hobbled to a wooden stool and sat down hard. Carefully she grasped the sliver, then shutting her eyes tight, yanked it out. "Ow!" she cried again softly. Then, as she dabbed at her toe with the moistened end of one finger, she tipped her head back and shrieked. "Joshua Steed!"

From outside, near the rain barrel, there was a muffled response.

Mary Ann stepped out from behind the curtain that divided hers and Benjamin's sleeping area from the rest of the cabin. She was just finishing pulling down her dress and smoothing it out. "What is it, Melissa?"

Melissa held up the sliver, as if her mother could see it across the room in the dim light. "I just ran a sliver in my toe. You told Joshua to smooth out the planks."

Shaking her head, Mary Ann stepped back behind the curtain. "You know better than to go barefoot before a new plank floor wears down smooth."

Melissa pulled a face at no one in particular. So much for sympathy. And yet she knew her mother was right. These planks had not come from a sawmill. That was too expensive. One of the first things her father and brothers had done after the family's arrival was to go down to the creek and select eight to ten of the straightest pine trees growing there and cut them down. Left for the next several months, the logs had seasoned nicely. When winter finally shut down the outside work, there had finally been time to give the cabin a wooden floor.

The logs were dragged into the barn and the work begun. Using "gluts," or hardwood chisels, and a "beetle," a large wooden mallet, the planks were sheared off one at a time. Though sawing off planks gave a much smoother surface, even if they had used the big two-man handsaws it would have taken four or five days to get enough to do the cabin floor. With the beetle and gluts, the men had split enough planks in one day to complete the job.

It had been Joshua's job to take the small adze and the hand plane and work the planks until they were smooth. *Smooth* was a relative word, however. With the floor barely six weeks old, it had not yet worn down to the polished smoothness it would eventually acquire, and a person walked on it barefoot at his own peril. Fresh from the iron bathtub placed behind the curtain near the fireplace, Melissa had been totally caught up in the excitement of going to town and she had forgotten about her bare feet.

She dabbed at her toe again, searching the floor for the offending splinter. Though the wooden floor had its drawbacks, Melissa knew she wouldn't trade it for the hard-packed dirt one they had endured for the first several months in the cabin. In addition to being cold and clammy, especially when it was damp, the dirt had to be constantly packed and repacked. It had also been Melissa's job to scratch intricate patterns into the dirt to give the impression of carpeting—floral patterns for the fall, holly leaves and berries for Christmas. It was the popular style among settlers, but she found it tedious, boring work, the effects of which only lasted for a short time under the feet of the family anyway.

Joshua came through the door, shirt open, suspenders hanging down below his waist, still drying his face from shaving. He took one look at Melissa, towel wrapped around her hair, and stopped dead. "Melissa!"

"What?"

"We're late. Get movin'."

She stuck out her foot and wiggled her toe at him. The dark spot of blood was still evident. "I just got a sliver in my toe, thanks to you."

"Come on. Pa and Nathan almost have the wagon hitched. We're gonna be late."

At sixteen, Melissa was fully a woman now, and Joshua's gruffness in no way intimidated her. She smiled sweetly, pulled the towel away from her hair and shook it loose, then started to rub it with exaggerated slowness.

"Ma!" Joshua bellowed. "Tell her to hurry." Without waiting for an answer he stepped to the stairs. "Rebecca! Matthew! It's time to go." He threw his towel in the general direction of one corner and started buttoning his shirt.

"My, my," Melissa taunted, "aren't we the impatient one?" She gave him one of her most radiant looks. "There's really no hurry. Lydia McBride will have so many beaus waiting to talk with her, bet you don't even get a turn."

Mary Ann came out into the main part of the room again. "All right, Melissa, that's enough. Hurry yourself along."

As her oldest daughter took a comb and brush and went to the small mirror hung on one wall, Mary Ann smiled. As she had grown up, she had only one brother, just eighteen months older than she was. And while Ezra Morgan had treasured each of his seven daughters, he made no attempt to hide the joy with which he viewed his firstborn and only son. Joel Morgan got the best of whatever came to the Morgan family, and that included the lightest assignment when working on the turnpikes.

Because of that, Mary Ann had learned at an early age how to goad Joel to the point of exasperation. It was her way of getting a little justice, and her father, probably shouldering a little guilt for his blatant favoritism, had never tried very hard to stop her. He knew that beneath the surface battles lay a deep bond between Mary Ann and her brother.

Mary Ann knew how it was with Melissa and Joshua. Though her oldest daughter had a large measure of her mother's patience and gentleness, there was also in Melissa a broad streak of her oldest brother's temperament. This led to constant fireworks, but for the most part these were benign and always laced with an underlying affection. Actually, they were closer than any other of the children, and in the last year or so Melissa had taken upon herself the role of mediator when Joshua and their father clashed.

There was a solid thump above them as Matthew, in typical fashion, reached the third-from-the-bottom notch in the log ladder that led to his loft, then jumped. In a moment he came down the stairs. He wore brown shoes and long socks tucked into his pant legs. His dark knickers were held up with miniature suspenders. A white shirt, buttoned at the collar, completed his outfit. His hair was plastered to his head as though he had stuck it in the rain barrel. But one rooster tail near the crown had managed to elude his efforts and waved like a flag of surrender.

In a moment Rebecca followed. She came down the stairs primly, stepping carefully as she held her long skirt up from touching. Her hair was combed out long, and bounced lightly on her shoulders. A red ribbon, saved from Christmas the previous year, added a splash of color to her fair skin and pale blue eyes.

Without waiting to be told, the two of them lined up for inspection, cheeks scrubbed, eyes eager. Mary Ann stepped forward, starting to smile; then suddenly tears welled up in her eyes, and she had to turn her head. She brushed them away quickly, before Benjamin should come in and see them. He always chided her a little about letting her emotions run too close to the surface. But here stood her two youngest—Matthew, looking like one of those posters you saw in the store window, squirming with anticipation, and her Becca, destined to be the prettiest of the Steeds, and already aware of it.

What brought the tears was the sudden remembrance of those who should have been standing alongside these two —Mary, their firstborn, named for her mother and grandmother, and dead in her mother's arms within an hour of birth; Rachel and Leah, identical twins, six weeks premature, with their long dark hair and perfectly formed little fingers and toes, and both stillborn; Jacob, next after the twins, and dead at four of pneumonia; and Laura, likewise stillborn. Each one had torn a piece out of Mary Ann's soul. She was grateful for those who had been spared, but times like this brought the memory of those who were missing back like a spear to pierce her heart.

The door opened, and Nathan entered the cabin. "Hey, look at this!" He stepped to where the children were standing at attention. If he noticed his mother's quick brushing at her eyes, he didn't give any sign. He walked back and forth, inspecting each one carefully, both of them positively beaming under his scrutiny. "Don't we look somethin'?" He turned to his mother. "I say we just have church right here and forget about the picnic."

"We may as well," Joshua snorted. "The way Melissa's going, it'll be Sunday before we get there."

"Nathan," Melissa said airily, "would you mind riding ahead into town and seeing if you can get that Lydia McBride girl to save five minutes' time for your brother? Why, he's more frazzled than a brood hen with a weasel in the henhouse."

Mary Ann cut in quickly before Joshua could retort.

"Nathan, you and Joshua take the bathwater out and empty it. We'll be right there."

"All right. The wagon's out front."

As Joshua and Nathan grasped the heavy iron tub filled with soapy water, Mary Ann turned and took down a heavy knitted shawl from a peg on the wall. "All right, then," she said to her children, "let's go."

Melissa had just finished slipping into her shoes. She set down the comb and brush, did a slow pirouette for all to see, then curtsied primly. Though her hair still gleamed with wetness, it was brushed back and looked attractive. The dress, chosen from the finest bolt of material in the Rutland Country Store two weeks before the family had come west, was a soft blue, and it heightened the flush in Melissa's cheeks. Though she would never quite rival Becca, there would be more than one head turned at today's village picnic.

Mary Ann smiled at her proudly. "Are you ready?"

She nodded sweetly. "I've just been waiting for Joshua."

He was at the door, and turned to howl in protest, but Melissa quickly stepped up beside him, slipped her hand through his free arm and said, "Come on, Josh. Let's go meet this Lydia McBride of yours."

Originally the charters of Massachusetts and Connecticut provided that their boundaries would extend from the Atlantic seaboard to the Pacific Ocean and would include all lands not currently inhabited by Christians. During the American Revolution the states had agreed to relinquish title to the western lands, but a vast region of western New York was left in dispute. In 1786 a convention was held in Hartford, Connecticut. In return for some other concessions, New York granted Massachusetts rights of preemption over some six million acres running west from the Finger Lakes region to the Pennsylvania border. Fearing the agreement would not last, Massachusetts decided to dispose of this property immediately and sold it to two wealthy speculators for what amounted to about three cents an acre.

Surveyors moved in quickly to divide the region into six-mile square blocks called "townships." When people began to build villages within the townships, these settlements would often take on the name of the township. Thus the Steeds had purchased property in "Palmyra Town," or "Palmyra Township," but now drove the mile or so south to "Palmyra Village." And because the village lay right in the southwest corner of the township, it was the closest village for many of the people in the three surrounding townships.

So on this mid-April day of 1827, as the Steed family approached the main intersection of Palmyra Village, people from Macedon, Farmington, and Manchester townships joined them in a steady stream. Wagons, buggies, buckboards, even an ox-cart or two, were all moving steadily toward the center of the village proper. Children called excitedly to one another, neighbors waved, strangers nodded pleasantly to those passing by. Occasionally a settler drove a few head of milk cows in for possible sale.

Here and there, some of the more enterprising residents of the village pushed small handcarts filled with sugar cakes, pies, molasses, maple sugar, root beer, or dried fruit. Others hawked such home-produced items as birch brooms, baskets made from black ash, or hand-painted oilcloths for the table.

Matthew and Becca's eyes were filled with wonder, barely able to dart quickly enough from one thing to another, pointing and oohing and aahing. Melissa, more prim, was determined to act the young woman. Her mother had to smile, for she knew her daughter well enough to know that the hand constantly picking at unseen pieces of lint on her dress was a sure sign of her inner excitement. Melissa had waited long for a chance to come into town, and to do so for a picnic and barn raising was more than she had hoped for.

They moved up Main Street, past a two-story brick store, a

clothier with women's dresses in the window, Abner Cole's law offices, another store. Down a side street they could see the barges pulled up at the docks along the Erie Canal. Men staggered under the weight of bags and bales being unloaded and taken into the warehouses.

As they came to the corner of Market Street, Benjamin Steed pulled up on the reins and the mules shuffled to a stop. To their right was the two-story frame building which housed the tavern of Stephen Phelps, probably the best-known tavern in the area. From the noise coming through the open door it was clear not all of the people coming to Palmyra Village were headed for the stable which would be the site of the barn raising. At least, not yet.

"Look," Benjamin said, "there's Martin Harris's rig." He turned back to his wife. "I think I'll go in and say hello." He handed the reins over to Joshua, who was sitting next to him.

Mary Ann frowned and gave him a sharp look, but he just smiled. "I'll only be a bit, then I'll join you there."

Inwardly she sighed, then felt a quick twinge of guilt. Benjamin had been working hard, with only an occasional trip to town. She had always found it hard to understand this need of men to stand around with other men and lift a glass of beer or down a tankard of grog. She finally smiled and nodded. "All right. Don't be too long."

He jumped down and waved as Joshua got the wagon moving again. Then, as Mary Ann sensed the excitement of her family—even Nathan, normally hard to ruffle, was looking about eagerly—she forgot about taverns and men's ways. She felt her own heart quicken a little at the thought of being in town. She laughed softly and poked at Joshua's back. "It's all right to hurry a little if you want, Joshua," she said.

Getting more and more frustrated with each passing hour, Joshua took another deep swallow from his mug of stout, a dark beer brought over to America from Ireland. For almost an hour now he had tried every device he could think of to maneuver Lydia McBride away from her family and the other young men who constantly hovered around her. Twice he had managed to speak a quick word or two, but then almost instantly someone else would break in before they could really begin to talk.

One of the things which dug at Joshua the most was the way the young men surrounding her were dressed. There was no question but what they represented Palmyra's elite. The one who spoke with her now looked like some peacock strutting in front of a flock of hens. He certainly had not come to help with the barn raising. He wore a double-breasted, knee-length frocked coat with rolled collar. At his throat was a white scarf, every fold carefully crafted. Long, pin-striped trousers were strapped under brightly polished boots. The felt top hat was, Joshua supposed, the latest style—the brim turned up at just the right angle and the crown flared out slightly wider than the base.

Joshua had once seen in a book a picture of a French dandy holding a kerchief to his nose and sniffing daintily at it. At any moment he expected this one to do the same. He looked away, keenly aware of the plainness of his own heavy trousers made of homespun and the boots scuffed and worn and lacking any polish whatever.

But almost immediately his eyes came back to watch Lydia. She was no less fashionably dressed, but on her it was stunning. Her dress was a dark blue, but layered from knee-level to hemline with white ruffles and lace. A high collar, also white, came right up under her chin. It was also trimmed with lace, as were the cuffs of her sleeves. She wore white kid gloves which accentuated the slimness of her hands. Her hat was a large bonnet affair, trimmed with some kind of ornamental feathers and ribbons which dropped down to her waist. The overall effect made it seem as though she floated lightly just above the ground. Without question she was the loveliest thing he had ever laid eyes on, and the sight of her was more intoxicating than the liquid he now drank.

Once full dark had come, the work on the barn had stopped and the town supper had begun. He looked around. A huge bonfire burned brightly, throwing light across the crowd which had gathered in the field east of the livery barn. It had quieted considerably now the supper was over. The children were playing games off in one of the pastures, and from their squeals of delight, Joshua suspected they might be playing skipping and running games like Wink 'Em Slyly or Copenhagen. These involved a lot of catching and kissing the girls, the boys doing it strictly for the sake of the game, while the girls would shriek in horror and run just slow enough to get themselves caught. Joshua smiled ruefully. There were some advantages given to the young.

The adults had started to congregate in smaller groups—the women gathering around to compare notes on cooking or sewing while their fingers flew back and forth knitting this or that shawl or sweater. Melissa was with an older group of girls, too old for children's games and too young to be included in Lydia's circles. But Joshua noted there were sufficient young men standing around to keep them tittering and smiling demurely.

He saw his father, who had rejoined the family not quite as promptly as he had promised, standing with Nathan near the fence of one of the corrals, examining a beautiful team of shire draft horses. For a moment Joshua almost moved over to join them. The animals were the personal property of Zachariah Stoneman, who owned the blacksmith shop and a stable. Standing nearly six feet high at the shoulder and weighing over a ton each, these magnificent animals were descendants of the great war horses of medieval Europe which had carried the heavily armored knights into battle. They were a dramatic contrast to the two ill-tempered mules the Steeds kept, and it was something to just stand and admire their grace and power.

But he was hardly in a mood for his father either, and finally he turned back to watch Lydia, brooding as he watched her over the top of his mug. Two other dandies had now joined the first. The sound of her laughter floated across to him on the still night air. She turned, seeming to sense his gaze, flashed him a smile, and then gave a helpless little shrug of her shoulders. He gave a short bark of disgust. Near as he could tell, she was not suffering too much under all the attention. And in fact, it seemed to Joshua she was giving each and every young man who gathered around her exactly the same treatment she was giving Joshua.

At that moment something else caught Joshua's eye. Three young men were moving away from the huge bonfire which lit the area. As they passed by him, he recognized the stocky figure and wild thatch of hair that belonged to Will Murdock. He also identified Mark Cooper, and he was pretty sure the one on the far side of the group was Will's brother, David. As they passed, he saw light glint off a heavy jug. He also saw two or three of the women shoot disapproving looks in their direction.

Curious, Joshua watched them as they left the circle of fire-light, passed the corral, and moved behind the dark mass of the barn. He glanced over to where Lydia was keeping her three young men totally engrossed. Again she glanced at him, and with a slight motion of her head, invited him to come over. He turned away, angry. He wasn't about to stand in line for her attentions. With sudden determination he emptied the last of the stout, deposited his mug on a table, and moved swiftly toward the barn, keeping one eye on his mother, the other on his father and Nathan standing near the corral.

As he came round the barn, there was a burst of laughter. Will Murdock had the jug propped up on one shoulder and was taking a deep swig from it. He swung the jug down and then across to his brother in one smooth movement, then started at the sight of Joshua. The others fell silent, instantly wary. For a moment Will peered at Joshua in the darkness, then slowly wiped his mouth with the back of his hand. "Steed, isn't it?" he finally asked.

"Yes. Joshua Steed." Joshua stepped forward and stuck out his hand.

Beneath the heavy brows, and in the deep shadows of the barn, Murdock's eyes seemed like two black pits, and there was no way to read his expression. But finally he stuck out his hand

and shook Joshua's; then he turned slightly and spoke to the others. "You remember the Steeds. Bought the Jenningses' land up next to the Harris farm."

There were nods and murmured greetings, but warm cordiality hardly filled the air. David Murdock, his eyes never leaving Joshua's face, lifted the jug of rum and drank noisily. Joshua guessed he was three or four years younger than Will, but it was obvious he was trying to emulate the hard exterior of his older brother. He lowered the jug, mouth pulling back into what was half a grin, half a grimace, then extended it slowly toward Joshua. "Have some rum," he leered.

For a second Joshua hesitated, keenly aware of each set of eyes on him, particularly Will Murdock's. He fought the urge to look over his shoulder and see if his mother or father had followed him. With forced casualness he reached out and took the heavy jug. The strongest drinks he had taken to that point had been the various kinds of beer purchased from the local tavern. He was not prepared for the stream of fire that hit his mouth. He nearly gasped and spewed the liquor out, but at the same instant he saw Will Murdock's eyes, watching him steadily. With every ounce of willpower he could muster he forced himself to swallow. It was like drinking liquid lye. Tears sprang to his eyes as the rum seared his throat and everything else on its way down into his gut. Still, Will Murdock stared at him. Joshua swallowed again. And then again.

Finally, he lowered the jug, praying his tear-filled eyes would not show in the darkness. With the same studied slowness with which David had moved, he wiped his mouth and handed the jug back to Will Murdock. "Thanks," was all he said.

For a moment everyone stood motionless. Then Will finally took the jug and passed it to Cooper. Then he stepped forward and clapped Joshua on the shoulder, giving him a resounding smack. "Good stuff, ain't it?"

"So why you takin' on with ol' Joe Smith?"

They had moved deeper into the shadows of the barn now and were sitting with their backs propped up against the rough boards, Joshua between Will and David Murdock. The jug was considerably lighter now as it was passed up and down between the four of them. Joshua's head seemed strangely detached from his body, and somewhere he was still vaguely aware of a fire burning inside his stomach, but he was also filled with a sense of lightness and ease, as though there were not one thing in all the world which at the moment was out of kilter. But he was nevertheless aware of the hard challenge in Will Murdock's question.

"I ain't taking on with him," he said shortly, his words slurring a little. "My pa hired him and his brother to help us clear land."

Will belched heavily, then nodded, only partially satisfied. "Well, if I was you, I'd tell your pa to think twice about that. Them Smiths are daft as lunatics."

Joshua ignored the pointed advice. "What's all this stuff you were talkin' 'bout the other day? Angels? A gold Bible?"

David Murdock was sitting next to Joshua, half leaning against his shoulder. "You mean you ain't heard?"

"Heard what?"

Will leaned forward. "Smith claims an angel came to him one night in his room. Seems like this angel knowed where some old book is buried. Joe says it's like the Bible." His eyes widened with greed. "It's written on gold plates."

"And you believe that?" Joshua hooted.

"Course I don't believe it," Will said, his mouth twisting angrily. Then he grabbed at Joshua's shirt. "But suppose it's true," he said, suddenly eager. "And suppose we followed ol' Joe when he goes to get it."

Mark Cooper pointed a finger at him, though it weaved back and forth as he spoke. "There's been lots of treasure hidden in these parts. The Spanish brought a lot of treasure up here. Pirates. People round here know about things like that."

Joshua pulled Will's hand away from his shirt. "Sounds like old wives' tales to me."

"Oh yeah?" Will blurted, his mood quickly turning ugly.

"Yeah," Joshua shot right back. "Suppose he did see an

angel—which I don't believe for one minute. Then where's the gold?"

"It's buried in a hill not far from where the Smiths live down in Manchester Township."

There was a poking at Joshua's shoulder. It was David. "The angel said Joe had to wait some time before he could get it."

"Oh," Joshua said, not trying to hide his amusement. "Of course."

Going up on his knees, Will leaned over him, so close Joshua could smell the foulness of his breath. He jabbed his finger hard into his chest. "Laugh like some drooling idiot if you like, but word is, the time's up this fall. Me and the boys are aiming to find out when, and be there when Smith takes them gold plates out."

Cooper broke in again. "That ain't all. Joe claims he saw God himself out in the woods one day."

"What?" Joshua was staring at him.

"Yeah. He went out to pray. He told the Methodist parson about it later. Said Jesus came down too. God and Jesus, just standing there in the air." He waved his hand drunkenly to show where in the air they were.

David now crawled around to face him too, completing the circle around Joshua. "Ya ask me, it was the devil, not God, he saw."

Will Murdock nodded soberly, then they all fell silent, chilled a little by the talk of the devil. Finally, Will sat back. "You know, I like you, Joshua. For a while I was afraid you might be friends with Smith. But I like you."

He grabbed the jug and took a quick draw from it, wiped his mouth, then got deadly serious. "But you ought to know. People are already startin' to talk about your family. They're wonderin' if you're takin' up with them Smiths, if you believe all that crazy stuff."

"Well, we don't. This is the first I even heard about it."

Will nodded. "I believe you. But you better tell your pa. Tell him to hire somebody else. Somebody who don't go out in the woods and talk with the devil."

Ⅰt is well known that some of the first people to cross the stormy North Atlantic to the New World came in hopes of escaping the religious oppression sweeping Europe in the wake of the Reformation. Puritans, Pilgrims, Quakers, Roman Catholics, Huguenots, Anabaptists, Jews—they came to America in pursuit of religious freedom. For these devout and God-fearing souls, religion permeated their lives. These were not just Sabbath worshippers. They sought to live as they believed. They read from the Bible daily, often using it as the primary text in teaching their children to read.

But not all who came shared those feelings. Many saw the New World as a land of tremendous opportunity. There were fortunes to be made, new lives to be carved out, and all of this in a political climate of unheard-of freedom. So along with the pious came the promoters, with the devout came the destitute. Nonconformists, radicals, free spirits—these came as readily as the godly, the reverent, and the dogmatic.

Following the revolutionary war and the ratification of the

Constitution, the winds of freedom which had helped forge a new nation took their toll on religious fervor. In this new climate, many found the doctrines of Calvinism—the idea that man was depraved and saved only by the grace of a benevolent deity—as deeply abhorrent as the arrogant demands of King George. They began to challenge traditional religious dogma. Called Deists, they believed in a supreme being, but rejected the idea that this being tightly controlled the lives of men. They felt he set in place immutable laws, laws upon which the universe was based and over which man had little or no control. If man was in harmony with those laws, then he was in harmony with Deity. Deists preferred such terms as Nature or Divine Providence to the more traditional God or Heavenly Father.

Others, called Unitarians, rejected the three-in-one concept of Deity, accepting God as an absolute unity of mind, spirit, and personage. To the Unitarians, God was Divine Mind or Spirit, and man's resemblance to God was purely spiritual. Imported from England, the Universalists rejected Calvin's idea of election to grace. They believed God would eventually restore all mankind to a state of holiness and happiness, two conditions which are inseparably intertwined.

Deists, Unitarians, Universalists—the theological forces in post-revolutionary war America were as diverse and divisive as the forces which led to the rebellion against Great Britain. Rationalism and secularism swept through all levels of society. By the late 1700s fewer than ten percent of the population attended formal church services. The universities could hardly boast an enlightened student who still belonged to a church.

It was into this climate of religious turmoil that Benjamin Steed was born. Jacob Steed was a hardheaded Connecticut farmer and veteran of the revolutionary war, including Valley Forge. He was a true theological eclectic, picking and choosing from the various movements of his day the concepts which fitted his own nature most comfortably. Deeply influenced by the "enlightened skepticism" of the age, he largely rejected formalized religion as exploitive and out of touch with the spirit of the age. Being of the common people and not from the intellectual elite populating the cities, his theology was also mixed with a generous portion of good old-fashioned folklore—water witching, divination, spells to ward off bad luck, and the like—and he saw no fundamental conflict between the two. While this might have been confusing to the more academic-minded theologians, one word really summed up the core of values which motivated—if not drove—Jacob Steed. That word was *duty*. It embraced many things—hard work, integrity, commitment, honor, respect for the rights of others, loyalty, patriotism. These constituted his theology, and he held to them as fiercely as any Bible-thumping churchgoer. And he had indoctrinated his children with them as religiously and thoroughly as any catechism. Of organized, formalized religion; of preachers, Bible study, baptism, and communion; of Sabbath worship in some man-made structure—well, there had been more than a few solemn warnings from Benjamin's father about the hazards which lay in those directions.

Born in Massachusetts about seventeen months after Benjamin, Mary Ann Morgan was also a product, albeit of a different kind, of the religious forces sweeping America. Her father, the youngest son of an arch-conservative Congregational minister, did not undergo any deep intellectual processes related to his faith. By his teen years he had broken out in open rebellion against his father's draconian code of behavior, and when he reached adulthood he simply abandoned all commitment to the church.

Mary Ann's mother came of Quaker stock. The Quakers had always stressed the importance of religious experience over formalized sacraments or worship services. When she married Mary Ann's father, it was not surprising in the Morgan home that there was no commitment to any one church or participation in organized religion. In the first seventeen years of her life Mary Ann had never attended a formal church service, though just prior to her marriage she and her next youngest sister had, out of curiosity, attended a camp meeting or two as they came through the area.

But that did not mean the Morgan home was one filled with secularism. Religion was still a powerful force in the lives of both parents. There were few days when Mary Ann and the other children had not sat at the feet of their mother and father and read together from the Bible. With equal frequency she had been taught that the Savior was the perfect model upon which one could pattern a life of honor and joy.

When Benjamin Steed met the young girl who worked like a man alongside her father on the turnpikes, there was little talk of religious matters during the brief courtship. One might have thought the religious differences between Mary Ann Morgan and this down-to-earth New England farmer were deep enough to eventually bring conflict to the marriage. But such was not the case. Mary Ann felt some disappointment that her husband did not take the lead in spiritual matters, but he had never balked at her attempts to carry on the traditions she had experienced in her own home.

For a time, when Joshua and Nathan were small, she had gone to several churches, trying to find one which suited her. Though he made his feelings about organized religion clear, Benjamin had never tried to stop her. And while he chose not to lead out in the morning Bible reading, he always joined the family without complaint or resentment. She knew he found her unshakable faith a little quaint, but he also readily admitted a person could do worse than model his or her life on that of the Carpenter of Galilee.

So while they could hardly be described as being one in their spiritual outlook, she and Benjamin had few conflicts over the matter. Most important, he loved his wife deeply and seemed to admire her steadfast determination to teach their children things of value. And that counted for a lot with Mary Ann Morgan Steed.

It was Easter morning, 1827. The fundamental religious differences between Mary Ann and her husband were clearly illustrated by the fact that Benjamin still slept heavily in their bed while Mary Ann was outside in the spring sunshine, the Bible open on her lap. That was due, in good measure, to the ale he had drunk the night before. Normally he was up at first light and out milking the cow or doing the other chores. But Mary Ann had quietly done what needed to be done, then got her Bible and slipped out of the door again.

On New Year's Day she had promised herself she would read all four Gospels through once again by Easter time. The day had arrived and she had the last three chapters of John to go if she was to finish her commitment.

She sat on a log near the creek, the sun lighting her hair and warming her back. It was another glorious spring morning. Beads of dew dimpled the grass, and the newly developed leaves had a softness to their green that would not be seen again. The whistling call of a cardinal floated up from the trees which lined the stream. A sense of happiness and peace filled her soul, and sudden tears sprung to her eyes. How good was life! How good was the majesty and grace of God!

There was still some lingering guilt about not being in a church somewhere with her family on this sacred day, but when she had suggested it to Benjamin two or three days earlier, he had flatly refused. If she wanted a special worship service at home, there would be no objection, but crowding into a pew to hear some mortal expounding on the divine seemed pointless.

She had once thought she might raise the issue again when the day arrived, but the disappearance of Joshua clinched that. When the activities in the village finally began to break up about nine-thirty the previous evening, they had searched for Joshua to no avail. At first Benjamin had only been irritated. But when a young boy reported seeing Joshua with the Murdock boys, and another added they were half-drunk and still drinking, Benjamin was furious. When he saw the pinched mouths and heard the whispered clucking of the women lingering around the fire, he came as close to a rage as she had seen in a long time. They had finally come home without him. That was another thing which had driven her to get out of bed and come outside with her Bible. There was an ugly confrontation brewing, and this might be the only ray of spiritual light she would find today.

About thirty yards away the cabin door opened and closed softly. Nathan was on the narrow porch, still tucking his shirt into his trousers, squinting into the bright sunshine. Mary Ann straightened and waved. Surprised, Nathan blinked again, then came toward her.

"Hello, Mother. I didn't know you were up."

"Yes. It was such a beautiful morning, I couldn't bear to stay in bed."

He sat down next to her, glancing at the Bible, then moved enough so he could lean against another tree. He raised his face to the sun and closed his eyes. "It *is* a beautiful day."

She smiled at him, feeling a quick surge of affection. How like Nathan, of all her children, to leave the comfort of his bed to enjoy the simple bounties of nature! She touched his arm briefly, then turned back to the Bible.

"What are you reading?"

She answered without looking up. "The twentieth chapter of John. It is dawn of that first Easter morning. Mary has just come to the tomb to see if there is anything more she can do for the crucified Master."

Nathan murmured softly. "That's appropriate reading for this morning."

"Yes. I could have finished it three or four days ago, but I wanted to save it for today. Do you want me to read it aloud?"

"Yes, I would like that."

She read softly: Mary had come to the tomb only to find to her horror it was empty. She raced back to Peter and John. "They have taken away the Lord," she cried. The two—chief

Apostle and beloved disciple—also came, and stooped to go in. Seeing the burial clothes folded neatly and laid aside, John said simply of himself, "And he saw, and believed."

Now Nathan's mother came to the account of Mary, tearful and stricken, lingering still at the garden tomb. Her voice slowed and deepened. Nathan opened his eyes, startled by the sudden realization that this woman was his mother's namesake. Strange, he had never made that connection before.

" 'And when she had thus said, she turned herself back, and saw Jesus standing, and knew not that it was Jesus.' "

Nathan leaned forward, peering at her. Completely engrossed in the words, she took no notice of him. He marvelled at the beauty which lit her face. The sun was behind her, but her skin almost seemed to glow, as though the light came right through her body.

" 'Sir,' " she continued, " 'if thou have borne him hence, tell me where thou hast laid him, and I will take him away.' "

At that moment tears welled up and spilled over, tracing glistening tracks down his mother's cheeks. She stopped, then took a breath, fighting for control. Nathan felt his own eyes suddenly burning. " 'Jesus saith unto her,' . . . 'Mary.' "

And there it was. A single word, and in one blinding, glorious instant grief was turned to joy, shock and horror to exultation. For the first time, Nathan had the tiniest glimmer of how Jesus must have spoken Mary's name—the tone of his voice, the depths of his love, the expression on his face.

His mother had stopped and now wept openly, too moved to continue. He slid over and took the book gently from her. "Let me go on, Mother."

She nodded, brushing at her cheeks, smiling at him through the tears. "I'm sorry. I just love that part so much."

"I know. It's beautiful." He swallowed and continued on. And suddenly they were no longer words on the paper for him either. He was there in the upper room, marveling at the power of the resurrected Christ. He dropped to his knees with Thomas, burning with shame for doubting the disciples' testimony and demanding to see for himself. He was on the shores of the Sea of Galilee, and the words of the Master to Peter burned into his mind: "Feed my sheep."

He finished quietly, then closed the book, and leaned back. For several minutes they sat there, neither wanting to break the spell which had fallen over them. Even the bubbling of the brook and the trilling of the birds seemed muted and reverential.

With one finger Nathan traced an aimless pattern on the cover of the old family Bible. His mother finally leaned over and placed one hand over his. "Tell me what is in your thoughts, son."

He looked up, a little startled at the question and at where his thoughts had taken him. "If the Savior was resurrected, does that mean he still lives?"

"Of course."

"As a real being?"

She was peering deep into his eyes now, puzzled. "Yes. Thomas felt the wounds in his hands and feet. That seems pretty real."

"But that was two thousand years ago."

She leaned back, eyebrows lifting a little. "What has time got to do with it?"

"Could he still appear to people?"

"Yes."

He finally turned to her. "Think about it, Mother. I mean the Savior himself. Do you think he could appear to someone today? Now?"

Mary Ann took the book from his hands and set it in her lap, looking down at the cover. "If he lived then and appeared to men, I suppose he could—"

"I know he could," Nathan burst out, "but will he? Does he?"

"I . . ." She stopped. "I've never thought about it in those specific terms. But yes, I guess he could." She looked at him again. "Why?"

For several moments Nathan did not respond, just frowned, lost in his own thoughts. Finally she could bear it no longer. "What, Nathan? What is it?"

"All right." He sighed. "Joshua told you about what happened the other day in town with Joseph Smith."

Mary Ann frowned. "Yes, but you know we don't hold with gossip, Nathan."

"I know. But . . ." He was struggling with his feelings. Finally he decided to plunge ahead. "The other day, when I walked part of the way home with Hyrum and Joseph—"

"Yes?"

"Well, I kind of asked Joseph how come people were saying those kinds of things about him."

"Nathan, you shouldn't have. It's not our affair."

"I know, but . . ." He shrugged. "I wanted to know."

He looked away, staring at nothing as he began to rub idly at his trouser legs.

"Well?"

Nathan turned, then straightened. Slowly he began, starting with Joseph's account of his troubled quest for which church to join. To his surprise, his mother nodded at several points, as though understanding exactly the frustration Joseph had gone through. But when Nathan moved on to tell of Joseph's experience in the grove of trees near his home, she fell silent. He had been tempted to tell all of this to Joshua that night after he had talked with Joseph, but something had held him back. Now after learning Joshua had been with the Murdocks, he was glad he hadn't. And somehow, Nathan also knew he could not share it with his father. But now with his mother, on this beautiful morning, the time seemed right, and he unburdened himself of it all. Throughout the entire narrative she never said a word, just watched him intently, only glancing away for a moment now and then, as though trying to comprehend it all.

Nathan finally finished and sat back. Still his mother did not speak. "So, there it is," he said.

"That is an incredible story," Mary Ann said softly.

"I know," he responded, unable to keep the glumness out of his voice. "I've never had anything leave me in such confusion. As I listened to him, one part of me believed—" He stopped, the very word giving him pause. "Yes, I guess I wanted to believe every word Joseph was saying. Before he told me, I would have fought any man who called Joseph a liar."

He exhaled wearily. "But at the same time, another part of me was almost reeling, like I'd been poleaxed. I don't know what to think anymore."

Mary Ann nodded absently, as though she had only barely heard him. Finally she came out of her thoughts and looked at him. "The Smiths are fine young men. I don't think Joseph is a liar either."

"But Mother. He said he actually saw God and talked with him." His voice lowered, partly in awe, partly in disbelief. "That just doesn't happen, Mother."

She picked up the Bible again, letting her fingers run softly along its spine. "It used to."

"That's why I asked you what I did. Do you think men could see the Savior today?"

"I don't know. It doesn't seem possible, and yet . . . oh, Nathan, I would like to think it is still possible."

"No wonder people are talking about him. They think he's either mad or possessed of an evil spirit."

She looked at him for a long moment, her face unreadable. "I suppose that's what people said about Paul and his vision, too," she finally said.

Nathan stiffened.

"What?"

"That's exactly what Joseph said."

"What?"

"He said he felt exactly like Paul. No matter what they say about him, he knows he has seen a vision and if he denies it, it will be like he is denying God."

For almost a full minute they sat there, mother and son, lost in their own thoughts. Then Mary Ann swung around so she was facing Nathan directly. She laid the Bible down, then clasped her hands around her knees and leaned forward. "I want you to tell me the whole story again. As much as possible, try to remember Joseph's exact words. Especially what God and Jesus said to him."

Nathan took a deep breath, letting his mind go back to the evening two days previous as he had sat with Joseph and Hyrum. This time he went more slowly, interspersing the account with other details, how Joseph had looked as he recounted his vision, Hyrum's occasional comment in support of his brother. When he was finished, his mother barely moved. Her eyes were down, looking at the Bible she had set on the log beside her. Then slowly, as if coming out of a daze, she straightened. Picking up the Bible, she opened it, turning pages toward the back of the book. She found what she was looking for and read it to herself.

Nathan leaned over enough to see she was reading in the book of James.

She looked up. " 'If any of you lack wisdom, let him ask of God,' " she quoted softly. "That's quite a promise." Suddenly she closed the book and stood up, brushing off her dress. "I've got to get breakfast. Your father will be waking."

She turned to go, but Nathan stood quickly and grabbed at her arm. "But Mother."

She smiled gently at him. "What?"

"Do you think it's possible?"

Her face softened with affection, and she reached up and touched his cheek. "With God, all things are possible, Nathan."

"I know that," he said, frustrated by her evasiveness. "But do you think it really happened, or is Joseph being deceived?"

She shook her head. "I don't know." She held up the book for him to see. "You know how I love the Bible, Nathan."

"Yes."

She looked away, gazing out across the cleared land, now plowed and readied for planting. "For many years I've felt like the Bible, as wonderful as it is, is not enough. I've felt like there has to be more. The Bible talks of baptism, for example. But how can you be baptized without a church? And communion. We need to take communion. You need more than the Bible to do that."

Nathan looked at her closely, surprised by her words. She had never given even the slightest hint she held such feelings.

Finally she turned her gaze back on him. "Remember when we lived in Vermont, we went to different churches for a time?"

Nathan nodded, puzzled by the direction the conversation had taken.

"I was searching for the right one. Even back then."

"But I thought we never joined one because Pa didn't hold much with organized religion."

A quick shadow darkened her eyes. "He doesn't. And that was part of it. But I don't think he would have stopped us if I had insisted on it."

"But you didn't."

"No."

"Why?"

For several moments she was silent, running the palm of her hand softly across the leather cover of the old Bible. "I've never told anyone this. Not even your father."

Again she had managed to surprise Nathan. "Told him what?"

Still she hesitated, as though not yet sure whether to share her secret. "What, Mother?"

She took a deep breath, then let it out slowly, her eyes closing momentarily. "You said Joseph Smith went into the woods because he wanted to know which church he should join."

"Yes."

"Well, during that time, when I was searching for answers to the same question . . ."

"Yes?"

"I didn't read James, but I came to the same conclusion. I decided I had to pray. Without God's help I couldn't know for sure which one was right." She closed her eyes for a moment. "I prayed a great deal about it as a matter of fact, over a period of several months. I never went off into the woods, but hardly a day went by I didn't ask God the same question Joseph asked him."

She stopped and gave him a strange look.

Nathan felt a sudden prickle up the back of his neck. "What? What happened?"

"One morning I had gotten up very early to pray. Your father was still asleep. I . . . as I was praying, suddenly this feeling came over me. It was like . . ." She stopped, groping for the right words. "I don't know. Thoughts just came into my mind. Afterwards I wasn't even sure it had happened."

Nathan was watching her intently, searching her face. "What kind of thoughts?" he asked in a low voice.

"I suddenly felt—very strongly—that for now I was to join none of the churches."

She stopped, her eyes far away, lost in the memory of that morning. Nathan was tempted to nudge her, to bring her back. When she finally went on, she spoke softly. "I felt that sooner or later I would be shown which church I should join, but for now I was just to be patient."

Nathan was staring at his mother openly, his eyes mirroring his surprise. No wonder Joseph's account had struck her with such force.

Again she smiled, her eyes misted with a faraway look. "I'm going to talk to the Lord. Maybe the time has come to ask again."

And with that, she took his arm and they started back for the cabin.

Sixteen-year-old Melissa Steed put the bowl of corn flour mush on the table and walked to the stairs. She cupped one hand to her mouth and called loud enough for her voice to carry clear up into the loft. "Matthew, Becca. Breakfast's ready."

"Comin'." It was Rebecca's voice, but it was Matthew's body that came shooting down the stairs and into the main room of the cabin.

Melissa smiled. Her youngest brother never did anything at normal speed. "Happy Easter, Matthew," she called.

His head shot up in surprise. Then he scanned the room, with his usual lopsided grin. Nathan was at the table cutting thin slices of bacon off the side of pork he'd gotten from the smokehouse. His mother was at the fireplace tending a large black frying pan, where the bacon sizzled and sputtered. Melissa was still at the table, arranging the dishes.

"Happy Easter, everybody," he crowed to them all.

"Happy Easter, son," Mary Ann said.

"Happy Easter, Matthew," Nathan said.

"Do you think there are Easter eggs, Mama?" Matthew asked eagerly.

Melissa shot Nathan a quick wink. After their return from Palmyra the previous evening, the two of them had spent a half hour hiding some boiled eggs and a few pieces of hard candy in the barn. "I thought Easter eggs were only for when children were especially good," Melissa said to Nathan gravely.

"I have been good," Matthew cried. "Real good."

Nathan shook his head. "I don't know. What about last week when you let the dog chase the chickens?"

Matthew whirled, his face outraged. "It wasn't me." Then he saw the look on their faces and grinned again, turning to his mother. "Can I go look, Mama?"

She stepped to her youngest and gave him a quick squeeze. "Get the spoons on. We'll have breakfast, then we'll go out to the barn and see."

Becca had come down in time to catch the last part of the conversation. Though two days before she had loftily sniffed that she was too old for childish things, Melissa noted, her nine-year-old sister now went to work helping Matthew set the table without being asked. For the girl who could find a dozen excuses for avoiding unpleasant tasks, this said a lot.

A moment later the door opened and Benjamin Steed came in, carrying a bucket of milk, still topped with foam.

"Happy Easter, Papa!" Matthew cried.

"Happy Easter, Matthew." He swung the milk up to the counter where Mary Ann had set out the five-gallon milk can with a muslin cloth over the opening. Melissa stepped up beside him and held the cloth down as her father poured the milk carefully through it to strain out any particles of dirt that had fallen in the bucket.

"Thank you, Melissa." He capped the can and turned. "Nathan, put this out in the icehouse till it cools down."

As Nathan came over, Benjamin suddenly looked around the room and frowned. "What time did Joshua finally come in last night?"

Melissa whirled in surprise and shot a look at her mother. Mary Ann was equally startled. The first thing she had done before going out to read the Bible was check to see if Joshua had returned. She assumed Benjamin had done the same.

"Joshua isn't here," Mary Ann said quietly.

Benjamin jerked around. "What?"

Melissa tensed.

"He hasn't come home yet, Pa," Nathan inserted quickly. "He must have stayed in town last night."

Melissa felt a clutch of anxiety as she watched the anger flash across her father's face. She, more than any of the children—perhaps even more than her mother—understood the complex of emotions which drove her oldest brother and which led more and more to the clashes with his father. Melissa also seemed to have a special closeness to her father, understanding the New England stubbornness and rock-hard integrity which formed the foundation of his character. Normally she could cajole him out of his frustrations with his oldest son and help avert the more violent confrontations. But she sensed that a new and frightening dimension in the relationship between Benjamin Steed and his oldest son had been opened.

Disappearing was one thing; drinking in company with the

Murdocks was something else again. The Steed family had been shamed, and Benjamin Steed took great stock in one's name and reputation. Forgiveness for any damage done there wouldn't come easy from him.

Her father spun around without a word, stalked to the door, and took down his hat. "I'll be back," he muttered.

Mary Ann moved quickly to his side and laid a hand on his arm. "Breakfast is ready, Ben. There's no use going into town now. You don't even know where he is."

"He's probably on his way home right now," Nathan jumped in.

Benjamin just stood there, his eyes hard, his jaw working as he clenched and unclenched his teeth.

Melissa took a quick breath. "Pa, Josh had his heart set on getting to talk with that Lydia McBride girl. But she paid him no mind. I think he took it kinda hard."

"He don't need you sticking up for him." He snapped it out at her, like the crack of a whip.

Melissa felt her temper leap, but she caught the warning look from her mother and dropped her eyes. She felt a deep ache for Joshua.

"Please, Ben," Mary Ann pleaded. "It's Easter morning. Come and eat. He'll be comin' along."

Finally he jammed his hat back on its peg and moved to the table. He sat down hard, staring at nothing. Nathan motioned sharply with his head and Becca and Matthew jumped to sit down as well. The others joined them, the silence heavy in the room.

Finally Benjamin looked up. "Becca. Offer grace, please. We'll wait no longer for your brother."

Chapter Six

The first thing to penetrate Joshua Steed's awareness
was the brightness pounding down on his eyelids, jabbing at
him like needles. He groaned and rolled over to get away from
it, and instantly regretted it. Waves of hammering pain exploded inside his skull. Pressing the heels of his hands hard
against his temples to suppress the waves of pain, he pulled
himself up into a sitting position. He opened his eyes slowly,
then blinked in bewilderment. His shirtsleeves and his pant legs
were covered with straw. There was a strong smell of cows. His
mouth was dry and foul, his tongue covered with a thick scum.
Through the cracks in a board wall in front of him, rays of sunshine were streaming, turning the myriad specks of dust into
drifting pinpoints of light. He realized it was the sunshine that
had awakened him.

He closed his eyes, struggling to push his way through the
heavy creek-bottom mud that clogged his mind. Cracking one
eye open again, he turned his head slowly to survey his sur-
roundings. A mound of hay was to his left, a pitchfork stuck in

one side of it. The collar of a harness hung against a wall. He turned the other way as the sound of heavy snoring finally registered in his brain. Then in an instant it all came flooding back. Will Murdock lay sprawled across the straw-strewn floor, the empty jug of rum lying on its side next to his head. His brother, David, was a few feet further on, lying on his back, twisted at a crazy angle, the flap on his pants unbuttoned, showing a corner of dirty underwear beneath it. Mark Cooper had collapsed on another pile of hay in the far corner.

Joshua dropped his head into his hands, massaging his temples carefully as the recollection returned. The last he remembered was hearing voices approaching and Will Murdock motioning frantically for the others to follow him into the dark recesses of the barn. They must have collapsed there and slept through the night.

He jerked up sharply, then groaned, not for the flash of pain which the sudden movement caused, but for the image of his father which leaped into his brain. His family! Last night he had simply walked away from the activities, following after Will Murdock. He had said nothing to anyone. He groaned again. Going home was gonna be right down ugly. He could feel it in his gut.

Joshua pulled himself up and leaned heavily against the wall until the barn's interior stopped whirling slowly around him. He stepped over Will Murdock, not much caring whether he waked him, then staggered outside, clamping his eyes shut against the bright sunshine. Still moving slowly, he tucked his shirt back into his pants and brushed at the straw on his trousers. Crawling between the rails of the corral fence, he shooed two horses away from the watering trough. They snorted and moved away, eyeing him warily. Ignoring them, he took their place and buried his head in the cold water, holding his fists against his eyes, trying to blot out the picture of his family—especially his father—waiting for him at home.

At eighteen years old, Lydia McBride was already fully aware of her beauty and the effect it had on men. So in spite of the grumbling of her father, she stood in front of the mirror to make sure everything was exactly as it should be.

Her mother, who had nearly died giving birth to Lydia and who had not been able to have any more children since, shamelessly doted on her only offspring. This dress, ordered special from one of New York City's leading dress designers, had arrived the week before. Lydia felt a quick twinge of guilt, knowing what the dress had cost her father, but today was Easter Sunday, and her mother had brushed aside any protests. There was an unspoken competition developing among the mothers and daughters of Palmyra as the effect of the Erie Canal's commerce began to be felt in the town. And Hannah Lovina Hurlburt McBride was not about to be bested in the competition.

As Lydia gave her hair one last brush, her mother stepped to the door. There was an audible gasp. "Oh, Lydia," she breathed.

Lydia turned slowly, doing a full three-hundred-and-sixty-degree circle for her mother's benefit.

"It's perfect! Absolutely perfect."

"I love it, Mama. Thank you so much for getting it for me."

"Hannah!" Josiah McBride's voice bellowed up the stairs.

Hannah McBride moved to her daughter and fussed for a moment at the lace on the collar. Then she smoothed down the back of the dress and stepped back to look again, moving back and forth slightly with a critical eye. Finally she nodded. "You are so lovely, Lydia. It's just perfect."

"Hannah! Lydia!" Her father's voice was much sharper now. "It is ten minutes to ten. We are going to be late."

Lydia smiled. Most people found her father to be stern and humorless, but she knew that beneath his public exterior he was not nearly as gruff as he seemed. And he was only marginally behind his wife when it came to indulging and pampering his daughter. But Lydia also knew that his recent appointment as one of the ruling elders in the church had been a thing of great importance to him and that it was wise not to push him on this matter.

"Coming, Papa," she called. Her mother handed her the parasol and white gloves and they started down the stairs.

Joshua moved slowly along Main Street in Palmyra Village. He still walked slowly and placed his feet on the boardwalk gingerly, but he felt considerably better. The plunge in the watering trough had helped somewhat, but to his surprise, as he had approached Church Street, he noticed two horses and a wagon pulled up in front of Asa Lilly's tavern, where he used the last of his money to nurse his way through two cups of very strong and bitter coffee. The girl who served him, a plump seventeen-year-old who constantly giggled when he looked at her, offered him a brush and a mirror as well, and when he walked out he was considerably more presentable than when he entered.

He moved slowly, enjoying the warmth of the spring sunshine on his back. One part of him urged him to stride out, getting home as quickly as possible so as not to add to his already troubled situation. Another part of him lagged back, postponing the inevitable clash which lay before him.

The sound of a buckboard driving by brought him around. A man, woman, and three children, all dressed in Sunday best, looked him up and down as they passed. The mother looked away quickly as Joshua caught her eye, the faint look of distaste evident on her face. Only the youngest girl, a cherub-cheeked three-year-old, waved happily to him. The family looked vaguely familiar, and he supposed he had seen her at the supper the previous evening.

Now Joshua noted there were others moving along the street as well, both on his side and the other. All were dressed in their best finery, and he suddenly remembered this was Sunday. Easter Sunday. A block and a half ahead of him he could see a dozen or more buckboards and carriages pulled up in front of the Presbyterian church.

He stopped. Josiah McBride was an elder in the Presbyterian church. Certainly he wouldn't miss Sunday morning services. Perhaps they hadn't left yet and he could get a glimpse of Lydia.

The image of Lydia surrounded by other young men flashed into his mind and he expelled air with a short burst of derision. Only fools were blind to reality. It was time to put fantasy aside. The tavern keeper's daughter, the one who had served him coffee a few minutes earlier—now there was realism. Not some beauty who was the daughter of one of Palmyra's most respected citizens.

But in spite of himself, Joshua turned and moved slowly back up the street until he stood a few doors down and across from the McBride home and store. He leaned against a post, hoping the shade of the overhang would keep him from being too conspicuous. The door to the McBride store and home was closed. He turned around and looked at the clock in the store window behind him. It showed eight minutes to ten o'clock. Services must begin at ten, he decided.

He shook his head. Being one of the ruling elders in the church, McBride would probably be one of the first ones there, which meant Lydia was at this very moment already sitting in the McBride family pew inside the church. Across the street another couple hurried quickly along, their four children in tow behind them.

Disgusted with himself, Joshua turned to go. But at that moment a sound from across the street swung him back around. He felt a quick catch of breath. Lydia McBride and her mother had just come out of the front door of the store. Both were wearing long dresses puffed out with petticoats, but Joshua had eyes only for Lydia. Her dress was of a soft blue with sleeves down to the wrist. A lace bodice was matched by lace trim around the collar and sleeves. Once again she carried a parasol which matched her dress, and she also wore a white knitted shawl across her shoulders. Even at twenty or thirty rods' distance, her dark hair glistened beneath the small hat she wore, and the sight of her took his breath away a little.

She nodded and smiled at the passing family, and Joshua heard the soft murmur of her voice float across to him on the still morning air. He couldn't help himself. He just stood and stared, feeling the odd mixture of excitement and panic welling up in him again. He took a step forward, then moved back quickly into the shadows. Josiah McBride had followed his wife and daughter out of the store. He turned to lock the door, then took his wife by the arm.

"Come on," he said, the irritation in his voice clearly evident even at this distance, "we're going to be late."

When they stepped out into the bright sunshine, Lydia had to blink quickly to adjust her eyes to the light. It was a glorious Easter morning. She nodded and spoke to the Baxters, noting with pleasure the sudden widening of the eyes as Mrs. Baxter saw her dress. *Let them covet*, she thought happily. *Let them all covet.*

As they started up the street, Lydia saw they were indeed the last of the people moving toward the church. She gave a quick toss of her head, not displeased with the knowledge that all eyes would be turned to them as they entered the church.

A figure standing in the shadows caught her eye. She started, peering more closely. It was Joshua Steed. Lydia instantly glanced at her father and mother to see if they had noticed. They hadn't. Her father had his arm through his wife's and was striding along with determination. She fell back a step and let her hand stir in a small wave.

She saw his hand start to lift, then it fell immediately when her father glanced back at her. "Come, Lydia, do keep up."

She nodded and hastened her step a little, but still hung back a pace from her parents. There was a sudden stir of excitement as she saw out of the corner of her eye that Joshua had started to move now too, lagging back a little so as to be out of her parents' peripheral vision, but matching his pace with theirs.

Her mind went back to the night before. Even from a distance she had seen the longing in Joshua's eyes. Did she have the power to draw him over, even though it was obvious his courage was wavering? She had enjoyed tantalizing him a little, testing her attractive pull. But he had not come, and when she had turned back after a time, he was gone. He had not re-appeared for the rest of the night, and it had surprised her how sharply the pang of disappointment had cut her.

So far her parents suspected nothing concerning her interest in this muscular young man who had moved into Palmyra Township the previous fall. Taken aback, Lydia considered her own choice of words. Interest? Was that what she was feeling for Joshua Steed? She had well over a dozen young men who fawned over her, some from the finest families in the village. Lydia had become quite bored with it all—bored with the end-less matchmaking attempts by hungry mothers, bored with the effortlessness with which she could turn heads.

But Joshua Steed was different. Oh, there was no mistaking the fact he had been smitten. When he had first come into the store and stopped dead, the stunned wonder at her so evident in his eyes, it made her laugh inwardly in complete delight. Yes, her power over him was there, but it had not knocked him off balance. And she liked that. Joshua had not joined the circle of hovering males. Instead he had walked away.

If she had been completely honest with herself, Lydia would also have acknowledged that part of the intrigue with Joshua Steed was the instinctive sense that her parents would abso-lutely disapprove of any relationship with him. Her mother had high hopes for a marriage of appropriate status for her only daughter. On the other hand, eighteen years of being an only child had left Lydia strong minded, strong willed, and totally, irrevocably determined that no one, not even her mother and father, would make the determination of whom she was to marry.

Lydia stopped. "Oh, Papa," she exclaimed. "I forgot a hand-kerchief."

Her father whirled, exasperated. "Lydia, we are late for church. You'll have to do without."

"Father, I must have a handkerchief."

Hannah McBride turned, a little annoyed herself. "I laid one out for you, Lydia."

"I know, Mama, but I must have left it there." She pushed the hanky deeper into the pocket of her dress, then pulled the corners of her mouth down. "You know I always cry on Easter Sunday, Mama. I must have a handkerchief."

Mrs. McBride turned to her husband. "She does need a handkerchief, Josiah."

Lydia was all contrition. "You go on ahead, I won't be long."

Josiah McBride threw up his hands in disgust. He fumbled in his pocket for the keys, then thrust them at her. "You hurry now. I don't want you making a grand entrance after the parson has started his sermon."

"It will only take a moment," Lydia called back over her shoulder.

From across the street Joshua had stopped to watch, not hearing the conversation clearly but sensing it had to do with Lydia's seeing him. Not daring to hope, he watched as Lydia hurried back to the store and unlocked the door. But as she opened it, his heart leaped. She was looking directly at him, motioning quickly with her hand for him to come across the street. Then she stepped inside.

All thoughts of headache and hangover instantly banished, Joshua crossed the street swiftly and approached the store. The door to the store was now nearly closed and there was no sign of her. He stopped, confused. Had he misread her signal? Then came a whispered voice. "Not here, Joshua. Come around to the back of the store. Go up between the saddlery and McIntyre's pharmacy. I'll be at the window."

By the time he had made his way between the two buildings, then to the back of the frame structure which housed the McBride residence and store, Joshua found himself filled with a growing excitement. And yet it was mixed with a faint irritation as well. The memory of the previous evening was still painfully sharp in his mind. He slowed his step, suddenly not wanting to appear too eager.

The window opened and Lydia leaned out. "Joshua. What are you doing in town?"

There was no missing the breathless excitement in her voice, and suddenly any irritation in Joshua vanished. She was genuinely glad to see him. He shrugged. "I stayed over last night. I'm just on my way home now."

"What happened to you? I looked for you after the supper."

"I was there, but you already had a lot of people there with you." He had almost said "young men" but quickly substituted "people" instead.

She brushed it aside with an impatient shake of her head. "That's partially my father's doing. He's convinced it's time for me to marry, and he keeps dropping invitations to what he thinks are eligible suitors."

She looked down swiftly, blushing. "I kept hoping you would come over too."

"I . . ." He let it trail off, not sure what to answer.

"I saw you standing over beyond the fire, but when I finally got a chance to walk over there, you were gone. I saw your family, but I couldn't find you."

Joshua felt a quick stab of regret. He had left in frustration, and missed the very solution to his frustration. But if she had really come looking for him, that meant something, didn't it?

She reached out a hand and laid it on his arm. "Joshua, I must go. My father will be furious if I'm late."

He nodded. "Thank you for coming back."

She squeezed his arm. "I wanted to see you."

He felt his heart leap. "I wanted to see you too."

Glancing quickly over her shoulder, she leaned even a little further out the window, lowering her voice. "Joshua, I wish you hadn't gone." She stopped, a little taken aback by her own forwardness, then rushed on. "I like you, Joshua."

He stared at her, a little dazed. "And I like you, Lydia."

She smiled, and at that moment, she was prettier than any-thing Joshua could ever remember seeing in his twenty years of living.

"Listen," she went on quickly, "Wednesday my father has to go to Waterloo for supplies for the store. He's taking my mother. They'll be gone for three days. I'll be staying at my aunt's house. It's about a mile south of town on the Canan-daigua Road. It's a big white two-story house on the east side of the road. There's a red barn out back."

"All right," Joshua said slowly, not sure what she meant.

"My aunt isn't nearly as strict as my father." She smiled, blushing a little. "And she doesn't feel like she has to tell him everything."

He grinned foolishly. "So if I were to come, I could see you."

She nodded, laughing softly. "Can you come?"

Getting away from the farm during the week would be an in-teresting challenge, particularly in light of what was waiting for him at home today, but he didn't hesitate a moment. "I'll be there."

"Good. It's the Johnson farm." And just that quickly she pulled back inside, gave him a quick wave, and shut the win-dow.

For several moments Joshua stood rooted to the spot, star-ing at his reflection in the rough glass. Then he clenched his fist and punched the air with one sharp jab. "Yes!" was all he could think of to say.

It was just before noon when Joshua stepped up onto the front porch of the cabin. He took a deep breath. The soaring elation he had felt when Lydia came back to talk with him had long since vanished on the walk home. He took another quick breath, then hunched his shoulders slightly, as though bracing for a sudden blow, and opened the door.

He saw instantly he couldn't have returned at a worse time. He had hoped the family would be scattered about, engaged in various activities, so his entrance would not be quite so dramatic. But they were all there, gathered around the table, the old family Bible opened in front of them.

For a moment it was like the scene was frozen in time. Matthew and Rebecca stared at him, eyes wide and round. Melissa's back had been to the door, but she jerked around and now her eyes were riveted on her brother's face. Joshua saw the sorrow in them and knew it was for him. Nathan had evidently been the one reading from the Bible when they heard Joshua's footsteps on the porch. He shot a quick glance in Joshua's direction, then suddenly became intensely interested in the page before him. His mother's head came up slowly, first to search Joshua's face and then, almost imperceptibly, turning enough to watch her husband, the anxiety etching deep lines around the corners of her mouth.

But it was to his father that Joshua's eyes were drawn, pulled by the power of the dark eyes boring into him. Benjamin Steed did not move, not even so much as the flicker of an eyelid, but Joshua could feel the anger seething just below the stone-cold exterior. He took another quick breath. It was going to be worse than he thought.

He walked over and sat down next to his mother. "Mama, I'm sorry I didn't come home last night. I was with some friends. I didn't realize it was as late as it was. We fell asleep and—"

Benjamin Steed came straight out of his chair. "Friends?" he asked incredulously. "That wouldn't be the Murdock boys, would it?"

Mary Ann took a quick breath. "Becca, you and Matthew go outside and feed the chickens."

Rebecca, frightened by what was erupting around her, stood quickly, but Matthew started to protest. One look from his father silenced the boy instantly. They hurried out and Benjamin went to the door, shutting it hard behind them. He whirled, his eyes blazing. But if he had expected it to somehow cow Joshua it didn't work, for Joshua had dropped his eyes and was looking at his hands.

"Well?" Benjamin demanded.

Joshua didn't look up. "Well what?"

"Look at me!" his father thundered.

Slowly, Joshua raised his head. "Well, what?" he repeated, no longer trying to hide the weariness in his voice.

"I asked you if you thought those two rum-soaked pieces of river trash were your friends."

"You don't even know the Murdock boys," Joshua shot back. "How can you say what they are?"

"Benjamin," Mary Ann broke in, both her eyes and her voice pleading with him, "we can talk this out without shouting."

Benjamin threw her a withering glance and stalked back over to where the others sat. He leaned across the table to face Joshua. "I may not know them, but every person in Palmyra Village knows of 'em. They're tavern rats. Riffraff that good folks stay clear of."

For a moment Joshua stared at the flaring nostrils and clenched teeth, almost feeling his father's hot breath on him. Then something inside him snapped. Reasoning with this man was impossible. And there was no pleasing him. No matter how hard he tried. He had learned that again and again. He straightened slowly, squaring his shoulders, the anger in him suddenly hard and cold. He was tired of being treated like the slop they fed the hogs.

He stood, bringing his face to within inches of his father's. "I guess you would recognize tavern riffraff, Pa," he said quietly. "After all, we only had to wait an hour while you and your *friends*"—he spat out the word with heavy sarcasm—"lifted a mug or two of your own."

Mary Ann jerked up, her eyes shocked. "Joshua!"

Melissa and Nathan were likewise stunned.

Benjamin leaned even closer, his voice dropping to barely a whisper. "What did you say?"

Even Joshua realized he had gone further than he had intended. He straightened, turning away. "Sorry," he muttered. "But they're my friends. We had a few drinks together, that's all."

Benjamin stared at his back, his chest rising and falling. Finally he turned to Mary Ann and threw up his hands in disgust. "And that's it. With that weak apology we're supposed to forget it? Let it all pass? This lovesick calf gets his feelings bruised because a little snippet named Lydia McBride won't give him the time of day and we're supposed to overlook it all."

Joshua whirled, first to glare at his father, then at Melissa. She shook her head quickly, her eyes pleading, but the damage had been done. He turned away, starting for the stairs. "You leave Lydia McBride out of this," he said darkly.

"Lydia McBride is the spoiled daughter of a high-minded storekeeper who thinks farmers like us are little better than stray livestock. If you think for one minute you can waltz in there and impress her with your patched-up trousers and manure-covered boots, then you're even a bigger fool than I thought."

Joshua's mother jerked around to face her husband. "Benjamin Steed! That was uncalled for."

He barely glanced at her. "You stay out of this, Mother! Joshua's being a fool and it's time somebody told him so."

Joshua turned slowly, his fists clenching and unclenching. Anger rose in his throat like a surge of bile. He took two steps toward his father. "I told you to leave Lydia McBride out of this."

Nathan leaped to his feet and jumped between Joshua and his father. He grabbed Joshua's arms. "It ain't true, Josh. Pa didn't mean it." He swung around to face his father. "Lydia McBride isn't the issue, Pa. Last night is the issue."

With equal swiftness, Melissa rose and moved to face her father. She reached out and touched his arm. "Papa," she said softly. She had not used that form of address with him since she had been twelve. "Papa, Papa," she pleaded.

Finally he pulled his eyes away from Joshua and looked down at her.

"Maybe Joshua did have too much to drink last night. And he was wrong not to let us know where he was. But can't we talk it out?"

Mary Ann jumped on that. "Melissa's right, Ben," she said. "Last night is the issue. Now, let's sit down and deal with the issue."

Joshua only half listened as the rest of his family stood as buffer between him and his father. Manure on his boots? No one was more keenly aware of the gap between himself and Lydia than he was. Every time he was around her he felt like an oafish teenage boy hanging around trying to get a glimpse of the royal family. His father's words came too close to the hard-edged truth, and they cut deep. Oddly, what hit him the hardest was the sudden knowledge that there would be no asking for a chance to go to the Johnson farm on Wednesday. He turned and walked to the fireplace, the disappointment as bitter as milkweed in his mouth.

Joshua's father swung around to follow him, and Joshua knew his family had lost.

"You want to talk about the issue?" he said, his voice trembling with indignation. "All right. The issue is *not* whether Joshua came home last night. He's a man now, or supposed to be"—it was flung out with open contempt—"and able to take care of himself." He glared at Nathan and Melissa, his expression daring them to disagree. "Nor is the issue that he shamed his family in front of people from three different townships."

Joshua snorted in disgust. "What do you—"

But his father rode over him, his voice rapidly raising in both pitch and volume now. "We won't even mention how this son of mine talks to me like I was some kind of mongrel dog or something."

"Pa—," Nathan started, but Benjamin whirled on him, cutting him off.

"Stay out of this, Nathan. Your mother wants to talk about the issues. Well, that's exactly what we're going to do."

"Whatever you say, Pa," Joshua said, forcing boredom into his voice, knowing it would further infuriate him, and suddenly wanting to do just that. He wanted to cut, to jab back as hard and as painfully as his father was striking at him. "Why don't you tell us, Pa. What is the issue here?"

His father's face was flushed now, a deep, mottled, angry red. "The issue is, you chose to be with trash, and now people are starting to wonder if Joshua Steed is trash too."

Now it was Joshua's turn to be incredulous. He threw up his hands and gave a hoot of derisive laughter. "You think that bothers me? Let them think what they want."

"Well, it better bother you!" Benjamin roared. "You don't walk barefoot through a corral without a whole lot of stink sticking to you."

"You don't give one hoot about what people think about me," Joshua shot back, now shouting as well. "I'll tell you what's bothering you. You're afraid if Joshua Steed stinks, someone might think his almighty righteous father stinks too! *That's* the real issue here."

Benjamin's eyes narrowed and he stepped forward. "You watch that smart mouth of yours, boy."

Joshua leaped forward and crashed a fist down against the table, causing his mother and Melissa to jump. He dropped his voice to a menacing hiss. "No, Pa. Let's have it out. Let's get down to the real issues here."

His reaction startled his father into momentary silence, and throwing all restraint to the devil, Joshua pressed in. "You're so worried about what people think of us Steeds, maybe you'd better be thinking about firing them Smith boys you hired."

The change of direction caught everyone by surprise. His mother's head jerked up. Nathan swung around and stared at Joshua in shock. Melissa too was staring, baffled by the unexpected direction the argument had just taken. Even his father rocked back a little. "The Smith boys?" he echoed.

"Yeah, the Smith boys. Particularly Joseph." He shook his head. "You're so worried about the Murdock boys. Well, at least they ain't goin' around sayin' they've seen God and angels."

Nathan shot his mother a quick look. She met it, then shook her head quickly.

"What are you talking about?" his father demanded, clearly caught off balance by Joshua's offensive.

"Why don't you go into town and listen to what people are saying about Joe Smith. And about you for hiring him as your helper."

"What are they saying about Joseph?" Melissa asked, truly puzzled now.

"That he claims he saw God and the devil out in the woods near his house."

Again, Nathan's eyes darted to his mother. And again she shook her head quickly. Joshua noted the interchange and was momentarily puzzled by it. But his father was still staring at him, so he forgot it and pressed his advantage. "He also claims an angel brought him a gold Bible. It's buried in a hill somewhere. He's going to translate it and save the world."

"Joshua," his mother said quietly, "the Steeds don't pay no mind to idle gossip, and I think it's shameful you'd use it against Joseph and Hyrum."

He turned to his mother. "Is it idle gossip, Ma?" He knew he was pushing this further than he had intended, but it had deflected the attention away from him and Lydia, and his father was now suddenly on the defensive.

"Joseph and Hyrum are good men," Nathan broke in.

"Then why won't they answer any questions about this whole thing when we ask them? You were there, Nathan. I asked them twice and all I got was the smoothest runaround you ever seen." He swung back to his father. "And people are starting to say Benjamin Steed must be believing all that stuff or else why is Joseph out here all the time."

"Who I hire is my business and—"

"Oh, no, Pa," Joshua shot back. "You're worried about stink. Well, Joseph Smith and all these wild ideas about angels and his gold Bible make him stink to high heaven. You don't care about that, then you'd better stop caring who I choose as my friends."

Somewhere, far back in some corner of his mind, the ridiculousness of the situation hit Joshua. He was not really taken with Will Murdock and his brother. They were loud and dirty, coarse in both language and demeanor. But that was neither here nor there. He wasn't about to let this bullheaded, narrow-minded man run his life any longer. He let his voice drop to a hoarse whisper. "Pa, you understand one thing. I'm a man now. I decide who my friends are and who they are not. I don't need your help." He lifted his chin in defiance. "And I don't need your permission."

Benjamin Steed leaned forward slowly, his eyes baleful and dark with fury, and Joshua felt a sudden prickle of fear. "Now you listen to me, mister," he said, his voice low and ugly, as full of menace as Joshua could ever recollect hearing. "As long as you live in this house and eat at this table, you need my permission to blow your nose! And if you don't like that, then maybe it's time you just find out what kind of man you really are."

Joshua stared back into the depths of his father's dark eyes, then suddenly he laughed, partly in anger and defiance, but mostly in sudden relief. That was it. There was the solution. A way to get out from under it. A way to get clear to visit Lydia on Wednesday. A way to stop the constant hassle and the battles.

He stepped back. "Fine. I'll be getting my things and moving into town."

Mary Ann shot to her feet. "Joshua, no."

Melissa was up and rushed to his side. "No, Joshua, no."

His father was staring at him, not sure he had heard correctly.

Joshua rushed on, his resolution solidifying even as he spoke. "Yes." He patted Melissa's arm, then looked to his mother. "I'll come each day to help with the farm work, but I'll be staying in town from now on."

The emotions on his father's face were a study in complexity—shock, bewilderment, anger, betrayal, hurt. Finally he stepped back and turned away. "Don't be doing us any favors," he growled. "We can manage without you."

Joshua smiled sadly, amazed at the calm which had come over him. "I won't be coming for you, Pa. I'll be coming for Ma and the family. I won't be letting them go hungry next winter because of me."

He turned to his mother and took her hands in his. Her eyes were shining with wetness. "It'll be all right, Ma." He took a deep breath. "It's time."

Her lips trembled and then she suddenly threw her arms around him, and he could feel her body shake convulsively. Joshua pulled her close and hugged her tight.

From behind them there was a gruff bark. "I'll be going into town." Benjamin swung around, grabbed his hat from the peg, and disappeared out of the door, slamming it hard behind him.

"It's time, Ma," Joshua said again softly, patting her shoulder. "It'll be for the best."

It was after dark when Benjamin Steed came out of the front door of Phelp's tavern in Palmyra Village. He stopped, torn with conflicting emotions. He had been born and bred to the idea that a man's private life was his own business and that when it came to religion, a man's heart was his own affair. It had always been his way, as Mary Ann had said, to give short shrift to gossip and rumor making.

He sighed. The Smiths had been good, solid workers. More than that. He had liked them. Even Joseph.

He shook his head with his usual unflinching honesty. Especially Joseph!

But the stories had been even worse than Joshua had intimated. His first inquiries in the tavern met with suspicion or open contempt, but when the men found out he was new to the area and had only hired the Smiths as day labor, the mood quickly changed. He was inundated with tales of wild doings in the night, fantastic accounts of bizarre and frightening behavior. Joshua had been right. The people were talking, and already Benjamin Steed's name was being linked unfavorably with that of Joseph Smith's. He was strongly advised again and again to break off any relationship as soon as possible.

Not that he believed it all. Benjamin well knew how stories could get started and then multiply like a litter of mice in a grain silo. But he also knew that in many cases stories usually had at least some basis in fact. And that troubled him deeply.

Part of what troubled him lay in his natural suspiciousness about any kind of open spiritualism. He had seen too many handwringers, people on fire with the "Spirit." Religion was like a lifeline cast at them in a dark and stormy sea, and they clung to it with wild desperation. That Joseph turned out to be one of these kind was a surprise to him, for he had not seemed that way in the fields.

He sighed again, his thoughts turning to Joshua and the events of the afternoon. But he brushed it aside quickly. Thoughts in that direction were too painful, and he straightened abruptly, making up his mind. He walked over to where the horses and buckboards were tied. An older teenage boy was lounging in one of the wagons, just as his father had said he would be. Benjamin fished a coin from his pocket and motioned to the boy.

"Yes, sir?"

"Do you know where the Smith farm is, down on Stafford Road?"

"Yes, sir, I do."

"Here's two bits. Will you take a message to young Joseph Smith for me?"

The boy glanced at the money, his eyes suddenly interested. "Yes, sir!"

"This is Joseph Smith, Junior, the son, not the father."

"Yes, I know."

Benjamin hesitated, then with a shake of his head, handed the boy the money. "Tell him Benjamin Steed has finished up the work he has for them. I won't be needin' him and his brother anymore."

Chapter Seven

Using the heel of a loaf of bread, Benjamin Steed mopped up the last of the gravy from the squirrel stew and put it in his mouth. Mary Ann watched him, feeling her heart sink a little. It was the midday meal on Thursday, and there had been no word from Joshua since he had left the previous Sunday with a few of his things stuffed into a burlap bag. In that time Benjamin had not once spoken of the events of that terrible Easter Sunday nor had he even once mentioned his oldest son. Late that same evening he had come back from town with the smell of ale on his breath and had gone to bed without a word to either her or the children. The next morning, when Becca had slipped at breakfast and made a comment about Joshua, Benjamin had shot her such a look that no one of the family had dared bring up the subject again. She had borne it in silence to this point, but she could bear it no more, and confrontation or not, she was ready to take action.

Melissa was taking the dishes to the small table where Becca was starting to wash the dishes in the iron kettle. Nathan, who was sitting across the table from his mother, started to get up, but she reached out and grabbed his hand. "Nathan?"

"Yes, Mother?"

Mary Ann took a quick breath. "I'd like you to go into town for me."

Benjamin was licking the gravy from his fingers. He stopped and his hand lowered slowly to the table as he turned and gave her a sharp look. "Nathan and me have got to finish harrowing the southeast corner before dark."

Mary Ann didn't look at her husband, just rushed on quickly. "I want you to go into the village. See if you can find where Joshua is staying."

Melissa stopped in mid-stride and turned back around slowly. Becca froze in the act of slipping one of the plates into the water, but she didn't turn around. Matthew was lying on the floor playing with the dog. He looked up, eyes suddenly anxious. Even the dog raised its head and cocked an ear, sensing the sudden change of atmosphere in the room.

Benjamin stood up slowly. He looked down at Nathan, studiously avoiding his wife's face. "You get the mules hitched up and bring 'em on down to the field."

"Ben!" The sharpness in her voice surprised her as well as him.

He turned, his eyes challenging. *Don't press this, woman,* was clearly written across his face. But Mary Ann Morgan Steed, normally a quiet and gentle person, couldn't stop now. She had lain awake the previous four nights brooding over what had happened. For nearly twenty-two years she had lived with this man. She knew the unbendable stubbornness of which he was capable. She also knew that Joshua had pushed him beyond any limits previously reached and that his forced silence covered a deep sense of betrayal and hurt.

"I'll not be asking him to come back, Ben," she said quietly. "But I can't go on not knowing if he's all right."

"Isn't this the same son who promised he'd be back to help with the farming?" He gave a short, bitter laugh. "More of his big talk, I suppose."

Melissa came back to the table to stand by her mother. "Pa, it takes time to find a place to stay."

Her father looked at her, and Mary Ann could see the hurt in his eyes. The whole family was lining up against him, or so it must seem to him.

Mary Ann stood and came around the table to lay a hand on her husband's shoulder. "Ben, I know Joshua did wrong. No one is sayin' he didn't. But I can't go on acting like he never was our son."

"He ain't been actin' like our son." It was said low, almost grumbled, but Mary Ann felt a quick leap of hope. Benjamin, too, wanted to know where Joshua was. His pride wouldn't let him admit to that, but she knew him well enough to read the concern beneath the outer gruffness.

She decided to take a chance that she had read him correctly. "If you say so, I won't send Nathan. But I think we need to try and at least find him."

He searched her face, then finally turned to Nathan. "I've got some work I can do on the fence along the creek. We'll finish the harrowing tomorrow."

Nathan nodded soberly.

"You could ride one of the mules, I suppose."

Nathan nodded again. "That would be good. I'll go saddle up."

Mary Ann watched her second son leave the cabin, then spoke. "I'll get some bread and things together." She smiled up at her husband, her eyes suddenly moist. "Thank you, Ben."

He brushed it aside gruffly, a little embarrassed, and moved to the door to get his hat. Melissa on a sudden impulse went to his side. She went up on tiptoes and kissed him on the cheek. "Thank you, Pa," she whispered.

Five minutes later Mary Ann came out of the cabin. She had two warm loaves of bread wrapped in a cloth. There was also a crock of pickles and some crab apple preserves. All were carefully placed in a flour sack. Nathan was at the head of the mule, which was now saddled and flicking its ears lazily back and forth. Matthew and Becca stood next to him, Matthew patting the mule's neck absently. Melissa followed her mother out with Joshua's jacket and a brush he had missed when he had packed so hurriedly.

Nathan helped them put the things into his saddlebags, then he swung up onto the mule's back.

"You'll just have to ask in town if anyone knows where he is," his mother said, touching his leg.

Melissa stepped forward, looking grave. "I'd start with Lydia McBride. Joshua won't admit it, but he's got it pretty strong for her. I'll bet she's at least seen him."

"I thought about that," Nathan nodded.

She smiled and waved. "I'm going down to see if I can help Pa with the fence. Matthew, Becca, why don't you come with me?"

"That's a good idea," Mary Ann said. "You go on along. I'll finish the dishes."

As the three of them trooped away, Nathan watched them go. Then he looked down at his mother. "I'll find him, Ma. You know Joshua. He'll be all right."

Mary Ann felt a sudden lump in her throat. "I know. It's just that . . ." She stopped and sighed. "If we don't do something now, he may never come back."

A look of surprise crossed Nathan's face, but almost immediately he nodded, sensing she was right. "I'll find him."

He picked up the reins, but stopped again. "Ma?"

"Yes, son?"

"I asked Pa why Joseph and Hyrum didn't come to work this week."

She nodded. "I know. I asked him too."

"Did he tell you what he did?"

"Yes."

"I'm afraid Joseph will think it's because I told Pa about the—" He stopped, not sure of what word to use. "About what happened to him when he prayed."

"Joseph is a good boy," she said, shaking her head. "I think he'll understand."

Nathan considered it, then nodded, a little relieved.

Mary Ann smiled up at him. What a good heart this one had, she thought. Not so filled with intensity. Not so insecure that he had to prove his worth to himself. "Nathan?"

"Yes?"

"Have you given any more thought to what Joseph told you?"

His brow furrowed. "Yes."

"And?"

"I don't know, Ma." He stared at his hands, which were toying with the hair on the mule's mane. Finally he looked down at her. "What about you? Have you given it more thought?"

"Yes. A great deal."

"Well?" he prompted when she said nothing more.

She turned and gazed out across the field, watching her three children disappear into a small stand of trees and brush. Finally she looked up at her second son. "I think it's true, Nathan. I'm not for sure positive, but the feelings just keep coming. I think it's true."

For a moment Nathan looked envious. "That will please Joseph."

A fleeting, wistful smile touched the corners of her mouth. "I suppose it will. But your father will not take to it kindly. Not now."

Nathan exhaled slowly. "I know."

She brightened, patting his leg. "Go find Joshua, Nathan. Let him know we still care."

"I will, Ma. I will."

Nathan knocked twice on the door, then knocked again a little louder. There was a rustle of noise, then a floorboard creaked and he heard a woman's footsteps approaching. He took off his hat.

The woman who opened the door was plump and grandmotherly. The first streaks of gray were noticeable in what hair was visible beneath a white linen bonnet, and the eyes were lined with crinkles which gave her a pleasant air even before she smiled. Nathan had seen Lydia's mother only one time in the store, but the resemblance between this woman and Mrs. McBride was immediately evident, even though Lydia's mother was probably a good ten years younger than her sister.

"Yes?"

"Mrs. Johnson?"

"Yes."

"My name is Nathan Steed. I was told your niece, Miss Lydia McBride, might be staying with you."

"Yes. Yes, she is."

"Good. Actually, I'm trying to find my brother, Joshua. I've been looking all over in town for him, and someone said Miss Lydia might know where he's staying. They suggested I might find her here."

Her head bobbed up and down, and her smile deepened. "Actually, your brother was here for a time last evening."

"Oh, good. So Lydia might know where I could find him."

"Quite likely. Go on around out back of the barn. You'll find her in the orchard." The grandmotherly eyes twinkled. "The apple trees are in blossom."

"Thank you, ma'am."

She squinted up at him. "You're not quite as stocky as your brother. How much older is he than you?"

He smiled. "I'm eighteen. Joshua's twenty."

"Hmmmm." She looked at him again, sizing him up, then wiped her hands on her apron. "Well, you can tie your mount on the side of the house there. She's out there somewhere."

"Thank you."

As Nathan tied the mule and started across the yard, he took a quick appraisal of the Johnson farm. The home was a spacious, two-story white frame building with well-kept yard. A large red barn stood behind it, surrounded with other outbuildings—forge, smokehouse, a vegetable cellar, carriage shed, and icehouse. A matched team of Belgian workhorses were in the corral along with a sleek-looking sorrel mare. The rail fences were neat and in excellent repair, and as he passed the barn's open door, Nathan saw everything was in its place.

As he came around the barn, his opinion of Lydia's uncle as a farmer climbed even higher. The rows of apple trees had been carefully pruned to keep them low enough so come fall the pickers would not need high ladders to harvest the crop. It was now well into April, and it had been an unseasonably warm spring. The buds were just opening, providing a veritable explosion of pink blossoms for as far as the eye could pierce into the orchard. The air was filled with a soft fragrance as well as with the pleasant hum of ten thousand bees moving from blossom to blossom, their legs and round bodies heavy with pollen.

He passed a cider press with its huge double wheels. Turned by horse or ox power, the wheels would crush the apples into pulp. The juice would be drained off for making apple cider and vinegar. The pulp, or pomace, as it was called, would be left out in the air for twelve hours, then pressed between layers of straw to form "apple cheese." That was a favorite of the Steeds, including Nathan, and he realized perhaps some of the apple cheese they had bought in town during the winter had come from this very orchard.

He slowed his step to look more closely at the cider press. It was small but modern and well maintained. He nodded to himself. Someday he would have a farm like this. So many farmers, especially on the frontier, did all right. They survived, and not much more than that. But with effort and care one could do more than just raise crops and cattle. One could build something lasting, something which bore witness to the labor and love of the husbandman.

The clusters of blossoms were too thick to allow him to see more than a few yards beyond where he stood, so Nathan bent down now and then to try and see below the branches of the trees. Now he understood the aunt's simple declaration about the trees being in blossom. That was explanation enough as to why a young woman might be found out here. The sun was dropping low in the sky now, and the air still. It was a moment of serenity and peace.

About twenty or thirty yards in, a flash of yellow a few rows over caught his eye. For a moment he saw her clearly, then she moved on behind another tree. He stopped for a moment, remembering how he had gaped at her like a kid in a candy shop that day outside the store when Joshua had introduced them for the first time. Even now he felt a quick rush of envy that Joshua should be courting this storekeeper's daughter.

Suddenly he wanted to move up quietly, get another look at her before she saw him. Feeling a little foolish, he moved quietly through the thick green carpet of grass and weeds. As he closed in on her he stopped again. She was leaning against an apple tree, half-turned away from him. She had broken off a small branch from one of the trees and now had the blossoms pressed up to her face. He caught a soft sound and realized she was humming to herself.

Stepping back a little, not wanting to break the moment, he watched her closely, almost struck immobile with the beauty of her. Her face was in half profile, highlighting the fineness of her features—the high cheekbones, the firm chin, the softness of her lips. She had combed out her hair full, and it fell in a full cascade over her shoulders and partly down her back, the ebony glossiness contrasting sharply with the pale yellow of her dress.

Suddenly, with the grace of a forest fawn, she tossed the blossoms aside, pushed away from the tree and began to sing.

> In London city where I once did dwell,
> There was a fair maid dwellin'.
> Made every youth cry, "Well-a-day."
> Her name was Barbara Allen.

Her body began to sway back and forth, barely moving but somehow, in that restraint, conveying the mournful sorrow of unrequited love and young womanhood denied.

'Twas in the merry month of May
The green buds were a swellin'.

She threw one hand out, taking in the richness of the spring's bounty which surrounded her.

Sweet William on his deathbed lay,
For the sake of Barb'ra Allen.

Nathan felt a quick chill scurry up his back. It was a haunting melody brought to America generations earlier by English immigrants. Its sadness had always moved him, but now as her voice carried to him, clear and true as the soft chiming of a crystal bell, he found himself mesmerized.

Barbara Allen. As Lydia sang the verses, the story unfolded. Unmoved by William's deathbed plea that only her kiss could save him, she tripped lightly down the stairs and out of the door. But when the death knell began to sound, the bells cried out in accusation, "Hard-hearted Barbara Allen." Pierced with sorrow, the lass stopped the funeral bier and peered into the face of the dead man.

Lydia's voice dropped in pitch, taking on a sudden huskiness, and the tempo slowed. The swaying stopped and she stood motionless, eyes closed, to finish the tale of Barbara Allen.

"Oh, Papa, Papa, go dig my grave,
And dig it deep and narrow.
Sweet Will has died of love for me,
I'll die for him tomorrow."

They buried him in the old churchyard;
They buried Miss Bar'bra beside him.
From his grave there grew a red red rose,
And from her grave a briar.

They grew to the top of the old church tow'r,
They could not grow no higher.
They hooked, they tied in a true love's knot,
The rose around the briar.

Her voice died, the last notes seeming to hang forever in the still air. She did not stir, nor did Nathan. He felt a sudden stab of shame. He had intruded on her, without her permission or knowledge. And he knew she would be embarrassed to know he had done so. Ashamed, he began to back away. He would wait near the barn until she decided to come out of the orchard.

Perhaps his feet made a noise in the orchard grass, or maybe she caught his movement out of the corner of her eye. Whatever it was, she suddenly whirled. "Oh!" he heard her gasp. One hand flew to her mouth and she fell back a step.

Blushing furiously, Nathan stepped out into full view. "Miss Lydia?"

Her hand was still up and there was fright in her eyes.

He swept off his hat and rushed on. "I'm Nathan Steed, Joshua's brother."

Her hand came down slowly as recognition dawned. "Oh."

"Your aunt said I could find you out here. I . . ." He stopped, unconsciously twisting the hat around and around in his hands. "I'm sorry for sneaking up on you. I was about to speak when you started to sing."

Her cheeks colored and her eyes dropped.

"It was so lovely I couldn't bear to stop you."

She blushed even more deeply, but smiled quickly up at him. "Thank you."

There was an awkward pause, then the smile broadened and she stuck out her hand. "Yes, Nathan, I remember you. Hello again."

"Hello." Nathan took her hand and quickly dropped it, startled a little by her openness. "I . . . I'm looking for Joshua . . ."

Seeming to sense his discomfort, and delighted by it, she stepped back, still appraising him with those wide brown eyes. He suddenly realized he was mangling his hat and forced his hands to stop. Then the smile faded and a shadow darkened her eyes. "Yes, Joshua told me what happened with your father. I'm sorry."

Nathan's mouth twisted in frustration. "He and Pa . . . well, they're a lot alike."

"Stubborn, you mean?"

He smiled. "Yes."

She cocked her head to one side impishly, causing her hair to fall around her face. "I've noticed that about Joshua too."

Nathan pulled his eyes away from her and looked down at his hands. The effect she was having on him was very disconcerting, and he found himself wanting to stare at her. "Ma sent me with some bread and other things. She's worried about him."

Her head bobbed quickly up and down. "I told him he needed to go back home. Talk to your father." She shook her head wearily. "He says he won't go back."

"I know. Do you know where I might find him? Is he staying in the village?"

Again there was a quick frown. "He's staying with Will Murdock until he can find something in town."

Nathan blew out air in a quick sound of discouragement. "That's not going to help."

"I know. I started to suggest that maybe Will Murdock was not the best company. He really snapped at me. Said who he picked as his friends was his affair and I was not to start acting like his pa."

Nodding glumly, Nathan kicked at the grass with his foot, digesting what she had told him.

"You knew he got work down on the docks."

Nathan's head came up with a snap.

She nodded. "One of the warehouses. He told me he was

going to help your family with the farming, but he's got to make his own way first."

Memories of the previous Sunday crossed Nathan's mind. "Maybe it's just as well." He took a breath. "Do you know where the Murdocks live? I'd best try and find him."

"They're east of town, out on Geneva Road. But there's no need to do that. Joshua said he would finish work at sundown, then come right out here."

"Oh?"

She looked up at the sky. The sun was perhaps five or ten minutes from setting. "Why don't you just wait. I'm sure he's coming."

"Well, if it wouldn't be a bother." He looked away quickly. "Once he comes, I won't stay long."

She laughed gently at his embarrassment. "It's no bother. Come on, we'll walk in the orchard." She waved her hand at the trees. "Isn't this wonderful?" She laughed again and started walking slowly away from him.

Nathan stood for a moment, marvelling at her. He wanted to make her laugh again. It was a sound of lilting joy, light as a breeze darting across a summer meadow. He jammed his hat on his head, poked at the back of his shirt to make sure it was in his pants, then fell into step beside her.

Joshua had come south out of Palmyra Village on the main road which ran on down to Canandaigua. As he approached the Johnson farm, he left the road and cut across a field of alfalfa toward the big red barn behind the house. Lydia had told him she would be in the orchard, and while he found her aunt much less intimidating than her mother, he still squirmed a little under her scrutiny. So he simply bypassed the house.

As Joshua came around the house and started past the barn, he suddenly stopped. A mule was tied at the hitching post on the south side of the house. To city folks, all mules may look alike, but there's no farmer that doesn't know his stock by sight. He changed direction and walked to the animal, feeling a sudden rush of anger. He looked in the saddlebags, saw his jacket and the flour sack filled with things. Lips tightening into a hard line, he walked around to the front door and knocked firmly.

After a moment, Lydia's aunt came to the door. "Oh, hello, Joshua."

"Hello, Mrs. Johnson." He glanced over her shoulder. "Is my father here?"

She looked surprised. "Your father? Why, no."

That took him aback a little. "But . . . our mule is tied up alongside the house."

Understanding dawned. "Oh, of course. No, that's your brother."

"My brother?"

"Yes, Nathan. He came about half an hour ago, looking for you. Lydia must have told him you were coming this evening, and he decided to wait for you. They're probably out in the orchard."

He let out his breath, the relief coming in a sudden rush. "Thank you."

As he came around the back of the barn, Joshua stopped. Lydia and Nathan were just emerging from the orchard, walking slowly. Nathan was saying something to her. Lydia's head was down, concentrating, hands clasped together behind her. Suddenly she threw her head back and laughed. Nathan smiled as he watched her.

Joshua felt a stab of—what? Envy? Jealousy? He pushed it away, surprised at the gladness he felt too. He raised his hand and waved. "Ho, Nathan!"

They both looked startled, then Nathan grinned and waved. He strode quickly toward Joshua, hand outstretched. "Joshua." They grasped hands, then suddenly Joshua swept his younger brother up in a bear hug.

"Ma sent you some bread and pickles," Nathan said when they pulled back and faced each other. "Melissa found your jacket and some other things you left. They're in the saddle-bags."

"Great." He turned to Lydia, who had been watching them with a smile. "Hello, Lydia."

"Hello, Joshua. I was hoping you would come."

He could see she meant it, and he felt a little bit ashamed for what he had felt a moment before. "I told you I would."

"I know. That's what I told Nathan."

Turning back to his brother, Joshua sobered. "How is Ma?"

"Fine. She's been worried about you."

He looked away. "I know. I planned to come out and help with the work, but I found a job in town."

Nathan nodded. "Lydia told me."

"It pays thirty-five cents a day."

Joshua noted the look in Lydia's eyes and felt a pang of disappointment. It was the same look he had seen when he first told her of his new job. He had expected as much, but it still hurt a little. To the villagers of Palmyra, the Erie Canal was a great boon which had brought economic prosperity and considerable growth to the region. But the dock area was a source of discomfort and embarrassment to them as well. Just a block away from their well-manicured homes and businesses, the lusty and bawdy nature of Canal Street stood in sharp contrast to the rest of the village. It was a necessary evil, but it was to be carefully avoided and its principals viewed with faint distaste.

"I know what you're thinking." He addressed Nathan, but he really spoke for Lydia's sake. "But if I'm going to make my own way, I've got to earn my own keep. This is more than what I could make doing day labor, and it's steady too."

Nathan nodded, trying to push back some of the disappointment. "I suppose."

Out of the corner of his eye, Joshua noted that Lydia seemed unconvinced too. Irritated, he changed the subject. "How's the family?"

"They're fine. Matthew wants you to see a racoon's den he found down by the creek. Becca said to send her love. Melissa is especially worried about you. She said to tell you she'll not point out all your faults if you decide to come back home."

Joshua smiled, warmed by the simple report. He had not really expected he would miss them quite like he had. The smile slowly died away. "And Pa?"

Nathan took a deep breath. "He knows I'm here. He told me to bring the mule."

A puzzled look crossed Lydia's face at the reference to the mule, but Joshua understood exactly what it implied. It was his father's way of telling Nathan it was all right to go. He took a quick breath. "I'm not going back, Nathan."

"I know." He looked away. "Ma knows too. But that doesn't mean you can't come see the family. Ma wants you to come for supper next Sunday."

Joshua considered that, knowing the difficulty it would be to face his father again, and yet wanting to be back, to sit around the table after the dishes were cleared, listening to Matthew's chatter, watching Becca's face which always mirrored whatever she was thinking, feeling the soothing spirit of his mother. He finally shrugged. "Maybe I could."

"Think about it. It would be good."

"Tell Ma I feel bad about not being able to come out and help. But I'll be sending out some of my wages. Pa can use it to hire enough help to make up for it."

They had come around the barn and now came to where the mule was tied. As Nathan began to get the stuff out of the saddlebags, he stopped, his mouth turning down into a slight frown.

"What?" Joshua asked, noting his expression.

"Pa fired Joseph and Hyrum."

It startled Joshua, but his reaction was quick. "Good for him."

"Joshua!"

"Well, it is. People in town were starting to talk."

For the first time Lydia spoke up. "Joshua's right, Nathan.

Even my father, who doesn't believe in stepping into other people's affairs, was real pleased to hear your father had ended his agreement with them."

Nathan shot her a look, then turned back to Joshua. "Joseph and Hyrum were good workers, Joshua. As good as they come. It ain't fair to fire them on account of wild stories being told around."

"They're not wild stories," Lydia said earnestly. "The parents of a friend of mine heard it straight from Joseph's father. 'Bout him going into the woods and seeing the devil."

"He never said he saw the devil," Nathan retorted.

Joshua leaned forward, peering at his brother. "How do you know what he said? Did Joseph finally say something?"

Nathan was caught. It showed on his face.

"Well, did he?"

Nathan sighed. "Yes, he told me about his experience when he was trying to find out which church to join."

Lydia stepped closer, suddenly eager. "Really, what did he say?"

Reluctantly, Nathan began. He related briefly what Joseph had said. It was obvious as he spoke he was feeling guilt, as though he were betraying a confidence.

Joshua threw back his head in a derisive laugh when he finished. "And you believe that?"

Nathan just stared at the ground.

Lydia reached out and touched his arm. "Do you, Nathan? Do you really believe such a fantastic story?"

He looked at her, then at Joshua, then back at her. "I don't know," he finally said lamely.

"Well, I know!" Joshua blurted. "That's the kind of talk you hear down at the asylum, and I say Pa is wise to be rid of them."

Nathan's head shot up, his eyes angry. "If you're so worried about people talking, why are you staying with the Murdocks?"

Joshua shot a quick look at Lydia, but she looked away. He felt a sudden anger at his feelings of defensiveness. "Till I earn some money, I can't be affording no room in town," he snapped. "The Murdocks have a place in their barn. They're not chargin' me anything for it."

"They're no good, Joshua," Nathan said flatly. "Joseph Smith's ten times the man Will Murdock is."

There it was again. Somebody always trying to tell him how to live and who to live with. He shouldered Nathan aside and took the things from the saddlebag. He stood there for a moment, then looked into the sack, smelled the wonderful aroma of the bread, fingered the crock of pickles, letting the anger die. He knew Nathan meant well and it was his frustration at his father's stubbornness that triggered this reaction in him. When he turned back around his face had softened a little. He held up the sack. "Tell Ma thank you. And Melissa too."

Nathan was anxious now to back away from the near confrontation too. "I will. What shall I tell her about Sunday?"

Joshua shook his head, thinking about the ugliness of the previous Sunday. "I don't know . . ."

"You need to go, Joshua," Lydia said, stepping to look up into his eyes. "It's not right to cut yourself completely off from your family."

He smiled suddenly. Like he said, everyone was trying to get into his life and run it for him. But he couldn't be angry with Lydia. Not when she looked up at him like that. "All right," he said, "I guess I could come."

"Good." Nathan untied the reins and swung up into the saddle. He looked down at Joshua. "You don't have to wait until then, you know."

Joshua grinned up at him. "I know. But I'm a working man now. I can't just be goin' places any time I feel like it."

"I know." Nathan reached out and gripped his hand. "Take care, Joshua."

"I will, Nathan." He hesitated for a moment, then softly added, "Tell Pa I'm sorry for what I said the other day."

Nathan grinned. "I will." He swung the mule around and dug his heels into its flanks, waving to both of them as the animal jumped into a trot and turned north onto Canandaigua Road.

It was almost full dark when Lydia waved good-bye to Joshua and went back into the house. As she shut the door, she stopped and leaned back against the door frame, smiling wistfully.

Across the room her aunt was on the sofa, working on a needlepoint cushion for one of the sitting room chairs. Her uncle was in the next room at the table, supposedly doing the books for the farm, but he had fallen asleep, his head on his chest, mouth partly open, snoring softly. As Lydia straightened, her aunt gave her a sharp look.

Lydia noted it and smiled, moving over to sit next to her favorite relative. So unlike her mother, Aunt Bea was easygoing, quick to smile, filled with gentle patience and wisdom. Lydia reached out and took her hand. "What was that look for?" she whispered, not wanting to awaken her uncle.

"What look?"

Lydia laughed softly, not fooled. "Come on, Aunt Bea."

She looked at her niece sharply. "Sometimes the forbidden fruit is the sweetest on the tree."

Lydia's eyes widened in surprise. "What does that mean?"

"Your father is not going to look upon a dockworker as the ideal beau for his only daughter."

"Oh." So her aunt had already heard.

She went back to her needlework, fingers flying. "If your pa finds out . . ." She didn't have to finish the sentence.

For a moment Lydia was tempted to brush it aside with a quick laugh, but it hit too close to her own concerns. "I know," she finally murmured.

Aunt Bea put her sewing aside. "And there's something kind of exciting about knowin' he will be furious with you for encouraging this Joshua Steed on, isn't there?"

Lydia was caught off guard. "It's not that, Aunt Bea. I—"

"Isn't it? You be honest with yourself, child."

Lydia leaned back, closing her eyes. Joshua was tall, and she found the combination of his rugged handsomeness and his bold manner exciting. But she had to admit there was something a little bit titillating about knowing her father—and especially her mother!—would highly disapprove of her relationship with Joshua Steed. Not that she didn't love her parents. She did, sometimes fiercely. But they were so . . . She sought for a good word. Traditional. Yes, traditional. They were so set on having her do things as they saw fit. Sitting in the parlor with your hands folded in your lap as you sipped tea from the china service. A proper courtship, a socially acceptable marriage.

"Don't ever forget the folly of perversity."

Lydia opened her eyes, startled by her aunt's statement. She raised one eyebrow, questioning.

"Sometimes we do things just to be perverse. Not because we enjoy it. Not because it's right. But just for the sheer joy of being perverse. But it's folly, pure foolishness."

"I'm not sure what you're trying to say, Aunt Bea."

She smiled and patted Lydia on the hand. "I'm not sure of what I'm trying to say either, dear. Don't pay any attention to an old lady's ramblin's."

Lydia smiled, knowing her aunt never rambled. "Well," she said, standing, "I've got to be up early if I'm going to get the store straightened before Mother and Father return on Saturday. I think I'll go to bed."

She reached down and kissed her aunt on the cheek. "Good night, Aunt Bea."

"Good night, Lydia."

As she started up the stairs, her aunt called to her again. She turned. "Yes?"

"Did you know the brother is your age?"

Lydia looked at her sharply. "What brother?"

"Joshua's brother. Nathan."

"Oh."

Her aunt looked up, her face full of innocence. "Seems like a nice boy. Doesn't have the fires of rebellion burning inside him that his brother seems to have."

Lydia frowned at the accuracy of the assessment about Joshua, then smiled fondly. "Good night, Aunt Bea."

She turned and went up the stairs, thinking about Joshua Steed. And as she stood before the mirror brushing out her hair, she found her thoughts turning to Nathan Steed. She thought about his gentleness, the way he had of saying something with almost a droll somberness that would instantly make her laugh. Without thinking, she began to sing softly as she counted the brush strokes.

> In London city where I once did dwell,
> There was a fair maid dwellin'.
> Made every youth cry, "Well-a-day."
> Her name was Barbara Allen.

Erie Canal, Palmyra

If a village of less than five thousand could be said to have an unsavory part of town, for Palmyra it would certainly have been that portion of the village which paralleled the Erie Canal. Barely a block north of the more sedate Main Street, Canal Street was almost like another country butted up against Palmyra. Each had its own distinct citizenry, its own set of mores and traditions, even its own language—that of Canal Street being considerably more profane than that of the rest of the village.

With such close proximity, it was difficult for the more re-spectable residents of Palmyra to totally ignore Canal Street and its denizens, but they did their best. Merchants and farmers had to go to the docks frequently to keep the flow of commerce moving, but they went only when required, and they rarely lingered once the transactions were complete. Women of any reputation at all totally avoided it, would blanch at the prospects of intermingling with the canawlers, the mule skinners, the dockworkers, and the bawdy women who served them. More than one child had his bottom warmed for heeding the siren call of such a forbidden and fascinating world.

This was not a place of picket fences, green lawns, or neatly tended gardens. The alleyways and fence lines were lined with trash, blown along with the dust whenever the wind blew. Empty lots were littered with shards of rope, shattered crates, or even an occasional wagon box or broken wheel. The street itself was filled with the droppings from hundreds of ox, horse, and mule teams, filling the hot summer air with stench, breeding flies by the thousands, and making it imperative to step carefully.

And yet this evening, just at dusk, Lydia McBride was heading for Canal Street. In her hand she clutched Joshua's handwritten directions on how to find the Erie Warehouse Company. She was coming back into the village from the east. Even with her natural daring she had not had the courage to cross directly over to Canal Street from her home—a matter of a hundred yards or less. Her parents were at a dinner social sponsored by the Palmyra Merchants Association and had given her permission to stay overnight at the home of her best friend, Elizabeth Ann Rowley. Elizabeth Ann's mother was in Ithaca awaiting the birth of a new grandchild, and her father was at the same meeting as Lydia's parents. Elizabeth Ann, co-conspirator in the evening's plan, watched wide-eyed, half shocked, half envious, as Lydia exchanged the white shawl she wore for a dark one, put aside the parasol and gloves, and stuffed her long hair up under a drab-looking bonnet that shadowed her face.

With a whispered thanks and a promise to be back before nine, Lydia had set out, continuing east on Main Street until she left the last of the village houses behind. Only then did she turn north and cut across the open fields to the canal and start back toward the main section of town. But as she approached the banks of the canal she gave a start. There was still enough light in the western sky to see by, and about twenty or twenty-five yards ahead a strange apparition appeared.

She stopped dead, peering at the figure, trying to push down the instant rush of fear. There was a fleeting impression of some gigantic, two-legged spider, tall as a man, coming toward her. Then in a flood of relief, she realized she had come upon Abner Jenkin's "ropewalk." The last building on the east end of Canal Street was the Finger Lakes Hemp Company. But that was merely the warehouse. The actual making of the rope was done on the ropewalk, a path stretching almost a quarter of a mile eastward, out of the way of the traffic of the village. What Lydia saw now was the "rope spinner." And as she looked more closely, she could see it was Abel Jenkins, Abner's teenage son. "Ninety percent legs and ten percent freckles," her father had once described Abel Jenkins, and that was what had startled her. The rope spinner moved slowly along the ropewalk, drawing hemp fibers from a large bundle of fibers wrapped loosely around his waist. He would twist the fibers into long, thin cords. It was the bundle of fibers that had looked like the hairy body of a spider, and Abel's gangly legs only added to the impression.

Lydia veered to the left to avoid him. A few yards behind Abel she could see another figure, and assumed it was his father. The rope spinner was always followed by another person who would weave the cords together to form the thick rope which was so important to the canal boat traffic. But the last thing Lydia wanted right now was to meet someone who knew her. And both Abner and his son came in the store often. She averted her face and hurried on, feeling the boy's curious stare on her back.

As she entered the main section of Canal Street, she slowed her step, staying close to the buildings so as to stay out of sight of any curious eyes that might look in this direction from Main Street. In a moment the smell of the street almost overwhelmed her, and she groped in her purse for a handkerchief and held it to her nose. She was the only woman in sight, and the curious looks or brazen stares of the men she passed frightened her a little. But she also felt a rush of excitement to be in this part of the village again. She had not been here since the canal had been finished two years earlier, and the rush of commerce had drastically changed its nature.

At the corner of Market Street she stopped and held Joshua's note up to the last of the fading light. Go to Market Street, then two buildings more. Enter the narrow alley there, go back about fifty paces, and enter the door on the left marked "Erie Warehouse Company." It would be unlocked for her.

As she took a breath and started to turn, she saw three men approaching. They slowed their step as they saw her. One leered hungrily at her, and again she felt a quick stab of fear. Then the other mumbled something. There was a burst of laughter and they passed on. Suddenly any exhilaration she felt was gone, and the foolishness of what she was doing hit her. And with it came a sudden burst of irritation that Joshua would ask that she venture into this part of town on her own. Just last week the *Wayne Sentinel* had reported that a wheat broker from Syracuse had been knifed and nearly killed. Joshua had brushed that aside, pointing out that the man had been down by the docks after midnight, for heaven only knew what reason. Joshua assured her that as long as she came before dark there was no reason to be nervous.

When Lydia had told Joshua she would be free this night, he had told her of his problem. The night watchman at the warehouse was sick and Joshua could earn another twenty-five cents a day by sleeping there after his regular twelve-hour shift. There was no way he could leave, but why couldn't she come to see him? She shuddered a little. Canal Street was bad enough. To be in a building, unescorted, with a man was something else. To have those two unthinkables combined. If her parents ever found out . . .

She frowned, chiding herself. No one had made her come. And she was honest enough to admit it was partly the very daring required which had prompted her to accept Joshua's invitation. Angry at her own hesitation, she thrust her handkerchief back into her purse, took a deep breath, breathing through her mouth, and moved on. In a moment she came to the alley. It was a narrow passageway between clapboard warehouses two stories high. The alley was in almost total darkness, and the smell of urine and something long dead assaulted her nostrils.

She chewed at her lip as she stared down the darkened passage, then peered at the instructions one more time. One part of her whispered with some insistence that if she had one lick of good sense she would bolt back the way she had come. Another voice jeered at her, reminding her that Joshua would know why she had not come. He had an uncanny ability to cut through any subterfuge, and she knew he would laugh quietly at her timidity.

Behind her, a man came around a corner. He was smoking a cigar and carried some kind of bag slung over his shoulder. In the semi-darkness he looked big and foreboding. Lydia made her decision. Gulping in a quick breath of air, she plunged into the foul smell of the alley. She walked quickly, fighting the rising panic, wanting to dart a look back over her shoulder. What if the man chose to follow her? Or what if Joshua weren't at the door? Her breath exploded from her lungs, and as she drew in another, she nearly gagged. The stench was overpowering.

There was the door! She nearly flew to it, and knocked sharply, fighting back the overwhelming desire to batter at it with her fists. It opened almost instantly and Joshua was there, standing large and strong in the doorway. Never had there been a more welcome sight. She fought back the panic, fought back the overpowering temptation to throw herself into his arms. She smiled demurely, then curtsied slightly. "Hello, Joshua."

"Hello, Lydia." He stood back, opening the door wider and bowing low as he motioned her in. The smell of wheat and flour, hemp rope and molasses was heavy on the dusty air, but after the alley it was like the breath of cherry blossoms in spring, and she breathed it in deeply.

Joshua shut the door and secured it with a cross beam. He

turned back to her and grinned. "I about decided you weren't coming."

She laughed lightly, catching her breath quickly now. "Isn't being late part of a woman's way?"

He laughed with her, obviously happy she had come. A whale-oil lamp sat on a table and another burned from its holder on the wall, giving the windowless room a warm and cheerful glow.

He pulled out a crudely made wooden stool and she sat down. He leaned back against a table built into one wall of the small office. "I know this is a bad place to have you come, but I'm glad you did."

"I can't stay long, Joshua. If anyone sees me before I get back to Elizabeth Ann's house, I'll be in more trouble than I even want to think about."

He nodded. "I know, but it's been almost two weeks since we had a chance to be together. And they found out the watchman has tuberculosis. It could be another week or so before they find someone to take his place."

She nodded, studying him as he talked. He had changed noticeably in the three months since he had left his family and moved into town. Much of that was attributable to the heavy dark beard which covered the lower part of his face. Normally, Lydia didn't care much for beards, but Joshua's was neatly trimmed, and she found it enhanced his narrow face and prominent features, making him even more handsome than usual. He had also filled out under the rigorous demands of dock work. He was still lean through the waist, but his upper body was more muscular, his shoulders broader, his step more firm and sure.

But the changes ran deeper than just the physical differences. When he had first come into the store the previous fall, he had still been a mostly gawky, awkward boy, fumbling for words, quick to blush. Now most of that was gone. He spoke quietly for the most part but with a surety of word and purpose. He rarely blushed anymore, a trait Lydia had watched disappear with a trace of longing. He was confident, sometimes almost brash, moving out to grasp life before it slipped through his hands. Two weeks ago he had kissed her for the first time. It was the only hesitation she had seen in him in almost a month.

He was watching her with a sardonic grin. "And what is going through that pretty little head of yours?"

Startled that she had gotten lost in her thoughts, she shook her head quickly. "I was just thinking how much you've changed since you started working here."

He hooted softly. "What? Turned from a man into an ape?" He hunched over, scratching under his arm pits and making grunting noises.

She laughed.

"That's what the foreman here wants. Apes. Don't stop. Don't think. Don't even sweat. Just keep moving them bales of cotton. Keep them bags of wheat moving onto the barges. Here comes another wagon. Up and at it you animals." His voice had gone from light humor to heavy bitterness.

She slowly sobered. "If you hate it that badly, why don't you get something else?"

He shrugged.

"I saw where Stephen Phelps is looking for a store clerk."

"Yeah," he retorted. "At half the pay I'm making."

"Half the pay but twice the working conditions."

He shrugged. "I can take the working conditions." He leaned forward and dropped his voice a little, though they were alone. "I send the family two dollars a month to help out. It costs me two more for room and board. The other six dollars I'm putting away."

That was the first Joshua had ever talked about savings, and it surprised her. "Good for you, Joshua."

He sat back, openly pleased with himself. "I figure a year, maybe a year and a half, and I'll have enough to buy me a wagon and a team of my own. There's real money to be made in the freight business."

"That's a wonderful idea." It occurred to Lydia that being a teamster might be fine for a man but not quite as wonderful for his wife and children, but she didn't say anything. It pleased her that he had plans beyond the noise and filth of Canal Street.

"Speaking of your family," she said, "they were in the store last week."

He frowned a little. "Nathan too, I suppose?"

Lydia did not miss the sudden petulance. She had mentioned Nathan once or twice in their recent conversations, and learned quickly that Joshua was jealous of any attention his younger brother paid to her. She was pleased she could shake her head. "No, just your mother and the other children."

What she did not add was that Nathan had come in by himself just that morning, something that was happening with increasing frequency.

Joshua didn't say anything.

"They asked about you."

"And did you tell them everything was wonderful?"

"Joshua," she said softly, "why are you so bitter about this? It's not your mother's fault you and your father don't get along."

He softened immediately. "You're right. I'm sorry." He took a quick breath. "How were they?"

"Melissa gets prettier every day. And blushes to the tips of her toes when I suggest it to her."

Joshua smiled at that. "Melissa is a special girl. She'll make someone a wonderful wife."

"Rebecca is an imp and Matthew is adorable. I can't help but slip those two a piece of candy each time I see them."

He laughed, the hardness completely gone from his face. "Those two I do miss."

"Your mother said the harvest is looking very good. It's been a good year for everybody."

"And Pa? Did she say anything about him?"

"She said if I saw you I was to tell you he sends his greetings and hopes all is well with you."

"Hmmmph!" he snorted. "I'll bet that's just Ma's way of trying to smooth things between us."

Lydia let it pass, watching the emotions working across his

face. She found herself comparing him to Nathan. There was a softness in Nathan which at first had seemed like weakness, but which now she found intriguing. She had been around his mother enough to realize Nathan had inherited her gentle nature. That was a good word. Gentleness. Not weakness. Nathan was gentle, but there wasn't much that was gentle in Joshua Steed.

Lydia thought of their father. Benjamin Steed had also been into the store several times now, and Lydia had no trouble understanding why there was bad blood between the father and his oldest son. They were so much alike in some ways— unbending, proud, quick to take offense at anything perceived to be a threat.

"Have you thought about moving back?" she asked, knowing she was moving onto sensitive ground. "You could still come here to work, and it would save you paying two dollars a month room and board."

He shook his head quickly in disgust. "Two dollars a month is worth it not to have to face Pa every day."

"But you could put that away too. That would get you out of here all the sooner."

He looked at her sharply. "Working the docks is honest work."

She realized she had touched a nerve, and backed away quickly. His mother had also raised concerns about the environment of the docks, and he was getting to be more and more defensive about it. But his determination to stay with it had also clinched any feelings Lydia's own father had about Joshua. A farmer was hardly what the McBrides had in mind for their only daughter, but at least it was an honorable profession. When her father had learned Joshua was working on Canal Street he had absolutely, irrevocably forbidden Lydia to have any more contact with him.

Lydia sighed. "It's not that, Joshua, and you know it. But it's just not right, you being separated from your family and all."

"Well, I ain't going back. So let's talk about something else."

Nodding, she stood and moved away, looking past him into the dark recesses of the warehouse. She had pushed him enough and knew he would not be pushed any more on the issue of his family. Joshua stood too, and offered to show her around the cavernous building. It was safer ground, and she immediately accepted. They moved slowly among the organized clutter, Joshua pointing out the various stacks of bales and boxes and barrels that constituted his working life. Next to a towering pile of crates he stopped. A faint fishy smell came from the boxes. She read the stenciled label. Dried cod from Boston on its way westward to the Ohio River valley.

They were standing close, and Joshua reached out and took her by the shoulders. He turned her to face him. She smiled up at him, but it was forced and faded quickly. For some reason she was suddenly depressed. The rush of adrenalin which had sent her plunging into the alleyway was gone now. The folly of her rashness hit her heavily, knowing what it would mean if her father ever learned of this. And coming to Canal Street alone at night had taken more out of her than she had expected. What if someone had been waiting there in the darkness of the alley?

"What is it?" He sensed her change of mood. His dark eyes were grave, probing.

She gave a little shrug. "Nothing, I . . ." She shook her head. "I'm going to have to go, Joshua. I shouldn't be here."

His hand came up and gently touched her cheek, tipping her head back. He leaned down and kissed her, at first his lips barely brushing hers, then quickly becoming firm, hard, almost insistent.

Lydia kissed him back, but it was with a curious detachment, almost analytical. She found Joshua immensely attractive, and the excitement of arranging each secret rendezvous and flirting with the risks that attended them was scintillating. But . . .

She pulled back and turned away, running her finger along the rough lumber of the crates. But what? She gave a little, impatient shake of her head, not sure exactly what was bothering her.

He turned her around. "Something is the matter, Lydia. What is it?"

She looked up at him, her eyes round and troubled. "If my father ever learned I had come here . . ." She let it trail off. "I told you they're talking about sending me to Boston. My aunt—father's youngest sister—runs a private boarding school for girls there."

"I know," he said glumly. Then suddenly he was angry. "Just like my pa. Wantin' to run everybody's life."

Surprisingly she wanted to defend them. "They just want what's best for me, Joshua."

"*You* decide what's best for you," he snapped. "No one else does."

She sighed again, the depression deepening. There were so many problems, so many challenges in all this.

He leaned forward, suddenly earnest. "Your father's feelings will change, Lydia. When I get my own freight business, he won't be lookin' down his nose at me any longer."

Maybe not quite so imperiously as now, she thought sadly, but she knew the depths of her father's feelings. Joshua's own-ing a team and a wagon wouldn't change those feelings or Josiah McBride's plans for his daughter. And besides, that kind of talk was marriage talk. Joshua had never spoken of it directly, but it was clear what was on his mind. She had those thoughts too, but it was with more and more reservations. Did she want this man as her husband? Was this really love or just a wild, irrational attraction? How did she feel about him?

He touched her face again. "I think I love you, Lydia. You're all I think about. Even when I'm working, I see your face in my mind."

"I . . ." She couldn't bring herself to say it.

"You'll see, Lydia," he said fiercely, reading her hesitancy as doubt about his abilities. "I will get my own wagon. Then another. I don't plan to spend my days in this stink hole."

"I know that, Joshua. I believe you. But . . ."

"But what?"

Thankfully, she was spared having to answer, for there was a sudden, heavy pounding on the outer door. Joshua turned, frowning. Then his face changed. "Oh, that must be Will and David."

"The Murdocks?" Lydia asked in surprise.

"Yeah, they promised to bring me some supper."

"Oh." Her face clearly reflected her dismay. She knew Will Murdock well enough to know that with one mug of stout her visit to the warehouse district would be common knowledge throughout all of the Finger Lakes region.

Joshua turned toward the door, but Lydia grabbed his arm quickly. "Joshua, they can't see me here."

He gave her a strange look. "Why not?"

"Because if they ever tell anyone and my father finds out, he'll ship me off to Boston before you or I can even snap our fingers."

He shrugged, brushing her concern aside. "So, we'll just tell them not to say anything." He started away again, but she dragged him back around.

"No, Joshua! Isn't there any other way out?"

"Well, yes." He gestured toward one corner of the building. "There's a small door there on the canal side—"

"Good." The hammering on the door was louder now and more insistent.

Joshua took her by the shoulders. "Lydia, it's full dark now. I don't want you out there alone. I was going to let Will and David stay here while I walked you back."

"No!" she blurted. The terrors of Canal Street were nothing compared to the thoughts of facing her father. She squeezed his hand. "I'll find my way. Just don't tell them I was here." She darted away and out into the night.

Chapter Nine

Nathan Steed finished tying the last shock of corn and stood it upright. He tossed the roll of twine and the corn knife aside, took off his hat, and mopped at his brow with his sleeve. The shocks of corn stood at attention where he had placed them, scattered randomly across the field like Indian tepees pitched in a broad meadow.

He let his gaze continue across the Martin Harris farm. Out behind the barn—big enough to be a church—the apple trees were bent nearly double with the opulence of the harvest. To the south of the house, almost an acre of pumpkin, squash, watermelon, and tomatoes was just starting to turn brown under the nipping of the first frost. In the yard, beneath the great elm trees, guinea hens strutted about like ill-mannered town gossips searching for any tidbit to snatch. A cock, comb scarred and flopping over almost to the point where it covered one eye, scratched lazily in the dust, his harem of hens scattered around him. Porkers who a few months before had been squealing, darting piglets now lay round and fat in their pens, snuffling as they dozed. By Christmas several would be stuffed with other things and lie on a platter next to the carving knife. He saw three pigeons bank and glide back toward the barn. They too had a destiny. They would soon be plucked and stuffed under a thick layer of piecrust for the Harris table.

Nathan felt a stir of envy. The Steed farm was coming along nicely, and they too would have a good harvest, but compared to this farm of Martin Harris's . . . He sighed, longing momentarily for Vermont and what the family had built for themselves there. But he brushed it aside. Things were going well, and for having been here only one year, there was much to be pleased with. Down deep, Nathan had quickly picked up his father's love of the Finger Lakes country. It was good land, a fine country, with good people.

But whenever he came to the Martin Harris farm, he always felt a tiny burst of covetousness. He let his eyes scan the split-rail fence that bordered the cornfield. Mr. Harris had hired him to cut and shock the corn. It had taken him almost a week, but now it was finished. He counted the sections of rail fence and quickly calculated. There were about fifteen acres of corn. He turned, squinting a little. Each section of fence was eleven feet long, or exactly one-sixth of a "chain." Surveyors used a chain consisting of one hundred links of equal size and totaling sixty-six feet in length. Nineteen fence sections were within an inch or two of being the same length as one side of a square acre. It was a simple way to calculate land area, and often a farmer would take down a length of his rail fence and use it as a giant ruler to measure off a new section he wished to cultivate.

It was a perfect Indian-summer afternoon, the air clear as fine crystal, the first hint of orange and yellows just barely touching the leaves. He wiped at the back of his neck, feeling the grit of the dust and the tiny bits of cornstalk that had worked their way inside his shirt. When he returned home, he would take a quick plunge in the creek. Then tomorrow his father and some of the other neighbors would come with their wagons and haul the corn to the Harris barn. The Steed corn —less than five acres—would come next, and thus they would move from farm to farm, helping one another, feeling the quiet camaraderie of men sharing a common labor. Satisfied with his work, Nathan stuffed the rag back into his pants pocket, picked up his equipment, and headed for the house.

The Harris home was located on the road which ran north from Palmyra Village up to the shores of Lake Ontario. It was an attractive clapboard house which sat about thirty feet back from the road. Nathan went to the front door, noting the profusion of flowers bordering the stone walk, and he remembered Mrs. Harris had promised to send some seeds to his mother.

As he knocked on the door, he felt a little ashamed for hoping Mr. Harris would open the door. Nathan had seen him come from the barn about an hour earlier and go into the house. He had not seen him come out again since then. Not that Mrs. Harris hadn't always treated him with courtesy, but she was a cheerless woman, and Nathan always felt a little uncomfortable in her presence. She was hard of hearing, and, as some with that affliction do, she had developed a paranoia that people were talking about her behind her back. She dressed well, and he guessed that Lucy Harris fully enjoyed being the wife of one of Palmyra's more prosperous farmers. Part of the role seemed to require a certain lofty aloofness, which she carried off to perfection.

The door opened and Martin Harris was there. He immediately smiled and opened the door wider. "Yes, Nathan."

"I've finished the corn, Mr. Harris."

"Already?" He turned to look at the clock on the fireplace mantle. It showed quarter past four o'clock. He stepped out on the porch far enough to survey the cornfield, then nodded, pleased. "Good, good. Come in, Nathan, and we'll settle up."

Nathan looked down. His boots were dusty and his pants and shirt covered with bits and pieces of the cornstalks. "I'd better wait out here."

"Nonsense." He clapped him on the shoulder. "Come in. I'll bet you could use something to drink."

Nodding, Nathan brushed at his clothes, then stepped inside. The older man followed him and shut the door. "Lucy!" he shouted.

From somewhere in the back of the house an answer floated back.

"The Steed boy has finished the corn. Can you fetch him something to drink?" He yelled it loudly, with just a touch of exasperation, then turned back to Nathan. "Sit down, Nathan, and I'll get my purse."

Nathan shook his head quickly. The chair he had pointed toward was upholstered in a rich-looking red velvet. In the Steed cabin, dirt and dust on one's clothes had little effect on the hand-hewn wooden benches and stools which served as their furniture. Here it was different. "I'm fine, thank you anyway."

Harris looked him up and down, nearly protested again, then nodded. "I'll get your money, then."

As he went up the stairs to the second floor, Nathan looked around. In sharp contrast to the Steed homestead, the evidence of prosperity was everywhere. This was the sitting room, and across the small vestibule where they had entered he could see into the parlor. It was furnished with the same good taste and elegance as the room in which he now stood. Both rooms had fireplaces with handsomely carved mantles of polished oak. These were not the large stone fireplaces of a backwoods cabin, but the work of craftsmen.

He heard a noise and turned. Mrs. Harris was standing at the door which led to the hallway and back to the kitchen. "Oh," she said. "I thought I heard Mr. Harris call."

"Hello, Mrs. Harris." She cocked her head, leaning forward slightly. More loudly, he spoke again. "Hello, Mrs. Harris. I'm Nathan Steed. Mr. Harris went upstairs for a moment."

Her eyes swept over his clothes quickly, and he felt her

quick disapproval. He was glad he was not sitting on her velvet chair.

"And how is Mrs. Steed?"

"Just fine, ma'am, thank you. Ma says to give you her best."

She nodded, still eyeing him closely. She was a handsome woman, almost as tall as her husband, and always elegantly dressed, but her mouth pulled down in a perpetual frown, and her eyes, like now, were always sizing people up, as though try-ing to decide where to put them in the order of things. For a moment, Nathan considered asking her about the flower seeds, but thought better of it. He glanced away, concentrating on a winter scene that hung on the wall in front of them of a red fox just coming out of his burrow.

In a moment Martin Harris came back down the stairs, a small leather purse in his hand. He smiled, but it almost in-stantly vanished as he saw her hands were empty. "Lucy," he said, "I asked you to get Nathan something to drink."

She looked surprised. "Oh. I heard you call, but didn't hear you well."

At that moment Nathan knew she had heard exactly what he had called, and so did her husband. There was a quick flash of anger in his eyes, but Nathan quickly broke in. "That's all right, Mr. Harris. I've got to get going anyway. Thank you, Mrs. Harris."

She smiled, satisfied they both knew that she was not one of the hired servants. "Are you sure? I've got some elderberry juice in the smokehouse."

"Yes, I've got to get to the blacksmith shop before they close."

Harris counted out four coins and held them out. "Two dol-lars, as agreed."

"Thank you." Nathan slipped them into the watch pocket of his leather vest. "Pa and I will be here right after sunup."

Mrs. Harris smiled sweetly. "And how is your brother, Nathan?"

Nathan turned, suddenly wary. "Joshua? He's fine."

"Still working down on Canal Street?" There was no mistaking the faint disdain.

"Yes. Yes, he is." He fought down the irritation—at her for so obviously trying to bait him and at himself for the sudden defensiveness he felt.

"I'll bet that just breaks your mother's heart."

"That's enough, Lucy," Martin warned. "That's none of our affair."

She turned, her face innocent. "What did you say, Martin?"

"You heard me," he grumbled, but let it go. He turned to Nathan. "Thank you again for a job well done, Nathan."

"Thank you for the work, Mr. Harris. Now I have enough to buy that present for Ma's birthday."

"Anytime, Nathan. Anytime at all."

As Nathan left the Harris yard and started down the road toward the village, he glanced up at the sun. If he hurried he could get his business done at the blacksmith's shop and still be in time to buy some penny candy for Matthew and Becca. That brought a smile to his face. While there were several places one could buy candy in proximity to Zachariah Blackman's blacksmith shop and stables, without question Josiah McBride's dry goods store had the best penny candy in all of Palmyra Village—or at least, the best penny-candy clerk in all of the village.

And with that he forgot all about Lucy Harris and began to whistle.

Business in the store was slow, and Lydia was moving slowly through the three rooms, straightening shelves, mentally checking inventory, and dusting where necessary. Her friends would sometimes wrinkle their noses at such menial labor, but she loved the clutter and variety that made up a well-stocked dry goods store and found a surprising amount of satisfaction in being master of it all. She could instantly turn to any one of a thousand items and knew, without asking, exactly how much it sold for. There was powder and ball for the rifles; a bewildering array of farm and work tools; pins and thread and needles;

ladies' bonnets, belts, and ribbons; a few small artificial flowers; expensive earthenware and cheap crockery; tobacco, some for smoking and some for "chawing"; bolts of jean and linsey; homespun cotton cloth and the expensive satins shipped in from Boston; sassafras and sage and crop-vine teas.

She looked up as she heard the small bell on the front door tinkle. She was in the back room, working with the barrel goods, half-blocked from a clear view by some reed baskets which hung from a post. But she had a clear view of the man's face and with a quick start saw it was Nathan Steed. Moving a step back, so as to see him more clearly but keep herself out of view, she noted with satisfaction his quick scan of the store and the obvious look of disappointment on his face. Her mother was behind the counter waiting on another customer, and Nathan immediately hung back, as though not sure what he had come in for.

Surprised at the sudden rush of pleasure she felt, Lydia set down the feather duster, smoothed back her hair, and flicked at a spot of lint on her dress. She stepped out into view, pretending not to see him. Out of the corner of her eye, she saw him stiffen, then start slowly toward her. He came into the room and stopped. She fussed with a small barrel of molasses, then looked up in surprise. "Why, Nathan Steed."

"Hello, Miss Lydia."

"How are things with you today?" She winced inwardly, wanting to kick herself. She sounded like one of the young girls down at the grammar school.

"Just fine, thank you. And with you?"

"I'm fine. It's been a while since you've been in."

"With the harvest and all, it's been pretty busy. I've also been helping Mr. Harris get his corn in."

She nodded, stepped to a large barrel of pickled herring, and started to adjust its position.

"Here, let me do that." He stepped forward and tipped the heavy barrel up on the tip of its rim. "Where would you like it?"

She pointed to a corner and he rolled it over there easily.

"Thank you."

They stood there for a moment, both feeling a little awkward.

"I . . ." He turned and gestured toward the other room. "I was in town and thought I'd get some candy for the kids."

"Oh. All right." With Lydia moving ahead of him, they reentered the main area of the store and stepped to the large counter that ran the length of the store. On one end were several large glass jars filled with various hardtack candies and long strips of black licorice. Her mother, still with the woman at the far end of the counter, glanced up, smiled mechanically, as she did to all the customers, and promptly forgot about them.

Lydia felt a quick wave of relief that her father was upstairs in the storeroom taking inventory. Her mother suspected nothing about Lydia's interest in Nathan, and he came in infrequently enough that it had not roused her suspicions. Her father tended to be much more perceptive.

The Steed family, with the exception of Joshua, was rapidly winning the respect of the local townspeople. Benjamin Steed was hardworking and his farm showed it, even after only one season. Word had also gotten out that he had been a successful and well-to-do farmer in Vermont. And more and more, women came into the store telling stories of Mary Ann Steed—sickness had struck a home and she was there for three days nursing the mother back to health. If there was fruit to be dried, corn to be husked, or venison to be cut into strips and smoked, somehow she always knew and showed up to help. She was midwife to more than one of the babies born in the north part of the township.

No, it was not the Steeds in general that raised her father's concerns. The problem was Joshua. Josiah McBride had never liked Joshua for some reason, but when he left home and started work on the canal docks, that had settled it. With his frequent companionship with the Murdocks and others of Palmyra's more questionable young men, those feelings had cemented into a rock-hard determination to steer his daughter away from him. If Joshua came into the store he was barely civil with him, and if Lydia lingered at all with him, he was instantly hovering over them, brows furrowed in open warning.

When Joshua's younger brother started into the same pattern—coming in the store, looking around quickly, lighting up if Lydia was around, hanging back or leaving quickly again if she was not—Lydia saw the same wariness in her father's eyes.

So why is it I still find Joshua so intriguing? There was something about him that frightened her, and yet she still found it exciting to be with him. She thought of that night she had gone to the warehouse, and inwardly quaked again at the risk she had taken. She also remembered the relief she had felt when the Murdocks had suddenly shown up and given her an excuse to flee.

She jerked up, aware that Nathan was watching her quizzically. She blushed deeply, wondering how long she had wandered off. He smiled at her, which only added to her embarrassment.

"I'm sorry," she stammered. "I was just thinking about your family. I . . ." She turned to the jars of candy and waved her hand in front of them. "What kind of candy would you like?"

"Four of these"—he touched the closest jar—"four pieces of licorice, and . . ." His eyes narrowed as he considered the other options.

"These are Matthew's favorite," she added helpfully, glad for a chance to recover her composure. "Becca's too."

"Then I'll have five of those."

She got a small sack and put the candy into it. When she turned back to him he was watching her closely. "Have you seen Joshua lately?" he asked.

Her head shot up. But his face was innocent, his eyes merely curious.

"Yes," she finally answered, "I see him now and then when he comes in the store. But he works a lot now, so it's not often." *Less often than he wants.* Twice in the six weeks since that night on Canal Street she had found an excuse not to meet him.

"How is he?"

She considered that for a moment. He still talked about owning his own wagon. Bitterness still twisted his face when she spoke of his father or suggested he move back home. "Fine," was all she could think of to finally say.

"We were hoping he could come home for Ma's birthday on Sunday. I stopped at the boardinghouse and at the warehouse, but he's not there."

She almost asked him if he had checked the taverns but bit her tongue. It was common talk in the village that Joshua Steed spent more and more of his evenings drinking ale, playing cards or checkers, laughing loudly at some crude remark of Will Murdock. Twice Lydia had tried to raise the subject with him but got a curt reply and a clear message it was none of her affair.

Nathan picked up the sack of candy and handed her a coin. "I left a note for him at the boardinghouse, but if you happen to see him, could you give him that message for me?"

"What message?" a rough voice barked behind them. Lydia jumped and Nathan whirled around. Joshua had somehow come into the store without either of them seeing him and now stood directly behind Nathan.

Nathan flushed a little. "Joshua," he blurted, "I didn't hear you come in."

He ignored that, looking directly at Lydia. "Hello, Lydia."

"Hello, Joshua." She finally dropped her eyes under the challenge of his gaze. She caught the faint smell of ale and knew her guess had been right. He smiled, a cool, humorless flicker that barely touched his mouth, then turned back to Nathan.

"You're managing to spend a lot of time in town lately, aren't you?"

"I've been to the blacksmith's shop."

"Yeah, I saw you go by."

Nathan's head came up slowly. "I came to buy Ma a birthday present."

"At the blacksmith's?" Joshua retorted.

"I'm buying her one of those swing-out hooks for the fireplace."

Unconsciously Lydia nodded at the thoughtfulness of the

gift. In frontier cabins the large stone fireplace was generally in the main room of the home. It was used for cooking, heating water, making ashes for the lye soap, melting beeswax or animal tallow for candle making, and a hundred other necessary functions. The women in the home had to be on constant guard so that their long skirts did not sweep around into the coals and catch fire. More than one frontier mother had been horribly burned by such carelessness. Then, some years before, some enterprising blacksmith had developed a metal framework which could be placed inside the fireplace. Swinging on a metal pivot, the hooks which held the pots and kettles over the fire could be pulled clear of the fireplace where these could be filled or stirred away from the fire and then swung back in.

Joshua merely grunted. Lydia watched Nathan and saw the irritation in his eyes. *Good,* she thought. While she found Joshua's obvious jealousy flattering in a way, she was not his personal property, and resented the fact that he seemed oblivious to the effect his changing life was having on her. Besides, there had been nothing between her and Nathan except friendly encounters at the store. She was glad Nathan was not cowed by Joshua's open belligerence.

"Ma's birthday is Sunday," Nathan said quietly.

"I know that."

"She'd like you to come to dinner. I left a note with the lady at the boardinghouse."

"Don't know if I can."

Nathan shook his head, clearly fighting for patience. "Don't know if you can, or don't know if you will?"

Joshua's mouth tightened. "I said I don't know if I can."

"Suit yourself, but I think you owe it to Ma." Nathan turned to Lydia and nodded. "Thank you for your help with the candy. The kids will be grateful."

"You're welcome. Good-bye, Nathan. Tell your mother happy birthday from me, will you?"

"I will, thank you."

He strode out of the store, nodding curtly to Lydia's mother and the woman she was serving.

As Nathan walked along the board sidewalk, he jammed the sack of candy down deep into one pocket. He was still fuming over the confrontation with Joshua. He was so stubborn! So proud. And yet, Nathan was honest enough to admit to himself it was more than that. Joshua had been spoiling for a fight the moment he came in the store, and Nathan darn well knew what was eating at him. Months ago he and Joseph Smith had teased Joshua about finding any excuse to go into the McBride store. That was before Nathan had met Lydia himself. Now he found himself doing exactly the same thing. He still remembered the first day in front of the store, when he and Joseph had driven up in the wagon. He had been transfixed, staring at the raven-haired beauty with the fair skin, the winsome smile, and those dark, teasing eyes. And Nathan could still close his eyes and conjure up the image of her standing amidst the apple blossoms, filling the air with the sorrowful tale of "Barbara Allen."

He kicked at a small pebble on the walk, considering for the fortieth time the idea of leaving the field to Joshua. But that was another reason for his anger. Joshua was a fool. Nathan could still remember the way Lydia looked at Joshua back in those first days. One could almost sense the breathlessness of her spirit when Joshua was around. But that was gone now.

He sighed, wondering if this might not be his own hopes talking. Then he shook his head. There was no mistaking the dismay which darkened her face when Nathan had asked how Joshua was doing. He gave a short grunt of disgust. Everyone seemed to have dismay in his eyes when speaking of Joshua anymore, not the least of whom was his mother. Joshua's curt rebuff of the invitation to the birthday meal irked Nathan. Pa was one thing; that wasn't good, but it was understandable. But Ma? That really galled him.

"Good afternoon, Mr. Steed."

Nathan looked up, startled. An attractive, well-dressed woman was approaching him. She was tall and slender, perhaps two or three inches taller than Lydia, but had the same glistening, dark hair and wide, dark eyes. Her hair was pulled back from her face and fell at the back in ringlets.

Stopping, she held out her hand, smiling at his confusion. "I'm Emma Smith. And you're Nathan, aren't you?"

Joseph's wife! Of course! He shook her hand briefly. "Yes, I remember now. How are you Mrs. Smith?"

She smiled even more. "I'm fine, thank you. And please call me Emma."

A week or so after Nathan's father had told Joseph and Hyrum not to come back to work again, Nathan had met the whole Smith family in the village. It had been an embarrassing moment for Nathan. He had tried to apologize for his father's actions, but Joseph had simply smiled and brushed it aside and proceeded to introduce him to his family. Father Smith, as they called him, since his name was Joseph too, was a quiet man, and now Nathan could barely remember him. Joseph's mother, a tiny woman, not five feet tall and weighing less than a hundred pounds, had the opposite impression on him. Nathan had liked her almost instantly. She was full of spunk, with bright blue eyes that laughed merrily, or flashed with quick anger when Nathan mentioned what the townspeople were saying about Joseph. There had been a sister and two younger brothers, but Nathan couldn't remember their names now. And Joseph and Hyrum had both been accompanied by their wives. Jerusha, he remembered. Emma and Jerusha.

"Joseph was just speaking of you the other day," Emma was saying.

"Oh?"

"Yes. He was wondering how the crops had turned out for your family."

"We did well, thanks to the help he and Hyrum gave in clearing the land."

"Good, I'll tell him."

"Is Joseph in town with you?"

"Yes. He's at the livery stable, checking on some harness equipment."

"I'd like to see him. Would you mind if I walked with you?"

"Not at all. I'm going there now." As he turned and fell into step beside her, Nathan remembered a phrase Hyrum had once used when he spoke of Joseph's new wife. Or at least she had been new then. They had been married in January. He had said she was a gracious lady. Now as they chatted and walked along he had to agree with that assessment. It was not hard to see why Joseph had felt it worth his time to make the hundred-and-twenty-mile journey to Harmony, Pennsylvania, to court this woman. Her speech was cultured and precise, but she was warm and quick to laugh. Nathan found himself feeling comfortable with her almost immediately.

"I haven't seen Joseph all summer," Nathan said. "Someone said you two had returned to Harmony."

"Only to get my things," Emma replied. "We were gone about a month." A slight frown crossed her face. "My parents did not approve of my marrying Joseph. There's still a little strain there."

Surprised at her frankness, Nathan merely nodded.

She turned and looked at him. "Joseph said he told you of what happened in the grove near his home."

"Yes, I . . ." He stopped, not sure if she expected a response, or if so, what it should be. He had thought about the conversation many times since then. It still stirred him deeply. Stirred and disturbed. That was one of the reasons why he had been hoping to see Joseph again.

If she noticed his hesitation, she gave no sign. "And the gold plates, did he tell you of those as well?"

Nathan turned and looked at her, then slowly shook his head. The gold plates. They were part of the legion of stories circulating about Joseph, but he had never said anything to Nathan about them, and with the cessation of their employment at the Steeds, Nathan had no chance to inquire further about them. Now Emma was confirming it. Or was she?

She smiled, somewhat wistfully, again not noticing his distraction. "Well, my father finds all this about Joseph as difficult to accept as most other people."

Nathan gave her a sympathetic nod, wanting to ask for more details but sensing her mind was lost in other things. He determined at that moment to press Joseph further about the matter at the first opportunity.

"Would you mind if we crossed the street?"

Nathan looked up in surprise. Emma had slowed her step, her eyes clearly troubled. About four doors ahead of them, three men had just come out of Lilly's coffeehouse and tavern. They were staring in their direction. One man's arm lifted and pointed at them.

"No, of course not," Nathan said quickly, remembering the day in town when the Murdocks had confronted Joseph.

They stepped off the boardwalk, waited for a large wagon loaded with sacks of grain to pass, then hurried across the street.

"Thank you." She was on the verge of saying more but stopped abruptly. One of the men had darted back to the door of the tavern and was calling something inside. The other two were cutting across the street, coming directly for them.

"It'll be all right, Emma. I'm here."

"I know," she said, her voice barely above a whisper. "I just hate it so."

Nathan took her elbow, changing sides with her so he was on the outside and she was next to the buildings. Nathan didn't recognize either man, but there was no mistaking their intent. One was already leering as the two men stepped onto the sidewalk and planted their feet, blocking the way.

"Well, if it ain't Mrs. Joe Smith herself," the older man said, bowing low in a mock curtsy.

"Excuse us, please," Nathan said firmly, pushing past them.

The second man was shabbily dressed, carried three or four days of whiskers, and had bloodshot eyes. He had obviously had more to drink than his companion, or held it with less dignity, for he weaved precariously as he fell quickly into step alongside them. "Aw, now, Miz Smith. What's your hurry? Where's ol' Joe nowadays? Heard tell he fled the country."

Out of the corner of his eye, Nathan saw Emma's lips tighten into a hard line. He moved enough to gently shoulder the man off of the sidewalk. "Mrs. Smith is late for an appointment. Excuse us, please."

The first man turned and walked backwards so he could face them as he talked. "Why, ain't that sweet, Luke? Miz Smith here has done gone and got herself an escort."

Nathan felt his temper rising but he merely increased his step slightly, causing the man to nearly trip and to turn around to walk a step behind them. Across the street three more men came out of the tavern. They stopped for a moment to watch, then hurried across to the sidewalk, blocking any progress now. Nathan stopped, sensing this was quickly getting out of hand. Two women coming in their direction on the same side of the street also stopped, then moved closer, cautious but curious. A passing buckboard with a family in it slowed, then pulled to a stop, close enough to hear without actually joining in.

"Please let us pass," Nathan said quietly.

"He even says please and excuse me," the second man said with mock solemnity.

Emma suddenly went up on tiptoes, peering over the heads of the men. Her hand shot up. "Joseph! Joseph!"

Across the street, Nathan saw the tall figure of Joseph Smith striding along. He felt a quick stab of relief as Joseph looked up in surprise, then swerved to come across to them. He pushed through the men and quickly stepped to his wife. "Emma, are you all right?"

"Yes. Nathan was helping me."

Joseph reached out and gripped his hand. "Hello, Nathan."

"Hello, Joseph."

The grip tightened in a squeeze of gratitude. "Thank you."

Nathan nodded, but it was not over yet. With that mysterious ability of small towns to smell anything out of the ordinary, the people of Palmyra were suddenly being drawn to the scene in the street like ants to a spilled jar of maple syrup. The barbershop behind them contributed four men, including the barber in his long leather apron. A dress shop just ahead disgorged two clerks and three customers. More men were coming quickly from the tavern. A group of four or five boys, who had been rolling an iron hoop along with sticks, now raced toward them, a mongrel dog at their side barking furiously at, as yet, he knew not what.

"Where you been, Joe?" the man with the bloodshot eyes called. "I hear you been out looking for more treasure down Pennsylvany way."

"Hey, Joe," someone else called from the back, "seen the devil lately?"

Joseph took Emma's arm. "The wagon's down by the barn. Let's go."

Nathan stepped in front of them to make a way through the crowd. The man who had first accosted them fell back before Nathan's determined gaze, but there was nowhere to go. Those pushing from the back did not move.

"You got that gold Bible yet?" This was a woman's voice from behind them.

"Make way!" Nathan barked sharply. He straight-armed an older man gently but firmly. The crowd behind him began to shuffle back enough to clear a path. Nathan pushed into it with Joseph and Emma close behind him.

But just as they nearly cleared the crowd, someone stepped directly in front of Nathan. "Make way for what?"

It was Will Murdock, still holding a pewter mug half-filled with beer.

"We're coming through, Will." Nathan was finding his patience rapidly disappearing.

"Come on, Nate. We just want some answers from ol' Joe Smith here," Will said loudly. "Ain't nobody gonna get hurt. We just want to ask Joe some questions." He suddenly raised his arms to the crowd. "Ain't that it, folks?"

Interestingly enough, many of those looking on would not normally have so much as given Will Murdock the time of day if they had passed him on the street. But if he was willing to take the point for them, now they'd go along with him. "Yeah!" they cried. "Let him ask the questions." "All we want are some answers." "Tell us, Joe. Tell us."

"Get out of the way, Will," Nathan said sharply. "Leave these people alone."

Will threw back his head and laughed. Then his eyes narrowed dangerously. "Now that ain't no way to talk to an old friend, Mr. high-and-mighty Nathan Steed."

He turned and looked behind him. "This a relative of yours, Josh?"

Nathan was stunned. Joshua stepped forward to stand beside Will Murdock. "Reckon I'd have to say it was," Joshua said grimly. His eyes were cold and Nathan knew he was still smarting over his presence in the store.

Joseph stepped up to stand beside Nathan, with Emma close behind him. "Hello, Joshua," he murmured.

"Hello, Joseph."

"Are you part of this too?" Joseph let his eyes sweep the crowd briefly.

For a moment the calm demeanor and the simple question caught Joshua off guard. His eyes dropped. But Will Murdock swung around to glare at him and Joshua jerked back up again. "Well, to be honest, I'm kind of curious about those questions too."

"Joshua!" Nathan cried.

Joseph laid a hand on Nathan's shoulder, still meeting Joshua's eyes steadily. "No answers today, Joshua," he said easily. "Emma and I were just leaving."

Joshua stepped squarely in front of Joseph. "I asked you

once last spring, and you wouldn't answer then either. What about them gold plates, Joseph? Is there such a thing?"

"That's enough!" Nathan shouted, grabbing at his brother's arm. "You've shamed the family enough. Now let us pass."

Joshua whirled, flinging Nathan's hand away, his eyes blazing. Nathan fell back a step before the fury he saw on Joshua's face.

For a moment no one in the crowd moved, the tension as thick in the air as static electricity before a summer thunderstorm. Then suddenly Will Murdock pushed in and thrust his nose up into Joseph's face. "Ain't it true you're getting close to getting them gold plates, Joe?"

For a moment Joseph looked startled and Nathan saw Will's shot had hit home. But just as quickly as it had come the look passed. Joseph just shook his head, as though dealing with a naughty child. "Does this mean you believe all them stories you've been hearing, Will?"

There was a snicker from several in the crowd. Taking advantage of the sudden lull in the tension, Joseph took Emma's arm and pushed past both Joshua and Will Murdock. Will's brother, David, reached out and grabbed Joseph's sleeve. "Don't let him get away until he tells us what he knows."

Joseph turned slowly, staring down into the twisted features of the younger Murdock. He was half a head taller than David and probably outweighed him by thirty or so pounds. For the first time his eyes had turned the color of glacial ice as he looked first at David, then down at the hand clutching at his sleeve.

The boy tried to meet the icy gaze, but finally dropped his eyes and let his hand fall to his side. Without another word Joseph pushed through the last of the crowd and walked away, his back straight, one arm coming up to hold Emma close to him.

There were murmurs rippling through the crowd and a few catcalls as the couple walked away. Nathan whirled. "That's right," he cried, "show him what you're made of." Eyes dropped as he stared them down, his chest rising and falling.

"Go ahead. All you fine Christian people who get your courage out of a bottle or from hiding in the back of a crowd. Show him the color of your bravery."

One by one heads dropped and people started moving away. Some were whispering, some glanced back over their shoulders, their faces angry. Seething inside now, Nathan turned back to face Joshua and his two drinking companions. Will Murdock smirked openly. David was still trying to recover his swaggering bravado. Joshua just met Nathan's stare, his eyes hooded and dark.

For a moment Nathan was tempted to hurl one last withering remark, but something inside him warned it might lead to something both would later deeply regret. He finally just shook his head, not trying to hide his disgust, and started away.

"Tell Ma I won't be coming for dinner," Joshua called loudly after him. "I wouldn't want to shame the family."

Nathan turned back slowly. "Perhaps it's just as well," he said quietly.

Joshua spun around on his heel, and he, the Murdocks, and the other men who had poured out of the tavern retraced their steps and disappeared. Nathan didn't move, just stood and watched them go, vaguely aware the crowd was disappearing now as rapidly as they had assembled.

With a deep feeling of weariness, Nathan finally turned around. He stopped dead. Lydia was standing near the door to the barbershop, her eyes wide, her mouth open, staring at him. Something in him felt suddenly sick. "You too?" he asked in a hoarse whisper.

She rocked back. "I just came to see what was happening."

He shook his head, the revulsion welling up inside of him, and started past her.

"Nathan, I didn't say anything."

He stopped, his eyes raking across her features. Another face in the nameless crowd. It hurt him more sharply than he could have imagined. "You didn't have to," he said bitterly, and walked away.

Chapter Ten

S_{ir!"}

Nathan had stopped by a rail fence along Stafford Road. An older man was in the field about fifty yards away, raking meadow hay into neat windrows. He looked up, wiping his brow.

"Sir, could you tell me which house is the Smith family's?"

"Eh?" the man called back, cupping one hand up to his ear.

Raising his voice, Nathan called again, "Could you tell me where the Joseph Smith family lives?"

The man shook his head, and for a moment Nathan thought he was refusing to answer, but he laid the big wooden rake down and came over to where Nathan was standing.

"Sorry, son," he said, his voice heavy with a Boston twang, "my hearin' ain't what it used to be. Say again."

Nathan smiled. The man looked like a weather-beaten tree stump, lined with proof of the years, but solid as Vermont granite. "I'm looking for the Smith farm. I understand it's somewhere along here."

"Yeah," he agreed, turning to point. "Third house south of here. Another half mile or so. A white frame house on the east side of the road."

"Thank you."

He nodded, matter of fact. "Glad to be of help."

Nathan half turned, then had a thought. "You know the Smiths very well?"

"We been neighbors since 1818. That's going on ten years now."

Nathan stuck out his hand. "My name is Nathan Steed. My family bought the farm next to the Martin Harris place, north of town."

Again came the quick nod, as though the announcement was not news. "Heard tell your pa is doing well for his first season."

"Yes."

"Glad to hear that." He straightened. "Well, third house down, on your left."

"Tell me about the Smiths," Nathan blurted, before the man could leave. "We keep hearing all kinds of wild stories."

The lines around the mouth deepened. "You ought not to be listenin' to fool talk, son."

"I don't," Nathan amended hastily. "Joseph and Hyrum worked this spring for my pa, helping us clear the land. I thought they were fine young men. That's why the stories seem a little strange."

He softened a little. "The Smiths are a good family. They work hard, pay their debts, and mind their own business." The last comment was accompanied by a sharp look which clearly suggested that others, including Nathan, ought to do the same. "I don't cotton much to all this talk about angels and gold Bibles, but I figure a man's religion is his own affair. But all this nonsense about the Smiths being lazy no-accounts and dishonest blackguards is just plain slop for the hogs. Comes from people who ought to be working and not standing around flapping their jawbones."

Nathan laughed. "I agree. Thank you again."

He was still chuckling as he continued south, turning once to wave to the old man. It was refreshing to know someone had a kind word to say about the Smith family. Each time he thought about the narrow-mindedness of people, he began to seethe all over again. The old man was right. Maybe all this talk of angels and seeing God in the woods was crazy, but it wasn't like Joseph was trying to push it off on people. He had only told Nathan after he had pressed him for it. And three times now Nathan had seen him parry Joshua's attempts to get the whole story out of him.

The confrontation in town earlier that afternoon had left a sour aftertaste in Nathan's mouth, and he had not felt like going home. His mother would be waiting to ask if Joshua was coming Sunday, and Nathan couldn't bear the pain that would fill her eyes when he told her no. And if he said anything about what had happened in town, it would only further alienate and anger his pa against Joshua. So for a time he had sat on the grassy banks of the Erie Canal, watching the barges go by. He thought of Joshua, he thought of Lydia, trying to push back the disappointment he had felt when he saw her in the crowd. But mostly he thought about Joseph and what Emma said about the gold Bible.

That's when he had decided to come south, see if he could find Joseph, and ask him directly. Since the day last spring when they had sat in the meadow and Joseph had told Nathan of his vision, Nathan had gone over it and over it in his mind. One part of him recoiled at the thought of it. God himself coming down to earth? And to visit a boy? And a farm boy at that? He had said as much to his mother, and she countered with examples from the Bible in which the Lord had called common folk or young people to do his work. Samuel was but a child when the Lord called to him in the temple. Gideon, in the book of Judges, was an unknown farmer and the youngest son in his family when he was asked to deliver Israel from the oppressive hand of the Midianites. Peter, James, and John were humble fishermen. Joseph the son of Jacob was but seventeen when he was sold into Egypt and went on to become vice-regent to Pharaoh.

It had startled Nathan as his mother rolled off the examples. Clearly she had been thinking about it quite a bit. More surprising to Nathan, she believed Joseph. Even though she had only heard the story from Nathan's mouth, she believed it. Whenever Nathan and she discussed it—always out of the presence of Nathan's father—if he began to ask questions or express doubts, she would quietly defend Joseph and give answers that showed she had been thinking of some of the very questions which troubled Nathan. A few weeks ago she announced, quietly but with force and power, that she had gotten an answer to her prayers. Joseph was telling the truth.

Nathan wasn't sure her answer fully convinced him. On the other hand, he had worked side by side with Joseph Smith for almost a month. He knew him. He liked him. And of one thing he was absolutely certain: Joseph was not a liar. And even if he were, what possible motive could Joseph have for doing it? Gain? How had he profited from the deceit? He and Hyrum had to hire out as day laborers to help the family survive. Glory? Nathan shook his head at that, thinking about the ugliness of the crowd in town that day. If Joseph was after glory, he had chosen an odd way to get it.

For the past few weeks Nathan had largely put it from his mind, and he and his mother had not discussed it further. But the events of the day brought it all flooding back. Emma had referred to the gold plates as though they were reality. And though Joseph had once again neatly parried the questions thrown at him, he had not denied anything. When Nathan thought back, Joseph had never once denied having the gold book!

It was nearly dusk by the time he stopped in front of a house where a board with the word *Smith* painted on it was nailed to the gate. Nathan looked at the house with a bit of surprise.

Joseph had told him his family had recently moved from their log cabin into a new home which the sons had built for their parents. He turned and looked back the way he had come. About fifty or sixty yards up the road and on the opposite side was a small log cabin. It looked more like what Nathan had expected to find.

But this house was a large one, well constructed, with an upper floor over the spacious main level. A front porch ran the full width of the house. The roof came to a tall gabled point over the front door, with wings extending from there both on the north and the south. Two chimneys rose from each end of the house. He calculated quickly, concluding there must be at least four or five rooms on each level. The wood was painted a gleaming white and the yard was well tended. And surrounding the house was a handsome-looking farm. Most of the crops were either in or waiting to be brought in, but the land looked rich and well cared for. For some reason it was more than Nathan had expected. He nodded thoughtfully. Again this hardly fit the picture of a family of religious lunatics.

He walked swiftly up to the door and pulled on the door knocker. There were footsteps inside, then the door opened. It was Emma. For a moment she was startled, then instantly broke into a smile. "Why, Nathan, what a surprise!"

"Hello, Mrs. Smith."

She laughed merrily. "Emma, please. Remember, I'm not much older than you, Nathan. And I'm still getting used to this Mrs. Smith business." She pushed open the screen door. "Come in, come in."

Nathan stepped inside, suddenly feeling foolish about coming. But Emma swung around and called up the stairs. "Joseph, it's Nathan Steed."

Before he could speak she reached out and touched his arm. "I didn't get a chance to thank you for what you did today."

Nathan shrugged, embarrassed by the gratitude in her eyes. "I'm just glad I was there. They wouldn't have hurt you, it's just . . ."

"It's just that they can't pass up any opportunity to mock

us." There was no mistaking the soft bitterness which tinged her voice.

"I know. I . . . I'm sorry one of them was my own brother."

"You don't have to be, not after what you did." She brightened. "But I'm forgetting my manners. Come in and sit down. Joseph will be right down."

She led the way into the parlor. It was furnished simply but tastefully. A wooden rocking chair was in one corner, a worn but still-serviceable sofa next to the west window. A small table held a large family Bible, and there was a braided rug made from multicolored rags in front of the fireplace. Hand-painted oilcloth curtains hung at both windows, and Nathan remembered that Hyrum once told them his mother was good enough at such painting that she sold them in the village.

There were footsteps on the stairs, and before Nathan had a chance to sit, Joseph bounded into the room. "Nathan! I was planning to come see you tomorrow."

Nathan blinked. "You were?"

"Yes, to thank you for today."

"Emma already did."

Joseph was dressed in a long-sleeved shirt open at the neck. Suspenders held up woolen trousers which were tucked into boots that came almost to his knees. At Nathan's demure comment, he shook his head, his eyes troubled. "I usually get a few ugly comments whenever I'm in the village, but I didn't think they would confront Emma." He turned to her. "Or I would never have left her alone."

"Thank heavens Nathan came along."

"Yes."

Joseph turned as someone came into the room behind them. It was his mother, a tiny woman in a long dress. She had a dish towel and was drying her hands. Joseph immediately stepped aside and brought her forward. "Mother, this is Nathan Steed, the one who helped Emma in the village today."

The blue eyes immediately lighted with warmth. "Oh, yes. I remember. We met once before in the village."

"Hello, again, Mrs. Smith."

"We are so grateful to you for what you did today for Emma." There were sudden tears in her eyes. "Joseph told me what you said to the crowd as he and Emma walked away."

This gratitude business was getting out of hand and Nathan felt his face getting hot. He started to brush it aside, but Joseph clapped one hand on his shoulder. "It was wonderful. We are in your debt."

Emma, sensing his embarrassment, gestured to the sofa. "Would you like to sit down, Nathan?"

"No, thank you, I can only stay a few minutes. I . . . I just wanted to talk to Joseph for a moment."

"Nonsense," Joseph's mother said quickly, patting his arm. "I have some warm apple pie in the kitchen. Emma, you go fetch Father Smith and the other children. They'll be disappointed if they don't get a chance to meet Nathan. I'll get the pie on."

"Really, Mrs. Smith," Nathan protested, "I've got to be getting back."

Joseph laughed as his mother gently pushed Nathan toward the sofa. "You may as well give in. No one refuses Mother's apple pie."

To the west of the Smith home, across Stafford Road, a small creek ran through the farm. Joseph jumped across it easily, with Nathan following, then walked through the remains of a cornfield, his feet crunching pleasantly on the short stalks left in the ground. Nathan followed at his side, his face pensive. Neither man spoke. Nathan was trying to collect his thoughts, and Joseph seemed content to wait for him to take the lead.

About a hundred yards west of the house there was a large stand of virgin forest. It was common practice in the area to leave such stands of trees as woodlots. In fact, in earlier times many house leases included a clause that forbade the tenants from cutting any firewood except that which they could get "by hook or by crook"—that is, by using a hooked stick like a shepherd's crook to pull down dead or dying branches from the trees. Though the custom had largely passed away, every wise farmer kept a woodlot for lumber and firewood.

For a moment Nathan thought Joseph was heading into the woodlot. The sun had gone down and dusk was rapidly approaching. Within the trees it was dark, almost foreboding. But Joseph stopped on a small grassy knoll just before the trees began. He nodded, as though approving of his choice of sites, and sat down. Nathan followed suit.

A bird flitted overhead and landed in one of the nearby trees. In a moment the lovely song of "bob-o-lee, bob-o-link" floated down to them.

Joseph looked up. "Looks like that one forgot to head south."

Nathan looked up, not able to find the dark shape in the treetop until it jumped to another branch.

"Normally the bob-o-links start south in mid-July and early August. This one must be from Vermont."

Surprised, Nathan turned to look at Joseph. "Why Vermont?"

He grinned. "Even the summers in Vermont are so cold he probably developed so many feathers he can't tell it's autumn now."

Nathan laughed.

"And the winters up there. Whoo!"

"I know. Remember, my family comes from Vermont too."

"Oh, that's right, down Rutland way."

"Yes."

"That hardly counts. Why, the birds up in Windsor County used to fly south to Rutland to warm their tail feathers."

"Right," Nathan chuckled. Windsor County was less than a hundred miles north of Rutland, but this straight-faced exaggeration was the New England way, and it brought a quick pang of homesickness to Nathan. There were some things he still missed about Vermont.

"You tell that to my pa and see what he says. That's one of the reasons we left Rutland."

"Us too," Joseph said, sobering. "We had three successive crop failures. Remember the winters of 1815 and '16?"

"Barely, but my mother still talks about them."

With one last lilting cry, the bob-o-link flew away and the woods fell silent. Joseph leaned back on his elbows and closed his eyes, letting the soft breeze play across his face.

Nathan watched for a moment, then lay back himself, feeling the warmth of the apple pie and two glasses of milk in his stomach. "Joseph?"

"Yes."

"I . . ." He hesitated, feeling suddenly foolish.

"You can ask it, Nathan."

He turned his head, surprised at his perceptiveness. "I don't want to pry."

Joseph turned his head. "After what you did today, Nathan, you can ask."

Encouraged, Nathan started, hesitantly, not wanting to offend. "This is probably none of my affair, and if it isn't, just say so."

"I think it may be very much your affair. Go on."

He plunged in. "Well, every one keeps talking about you seeing angels and having a gold Bible. Today in town even Emma seemed to talk like there was something to all this."

Joseph sat up a little, and a slow smile stole across his face. "That wasn't a question, Nathan."

"No," he chuckled, "I guess it wasn't."

"So just ask it."

Nathan took a breath, and pressed on. "All right, then. Is there any truth to all this? Do you have gold plates or a gold Bible?"

"No."

For a moment Nathan stared at Joseph. That was it? A simple no? So all of the talk, all of the Will Murdock prattle, all the rumors and wild stories were just that? He felt a wave of relief wash over him.

"But . . . ," Joseph added, watching Nathan closely.

Nathan felt his heart drop. "But what?"

"May I ask you a question first?"

"Of course."

"Have you thought about what I told you before?"

Now it was Nathan's turn to sit back. He finally sighed, not able to be anything but totally honest with him. "Yes. A great deal."

"And?"

"And . . ." He finally threw up his hands in frustration. "I don't know. One part of me wants to believe it. I mean, I know you're not lying, Joseph. But another part of me thinks, 'This is absolutely incredible. God appearing to a fourteen-year-old?' " Instantly he flushed. "I'm sorry, Joseph, I didn't mean it that way."

"Sorry for what?" Joseph replied softly. "It couldn't seem any more fantastic to you than it does to me. Do you know how many times I've asked myself the very question? Why *did* this happen to me? And the answer always comes up the same. I don't know. I only know it did."

He turned, gazing into the darkness of the nearby forest. "It was right over there, you know."

"What?"

"Where it happened. After I read the Bible and decided to pray, I knew exactly where I wanted to go. I had been in this stand of trees many times, cutting wood, looking for livestock."

Nathan watched him, watched the memory filling his eyes. Finally, he spoke softly, "Mother believes you."

Joseph turned around very slowly, one eyebrow coming up. "She does?"

"Yes." Nathan told him quickly about her own experience

in seeking which church to join and how his story had touched her. "She prayed about it for almost a month. Then she said she knew."

Joseph looked away, but not before Nathan had caught a sudden glint in his eyes. "You don't know what that means to me, Nathan," he said, his voice husky. "Will you tell her that for me?"

"Yes."

There was a long moment of silence, then finally Joseph turned back to him. "Now, about these gold plates."

Nathan looked up quickly. "But you said there weren't any."

"No, I said I don't have them. And I don't." His eyes lifted to meet Nathan's. "Not yet."

"Not yet?" Nathan cried, going up to his knees to face him, the dismay making his voice crack a little.

"Once again, Nathan, I'd like to tell you the whole story. Then you can ask questions. Is that fair?"

Nathan sat back slowly. "Fair enough."

Now Joseph sat fully up, clasping his knees and putting his head down on his arms. "About three years passed after the vision of 1820. Nothing else had happened. I mean, I went about life as usual. I came in for a lot of ridicule and persecution because of my telling people." He shook his head slowly. "That scene in town today has been repeated many times. But other than that, it was pretty much a normal life for a teenaged boy.

"It was September, 1823. I had reflected a great deal about my experience and wondered why nothing else had happened. The Lord had told me that the fulness of the gospel would at some future time be made known unto me, then three years of silence followed.

"I began to feel it was my own sins and weaknesses that had caused this period of silence." There was a ghost of a smile, wistful, almost sad. "Not that I was guilty of any great sins. That is not my nature. But I often acted foolishly. I was guilty of too much levity." He grinned more openly now. "You know my nature, Nathan. I love to have a good time."

"Is that bad?"

"Of course not. But remember, I had been called of God, and such frivolity seemed out of character with the calling I had received. But anyway, one night I took myself to prayer and supplication to the Lord. I asked him to forgive my follies and imperfections. I also asked to know my standing with him."

He fell silent, smoothing the grass with his fingertips. The silence stretched on and Nathan was tempted to prompt him, but he waited, sensing that Joseph was gathering his thoughts. Finally, he began speaking, slowly and distinctly.

"While I was thus in prayer—this was in my bedroom in the cabin where we lived before we moved here, just up the road."

"Yes, I noticed it as I passed it tonight."

"Yes. That's where Hyrum and Jerusha live, now we have moved into the big house. Anyway, while I was praying, I suddenly noticed the room was getting light. The light grew brighter and brighter until the bedroom was brighter than at noonday. And there, standing in the air at my bedside, was a personage."

Nathan felt a familiar prickle run along the back of his neck. Was there nothing normal that happened to Joseph when he prayed? Again a part of him reeled at what he was hearing, but also once again Nathan felt his heart burning as Joseph spoke. It was like every word was piercing the flesh and penetrating his very soul. "Was it God?" he finally ventured.

Joseph shook his head.

"Then what was it? What did it look like?"

"Not it," Joseph smiled. "Him."

"It was a man?"

"Yes. He had on a robe of the most exquisite whiteness, whiter than anything I had ever seen on this earth. The robe came down his arms to a little above the wrist, leaving his hands uncovered. It also came down to a little way above his ankles. He wore no shoes or sandals. His head was also un-covered."

Nathan was staring at Joseph, transfixed at the verbal imagery he was creating.

"Not only was his robe of this incredible whiteness, but his very person was glorious beyond any description. His countenance was like lightning. That's the only thing which comes close to describing it. This was what made the whole room brighter than daylight."

"What did you do?"

Joseph laughed softly. "To be honest, at first I was frightened. I mean, suddenly here is this glorious being by my bedside, so brilliant he fills the whole room with light. But the fear quickly left me. He called me by name. He told me that his name was Moroni, and—"

"More-ohn-eye?" Nathan repeated the name slowly.

"Yes, that was his name. Moroni. He said he was a messenger sent from the presence of God." Joseph shook his head slightly. "In light of what happened today, this next part should interest you, Nathan. Would you like to guess what the first thing he said was?"

"I don't know."

"He said God had a work for me and that because of that work my name would be known for good and evil, or rather that people would speak both good and evil of me throughout the world."

Nathan digested that, thinking of the catcalls earlier that day.

Joseph had stopped and was peering into Nathan's eyes. In the near darkness the blue seemed to be almost black and Nathan could not read their expression. "He then told me . . ." Joseph took a breath and let it out in a burst, as though he were still a little dazed himself. "He told me there was a book, written on gold plates, deposited in a nearby hill."

Nathan had shot forward. "The gold Bible!"

Joseph shook his head. "That's what everyone is calling it, but all he said was that it was a record written on gold plates. He said it was a record of the people who lived on this continent before our time and told how they had come to be here."

Nathan was reeling. "You mean this is a record of the Indians?"

"The forefathers of the Indians," Joseph corrected. "Or at least part of them. He also said the Savior had visited these people and the book contained the fulness of his gospel.

"After that he began to quote some scriptures from the Bible, prophecies from Isaiah and other Old Testament prophets about the last days. When he was finished, he spoke again of the plates, telling me the time had not yet come for me to have them, but when I did get them, I was to show them to no one except those to whom I would be instructed to show them, or I would be destroyed. As he was speaking, a vision was opened to me and I saw the place where the plates were buried. It is not far from here, and the vision was so clear and distinct, I knew I would have no trouble finding it again.

"When he finished, the light in the room began to gather about him, as though it were collecting itself right into his person. Then, it was almost like there was a conduit which opened up into heaven. He ascended up that passageway, growing more and more distant, until he disappeared."

Full night had fallen now, and the sound of crickets and frogs rose like a soft chorus behind them. A mosquito buzzed near Nathan's ear and he brushed at it without thinking, his mind racing. "So there really are gold plates?"

"Yes."

"What do they look like, Joseph? How big are they?"

"You said you would let me finish before you asked questions."

Chagrined, Nathan sat back. "I thought you were finished."

Joseph chuckled. "So did I that night. You can imagine my astonishment. I lay there on my bed marveling greatly at what had happened, when suddenly once again my room began to fill with light."

"Another angel?"

"No. It was Moroni again. He commenced speaking and repeated everything he had said the first time, without any variation. Then he told me of great judgments that were to come upon the earth in this generation. Having done that he ascended once again to heaven as he had done before.

"By this time, so deep were the impressions his visits had made upon my mind, any thought of sleep had fled. But imagine my surprise when once again my room began to fill with light. For the third time he stood at my bedside. Once again he repeated all he had said before. Then he warned me that Satan would seek to tempt me to use the plates for personal gain."

Joseph shook his head in the darkness. "As you know, my family has gone through some hard times financially. The angel seemed to know about that, but said I was to have no other purpose in getting the plates than to glorify God and to build his kingdom, otherwise I could not have them."

He exhaled slowly, feeling the weariness of that night. "When he ascended the third time, I immediately heard the cock crowing and realized his three visits had taken all of the night."

"Where were the plates hidden?" Nathan burst out, the questions tumbling in his mind.

Joseph held up his hand, smiling at him in the darkness.

"You mean you're still not finished?"

"No. Because Moroni was not finished."

"What do you mean by that?"

"That morning I went out as usual to work with my father and brothers. We were in the midst of the harvest. But I was so exhausted with all that had happened and from being awake all night, my father noticed something was wrong. He finally sent me back to the house to rest, but as I crossed the fence I lost all strength. I must have fainted. I was unconscious for a time. The first thing I remember was a voice calling me by name again. When I opened my eyes, there was Moroni standing above me."

"A fourth time?" Nathan breathed.

"Yes. Once again he repeated everything he had told me." Joseph stopped, and gave a short laugh. "Now do you understand why I can remember everything so clearly?"

"I guess *so.* Four times!"

"Yes. When he was finished, he told me to return to the field and tell my father all that had happened, then I was to go to the hill where the plates were buried."

That caught Nathan by surprise. "What did your father say?"

"My father is a very practical man," Joseph said softly. "I am pleased to say he believed everything I told him. In fact, my family has always stood by me in this." He shrugged. "They at least have believed me. Anyway, Father simply told me to do exactly as the angel had commanded me to do. So I left the field and went immediately to the hill where the plates were buried. Having seen it the night before in vision, I knew exactly where it was. It's within walking distance of our farm. When I got there, I climbed to a spot near the top of the hill. There I found a stone of considerable size, half-buried in the ground. From above, it looked like a huge boulder, but I dug around it and found the bottom of it was flat. I got a large stick, and using it for a lever, pried the stone up."

He stopped, but Nathan leaned forward eagerly. "And? Joseph, don't stop now. What did you see?"

"Under the stone was a large box, made of flat stones laid in some kind of cement. And there in the box was everything he had said there would be."

"What do you mean, everything he said there would be?" Nathan demanded. "Was there something besides the plates?"

"Oh, I didn't mention the other things?"

"What other things?"

"Moroni said that with the plates I would find a Urim and

Thummim—two stones set in silver bows—which fastened to a breastplate, a piece of armor you would strap around a man's chest. The stones were to assist me in translating the book. The breastplate has a place to attach the Urim and Thummim so as to leave the hands free to work."

The shocks were coming like pelting rain. "So you are to translate this book? That's the work God has for you?"

"Nathan, Nathan," Joseph laughed. "Please let me finish."

"I'm sorry," Nathan replied ruefully. "This story has too many endings."

Joseph moved a little closer to Nathan. The air had turned quite chilly now. The harvest moon, now half waning, was rising above the trees to the east of them, turning their puffs of breath into silvery clouds. Also in the light Nathan saw Joseph had turned very sober. "What?" he said, puzzled by the sudden shift of mood.

"You believe me, don't you, Nathan." It was not a question, but a statement, filled with wonder.

It stunned Nathan.

"You believe it all. I can see it on your face."

For a moment, time seemed suspended as Nathan probed the inward recesses of his soul. There was still the incredulousness, still the sense of hearing something that couldn't possibly be true. And yet he knew it was. He knew without the least shadow of doubt that everything Joseph was telling him was true. And so, finally, with a wonder of his own, he said, "Yes, Joseph. I believe you."

Joseph leaped to his feet and dragged Nathan up to face him. He grasped him by the shoulders, then pulled him to him and pummeled his back. "Thank you, Nathan. Thank you."

After a moment Nathan pulled back, twisting his mouth into a sardonic grin. "Does this mean I get to hear the end of the story?"

Joseph laughed. "Yes." Almost instantly he sobered, shaking his head. They both sat back down again, then Joseph went on. "So I'm kneeling there, in front of this stone box, looking down at the plates and the breastplate, filled with wonder and amazement." He sighed, a sound heavy with pain. "And other things as well."

"What do you mean?"

"At that point, I unfortunately proved Moroni had been right."

"Right about what?"

"Remember, he had told me I would be tempted to use the plates for my own personal gain. In spite of that, on the way to the hill, I must confess, all I could think about was the gold. What it would mean to my family. A fortune! And suddenly mine." He passed a hand across his eyes. "And suddenly, there it was! Right at my fingertips."

He stopped, and the silence seemed deafening. Nathan was leaning forward, hanging on every word.

"There must be forty or fifty pounds of gold in those plates, Nathan. My parents have worked so hard and gone without so much. And now they're getting older. All I could think of was our troubles were over."

His voice dropped in pitch as he remembered the shame. "I reached down to grab the plates. But as I touched them, something jolted me so violently, for a moment I had no strength in my arms. Stunned, I reached for them again. Again I was hit with a tremendous shock. It was like being hit with a bolt of lightning. Bewildered, dazed, I tried a third time. The third time the jolt was so powerful it knocked me backwards. In pain and frustration I cried out, 'Why can't I obtain this record?' Almost instantly a voice beside me answered, 'Because you have not kept the commandments of the Lord.' "

"It was Moroni again."

"Yes. Imagine my shame. All of the feelings I had on my way to the hill came flooding back as I remembered his warning from the night before. He told me again I was not ready to receive the record. He said I was to return to that spot each year at the same time. Then, if I had prepared myself properly, I would get the record so I could translate it. As I said, that was four years ago now."

"Four years?" Nathan cried. "But why would he make you wait so long?"

"He said I wasn't ready." There was a soft hoot of self-derision. "Obviously I proved that was true. So I put the stone back into place, covered it with earth, and returned home."

Nathan sat back, feeling like he had just run a footrace. Then suddenly comprehension dawned. "You said this happened in September?"

Joseph nodded, stepping close enough for Nathan to see his features clearly. He was smiling, but sober too, filled with solemnity. He laid a hand on Nathan's shoulder. "Yes, Nathan. It was late September."

"But . . ." Nathan stopped, staring at Joseph.

"That's right," Joseph said quietly. "It will be four years next week."

"So how many more years are you going to have to wait?"

His face took on a radiant look as he just looked at Nathan steadily.

"Do you mean . . . ?" He stopped, suddenly feeling a little overwhelmed.

Joseph smiled slowly. "That's right, Nathan. I get the plates next week."

Chapter Eleven

Mary Ann sat in the rocking chair in one corner of the cabin's main room. Her fingers flew back and forth, the knitting needles clicking softly, as she worked on the shawl for Melissa's trousseau. But her mind was not on the knitting nor on Melissa. It was on her son, and she watched him closely as he finished his supper, sitting alone at the table. They had expected him shortly after dark, knowing that the Harris farm adjoined theirs on the south and was no more than a five-minute walk. But he had come in barely half an hour ago, saying only he had finished the corn earlier than expected and gone into the village. She had raised one eyebrow, curious at his sudden reticence, but something in his eyes warned her off.

Benjamin sat beside him, braiding some leather thongs into a bridle for the mules. He had not said much, but Mary Ann saw him once again look up and give Nathan an appraising look. He also sensed whatever it was Nathan was holding in.

You could feel it, like some inner excitement bursting to get out but held in restraint by force of will.

"Did you happen to see Joshua while you were in town?" It was said casually, with studied nonchalance. But it had the same effect as if he had hit the old tin tub with a wooden mallet. Matthew and Becca were playing checkers in front of the fire, using slices of corncob as the pieces and a short length of planking with the squares carefully etched into it as the board. Becca's hand froze in the midst of a move and she glanced at her mother quickly. Matthew turned to his father, eyes wide and suddenly anxious. Melissa, stretched out on her parent's bed reading a book Mr. Harris had sent over, put a finger in her place and looked up slowly. Even the dog, who had his head tucked comfortably against Matthew's leg, woke up. His head lifted, ears cocked, and he looked back and forth between the family members.

Nathan finally looked at his father. "Yes."

The silence stretched out for what seemed to Mary Ann like an interminable length of time. Then her husband grunted some kind of response, keeping his eyes focused on the bridle.

"I asked him to come to dinner Sunday, for Ma's birthday."

There was a quick stab in Mary Ann's chest. From Nathan's expression she already knew what the answer was going to be.

Again Benjamin merely rumbled something in reply. He was too proud to ask for the answer. From the bed, Melissa gave a soft exclamation, clearly exasperated. "Well?" she finally said, when it became obvious no one else was going to pursue it. "Is he coming?"

Nathan looked at his mother, then shook his head. "He's working long hours at the warehouse now. He may have to work Sunday."

She nodded slowly, seeing in his eyes that he was trying to soften it for her.

"How is he?" Melissa asked softly.

Nathan shrugged. "He's fine. Unloading freight is filling him out."

That was the problem with Nathan, his mother thought. His eyes always betrayed him. She tried to hold his gaze, see what was hidden there, but he looked away quickly, and the pain shot through her again. There was more, and it wasn't good, but with the strain between Joshua and his father, Nathan would not elaborate.

Gradually the tension in the room began to dissipate. The dog laid his head back down again. The two younger children went back to their game and Melissa returned to her reading, though Mary Ann noticed she too would stop now and then and look at Nathan quizzically.

For five minutes it was silent in the cabin except for the quiet murmur of Becca and Matthew at checkers. Then Benjamin gave one last tug on the bridle and stood. "I think I'll go up in the loft and see if I can find that leak in the roof."

Mary Ann nodded, understanding the tension in him and what was driving it. Nathan pushed aside his plate, now wiped clean. "You need some help, Pa?"

"No, there's not room enough for two of us up in that corner." He walked to the wall near the door, hung the bridle on a peg, then moved to where a lantern sat on a shelf. He found a match, lit the lantern with it, then moved to the stairs.

Nathan watched him go, not stirring until the sound of his footsteps on the floor above stopped as he climbed up the notched log ladder that led to the attic loft where Matthew slept. But then instantly he was up. He grabbed a chair and brought it over to sit beside his mother.

"Ma, I'm sorry about Joshua," he said. His voice was low, and he glanced quickly towards the stairs.

Melissa had missed none of this. She closed the book and sat up, leaning forward to listen.

Nathan sighed. "I stopped in McBride's store to get some candy—" He stopped suddenly, remembering. Thrusting his hand into his pocket, he drew out the sack. "Matthew. Becca. I brought something for you from the village."

Matthew was up like a shot and to Nathan's side in an instant, with Becca on his heels. "Yippee!" he crowed as Nathan divided out the spoils.

As they went back to their game, sucking on the licorice, Melissa came and sat on the floor in front of her mother. "May I listen?" she asked.

Nathan nodded, and began again. "Anyway, I was in the store getting candy. I happened to be talking with Lydia McBride—"

"Happened to be?" Melissa teased.

Nathan flushed. "Well, Joshua came in at that moment. All Lydia and I were doing was talking, but . . ." He lifted his shoulders in a gesture of frustration. "It probably wasn't the best time to ask him to come for dinner."

"Maybe he'll still come," Melissa volunteered. "Once he cools down. You know how proud he can be."

But Nathan was shaking his head. Again he darted a quick look toward the stairs. "He might have changed his mind . . . before."

"Before what?" Melissa prompted.

He took a deep breath. "But I saw him again, later today." With heavy heart he proceeded to relay the events of that afternoon on the street.

Nathan stopped, his eyes lined with pain. "I'm sorry, Mama. I shouldn't have confronted him like that." He sighed again. "I think he'd been drinking a little. And then whenever he's around Will Murdock . . ." He left it unfinished. There was really no need to say more.

Mary Ann stopped knitting long enough to pat his arm. "It's all right, Nathan. I'm glad you helped Emma. That's shameful they treated her that way."

Nathan slid forward on his chair, bringing his face closer to his mother's. His voice dropped another level so he was doing little more than whispering. "Afterwards, I went down to see Joseph, Ma." He paused, his eyes shining with excitement. "That's why I was so late."

Melissa started a little. It caught her brother's eye and he hesitated, searching her face. Mary Ann understood immediately what he was thinking. She and Nathan had an unspoken agreement that they would not talk of Joseph in front of Benjamin and trigger his ire. That meant they usually found a time when it was just the two of them. But Mary Ann had told Melissa of Joseph's vision and her own feelings. She had also been party to some of their discussions. She had not given any indication, one way or the other, how she felt about it, and that was the cause of Nathan's hesitancy. But her eyes were openly curious and showed no sign of questioning, so after a moment Nathan seemed satisfied and turned back to his mother. "He told me about the gold plates, Ma."

In moments, the knitting was forgotten as Nathan began to recount what Joseph had shared with him. They sat together, the three of them, heads huddled together, speaking in hushed voices. Melissa once asked him to repeat something he said, but other than that both sat quietly, listening intently. At one point, Mary Ann reached up and brushed at the corner of her eyes, causing Nathan to peer at her more closely. She motioned him to continue, not wanting him to stop.

Nathan sat back finally, eyes shining with excitement. "Next week, Mother. He gets them next week."

A noise behind them caused them all to jump, their heads snapping around. Benjamin was standing on the bottom step, the extinguished lantern in his hand. His face was an inscrutable mask.

How long had he been there? Mary Ann realized with a start that Becca and Matthew were both on the bed now, Becca looking at the pictures in Melissa's book, and Matthew asleep. She had been so engrossed in Nathan's narrative, she hadn't noticed their movement. Or her husband's presence on the stairs.

"Did you find it?" she asked, too quickly, picking up the needles again.

He shook his head, then moved slowly across the room and replaced the lantern on the shelf. Melissa's eyes followed him anxiously. Nathan was staring at his hands.

"You'll have to go up on the roof in the daytime," Mary Ann started, fighting to keep the guilt out of her voice. They had not been deliberately trying to hide anything from him, but it looked like an open conspiracy. "It's not a bad leak yet, but winter could make it—"

She stopped. He had turned now, his eyes narrowed and lips tight. He stood there, looking at Nathan. The silence was thunderous. Finally Nathan looked up and met his gaze.

"That's the biggest cartload of nonsense I've ever heard."

Mary Ann's head came up sharply. "There is no need to be insulting, Ben," she said quietly.

He swung back to his wife. "Since when is speaking the truth insulting? It is nonsense. Ridiculous nonsense, and I can't believe a son of mine sat there and listened to talk of angels and gold books without so much as even raising an eyebrow."

Nathan started to clear his throat, but his father rode over it. "Angels popping in and out of the bedroom like a gopher in a potato patch, God appearing in the woods, a gold Bible buried in a hill." He gave a soft hoot of disgust. "What's that lyin' fool gonna come up with next?"

"Whatever Joseph is," Nathan said evenly, "he is not a fool. Nor is he a liar."

"Right," he sneered. "First he says an angel shows him where there's this golden book. Then he tells him there's also a pair of magic spectacles so he can read it." He threw up his hands. "Just what *does* it take to convince you a man is a fool?"

"He didn't say they were magic spectacles, Pa, he only—"

But his father was having none of it. He whirled on his wife again. "And you and Melissa sitting there, not saying a word. Does that mean you believe this tripe too?"

Melissa's eyes dropped before the power of the challenging gaze, but Mary Ann did not flinch. She put down her knitting slowly. "Ben," she started softly, "I know how you feel about this kind of thing, but what if—" Her voice suddenly caught. "What if they're true? Think about that. The heavens opened again. God speaking to his children, like he did in Bible times. Oh, Ben, what if it *is* true?"

"It's not true!" he snapped. "This boy is crazy, a ravin' lunatic. Straight from the asylum."

"That's what some people said about Jesus, too," she said quietly.

He snorted his derision, then turned to his daughter. "What about you, Melissa?"

She flinched. "I . . . I don't know, Pa. It all seems so strange in a way, but . . ."

"But what?" he demanded.

"But I agree with Nathan on this much. We know Joseph. He worked for us all that time. I don't think he's a liar."

"He don't have to be lying!" Benjamin shouted. "You ever heard of being crazy? You ever heard of being deceived?" He stopped, chest heaving, his head shaking, like a bull about to charge. "This is devil's work, Mary Ann, and I won't have it in this house."

"But Pa—," Nathan started. At the look in his father's eyes, Nathan stopped.

"I said it's crazy talk, and God help the fool who listens to it."

Mary Ann shot to her feet, spilling the knitting and the needles onto the floor. It caught all of them by surprise, and even Benjamin fell back a step. She stepped forward, her face close to his, her eyes boring into him.

"Well, it is," he muttered lamely, cowed by the look in her eyes. "It's nothing but crazy talk."

"You have your feelings," Mary Ann said slowly, "and you're welcome to them, but I'll not have you taking the name of the Lord in vain in front of the children."

He glanced behind her. Matthew and Rebecca were both wide awake now, sitting on the bed, staring wide-eyed at their parents.

"Then you'd best get them to bed so we can continue this discussion, because we're not through with this yet."

Melissa jumped into action without being told. In a moment she had herded the children out of the door for a quick trip to the outhouse. The three of them stood quietly, not looking at each other. A minute or two later Melissa brought them back in and shooed them up the stairs. For once there was no protest from Matthew.

As Melissa came back down, Benjamin turned on his wife. "This has gone far enough, Mary Ann. I mean it. I'll not have my family mixing with crazies or sharing their ideas. People are already talking."

Something burst in Mary Ann. For years she had stood by this good man's side. They had shared the same bed, watched children die, fought the land, and stood miles apart on their feelings of religion. She loved him deeply. He was a good man, a good father and good provider. But she also knew the depths of his stubbornness, knew how foreign spiritual matters seemed to him. And she had accepted it all. For years she had longed for some sign in him of the inner fire she felt when she read the Bible or prayed. But it was never there. Oh, he joined with them in Bible reading. He made no objections when she taught the children to pray, but she could always tell it was a little beneath him. It was all right for the children, maybe even good for them. But he didn't need it. He had his own strength to rely on, his own values driving him.

She turned away, not wanting him to see the tears.

He assumed it meant surrender. Nodding in satisfaction, he turned to his son. "Nathan, there'll be no more Joseph Smith. No more going to his place, no more talking with him or about him. You understand?"

Mary Ann whirled. "And if he does?"

Startled, Benjamin stared at her, then his brows lowered. "He'd better not."

"What will you do, Benjamin? Drive him out of the house

too? Do we lose another son because you refuse to accept any-thing but what *you* feel?"

Behind her, Mary Ann was barely conscious of Melissa's gasp and Nathan's stunned look, but she was past the point at which wisdom was going to dictate her words.

She had shocked Benjamin too, but not into silence. "That's enough, woman," he warned, his voice low and filled with menace.

"Is it, Benjamin?" she cried. "Is it? And just how old will Nathan have to be before you let him choose who he talks to and what he believes? You tell him now, so he can make his plans."

His mouth opened, then clamped shut again. She saw the muscles along his jaw tighten and the veins on his neck swelling out. Not many times had Benjamin Steed been talked to in those terms, and never from his wife. He looked at Nathan, then at Melissa. Neither would meet his eye. He glanced once more at Mary Ann, then whirled and plunged out of the door, slamming it hard behind him.

Behind her, Nathan let out his breath slowly. "I should have waited to tell you," he said. "I should have known how Pa would feel."

"I know," she said wearily. "I know."

It was nearly midnight before he came back in. He shut the door quietly and dropped the latch. He had left without getting his coat, and the September air was close to freezing. Even in the barn it would be very cold. In bed, Mary Ann felt her eyes burning. There was so much pride in the man.

He went to the pail of water at the sink, got a dipper full, and drank it in two noisy gulps. Only then did he part the cur-tain that separated their bed from the rest of the room. She lay still, not pretending to sleep, but not wanting him to feel she was waiting for him either.

He undressed slowly, folding his pants and shirt neatly to

put under the covers at the foot of the bed. Carefully he climbed in beside her, shifted his weight a little as he pulled the covers up, then lay still. For several minutes they lay that way, silent but aware of the other, and both aware of the other's awareness.

Finally, Mary Ann turned over. "Ben?"

He stirred but didn't answer.

"I'm sorry, Ben. I didn't mean to get angry."

The silence stretched on and finally, sure he wasn't going to respond, she turned back onto her side, filled with a mixture of sadness and resentment.

After another minute or two he spoke. "Mary Ann?"

"Yes."

"I'll not be speaking of Joseph Smith again."

She waited, not sure exactly what that meant.

He took a quick breath. "If you and Nathan insist on it, I'd prefer you do it out of my presence."

Tears sprang to her eyes. It wasn't much, but she knew what even that much had cost him. This was a proud man, but a decent one. One who loved his family, maybe not perfectly, but loved them strongly nevertheless.

"I understand, Ben. We'll honor your wish."

She felt him nod, then he turned over, his back to her.

"Thank you, Ben."

There was no answer, but she felt him relax a little. In a few minutes his breathing deepened and he was asleep. But for a long time after that, Mary Ann lay there, staring into the darkness. She was glad for the truce, but felt an aching sense of loss that one was even necessary.

"Do you think this is it?" Lydia asked, anxiously peering up the dirt road to where she could see the small cabin with smoke curling upwards from its chimney.

"It's got to be," her cousin replied. "Mr. Harris said it was the next road up from him, just across the creek."

Lydia took in a quick breath, then let it out slowly, her courage slipping away rapidly.

Robert smiled, his eyes teasing. "Sure you don't want to just ride on up with me and get that little filly I've got to pick up?"

She was tempted for a moment and he laughed. "If you don't go in, no one will ever be the wiser." He was the youngest of her Aunt Bea and Uncle Karl's children and only two years older than she, and in many ways was the older brother she had never had. "On the other hand," he chuckled, "if you do go in and get this over with, maybe I'd get some conversation out of you on the way home."

"Oh, Robert," she burst out. "It looks so forward of me, coming to his home and all." It had been four days since the incident with Emma Smith, but she had not been able to get it out of her mind. And each time she thought of it, she could feel Nathan's gaze burning into her flesh as it did when he saw her in the crowd. The prospects of facing Nathan and trying to apologize had so occupied her thoughts on the way up from the village, she had hardly spoken.

"Would you like me to come up to the house with you?"

"Oh, would you, Robert?"

He shook his head, trying hard to look put out, but totally failing. "You know what Uncle Josiah is going to do to me if he finds out I brought you out here?"

"He won't," she answered, feeling a quick jolt of concern about her father knowing of this, "not unless you tell him."

"All right, let's go." He clucked at the horses, pulling on the reins so the buckboard swung into the dirt lane that led to the Steed cabin.

Matthew, who was feeding the chickens in the barnyard, spotted them first. He set the leather bucket of wheat down and came to the fence, squinting to see better. Then he gave a whoop. "Miss Lydia!"

"Oh, I should have brought some candy," she murmured.

Becca was around the side of the house pulling up a bucket

of water from the well. Matthew's call brought her around on the run. And she too gave a cry of joy. The two of them started toward the wagon, running pell-mell.

"Well," Robert observed sardonically, "it looks like at least two of the family are glad to see you."

As they swung the buckboard around in the yard, the children running alongside, Melissa came out on the porch. Lydia had talked with her once or twice and was pleased to note the instant recognition and the smile of genuine surprise. "Hello, Melissa."

"Why, Miss Lydia, what a surprise!"

For some reason, Lydia had always thought of Melissa as Joshua's little sister, but as she stood before her now, she realized she was fully a woman. With a start Lydia remembered that Melissa was only two years younger than Lydia's own eighteen years. She could see both Joshua and Nathan in her features, and her mother as well.

She turned to look down at the two faces peering up at her. "And how are my two favorite customers?"

"Fine, thank you," Becca said demurely.

"Great!" shouted Matthew. "How come you came to our house?"

"Matthew!" Mrs. Steed had come to the door and caught the last interchange. "You be polite now." She turned to Lydia. "Good afternoon, Miss McBride."

"Afternoon, Mrs. Steed." She had evidently been baking bread, for there was flour on her apron and she was rubbing pieces of dough off her hands. Then Lydia suddenly remembered she was not alone. "Mrs. Steed, this is my cousin, Robert Johnson. Robert, these are the Steeds—Matthew, Rebecca, Melissa, and Mrs. Steed, Joshua and Nathan's mother."

They exchanged greetings and pleasantries for a moment, then as it fell silent, Lydia knew the time had arrived. Matthew had been the only one open enough to ask her why she was here, but the curiosity was evident in all of their eyes. "Is Nathan here, Mrs. Steed? I needed to talk with him for a moment."

Lydia felt the quick surprise in his mother's eyes. This was so forward of her to come. Proper young ladies just didn't come chasing after men. She felt like she owed his mother some explanation. "I—" She took a breath. "The other day in town, I did something that hurt Nathan. I'm ashamed of it. I'd like to make my apologies."

Understanding came then and Mrs. Steed smiled. "Nathan's down by the creek, laying a rock wall to keep the mules out of the winter wheat."

"I'll take you," Matthew blurted, already starting around the wagon.

Becca cut him off. "No, you're feeding the chickens. I'll take her."

Melissa smiled sweetly at her sister. "And you're getting water for the baths tonight. Pa will be back from huntin' in an hour or two, and the water had better be nice and hot. I'll take Lydia."

Both of the children started to protest, but Mrs. Steed overrode them. Lydia blushed slightly, knowing these two Steed women were seeing to it that she and Nathan would have an opportunity to talk undisturbed.

"Well, it should take me about an hour to get that horse," Robert spoke up.

Lydia nodded. "I'll be waiting out by the road."

"No. I don't know exactly how long I'll be. Just wait here."

"All right." Lydia jumped down and waved as he drove out of the yard.

"Children," Mrs. Steed said firmly, "on with your chores." Then she smiled at Lydia. "I've got the first loaves baking now and we just churned some fresh butter. Why don't you bring Nathan back up when you're done and we'll sit a spell."

"I'd like that," Lydia replied, a little surprised that she really meant it. She had been dreading this moment for four days and now unexpectedly found herself feeling quite at home with this warm, open family.

As Melissa led out and Lydia fell into step by her side, they didn't speak, but it was a comfortable silence. The Indian summer that had prevailed earlier in the week had gone now as a gray overcast ran from horizon to horizon. But while it was cool, it was still pleasant, and the top leaves on the birch and maple trees along the creek were just starting to turn yellow and orange. Another week or two and the whole countryside would be a spectacular festival of color.

As they came around a patch of brush and small trees, Melissa stopped and pointed. Nathan was about seventy-five yards ahead of them, his back to them as he worked, moving stones from the creek and stacking them into a wall.

They watched him for a moment, then Melissa smiled mischievously. "I'd like to watch his face when he turns and sees you." She turned to go. "See you back at the house."

Lydia touched her arm. "Thank you, Melissa." *Thank you for fending off the children. Thank you for not taking me all the way to him, even though you'd love to see his face.*

Melissa nodded, half turned to go, paused for a moment, then shook her head quickly, as though chiding herself. She started away.

"What?" Lydia said quickly.

Melissa stopped, her back still to Lydia. Again there was the quick shake of her head.

"What, Melissa? What were you going to say?"

She turned, her dark eyes searching Lydia's face, but still she hesitated.

"Come on," Lydia urged. "Say it."

Her shoulders lifted, then fell as she gave in. "You've come because of what happened in the village the other day with Joseph's wife, haven't you?"

Startled, Lydia gave a quick nod. "Did Nathan tell you about it?"

"Yes."

"What did he say? I mean . . ."

"He was very angry with the people."

"I know," Lydia said in a low voice.

"The fact you were there bothered him most of all."

Her head came up quickly in defense. "But I didn't say anything. I just saw the crowd gathering and came to see what was happening."

"That's what I told him too."

Lydia blinked. "You did?"

"Yes."

"How did you know?"

Melissa smiled, her eyes softening. "I guessed."

Lydia laughed, really pleased. "And what did Nathan say to that?"

Now Melissa laughed, a low, husky sound of delight. "I think he wanted to believe me." Then instantly she sobered. "I'm glad you've come to talk to him about it."

She took a quick breath. "I hope he'll listen."

Again an impish smile stole across Melissa's face. "If he doesn't I'll talk to him tonight. With the razor strap." On sudden impulse she reached out and touched Lydia's arm. "It will be fine. Go do it."

For a moment Lydia just looked at her, feeling a great rush of warmth for this girl. Then spontaneously she gave her a quick hug. "Do you know what, Melissa? I think you and I could become very good friends."

"I think so too." Melissa smiled slowly, then instantly the mischievousness returned. "I hope we will, Lydia." She laughed as Lydia blushed, then turned and hurried back toward the house.

"Well?" Robert said as they turned out of the Steed lane and back onto the main road to Palmyra Village, the yearling mare trotting steadily behind the buckboard.

"Well, what?" Lydia answered, playing it coy.

"You know what. Did you get to talk to him?"

She leaned back, tipping her face to the sky and closing her eyes. "Yes. We had a nice talk. Thank you for bringing me, Robert."

He grunted, pleased for her. They rode on for several minutes in silence, then he turned to her. "And what about the brother?"

Lydia sat up quickly. "Joshua? What about him?"

He spoke with mock seriousness to take some of the sting out of his words. "Are you going to make a choice or are you going to create family warfare by driving both of them completely out of their minds?"

She laughed. "Oh, Robert," she said, shaking her head.

"Well, you told me you think part of Nathan's holding back is because Joshua thinks you're his girl."

"Well, I'm not," she snapped.

"Does he know that?" Robert asked quietly.

She hesitated. " 'He' meaning Joshua or Nathan?"

He shook his head. "Either one."

The corners of her mouth pulled down. "I don't think so."

"Then maybe it's time you made up your mind."

She looked at him for a long moment, then suddenly slid over to sit right next to him. She slipped her arm through his and laid her head on his shoulder dreamily. "I already have, Robert."

He gave her a sharp look, then slowly smiled. "Mother will be pleased. She's favored Nathan since he first came out to the farm that night."

Lydia laughed. "Not just favored, Robert. She's been doing her best to make sure I don't make any mistakes with him. Who do you think put me up to this trip today, anyway?"

Now it was Robert's turn to laugh. "That's my mother."

Again they both fell silent, lost in their own thoughts. Then finally Robert turned to her. "And when do you tell Joshua all this?"

Lydia did not move for several moments, just looked out across the sweeping farmland. Then with a deep sigh she shook her head. "He wants to see me night after tomorrow when Mama and Papa are in Canandaigua. I've decided to tell him then."

Chapter Twelve

Joshua looked up at the lowering sky, squinting against the dust that filled the air. The first serious storm of the fall was on its way into western New York, and while the rain would probably not come before midnight, the wind was gusting heavily now, at times almost reaching gale force. The village of Palmyra was already littered with broken tree branches and with rubbish plastered up against picket fences and anything else that blocked the wind's path.

"Bet you a tankard o' rum she ain't comin'."

Joshua let the wind push the livery-stable door shut again and turned to face Will Murdock. "I told you, her pa cancelled his trip to Canandaigua because of the storm. It ain't going to be easy for her to get away."

There were five others besides Joshua in the barn. The two Murdock boys and their cousin Mark Cooper; another cousin, Mark's sallow-faced, flat-chested fifteen-year-old sister named

Hope; and Sarah Black, a neighbor girl Will Murdock had brought along. Sarah was attractive enough, though shabbily dressed, and obviously taken with Will. Hope, on the other hand, couldn't have been more poorly named. Her hair was greasy and hung down straight as a horse's tail. Her clothes were patched and soiled. She rarely smiled, and her eyes, large and dark and sunk deep into her face, reminded Joshua of the expression of a yearling calf on its way to the slaughterhouse.

"That fortune-teller ain't gonna stay all night," David grumbled.

Sarah nodded quickly. "It may be our only chance to find where Joe Smith's got them plates hid."

Will had brought a jug of whiskey and had been sampling it liberally since they had arrived. He brought it up and took another deep draught. He offered it to Joshua, who shook his head. If Lydia knew he had been drinking . . . "Who is this man, anyway?"

"Don't know him personally," Will said, wiping at his mouth with the back of his sleeve. "But Willard Chase does. Chase lives on Canandaigua Road, directly behind the Smith farm. He's the one who sent down to Ithaca for this man. He's a conjurer." Will pronounced the word with a little shiver of awe. "He's gonna divine where the gold Bible is hidden."

"Yeah," Mark Cooper broke in. "He found a lost child once just by holding up the boy's shirt to his eyes."

Joshua hooted. "He sounds crazier than Joseph."

Will swore and slammed the jug down on a box of harnessing gear. "You got any better ideas how we find out where Joe's hidin' the gold?"

"We don't even know for sure he's got any gold."

Will grinned wickedly. "We know, don't we boys?"

By his look, Joshua assumed "boys" included Sarah and Hope as well. They all nodded, each trying to look like old Mother Wisdom herself.

"How? What makes you so sure?"

"Tell him, Mark."

Mark leaned forward, his voice dropping to a conspiratorial whisper. "The Smiths got company night before last."

"Company? Who?"

"Josiah Stowell and Joseph Knight."

Joshua looked blank.

"Josiah Stowell is a big rich farmer from South Bainbridge, down Pennsylvany way. Knight is his friend. Stowell is the one who hired Joseph to dig treasure for him down in Harmony. That's how he met Emma."

"So?"

"So!" David burst out. "These two men have helped Joe Smith from the beginning."

Joshua was still not impressed. "What does that prove?"

Will rolled his eyes. "You ever heard a Preacher Clark, one of the ministers in town?"

Joshua nodded.

"Well, Preacher Clark said he talked with Martin Harris a while back. Harris said Joe told him the exact day when he was gonna get them plates."

He had finally got Joshua's attention. "Martin Harris said that?" Joshua didn't know anything about any men named Stowell or Knight, but Martin Harris was something else. He and Joseph were as thick as two thieves. "And what day did he say it would be?" Joshua asked, feeling a sudden quickening of excitement.

Will smiled triumphantly, showing yellow teeth. "September twenty-second!"

Joshua snapped up. "But that's two days ago."

"Exactly," Will crowed. "Joe's got them plates right now. You think it's coincidence this Knight and Stowell have come more than a hundred miles to be with Joe on September twenty-second?"

Joshua just shook his head. It made sense, and yet . . . If Joseph really did have gold plates, Joshua was as ready to go after them as the next man. But if this was going to be just another long night of drinking whiskey and talking brave, he would pass. And Lydia only complicated matters further. When she found out they were going with the Murdocks, that would end it right there. He shook his head. But if Joseph really did have the plates . . .

"There's somethin' else."

Joshua swung around in surprise. It was Hope who had spoken, catching them all off guard. Even her brother, Mark, was staring at her.

"What?" Will demanded.

She took a quick breath, then started to speak, darting looks at them, then dropping her eyes again quickly. "I was with Pa in town today. A man told Pa Joe Smith was over in Macedon Township today digging a well for a widow woman there. He's earning money to pay old Mr. Barnham, the cabinetmaker, for a special wooden chest he's ordered." For the first time she looked squarely into Joshua's eyes. "A chest he said had to be real strong. With a lock on it."

Will and Joshua and Mark were staring in amazement at the little mouse. She fairly beamed. She had scooped them all.

Will turned cold sober and stepped up to thrust his face next to Joshua's. "You know what that means?" he demanded. "It means that tonight ol' Joe is gonna go after them plates and put 'em in that box." He turned grave. "If we don't get 'em tonight, he'll hide 'em good and we'll never find them."

Joshua made up his mind. "Where is this conjurer?"

"He's staying at Chase's house. They've got someone watching the Smith house. As soon as he makes a move, we'll be there to catch him."

Sarah sneered at Joshua. "Yeah, assumin' we're not still standing here jawin'."

"All right," Joshua said. "You go on ahead. As soon as Lydia comes, we'll meet you at Chase's."

Will nodded, then his mouth twisted. "Don't be too long.

Once we find out where the gold is, we ain't waitin' for nobody."

Now that full dark had fallen, the wind had picked up again. It hammered at the two figures riding south along Canandaigua Road. The temperature had dropped sharply, and Lydia pulled her long coat around her, trying to hold on to her hat with one hand and manage the reins with the other as the horses trotted steadily along.

They were nearing a large house and Joshua slowed his horse to a walk. She reined in beside him. "Is this the Willard Chase place?" He had to half shout it at her with the wind whipping his words away.

Lydia yanked on the reins, pulling the horse up to a halt. "Willard Chase?" she said in alarm.

Joshua pulled his horse around to face her. "Yes. Is this his place?"

Lydia felt her heart drop. "You didn't tell me we were going to his house."

Joshua seemed baffled. "I guess I didn't. What does it matter?"

"Willard Chase is a class leader in the Methodist church. My father is an elder in the Presbyterian church. They've worked together on several town committees."

"Oh," Joshua said, a little irritated, "then your pa shouldn't mind you bein' with him tonight."

"My father thinks I'm at Aunt Bea's house," she burst out, feeling her temper rising. She had come to the livery stable with the full intention of telling Joshua it was over between them, but he had swept her up with the talk of the gold plates and this being the very night they could finally get them from Smith. Palmyra had been buzzing about the gold Bible for four years now. To be with the group that would be the first to see it . . .

She had finally pushed down the voice which kept warning her to leave immediately, and agreed to ride south and join the "others" who were going to get the plates. Now she realized Joshua had been deliberately vague about who the "others" were. But Willard Chase? News of her presence would be back to her father before daybreak.

"No, Joshua, I can't let him see me. I'd better go back."

He grabbed at her reins. "Come on, Lydia, this is it. This is the night." When she continued shaking her head, his voice rose higher. "Look, I'll go in then. I won't tell him you're out here. Once we know where Joseph is, then you can go with us to get the plates." He didn't wait for her to answer, just pointed to a large elm tree. "Wait there. I'll be back in a minute."

As he spurred his horse and cantered away, Lydia nearly screamed at him to stop. Events were quickly getting out of hand and she felt a looming sense of dread. By the time she had reached the livery stable, she was already an emotional wreck. Just getting out of the house had been an incredible drain. Her father had cancelled his trip to Canandaigua because of the weather, and with the storm coming he had put his foot down. There was no need now for her to go to her Aunt's for the night. It had taken both tears and tantrum to finally win out and get out of the house.

Then all the way to the stable she had fretted about how she was going to confront Joshua with her news. She knew now that whatever she had once felt for Joshua—mostly a combination of physical attraction for his dark handsomeness and an infantile desire to flaunt her independence—was now gone, but he had not sensed it yet. He still assumed everything was wonderful between them. And that made the task twice as difficult. If she had been completely honest with herself, she would have seen that part of her willingness to ride south with Joshua was her desire to delay the confrontation for a while longer. But to her dismay, she now realized that waiting had only complicated things tremendously.

She tied her horse to a bush and moved around the trunk of the elm tree to its lee side, trying at least to blunt the force of the wind. Pulling her coat around her, she hugged herself, feeling more forlorn than she could ever remember feeling in her life.

Three times in the last day and a half she had started letters to Joshua. Three times she had torn them up. She couldn't choose evasion. She had to face him. Would he be hurt or would he be angry? Would he blame her or would he turn on Nathan? Glumly she answered her own question. A week ago in the store Joshua had caught them—she frowned at her choice of words. There was nothing to feel guilty about. They had just been talking. But she had seen the jealousy twist Joshua's features and watched the anger rise in a great surge within him.

And what would she say if he did ask if Nathan was the cause of her change of feelings. She had known it was over with Joshua before Nathan had started to dominate her thoughts, but . . . She shook her head, feeling guilty. As if there weren't enough hurt in the Steed family already.

Turning toward the house she peered at the warm glow of lamplight coming from the windows. She could see the shadows of people, moving against the blinds. They moved slowly and deliberately. No one seemed in any hurry to leave. She frowned, willing Joshua to hurry. The chill was seeping beneath her coat, through her gloves, into her riding boots. But it was more than the cold. There would be no telling Joshua anything until the search for the gold Bible was done with. Suddenly she didn't really care about Joe Smith anymore. She just wanted this thing with Joshua done with and behind her.

A half hour dragged by, seeming like twice that. The rain was still some time off now, but the temperature continued to drop, and Lydia moved back and forth, stamping her feet and blowing on her hands. Twice she had shrunk back as other men rode up and entered the house. But there was still no sign of Joshua. Her irritation had long since turned into a burning anger. The fact she was out here alone in the dark and cold meant nothing to him. They were probably drinking hot coffee laced with rum or other liquor and patting each other on the back and telling themselves how brave they were.

Twice she nearly got on her horse and simply rode away. She found the night foreboding and the promise of what was yet to come less and less attractive. Her aunt's house was just half a mile up the road, and the thoughts of it beckoned to her like the glow of a warm fire on a winter's night. But leaving now meant she would have to work out another time to see Joshua and confront him. Going through this emotional trauma again was more than she could bear. So she waited, getting more exasperated with each passing minute.

Suddenly she froze, peering toward the house. Joshua was coming, but he was not alone. There were four or five others with him. She stepped back quickly, letting the deep shadows of the overhanging tree embrace her.

"Lydia!" It was an urgent whisper.

She stepped out, her heart dropping. With the heavy overcast it was very dark away from the house, but she didn't need much light to recognize the figure of Will Murdock. Her anger flared. No wonder Joshua had avoided mentioning who was in on this night's activity! But almost instantly the anger gave way to fear as she recognized the others with Will. Mark, David, Mark's drab little sister, and another girl Lydia didn't know. There was not a one of them who was renowned for discretion. Had they known Joshua was bringing her? Yes, almost certainly. Had they told Willard Chase she was out here waiting for them? A new wave of coldness swept over her as a picture of her father flashed through her mind.

She spun around to face Joshua, as angry as she could ever remember being at anyone. In the darkness he took no note of it. "We were right, Lydia. Joseph's got the plates."

Will, likewise oblivious to her mood, jumped in excitedly. "The Smiths somehow got word of the conjurer being here. This afternoon Emma rushed over to Macedon to fetch Joe home. He got home 'bout an hour ago. He's getting ready to go out and find the plates."

Lydia turned, piqued in spite of her anger. "Where are they?"

David Murdock broke in gleefully. "The conjurer says Joseph has them hidden in the forest someplace."

"Oh, good," she cried, "in the forest someplace."

Mark's sister seemed stung by her sarcasm. "Joe's gonna get them tonight and bring them home. We're gonna follow him."

Lydia turned in disgust, but spun back around as her mind suddenly registered what she had just seen. Will Murdock had a rifle in his hand. She turned. Mark had a two-foot length of oak limb and was tapping it menacingly against his leg. Jonathan had a pistol stuck in his belt, and one hand caressed the butt lovingly. She whirled to face Joshua. "What is this?" She jerked her hand, pointing at Will's rifle. "What are you going to do?"

Joshua reached out and took her hand. She jerked it away. "You have guns?"

Will stuck his face next to hers, his eyes wide and yellow, like those of a lynx when caught in the lantern light. "By morning we'll have the gold and ol' Joe Smith will have a few lumps on his head." He threw back his head and howled. Lydia averted her face, the whiskey on his breath nearly making her gag.

Joshua stepped between them. "No one's gonna get hurt, Lydia. We're just makin' sure Joe doesn't get away."

She stared at him, not believing he couldn't see the ridiculous contradiction in his words. With sudden determination she spun on her heel and walked quickly to where she had tied her horse.

Joshua was beside her in a moment and grabbed her arm. "Lydia, what are you doing?"

She spun around, her eyes blazing. "This is insane, Joshua," she hissed. "Somebody *is* going to get hurt and I want no part of it."

"Come on, Lydia," he urged, keeping his voice low, so the others wouldn't hear. "Will just talks big."

"Why didn't you tell me the Murdocks were with you?"

He looked down, not meeting her eyes. "There are others too."

"You knew I wouldn't come if you told me, didn't you?"

From behind them, Will called in a contemptuous voice. "What's the matter, Joshua? Your woman losing her nerve?"

Joshua half whirled, his mouth tight. "That's enough, Will." He turned back to her, his eyes pleading. "Lydia, just for an hour. Then if nothing happens, I'll take you to your aunt's house."

She stuck a foot in the stirrup and swung up into the saddle. "I'm going now, Joshua."

Behind them the girl named Sarah made some comment, and they all laughed.

"Are you coming?" Lydia asked quietly.

"Maybe you'd better go, Joshua," Will jeered. "This is gonna be man's work tonight."

Joshua suddenly shook his head. "Lydia, all I'm asking for is one hour."

She stared down at him. Finally, she shook her head. "No, Joshua, you're asking for a lot more than that." She reined the horse around sharply. "Good-bye." She dug her heels into the horse's flanks and it leaped away.

"Watch out for the hobgoblins, Lydia, they'll—" But the wind whipped the rest of Will's taunting call away across the open fields. Lydia did not turn back but spurred the horse harder, squinting her eyes against the wind and the hot tears which sprang to her eyes.

The Steed family were having a quiet evening at home. Nathan was lying on his parents' bed, laboriously plowing through *The Autobiography of Benjamin Franklin*, which he had gotten from Palmyra's tiny library. His father was patching a saddle strap, trimming the new piece of leather with a knife and then twisting the blade point round and round to make the holes for the buckle. His mother sat at the table quietly reading the Bible to Matthew and Becca. Melissa was at the mirror, brushing her hair until it crackled with static electricity.

Nathan stopped and looked up, cocking his head to listen. For a moment he thought he had heard something. Finally he shrugged. The wind moaned around the cabin like a wounded animal, rattling the door and the oiled paper at the main window. He started to drop his head again when he saw the dog. His head was up, ears cocked forward, eyes staring at the door. A low growl came from his throat.

"Pa," Nathan said.

As his father looked up, Nathan gestured with his head. The dog came to its feet, growling more openly now, then trotted to the door and gave a low bark. Then Nathan heard it too. The clatter of horse's hooves on the hard-packed dirt outside.

"Someone's here," Melissa said unnecessarily.

Benjamin stood and went to the door as all the family paused in what they were doing, curious as to who would be out on a night such as this.

"Mr. Steed?"

Nathan jerked up sharply. He couldn't see past his father into the night, but there was no mistaking that voice.

"My name is Lydia McBride. Could I please speak with you and Nathan on an urgent matter?"

Joshua had had little time to worry about Lydia's moodiness and her sudden flight. She had barely gone when Willard Chase came bolting out of the house. Joseph was getting ready to move. In an instant, the men had been organized into teams to cover all of the possible routes he might take. Chase had tried to send Joshua and the Murdocks to the north on Stafford Road in case he went that way. But Will brushed the suggestion aside angrily. The long hill owned by Pliney Sexton, which supposedly was the site where the plates were buried, was south on Canandaigua Road another two miles or so down from the Chase farm. There was no way Will Murdock was going to be cheated out of his chance to be at the center of the action. The others had agreed quickly, partly because time was too critical for debate, partly because they sensed that Will and his party were willing to take whatever action was necessary to get the plates from Smith.

They had moved quickly to the place where Armington Road came east from Stafford Road, the road the Smiths lived on, and joined Canandaigua Road. If Joseph was headed for the hill, this would be the route he would have to take. It was interesting, for all of Will's bellowing and blowing, that it was Joshua who quickly took over the leadership of the group. He was the only sober one of the four of them—not counting the girls, who now huddled together quietly, trying to keep each other warm—and even Will seemed content to let him lead out.

For a half hour they squatted in the heavy undergrowth about fifteen or twenty yards off the road, getting colder and more frustrated with each minute. It was late enough in the month that the last of the waning moon was now gone, and the night would have been dark enough without the storm clouds deepening it even further. Joshua was still fuming over Lydia's cavalier performance and Will's vulgar comments about her, and now his nerves had frayed to a thread as he peered into the darkness trying to pick out anyone coming down the road.

"I say he ain't comin' this way," David pouted. "We're gonna miss him."

Joshua whirled. "Will you shut up!" he hissed. "If he does come, he'll hear you whining a mile away."

"Don't tell me to shut up, big man," David shot back, his voice rising. "Ain't nobody made you—"

But Joshua had swung around and grabbed him by the shirt front and yanked him up to face him. "You want that club stuffed down your throat?" He shoved him back and the younger Murdock crashed down to the ground. Will was up in an instant, but in the face of Joshua's height and fury, he finally turned to his brother. "Joshua's right, David. We've got to be quiet."

"They didn't say Joseph had left," Joshua whispered, fighting down the surge of emotion. "They said he was getting ready to leave. He could be another half hour. And we're gonna sit right here and be quiet until we're absolutely sure he ain't coming this way."

He glared down at David, daring him to disagree, but the boy was already cowed. Sarah pulled away from Hope and moved over to sit beside him, pushing her shoulder against his. Joshua turned back to his watch, squinting his eyes against the wind. He felt the first raindrop spatter against his face but ignored it. *Come on, Joseph! Don't you be going any other way.*

Five minutes later their wait paid off. At first, Joshua thought it was one of the trees beyond the road, writhing and twisting as the wind gusted, but then the shape materialized out of the darkness, tall and striding along purposefully. He signalled urgently with his hand, and they all crouched down even more tightly to the ground.

It was Joseph, all right. As he came to the junction, he stopped and looked around carefully, taking the most time to search the road in the direction he had just come, to see if he was being followed. Joshua held his breath, his eyes peeping through the branches which hid them. Finally, Joseph seemed satisfied, and strode off again, turning south on Canandaigua Road.

"All right," Joshua whispered, urging them in close to him. "That's him and he's headed for the hill. Will, you and me are gonna follow him. Mark, you and David head down Armington Road and hide yourself where it joins Stafford."

Mark rose up, a protest forming on his lips, but Will cuffed him back. "Joe's got to come back this way. If we miss him, you've got to get him."

Joshua turned to the girls. "You two hurry on back to the Chase house. Tell the others we've got him. Bring three men and stay with them here. Have the rest go south on Stafford Road in case he cuts across the fields. As dark as it is, we can't take a chance on missing him."

He didn't wait to see if they obeyed. Joseph was moving fast, and in a moment they would lose him completely. Joshua was appalled at the noise they made as they hurried along, but he knew it was just his nerves sharpening his perceptions. The wind was blowing straight out of the south and taking the sound away from Joseph. In the dim light, they could see him stop every now and then and search the night around him. But each time, they dropped down flat, and in a moment Joseph would continue, with no signs of having seen them. They followed him that way for almost ten minutes.

"Where'd he go? Where'd he go?" Will Murdock hissed the words into Joshua's ear and clutched at his arm.

Joshua shook his head in sharp warning, peering into the night, trying to distinguish the blackness of Joseph's shape from the surrounding darkness. After a moment he nodded, holding a finger up to his lips. He saw a shadow momentarily cross the path of a farmhouse's lighted window. He was still there ahead of them, striding along rapidly. There was no question; he was heading for the hill. Joshua felt his pulse quicken at the thoughts of the gold waiting there.

But suddenly, about a half mile north of the hill, Joseph stopped. Signalling frantically to Will, Joshua dropped to a crouch. It was hard to distinguish what Joseph was doing, but Joshua sensed that this time he was not checking his back trail. He seemed to be peering off to one side, as if looking for some kind of landmark. Then to Joshua's surprise, he suddenly plunged off the road and disappeared.

For a moment he stared, then realization dawned. He jumped up. "Come on, Will. He's left the road. We're gonna lose him."

When they reached the point where Joseph had stopped, Joshua stepped off the road, searching for some sign to aid them. Then in a moment he had it. In the rail fence there was what was called a wall stile, or more irreverently, the "fat man's agony." It was a very narrow opening between two posts, just wide enough for a man to slip through but too narrow for stock to pass. Normally a horizontal stick was slipped between the two posts about waist high to discourage the smaller calves or colts from trying to get through. That stick was out of its place and leaning against the fence.

"This is it!" Joshua cried softly. "He must have them hidden in the trees over there."

"We got him!" Will chortled. "We got him."

He started to push through the stile, but Joshua grabbed his shoulder. "No, Will. You stay here. In case we miss him."

"Forget it, Steed," Will snarled. "You just want them plates for yourself."

Joshua felt his anger explode. He jerked Will around, almost making him drop the rifle. "Listen! Have you got hay for brains? It's gonna be darker than the bottom of a well at midnight in those trees." He pointed to the cross stick. "Look, he left the stick out. That means he's planning to come back this way. We can't take a chance of missing him. Now stay here. And no shootin'!"

Without waiting for an answer, he slipped through the stile and started across the narrow width of an alfalfa field. A wood-lot, thick and pitch-black against the marginally lighter night sky, stood about fifty yards away. He moved swiftly but stepped carefully. If this was where the plates were hidden, Joseph would be especially cautious now.

Once into the trees, he stopped, momentarily blind. It was even darker than he had expected, but as he stopped, he found he could make his way, sensing more than seeing the shape of trees and the movement of bushes waving in the wind. The rain was still just coming in an occasional drop or two, but the wind had picked up and Joshua knew the front was almost on them. Another ten minutes or so and the rain would start in earnest. That would only darken the night further, a point in Joseph's favor, and it would be easy to lose him.

For several moments Joshua stood motionless, searching the sounds of the night, trying to separate them from the noise of the wind. He felt an eerie prickle at the back of his neck, and wished he'd been smart enough to bring his rifle too. But almost immediately he shrugged it off. Whatever Joseph was, he wasn't violent. If this were a case of going into the woods after

Will Murdock, that would be another matter. But Joseph . . . He shook off the mood.

Remembering all the techniques his father had taught him about stalking wild game, Joshua began to slip quietly from tree to tree. He would barely touch the ground with the balls of his feet to make sure there would be no telltale sound before putting his full weight upon them, stopping frequently to search the night for movement, holding his breath to listen better.

The crack of a branch to his right pulled him around sharply. He froze, straining to read the direction from which it had come. There it was again, this time louder. He felt his heart leap. This was not just someone or something walking through the woods. Whoever it was was pulling at the undergrowth, moving branches and brush. After the previous silence, broken only by the moaning of the wind, it sounded like someone driving a hay wagon through the trees.

In a half crouch, he started moving slowly toward the place where the noise was coming from. It stopped, and he froze, peering anxiously in the darkness. Suddenly a dark shape loomed up directly in front of him, less than ten yards away. With a sharp gasp, he dropped to one knee, pressing himself against a tree. For an instant he thought it was coming directly toward him, but just before it reached Joshua, it turned to the left and passed by him.

Heart thudding against his chest in great hammering blows, Joshua felt himself sag a little. Then it registered in his mind. The figure was tall and slender. Joseph! And he had something slung over his back, a burden of some kind. And there had been heavy breathing. It had to be Joseph, carrying something in a sack. Something heavy! And he was heading out of the trees again, for the stile. Right into Will's arms!

Joshua straightened, ready to plunge after him, then he stopped. Curious, he moved in the direction from which Joseph had come, head swinging slowly back and forth. Then he had it. It was a small clearing in the trees. Tree limbs and dead branches were strewn around on the forest floor. He moved to a fallen log that lay at the foot of a stand of birch trees. He knelt quickly, running his hands along the log. He felt a surge of elation. The wood was rotten and crumbling, but the birch bark was still firm. Someone had cut a large flap in the bark and hollowed out a sizeable area within the rotten wood. He felt quickly, then uttered a soft exclamation of amazement. It was large, almost two feet wide and the full depth of the log. He leaped to his feet. A hole that big could hold thirty or forty pounds of gold!

Throwing all caution aside now, he leaped to his feet and, holding his hands out in front of him to ward off any low-lying branches, broke into a lumbering run after Joseph. Carrying that much weight, he could only move so fast. Will would slow him down and Joshua would catch him from behind. *We've got him!*

But as Joshua reached the fence and located the wall stile there was no sign of either Will or Joseph. He stepped forward, then began to curse silently. The cross stick had been replaced in its slot.

A noise behind him jerked him around. A dark figure was coming at him across the alfalfa field. Will's voice suddenly barked out at him. "Stop! Stop right there or I'll shoot."

Joshua felt a rush of disappointment hit him like a punch in the stomach.

Will came pounding up, rifle high. "All right, put your hands—" He stopped, peering at Joshua stupidly.

Snatching his hat off, Joshua threw it at Will with all his fury. "You stupid dolt! I told you to stay here!"

Will fell back a step, stunned by Joshua's rage.

"You idiot!" He let his shoulders drop, tasting the bitterness like it was something he had bit into. "We coulda had him." He spun around and slammed the fence railing with his fist.

"I . . . I thought I saw Joe coming out of the trees over that way." Will was stammering. "I thought he'd gotten past you."

"No!" Joshua shot back. "You were afraid I was going to get the gold." He let out his breath, shaking his head. "Jackass! We had him and you let him go."

Will's spluttering turned to anger. "Watch your mouth, Joshua." The rifle came up slightly. "I told you. I saw him. He was getting away."

"Yeah," Joshua muttered. "Just like I saw that angel of Joe's." He removed the stick and squeezed through the fat man's agony. "Come on, we can still catch him."

Will grabbed his arm. "Has he got the gold?"

Joshua stared at him for a long moment, still fuming, then in spite of himself he grinned. "Yeah, he does!"

"Yahoo!" Will whooped, but cut it off instantly as Joshua cuffed him sharply and said, "We ain't caught him yet."

They picked up Joseph again ahead of them in less than five minutes. He was moving steadily, though more slowly now, back up Canandaigua Road. Whispering urgently, Joshua persuaded Will to hang back. Joseph was headed directly into the arms of Mark and David, and they would once more have him trapped. But their plan was foiled almost immediately. Now that they were moving north again, the wind was at their backs. Perhaps it carried their noise to him, or perhaps Joseph sensed their presence. Whatever it was, he suddenly plunged off the road again and disappeared.

Joshua ran forward, peering toward the line of trees. He had driven more than one wagonload of freight from the docks down this way, and now he tried to remember the lay of the land. This line of trees, varying in width from as little as fifty or sixty yards to as much as a quarter of a mile, ran nearly unbroken for about two miles. It angled somewhat off due north so it ran from the southeast to the northwest. His head came around and he stared into the darkness toward the north. If his memory served him right, the northern tip of the woods ended a short distance from Joseph's house, providing a virtual path of cover for him all the way home. And suddenly he understood.

He took Will's arm and dragged him into a run. "Come on."

"What?"

"I know where he's going. We can cut him off."

"Here," Joshua said in an urgent whisper. "Stay behind the tree." He raised a fist in threat. "And this time, Will, don't you move until I say."

They had come into the woods about half a mile further on from the spot they had last seen Joseph. Once within the woods, Joshua had moved them quickly in the same direction Joseph was moving until he found a place where the trees narrowed to no more than fifty yards across. Only then did he turn them around.

"I'll be right across from you over there. If you see him, wait until he's almost between us, then holler. I'll do the same." He started to turn, then swung back. "Will!" he hissed.

"What?"

"There'll be no shooting. You could hit me too."

There was a soft laugh of derision. "Right." He muttered something else, probably still angry at Joshua, but Joshua didn't stop to find out what it was he said. Joseph was making good time, even considering the load he was carrying. This time they couldn't miss him.

Three or four minutes passed with no sign of anyone approaching. The wind had almost died now, and the occasional spatter of rain had now settled into a light but steady drizzle, making the moldy floor beneath his feet slippery and even blacker than before. But the cessation of the wind left the forest hushed and still, and no living thing would be able to pass them, even if the darkness was almost total. Joshua began to wonder if he had misjudged Joseph. What if he had cut straight west and picked up Stafford Road, then turned north? A momentary wave of panic hit him as he considered the possibility, but he remembered there were others there to catch him if that was the case. Then he shook his head. No, Joseph would stay in the trees. It would slow him down, but it was the safest route back home.

He settled back, hunkering down deeper into his coat against the dampness and the chill. Two minutes more dragged by, then Joshua stiffened, his ears straining forward. It was off to his left and still maybe seventy or eighty yards south of his position, but there was no mistaking it. Someone was coming through the trees. He listened intently, trying to judge distance as the sounds drew definitely closer. Whoever it was—and there was no doubt now in his mind that it was Joseph—would pass almost directly to his left.

Moving like a cat in its final stalk of a bird, Joshua started back toward Will to cut the distance down a little. As he came up on a large windfall of logs and branches, the sound now seemed thunderous and came directly in front of him. With a leap of exultation, he realized there was only one way around the windfall and that way would bring Joseph into Joshua's path. Tensing, he crouched down, balancing on the balls of his feet, ready to spring.

Five yards away, so close Joshua could now hear the labored breathing, Joseph suddenly stopped. He had come to the windfall and was stopped at a place where a tree had fallen across the path, lodging up against another tree so the trunk was nearly waist high. Joshua watched as Joseph lowered the sack he was carrying to the ground, then put a hand on the tree trunk, preparing to vault over it. But again he stopped. Joshua could see the dark shape of his head swinging back and forth, probing the darkness. Joshua froze. Had Joseph somehow sensed Joshua's presence ahead of him in the darkness? The moment seemed to stretch on forever, but finally Joseph was satisfied. He vaulted easily over the log and bent down to retrieve the bag.

Joshua hurled himself forward, covering the ground in three great leaps. Quick as a cat, Joseph whirled to meet him. Their bodies struck hard, Joshua's weight slamming Joseph back against the log. There was a grunt of pain and a whoosh of breath.

"Will! I've got him! I've got him!"

A thunderous blow caught Joshua alongside the head. Lights flashed behind his eyes, and the next instant he was skidding in the dark wetness of the forest compost. For a moment he lay there, dazed. Somewhere it registered in his mind that Joseph had retrieved the sack from behind the log and was darting past him. He shot one hand out, grabbed at a leg. He caught the pant leg and held on. Joseph went down hard and Joshua was up on hands and knees, going for him. Joseph kicked out. The toe of his boot caught Joshua square in the breastbone. It was like he had been shot. The pain dropped him to the ground again and he retched, gagging for breath. Joseph scrambled out of his grasp and was up on his feet again.

"Will," Joshua croaked, "Will. Get him! He's getting away."

At that instant, there was a blood-chilling cry, and another dark shape hurtled from behind a tree. It was Will Murdock, rifle high, the butt swinging down hard toward the small of Joseph's back. There was a blur of dark shapes as Joseph spun, quicker than a startled rabbit. He took the blow high on his shoulder. There was a solid thud, a heavy grunt of pain. Will's rifle had connected. But even as he spun around to escape Will's blow, Joseph had swung the sack around to block the blow. The heavy weight crashed into the stock of the rifle. Will howled in pain and the gun went flying. Joseph crashed into the trees and disappeared, the sounds of his flight quickly fading.

Joshua stumbled to his feet, still gasping from the pain in his chest. He moved to Will's side. "Are you all right?" He started to pull him up.

There was a sharp cry and Will grabbed at his right arm. "He broke my arm. He broke my arm."

Joshua dropped to one knee and took the arm carefully, feeling up and down, ignoring the cries of pain. Finally he sat back. "It's not broken."

"He likely near killed me," Will bawled. "Where's my rifle? I'll put a bullet in his ugly head."

Joshua sat back and dropped his head, massaging his chest. "He's gone, Will. The others are gonna have to get him now."

Ten minutes later Joshua and Will nearly stumbled over Mark and David. It was raining hard now, and they could see no more than five or six feet in front of them. The two were sitting on the side of Armington Road, just east of where it connected to Stafford Road. Mark was holding his head and moaning softly. David held his wrist, whimpering like a scared puppy.

Joshua slowed to a walk, then stopped, his chest heaving. "You too?" he said in disgust.

Mark leaped up. "Will, Joshua, we saw Joe. He had two men with him. They jumped David before I could get in to help. Then one of them hit me from behind with a club."

Joshua gave a short, mirthless laugh, knowing at that moment they had lost. Too wet and cold and in pain to care anymore, he sat down heavily beside David.

"I think one of them had a gun," David started. "They—"

But Joshua's look cut him off. "Joseph Smith is as strong as an ox," he snapped angrily, "but he's alone."

"They poleaxed me," Mark cried. "I didn't have a chance."

Will snorted in disgust. "Joshua's right. There weren't anyone but Joe Smith. I thought at least the two of you could handle him."

"Yeah," Joshua said wearily. "Just like we did." He turned and looked down the road. They were less than half a mile from the Smith farm now. "Well, he'll be home by now." Suddenly he thought of Lydia. As she had ridden away, Will called her a silly fool. He could still clearly picture the anger, the hurt, and the bitterness in her eyes. He let out his breath slowly, feeling a sudden desolation. *Who's the real fool here?*

Chapter Fourteen

The storm that had been threatening upstate New York throughout the day had finally arrived. The earlier sprinkles had given way to drizzle, and the drizzle now to pouring sheets of rain. As the three riders turned into the yard of the Joseph Smith home, the hooves of their animals sunk into the muddy soil, then pulled out with a soft sucking sound. The animals—two mules and a horse—had lowered their heads and laid their ears back flat against the wetness.

The riders were no less miserable than their beasts of burden. As they came to the hitching rail, they swung down one by one. Nathan watched Lydia as she climbed down and tied her horse to the railing. He had taken one of his hats and insisted Lydia wear it, but once the rains came, hats were little protection. He could see the water now, dripping off the back of the hat's brim and down her neck. Her coat and the dress beneath were long since soaked through, but she seemed not to notice. She was too weary to notice much of anything.

Nathan glanced at his father. Tight-lipped and grim as a foot soldier on the battle line, he had barely spoken a word since Lydia had appeared at their doorstep. Nathan turned to Lydia and gave her a quick smile of encouragement. She smiled back, but it was a tired smile, almost bleak.

"All right," his father muttered, "let's get this over with."

They strode up to the door and Nathan knocked firmly. Quick footsteps were heard and the door opened almost immediately. It was Joseph's mother. For a moment she looked startled and confused, almost frightened, then recognition dawned. "Oh, Nathan."

"Hello, Mrs. Smith. Is Joseph here?"

Again there was a brief flicker of alarm. "Uh . . . no, no he isn't."

"Who is it, Mother Smith?" It was Emma. Her eyes widened instantly at the sight of him. "Nathan, what are you doing here?"

"Emma, this is my father, Benjamin Steed. I think you know Lydia McBride, from the dry goods store."

"Yes." She stepped back. "Please come in. You're soaked to the skin."

Nathan nodded absently and they all entered. The moment Emma shut the door he went on. "We have something urgent to tell Joseph. Do you know where we can find him?"

In the parlor, just off the entrance, there were more people. Joseph had three younger brothers, an older sister about the same age as Emma, and two younger sisters. They were all there, watching the new arrivals with wide eyes and just a trace of fear. The tension in the air was unmistakable. It was a little surprising to see the whole family gathered. It was now almost nine-thirty, and past the normal hour of bedtime for a farm family.

Emma touched his arm. "What is it, Nathan? Why do you need Joseph?"

He took a deep breath. Sensing his reluctance to speak in front of the younger children, she and Joseph's mother moved them to the other side of the house into the study.

Immediately Nathan plunged in, telling them of the experience Lydia had had earlier. When he finished, he sighed deeply. "One of those men out there now looking for Joseph is my brother Joshua." Out of the corner of his eye he saw his father look away, shamed to hear it spoken.

Benjamin cleared his throat nervously. "Mrs. Smith." Remembering his hat was still on, he swept it off, twisting the brim of it around and around in his hands. "I'm deeply sorry my son has a part in this. You may rest assured before the night is finished, it will be taken care of."

"I understand, Mr. Steed. Thank you for caring enough to do something about it."

Nathan straightened. "Do you have any idea where Joseph is? We can still warn him."

Again there was the quick exchange of glances between the mother and wife. Then Emma shook her head, her eyes troubled. "Father Smith was over to Willard Chase's house earlier today. He overheard them talking with this fortune-teller Miss Lydia has told you about. They were definitely after the plates. When Father Smith returned and told us that, I got worried enough I rode to fetch Joseph home from a job he was doing."

There was a pause, as though she were deciding whether to say more. She glanced quickly at Lydia, then Benjamin. Finally, she added softly, "He was worried about the plates. He's gone to find a better place to hide them."

"So he did get them?" Nathan asked excitedly.

"Yes, night before last. I went with him. We hid them in the woods."

Lydia started. Sarah—or was it Hope?—had used those exact words. The conjurer had told them the plates were hidden in the woods somewhere. She was staring at Emma, the implications of what she had said hitting her. Lydia had determined she would say nothing while at the Smiths, but now she almost blurted out her question. "Did you get to see them?"

Emma appraised her slowly, and Lydia blushed at her forwardness. But Emma smiled, and there was no resentment in her eyes. "No. I could see Joseph had something heavy in the sack, but no, he didn't show them to me."

Nathan was aware of his father's deepening frown. This was not his purpose in coming. "Do you know which way Joseph went?" he cut in bluntly. "Maybe we can find him and make sure everything is all right."

A sudden sound from the back of the house pulled them all around. A door had slammed. There were heavy footsteps, and Joseph burst into the room, breathing heavily, hair plastered to his face, his wet shirt torn and disheveled. He held the shoulder of one arm, as though it hurt him badly.

"Joseph!" Emma cried, moving quickly to his side. "Are you all right?"

He nodded wearily, taking in air in huge gulps. He turned to Nathan and his father, his eyebrows lifting. But before Nathan could speak, he turned to Mother Smith. "Mother, can you fetch me some water?"

Mother Smith hurried into the kitchen and returned in a moment with a dipper filled with water. Joseph took it, wincing in pain, then drank it hungrily. "Where's Father?"

"He's out in the barn with Mr. Stowell and Mr. Knight."

He turned toward the next room where the rest of the family was watching them. "Don Carlos, go find Father. Tell him I was attacked by some men. Up on Armington Road. Then run up to Hyrum's and fetch that wooden chest of his."

"What!" Mother Smith, Emma, and Nathan had all blurted it at once. The sisters jumped up, hands flying to their mouths. Don Carlos, about eleven and the youngest of the Smith brothers, gulped, then nodded and dashed out. Lydia looked away, sickened and yet grateful she had not stayed to become part of the attack on Joseph.

"Attacked?" Emma whispered, her face white.

"Yes. Three different times."

The shock rippled through the room. He moved to the rocking chair and sat down heavily. Again there was a quick grimace of pain, and he rubbed at his shoulder. He also seemed to be favoring one hand carefully.

Emma dropped to her knees in front of Joseph. "Did they get the record, Joseph?"

He shook his head. She rocked back, closing her eyes in instant relief. "They tried, but I've hidden it again just outside."

"Praise God," his mother breathed.

Joseph looked up at Nathan and his father. It finally seemed to register he had company. "Nathan, what are you doing here?"

Nathan explained quickly. Twice as Nathan spoke, Joseph nodded, as though it explained some things. "I'm afraid Joshua may have been one of those who attacked you."

Joseph noted the pain in Nathan's eyes and the shame on his father's face, but he was too honest to hold back the truth. "Yes. Him and Will Murdock."

Benjamin stepped forward, his face twisting. "You're sure?"

Joseph stood and laid a hand on his shoulder. "No, not positive. It was very dark. But . . ." He shrugged and it said enough. "I'm sorry, Mr. Steed. I don't hold you accountable in any way."

At that moment, Samuel, another of Joseph's brothers, stuck his head in the room. "Joseph, Pa and Mr. Knight and Mr. Stowell are going after them."

"It's probably too late. They'll be gone by now."

"Well, they're going."

"Come on, Nathan," Benjamin said grimly. "We'll join them."

Nathan turned to Emma. "Can Lydia stay here?"

There was a quick nod. Lydia started to protest, but Nathan grasped her arm. "We'll be back. It's better you stay."

She had already ridden close to five miles this night. She was wet and cold and weary as she had not been for a long time. She finally nodded, not wanting to stay with the Smiths, but not up to much more on this exhausting night.

Emma put an arm around her as the men went out of the door. "Come, Lydia. You are so wet. Let's get your coat off and sit you by the fire."

Though no more than fifteen minutes had passed, Lydia was feeling the strain of being the only outsider in the house. Once Nathan and his father had left, the children disappeared upstairs or to the back of the house. Emma had taken Lydia's coat and spread it out on a chair before the fire, then pulled a chair up for her as well. For a time she and Mother Smith and Sophronia, Joseph's oldest sister, stayed with Lydia, making small talk, but no one was in much of a mood for social amenities. After some desultory conversation, the women went into the kitchen to prepare something for when the men returned.

Lydia knew she should have volunteered to help, but she was too spent to make more small talk, and the chance to be alone was a welcome one. She had pulled her chair closer to the fire, letting its warmth steal slowly but deliciously through the wetness of her clothing. She found herself longing for the men to return so she could go to her aunt's house and put this night behind her once and for all.

She turned and looked at the man lying on the couch. Joseph had come in shortly after the women had exited, smiled pleasantly, and talked with her for a moment. But his eyes quickly grew heavy and he leaned back and was almost instantly asleep. Now she took the opportunity to study him more closely. From the time she had been ten or eleven, it seemed that Joseph had been the center of controversy around Palmyra. People could barely speak his name without open contempt. When he came into town, they pointed and laughed or whispered. Yet now, stretched out before her, eyes closed, chest gently rising and falling, he seemed an unlikely candidate for such attention. He was tall—at least six feet, she guessed—and his features were pleasant enough. His hair was still dark in its wetness, but he had combed it straight back and she could see it was full but neatly trimmed. His mouth was relaxed now, and this made him seem even younger than he was.

As one of the lay leaders in the Presbyterian church, Lydia's father was one of Joseph's most vociferous critics, and had often openly challenged—or better, ridiculed—Joseph when he came into the store. It was therefore natural that Lydia should have many of the same feelings towards him. And the tales of super-natural experiences, angelic phenomena, secret records buried in the ground—it all left her with a deep sense of uneasiness whenever she saw him. Tonight the uneasiness had only deep-ened. Lydia, along with most of Palmyra Township, had always thought of Joseph as an outright charlatan, inventing the fraud-ulent tales as fast as he could make them up to foster his own deluded ego. But if that were true, if there were no plates, no gold Bible, then tonight had been a most elaborate sham. Joseph's bursting into the room exhausted and disheveled, the demand that his pursuers be sought, the call for a chest. If there were no plates, then this could only be some kind of contrived little drama, played out to impress her and the Steeds. When the Smiths didn't even know they were coming!

She shook her head, troubled. No. There had to be another explanation. Emma, Joseph's mother, the brothers—there was no question but what the Smith family believed totally in their husband, son, and brother. And Joseph was clearly convinced of his mission too. That could no longer be comfortably denied. So what *had* happened to him? If he didn't have gold plates, what was he hiding in the woods? What was he going to put in Hyrum's chest? Was this what insanity was like? To be so con-vinced of something that it became totally real to you?

Suddenly she saw Joseph's eyes were opened, scrutinizing her as she studied him. She blushed and turned away quickly.

He sat up. "I didn't even take time to thank you for what you did tonight."

She turned back. His eyes were searching hers now. They were clear and blue and disarmingly pleasant. He smiled gently. "You could have just gone on home."

"My father thinks I'm staying with my Aunt Bea. If I went home, I would be in serious trouble." She laughed then, sur-prised she should answer him with that kind of honesty.

His eyes were twinkling now. "And how will your father feel when he finds out you helped"—his voice became low and filled with mock gravity—"ol' Joe Smith?"

Again Lydia blushed. What was there to say to that? But there was no animosity in his eyes, and in a moment he laughed again, brushing it aside. He shifted his weight, grimacing with pain. He lifted his right hand, laid it against his chest, and began to rub it absently. "Well, anyway, thank you."

"I should have come straight here," Lydia responded. "But I didn't know what to do. I thought—" She hurried on, worried he might begin to wonder why she was over at the Willard Chase farm with them in the first place. "I couldn't go to my father, of course. And . . . well, Nathan *is* Joshua's brother."

"You did right. You ought not to be riding out on these roads alone at night."

She let out her breath slowly. "I just wish we had gotten here sooner."

He grinned. "Me too."

He was so open, so relaxed. At that moment Lydia decided to ask him straight out. Did he really have some kind of gold Bible? Had he really seen an angel? But even as she phrased the questions in her mind, something inside her was repulsed. What if he said yes? Would she believe him? It was all so utterly fantastic. She gave a quick, almost imperceptible, shake of her head, irritated she had even considered it as possible for a moment.

Again he was watching her closely, his eyes amused, as though sensing her thoughts, but before he could speak there was the sound of footsteps on the porch. The door burst open and Hyrum came in, a wooden chest on his shoulders. Don Carlos followed, shutting the door behind them.

"Ah, there you are!" Joseph cried, leaping up.

"Here it is," Hyrum said, swinging the chest down into Joseph's arms. Again there was a soft grunt of pain as Joseph took it, and the image of someone leaping out to strike him in the dark flashed across Lydia's mind.

Hyrum turned to Lydia. "Evenin', Miss McBride."

The boy had evidently told Hyrum what was happening, for Hyrum seemed not in the least surprised to see her there. Then without waiting for her to respond, he swung back to Joseph, pulling a key out of his pocket. "Here's the key."

"Wonderful!" Joseph exclaimed. "This will do until I get the chest I ordered from the cabinetmaker in town." He swung it under one arm. "I'll be right back."

As he exited the room, Lydia looked at Hyrum in open surprise. Guessing her thoughts, he shook his head. "No one sees the plates, except Joseph. Not me. Not Mother or Father. Not even Emma."

She remembered what Emma had said earlier about seeing only the sack. *How convenient,* she thought. But she just nodded, hiding the doubt she was feeling. Then to her relief, there was the sound of voices in the yard, and she realized the men had returned.

Five minutes later they were all in the kitchen. They ate rewarmed slices of bread along with a thick stew Mother Smith had already had cooking on the stove. Lydia stood back, declining any refreshment, and watching the men. She was particularly interested in Mr. Stowell and Mr. Knight. Emma had told her they were from down Colesville and South Bainbridge, about twenty-five or thirty miles from her own home in Harmony, Pennsylvania. But that was well over a hundred miles south of Palmyra. What had brought them here to the Smith home? They seemed comfortable with the family, and they talked of the record as though there were not the slightest question about it in their minds either. Yet they were hardly wild-eyed fanatics. From both dress and deportment, they were clearly prosperous, educated farmers. It was another troubling piece in her puzzle.

She turned a little, watching Nathan's father. The fruitless search had done little to lighten his mood. His mouth twitched from time to time, particularly when reference was made to whom it might have been that had attacked Joseph. There was a fury burning in Benjamin Steed, and Lydia was glad they hadn't found Joshua. Not tonight. Let things simmer down a little. It would still be bad enough. But tonight . . . She felt a little chill run up her back and wondered how she had allowed herself to become entrapped in all this.

The back door opened and Joseph came in. Samuel quickly stood and Joseph took his chair. He looked first to Emma, then to his parents, with obvious relief. "All is safe now." There was a collective sigh of relief, and Emma ladled some stew into a bowl and handed it to him. As he reached for it, he gave a soft cry of pain.

"What is it, Joseph?" Mother Smith asked anxiously.

He was peering at his right hand, the one Lydia had seen him favoring on the sofa. He held it up, palm facing them. "Father," he said, "I seem to have hurt myself."

Lydia felt a sudden lurch in her stomach. The thumb on his right hand was noticeably out of line from where it should normally have been.

Joseph touched it and winced sharply. "The last man who jumped me came from behind, I heard him just before he leaped. I swung around and struck him a heavy blow. I must have dislocated my thumb. It hurts somethin' fierce."

Father Smith stepped to his son, taking the injured hand carefully. "That you have, son. Hold on, this will hurt." He grasped the thumb as Joseph gritted his teeth. He yanked on it sharply, and there was a soft popping sound.

Joseph gasped, then blew out air in a sharp burst of relief. "Yes," he cried. "That did it." He blinked back sudden tears of pain. He shook his hand, wiggled the thumb. "It's better already."

The group fell silent for a time as they continued eating. Joseph finished first and looked up. "This is exactly what the angel warned me about," he said matter-of-factly.

Lydia jerked around, and saw that Nathan's father was staring at Joseph as well.

"When he gave me the plates, he told me this kind of thing would happen."

"What did he say, Joseph?" Josiah Stowell had leaned over the table eagerly.

Joseph leaned back, his eyes reflective. "He said I was but a man, and that now the record was in my hands I would have to be very watchful and faithful to my trust. Wicked men would lay every plan and scheme to take it from me. He also warned me that if I do not take continual heed, they will succeed."

Lydia felt her skin begin to crawl. As she looked quickly at the other faces, it was clear no one in the room except herself was having any trouble with this talk of an angel and his eerie warnings. Well, almost no one. Nathan's father shot her a quick look and seemed relieved to see her dismayed as well. He stood and picked up his hat from the back of his chair. But before he could move away, Joseph Knight spoke.

"So you are going to translate the record?" Everyone turned to Joseph at that.

He nodded firmly. "Yes, with the Lord's help."

"How long, Joseph?" Nathan broke in. "How long before it's translated?"

Lydia felt a little sick. Nathan too? It was evident in his eyes, in the eagerness of his voice. She felt suddenly a little dizzy and filled with an overwhelming desire to be gone from this house.

Joseph was looking at Nathan, shaking his head. "I don't know." He looked suddenly forlorn. "I am in need of making a living to support my family." He looked up at Emma and smiled briefly. "We're hoping that Emma will soon be with child and I have to think about becoming a father."

There were quick nods of approval.

"And the opposition grows almost daily now," Joseph continued. "I do not know what we shall do."

"My parents have invited us to come back to Harmony," Emma said. "My brother has a small house nearby that he'll sell to us."

"Yes," said Stowell quickly. "That's a good idea. Come down to Harmony, Joseph. Mr. Knight and I can help you. You must start on the translation as quickly as possible."

"Perhaps we will," Joseph said, now quite weary. "We are considering that very seriously."

There was a moment's silence and Lydia seized upon it as the opening she had been waiting for. "I must go. My aunt will be worried."

"Yes," Nathan's father added quickly, putting on his hat. "Nathan and I also must be going. We've still got to find Joshua."

In a moment they were all standing. Joseph led them through the house to the front entryway. As Lydia put on her coat and hat, Joseph reached out and took her hand. "Miss Lydia, thank you again. It was noble of you to try and prevent what happened tonight."

He turned to Nathan. "And to you, good friend. Thank you for riding on this stormy night to help." He looked to Nathan's father. "Mr. Steed, I know you do not believe in what has happened to me. It says much for you that you didn't let it stop you from coming."

That caught Nathan's father by surprise and he didn't know what to say. He murmured something under his breath, shook hands quickly, and stepped out and onto the front porch. The rain had slackened a little but still came in a steady downfall. The temperature had dropped and the air was cold and moist. Their breath came in little clouds of white.

Lydia gazed out into the rain, dreading stepping out into it again. "My aunt just lives up the road from here," Lydia said. "I can find my way."

Nathan's father shook his head and Nathan immediately touched her shoulder. "We shall see you there. And I think your aunt deserves an explanation for your lateness."

She nodded gratefully, too tired to protest. She pulled her hat down low and stepped into the rain, moving around to where their mounts were tied. As she untied the reins, she turned to Nathan's father. "Mr. Steed?"

"Yes?"

"Do you really believe Joseph has gold plates?" She had nearly asked Nathan; then, knowing what his answer would be, had turned to his father instead. She was hoping to find at least one ally, for doubts still tumbled inside her.

Benjamin Steed undid the reins of her horse and offered her his hand to get up into the saddle. When she had swung up and settled herself, feeling the cold wetness instantly penetrate through to her legs, he looked up at her. When he spoke, his voice was low, and tight with anger. He shot a quick glance at Nathan. "I think the whole thing is madness."

He untied his mule and swung up into the saddle beside Lydia. He gave her a long look, deliberately avoiding Nathan's eyes now. "Personally, I wish Joseph Smith would take his sacred record"—the last two words were spat out with great contempt—"and all this talk about angels and get out of here. Pennsylvania isn't half far enough if you ask me."

She turned to see Nathan's reaction to that, but he didn't look at her. He was watching his father, the pain drawing the corner of his eyes into tight lines. His father glanced at him once, then reined the mule around and dug his heels into its flanks.

Nathan finally looked at Lydia, his face glum, then followed suit, waiting at the front gate to let her fall in between them. No one else spoke as they rode slowly northward.

It was after eleven when they finally found Joshua. Twice Nathan had tried to talk his father into going home, promising he would look for Joshua the following day. They were wet, they were cold, and they were very tired. The mules were also tired and miserable and had started to balk at every turn. But Benjamin was having none of that. His mood had not been helped by the experience at the Smiths'. Like Lydia, he had seen the eagerness, the trust in Nathan's eyes as Joseph spoke, and it left him filled with disgust. Nor had the search for Joshua done anything to change his mood. As they moved from boardinghouse to warehouse to the Murdock farm—Will and David were not home either—and back to town again, Benjamin could feel the anger deepening inside him until it was like a cold, hard lump settled in the pit of his stomach.

They rode through the deserted silence of Main Street, past the darkened houses and shops, disturbed only by the barking of an occasional dog. They came to Church Street, where they would turn north for home. As they reached the corner, Benjamin reined up.

Nathan's mule went three or four steps further before Nathan saw his father had stopped. "What?" he said.

Benjamin gestured with his head. Half a block further up the street was Asa Lilly's tavern. Lamplight still shone from two of the windows, and there were three horses and a buckboard tied up in front.

Nathan peered through the rain, then finally grunted. "One's a sorrel."

Benjamin nodded. Joshua had no mount of his own, but Lydia had said they were all on horses, so they had checked at the livery stable. Joshua had rented a sorrel mare for the night.

"Come on," Benjamin said gravely. "Let's take a look."

Joshua was at a table with the two Murdock boys, Mark Cooper, and a man Benjamin did not recognize. He was older, balding, his hair plastered to his head. It was clear that none of them had been long out of the rain. A bottle of whiskey sat in the middle of the table, better than three-quarters empty.

Will Murdock was speaking, or rather half shouting. His voice was slurred, the speech thick. "So close. We almost had that sneaking—"

He stopped. Joshua had looked up toward the door and frozen, his face going instantly ashen. Will turned slowly, struggling to focus his eyes. The others turned too, staring at the two dark figures in the doorway. Asa Lilly's oldest son was wiping down the counter. He stopped and slowly set down his rag.

"Well, well," Joshua said, recovering a little. He forced a smile, but it was battered, crooked, a feeble effort at bravado. "Hello, Pa. Evenin', Nathan."

Benjamin stepped forward into the light, Nathan following closely behind him. Benjamin felt the rage surging upward in his gut, making his hands tremble. He clenched them tightly, fighting to steady them.

"Care for a drink?" Joshua said, reaching for the bottle. "It's a cold night out."

"Nathan and I would like a word with you outside."

Three men at another table were talking quietly, laughing amongst themselves. They suddenly fell silent and turned to watch.

Joshua licked his lips, then feebly smiled again. "Come on, Pa, have a drink first. Then we can talk."

"I said outside," Benjamin commanded, clipping off the words with measured precision.

Will Murdock sensed Joshua's need for an ally. "Now, Mr. Steed, ain't no need to be unsociable."

"You shut your mouth!" Benjamin roared. "You've done enough for one night."

Will rocked back in his chair. Nathan reached out a hand and laid it on his father's arm. "Pa," he cautioned. Benjamin shook it off, barely aware of it. Behind the counter, the Lilly boy began to back slowly away. When he reached the stairs he turned and bolted up them.

For a moment, no one else moved. Every eye was riveted on Benjamin. Then finally Joshua pushed back his chair and stood up, the hangdog fear suddenly gone. "You got something to say to me, you say it here."

"That's right," Benjamin raged. "Let's shame the Steed family in public." He laughed bitterly. "Why not wake the whole village so they can see what a son of mine has done?"

"And just what have I done?" Joshua asked, his own voice now filled with venom.

"Gone after Joe Smith and his gold plates."

There was a start from the other table, and the men swung

around to look at Joshua more closely. Joshua was likewise taken aback.

"Lydia McBride came for us. She told us what you and these mongrel dogs were up to."

"Lydia?" Joshua echoed in a hoarse whisper.

"Lydia?" Will Murdock howled, leaping to his feet. He swung around to Joshua. "I told you she would be nothing but trouble."

Joshua whirled and straight-armed him, slamming him back into his chair. "Shut up!"

"Was it you that hid in the woods and jumped Joseph from behind? Like a real man does?"

Joshua's eyes darted away, unable to meet his father's. "I don't know what you're talking about."

Nathan spoke to Joshua for the first time. "Joseph said he recognized your voice. Heard you call out Will's name."

In one instant Benjamin saw it all—saw the reaction at the table, saw the quick look of fear Will Murdock and his brother exchanged, saw the alarm in the older man's eyes, saw Mark Cooper drop his head quickly, saw the guilt on his own son's face. They were all guilty. His son and this scum he was running with.

"You did it," Benjamin lashed out. "At least be man enough to admit it."

Joshua's eyes narrowed and he lunged forward a step, his fists clenched. "I didn't hit him," he hissed, "but only 'cause he was too fast for me. I tried!"

Benjamin stared, shocked into momentary silence by the open admission and the blazing defiance.

Nathan exploded. "Did it ever cross your mind that what you were doing was nothing more than plain robbery? Common thievery?"

"Them plates aren't his," the balding man snarled. "Smith himself admits he found them up top of old man Sexton's hill."

Asa Lilly came tumbling down the stairs in a nightshirt, followed by his son. He stopped at the bottom of the stairs, then came forward slowly, holding up his hand. He knew Benjamin from the several times he had been in the tavern since the Steeds had come to Palmyra. "Ben," he said soothingly, "have we got a problem here?"

"There's no problem," Benjamin spat, not taking his eyes from Joshua. "I've just come to fetch my son home. Seems like he's not old enough to be on his own anymore."

Joshua leaned forward, unable to believe what he had just heard. Then he threw back his head and roared.

Something inside Benjamin snapped. He stepped forward, swinging. Joshua saw it coming, strangled off the laugh, but was too stunned to duck. The flat of Benjamin's hand caught him square alongside the head with a crack that seemed to thunder in the room. He went crashing backwards and hit the table, sending the whiskey bottle flying. His feet tangled in a chair leg and he fell heavily, smashing his face on David Murdock's knee as he went down.

For several seconds, no one moved. "Joshua," Benjamin stammered. He stepped forward, his hand extended toward his son. Joshua rolled frantically away from him, then came up into a crouch, blood trickling from his nose.

"Joshua, I'm sorry. I—"

Looking around wildly, Joshua's eyes lit on the pistol stuck in Mark Cooper's belt. With a cry like that of a wounded badger, he leaped forward, snatching the gun. He swung around, the pistol coming up just as his father reached him.

"Joshua!" Nathan screamed. "No!"

Benjamin froze, chest heaving, looking down the barrel of the pistol, the hole seeming as large as a cave. He felt suddenly, terribly sick. Joshua's eyes were crazed, his hand trembling violently. Benjamin saw the thumb on the hammerlock of the pistol, white at the knuckle, and knew he was moments from death.

Then gradually, sanity returned to the eyes that stared at him over the barrel. Joshua fell back a step, the gun lowering, but only enough to point at Benjamin's chest.

"Don't do it, Joshua! Don't do it!" Nathan's voice behind them was almost a sob.

The pistol lowered a fraction more. "Don't you ever touch me again," Joshua cried, his voice trembling as noticeably as his hands. "Not ever!"

"Joshua!" There was no sound. "Joshua!" He could only mouth the word over and over.

In the room, everyone had frozen into immobility. Then Asa Lilly moved. Joshua swung around, the pistol waving wildly now. "Stay back!"

Lilly and his son cowered backwards. The men at the table dropped their eyes, huddling lower in their chairs. Those at Joshua's table could only gape at him, as stunned as the others.

Joshua slowly backed around the table, keeping the gun steady now. He passed behind Benjamin, passed on Nathan's left. Nathan, his face twisted with anguish, took a step toward him.

"Don't!" Joshua whispered.

"Joshua," Nathan cried, pleading.

"Just don't!"

Then suddenly he turned and plunged out of the door. In a moment there was a hoarse cry, the sounds of a horse's hooves pounding away. Then there was nothing except the soft sound of the rain on the roof overhead.

Chapter Fifteen

The month of June was closing out in western New York, and summer had now come with a vengeance. The afternoon temperature had climbed into the nineties, and a line of thunderstorms off to the west, spawned from the waters of Lake Erie, left the air laden with a muggy heaviness that effectively stifled any movement. Even the trees hung limp and lifeless, as though too weary to rustle their leaves. A raven circled lazily overhead, splitting the stillness with an occasional raucous caw, but no other birdcalls were heard. A few cows clustered together in a stupor beneath the spreading shade of an oak tree. Further on, a pair of horses stood side by side but facing in opposite directions, their flicking tails keeping the flies away from each other's faces.

Benjamin Steed snapped the reins once lightly just to remind the mules he was still there. An ear flopped backwards momentarily. Other than that there was no sign that they noted his presence. Benjamin sat back, content to let them set their own pace. Though he had left his home just a few minutes earlier, the sweat already trickled from beneath his wide-brimmed hat and into his eyes, and there was a stickiness in his arm pits, but he gave little mind to it. His thoughts were on other things, primarily on his oldest son.

Nine months had now passed since that dark September night and the bitter confrontation between father and son. Benjamin still felt sickened whenever he let his mind run over those few moments in Asa Lilly's tavern—the angry words, Joshua's mocking laughter, the stinging blow Benjamin had given his son. His mind always stopped at that point, freezing the imagery of the crazed blankness in Joshua's eyes as he had grabbed the pistol and come within a hairsbreadth of killing his father. They learned later that from the tavern he had gone to the boardinghouse and cleaned out his room, then disappeared.

Since he took the horse with him, technically he had stolen it, a charge even more serious than attempted robbery. But Benjamin, using some of their last cash reserves, had paid for it, and the charges were quietly dropped. The men of Palmyra keenly felt Benjamin's shame and let him know he had done all that was expected of a man.

Since that time, there had been no direct word from Joshua —no letters, not even as much as a note. There were only the rumors—he was fired from a job in Buffalo for drunkenness; he had made it to Pittsburgh and lost the horse gambling; he was working the keelboats along the Ohio; he had been in a brawl and nearly killed a man in Cincinnati. His mother had grown more despondent with the passing months, and they rarely spoke openly of Joshua anymore. But each time a rider came into the yard she would step quickly to the window, her eyes lighting with momentary hope, before she saw who it was and slowly lowered the curtain once again.

The latest report, brought in just three days before, was the closest they had come to hard news of his whereabouts. A teamster on his way east to pick up a train of wagons and take it back west reported that Joshua was working for a freight outfit in a little town called Independence, Missouri, on the western borders of the United States. Trailhead for both the Oregon and Santa Fe trails, it was a town with a bawdy reputation and wide-open opportunity. Ben had not told his wife the part about the bawdiness, only that the word about Joshua was positive, or at least it seemed to be, for a change. She had immediately sat down and written a letter and insisted Nathan take it into one of the stores and have it posted.

Swatting at a horsefly buzzing past his ear, Benjamin frowned. He understood Joshua's hurt and the pride that kept him from writing. Had it been strictly directed toward himself, he could have forgiven his son's silence. But Joshua's quarrel was not with his mother or the rest of the family, and it only galled Benjamin further that he wouldn't give in and write his mother a letter.

Benjamin had never been one to give credence to the idea of bad blood, but with Joshua he found himself wondering. At first he had been filled with a deep guilt. If he had treated Joshua more gently, not always jumped with both feet on his stubbornness, would things have been different? But he had finally put it aside. He had treated Joshua no differently than he treated the other children. Nathan had never reared back like a rebellious colt fighting the halter rope. Melissa spoke her mind freely enough, heaven knows, but it had never brought her into open battle with her father. And no Steed—not in all the eight generations since the first one stepped off the boat in Boston almost two hundred years earlier—no Steed had ever been taught to go after another man's property, be it gold plates or whatever.

Benjamin was jerked out of his brooding as a movement off to his right caught his eye. He was heading for Palmyra Village and was just passing the Martin Harris home. A man came out of the side door and started around the house. Benjamin yanked sharply on the reins, pulling the mules up. "Ho, Martin! Is that you?"

The well-dressed man turned and one arm came up instantly. "Benjamin Steed. How are you?"

"Fine, Martin," Benjamin called. He clucked at the mules and turned the wagon into the yard.

Martin strode over and stuck out his hand. "Ben, good to see you again."

"And you as well," Benjamin responded, returning the firm grip. "Heard tell you been away."

"I was, I was." Martin noted the sweat on his brow. "You look like you could stand a spell out of the sun. Come on, I've got some wine cooling in the icehouse. Or are you in a hurry?"

Benjamin shook his head and swung down.

Martin nodded, glancing up at the sun, brassy now with the haze which filled the air. "It's a scorcher today. Too hot to do much of anything."

As they walked around the back of the house to where a table sat beneath a large hickory tree, Martin called toward the house. In a moment a girl in her late teens appeared at the door. "Lucy, bring Mr. Steed and me some glasses."

As they settled back, Benjamin took off his hat and wiped at his brow. "Heard tell you were down in Pennsylvania."

"Yes. Just got back a few days ago. Hold on. Let me get the wine."

As Martin walked toward the icehouse, Benjamin felt a quick rush of envy. He looked around at the solidly built home and the outbuildings. According to reports in the village, Martin had left in mid-April. That meant he had been gone about two months. Someday, Benjamin vowed, he would bring *his* farm to the point at which he could leave it in the hands of hired help for two months if he chose. That was what it meant to be a gentleman farmer.

The door to the house opened and the girl came out carrying a small tray with two glasses. Martin also reappeared, a bottle of wine in his hand. "Benjamin, this is my daughter Lucy."

Benjamin nodded as the girl smiled and curtsied slightly. Mrs. Harris was also named Lucy, and Benjamin could see the resemblance between mother and daughter. "Thank you, Lucy." Martin uncorked the bottle and poured each man a glass as the girl went back into the house.

"You been gone on business?" Benjamin asked, sipping the cool wine, letting it roll on his tongue so he could savor its cool tang.

Martin leaned back, took a drink, then another, then reached for the bottle and refilled his glass.

Benjamin sensed his sudden reticence and was embarrassed he had seemed to pry. He turned and gazed out across the corn-fields to the south of the house. The corn was now over a foot high and had the deep green color which foretold a bounteous harvest. "It's a good crop you've got comin', Martin," he said quickly.

Martin nodded. "It's going to be another good year." He sipped at the wine, watching Benjamin over the top of his glass. "Your place is looking right smart now too."

Benjamin swung around to look to the north. The tree line along the creek mostly hid his property from view, but he nodded nevertheless, not trying to hide the satisfaction he felt.

"How many acres do you figure you've got cleared now?"

He calculated slowly, though he already knew the answer. "Well, we finished off about forty acres last season, and be-tween last fall and this spring Nathan and I cleared thirty or thirty-five more."

"It's a right handsome farm."

"It's good land. A place where a man could be happy to sink down his roots once and for all."

"Yes."

Both men fell silent. Martin stroked his beard thoughtfully. Although it was very much in fashion, Benjamin had never much cared for the Greek-style beard Martin chose to wear. It ran from ear to ear, but the chin and jaw were kept clean shaven so the beard looked somewhat like a bandage one wrapped around the face to cope with a toothache. Benjamin himself was clean shaven, and preferred it that way.

Feeling Martin's eyes upon him, Benjamin concentrated on his wine. In the heat it was quickly losing its chill. Benjamin drained his glass, now suddenly anxious to be on his way.

"I went south to help Joseph Smith translate the Book of Mormon."

Benjamin set the glass down slowly. "The what?" he finally said when the words sank in.

"I wasn't on farm business. I went down to Harmony to help Joseph translate the sacred record. It's called the Book of Mormon." He picked up the wine bottle and motioned toward Benjamin's glass.

Benjamin pushed it toward him, trying to keep his face impassive. After the events of that night nine months ago, Palmyra Village and the surrounding township was a turmoil of wild rumors and "confirmed" facts: Joseph for sure had the gold Bible. There was no such thing as gold plates. It was a hoax. It was absolute truth.

Several men swore they had seen the stone box at the top of the hill owned by Pliney Sexton. In fact, the hill south of town was pockmarked with holes dug by hopeful treasure-seekers. Benjamin had seen that for himself. One man claimed to have actually peeked through a window and seen the plates in Smith's hands, though the man was a known liar and no one gave him much credence. Reports of Joseph being shot at by unknown assailants were more likely true. The whole countryside was in an uproar, and more than one group was determined to get their hands on the gold.

The pressure on Joseph and Emma had finally gotten so intense that they had moved back to Harmony to live with her parents. That had been over six months ago, and gradually the furor which always seemed to surround Joseph Smith had died down a little.

Suddenly, Benjamin realized Martin had refilled his glass and the stern blue eyes were surveying him carefully. He cleared his throat. "And how is Joseph doing?" he said carefully.

"He's fine. Emma was big with child when I left. They should have a baby by now."

Not sure what to say, Benjamin just nodded. The whole tragedy with Joshua had been triggered by the business with Joseph and his gold Bible, and Benjamin wanted no part of it. Feeling the silence stretching out to the point of discomfort, he picked up the glass and gulped it down. "Well, I'd best be going."

Martin looked at him steadily. "He does have them, you know."

In spite of himself, Benjamin leaned forward. "Have you seen them?"

With a deep sigh, Martin shook his head. "The angel has forbidden him to show them to anyone."

Of course. But Benjamin kept his face expressionless.

"But Emma's felt them under a cloth." Martin reached across and grabbed Benjamin's arm. "And I got to write for Joseph as he translated. He would set on one side of a table, I would set on the other. There would be a curtain between us—"

Benjamin fought the temptation to openly scoff. "How can he translate anything? He's barely been to school."

"But that's the miracle of it," Martin burst out. "He translates by the gift and power of God. He has the sacred stones, the Urim and Thummim, that were buried with the plates. These help him."

Benjamin made no attempt to disguise his skepticism. It only heightened Martin's excitement. "Do you believe the Bible, Ben?" he asked eagerly.

"Of course, but—"

"In the Old Testament, the high priest had a Urim and Thummim, Ben. It was something God prepared to help men receive revelation. That's what the angel gave Joseph. They help him translate the record. God hid them up with the gold plates so Joseph could translate."

Benjamin sat back, feeling cornered. He had great admiration for Martin Harris and he had no desire to offend him, but magical stones?

Martin rushed on, leaning forward now, his wine forgotten. "Joseph would study the plates, then give the translation. I would write as Joseph read from the plates." His eyes were shining. "Oh, Benjamin. It was a marvelous experience. We've written a hundred and sixteen pages so far."

That startled Benjamin a little. He had never thought about the record as being real, so the length of it had never crossed his mind. A hundred and sixteen pages was—

"Benjamin, I'm telling you, it's true." Martin had leaned across and grabbed his arm. His grip was hard, the fingers digging into the flesh. "It's true."

Benjamin cleared his throat. This would have to be done delicately, but words didn't come.

Martin sat back. "I gave him fifty dollars, you know. To help him and Emma get down to Harmony." He pulled a face. "Lucy—Mrs. Harris—still hasn't forgiven me for that."

Fifty dollars! Ben sat back, a little dazed. That was two months' wages for a working man.

"I know what you're thinking, Ben. But I didn't go into this with my eyes closed." He turned toward the house. "Lucy!"

In a moment his daughter appeared at the door again. "Bring me the Bible." He turned back to Benjamin. "I had my doubts, too. Joseph is a good boy, but I was getting lots of pressure from Mrs. Harris and others. Everyone thought I was crazy." He sighed. "So I asked Joseph if he would copy some of the characters from the plates for me."

"And did he?"

"Oh yes. Joseph is very anxious to convince people he's really got the plates. He wishes he could show the plates to people, but the angel has absolutely forbidden it. It's been hard for him."

Or smart of him!

Martin's daughter came out carrying a large family Bible and handed it to her father.

"Thank you, dear." A slip of paper stuck out about midway in the book, and Martin opened the book at the place. He took the paper out and handed it across to Benjamin. Lucy leaned forward trying to see it better. Martin looked up sharply. "That's all, Lucy."

Blushing, she hurried back into the house. Benjamin took it, curious in spite of himself. It was a piece of foolscap, about six or seven inches long and four or five wide. On it was an assortment of strange characters arranged in columns. Benjamin was not a learned man, so all he could say was these looked like no writing he had ever seen before. He handed the paper back to Martin.

"Well?" Martin asked.

He shrugged. It looked like the scribblings of a child. "Who's to say what those are or what they mean?"

"That's what I thought too, to be honest with you. So I wanted to test it, see if I could get some kind of proof for those who were saying Joseph was crazy."

And yourself. Martin was passing over it quickly, but Benjamin saw more clearly now that, for all his trust in Joseph, Martin had reservations too.

"Once Joseph gave me a copy of the characters, I decided to find out for myself." He tapped on the table with one finger, emphasizing his point. "Benjamin, I didn't go into this blindly. I wanted to really know."

"So, what did you do?"

"I went to New York City."

Benjamin blinked. "You what?"

"That's right, I went to New York City. I wanted to find someone who could tell me if these were authentic or not."

Martin was lost in his own thoughts now, remembering. "I was referred to a Professor Charles Anthon at Columbia College. He is one of the leading authorities in ancient languages. So I got an appointment with him and showed him the characters. Then I showed him Joseph's translation of the same."

He was looking off now, at a point somewhere behind Benjamin's shoulder. Benjamin waited for a moment, then couldn't stand it any longer. "And?" he prompted.

"He studied it carefully, then pronounced Joseph's translation to be correct."

Benjamin felt the breath go out of him a little.

"I asked if he would write me a certificate stating his conclusions so I could bring it home and show it to the people of Palmyra. He agreed and did so immediately." Finally, Martin's eyes came down to meet Benjamin's. "I thanked him and started for the door. He called my name, and when I turned back, he asked me how Joseph had found these gold plates. I told him an angel of God had revealed to him where they were. He nodded, then asked if he could see the certificate he had written. I accordingly took it out of my pocket and handed it back to him."

Martin's mouth tightened in anger. "He took it and tore it up."

Benjamin leaned forward. "Tore it up? But why?"

"He was angry and said there was no such thing as the ministering of angels anymore. He said if I would bring the plates to him he would translate them. I told him I was forbidden to bring them, and . . ." His eyes dropped to the Bible in front of Benjamin. "And I also told him part of the plates were sealed."

"Sealed? What do you mean sealed?"

"About two-thirds of the plates have a band around them so Joseph can't read them. He's been told he is not to translate that part of the book."

Benjamin felt himself reeling. There were so many twists, so many bizarre aspects to this whole situation.

"Anyway," Martin was continuing, "when I said that, Professor Anthon said, 'Well, I cannot read a sealed book.' "

He said it with such solemnity while gazing directly into Benjamin's eyes. Benjamin began to squirm a little. There was some significance here, but for the life of him he didn't know what it was.

Martin reached across the table for the Bible, which still lay open to the place where the foolscap had been inserted. He turned the book around and slid it across in front of Benjamin. Benjamin looked down and saw it was opened to the book of Isaiah.

"Read verses eleven and twelve, there in the twenty-ninth chapter."

Puzzled, Benjamin ran his finger down the page and found the place. " 'And the vision of all is become unto you as the words of a book that is sealed—' "

Martin leaned forward eagerly. "That's right, Benjamin. A sealed book. Keep reading."

"—'as the words of a book that is sealed, which men deliver to one that is learned, saying, Read this, I pray thee: and he saith, I cannot; for it is sealed.' "

Martin leaned back, his eyes half-closed. "Ben, do you have any idea what it's like to be part of the fulfillment of a prophecy which is almost three thousand years old?"

"You mean . . ." Benjamin was getting more troubled by the moment. "You think this scripture is talking about this Book . . . this Book of Mormon?"

"Finish reading, then we'll talk."

Benjamin took a breath. " 'And the book is delivered to him that is not learned, saying, Read this, I pray thee: and he saith, I am not learned.' "

Face positively glowing, Martin waited for a response. Still puzzled, Benjamin read the verses again, this time to himself.

"Don't you see, Ben?" Martin finally blurted. "I took the characters to a learned man and he said he could not read the book if it was sealed. That's exactly what Isaiah predicted."

Exactly? Benjamin had to admit, the story disturbed him a little, but "exactly" seemed a little strong. "But this also says the unlearned man can't read it either."

"No," Martin replied firmly, "the learned man says he cannot read a sealed book. The unlearned man says only that he is unlearned. That is why the Lord had to provide help for him."

Benjamin was starting to feel a little badgered by Martin's enthusiasm. He had great respect for this man, but when it came to Joseph, his emotions were too firmly set to be swayed now. Finally, his mind fell on something Martin had said earlier. "You say you have finished a hundred and sixteen pages?"

"Yes."

"Can I see them?"

Martin's face fell. "No."

Benjamin turned away.

"I begged Joseph to let me bring the manuscript home. He inquired of the Lord. At first the Lord said no. But I'm getting so much pressure from Lucy—Mrs. Harris. She doesn't believe any of this and is angry that I'm spending so much time helping Joseph. She keeps demanding to see some kind of evidence he really has the plates."

Benjamin nodded, wondering if Martin knew his wife—a real shrew in Benjamin's book—had gone around the township telling people her husband had been duped by Joseph into giving him all his money. She brought items of furniture, clothing, or other personal belongings and begged people to hide them so her husband couldn't give them away. It had been the number one topic of conversation in the area for over two weeks. Martin was being shamed and probably didn't even know it.

"I pressed Joseph to ask the Lord again," Martin was saying. "Finally, after three times, the Lord agreed, but I had to promise with the most solemn covenant that I would show them only to certain people—to Lucy, also to one of my brothers, to my mother and father, and to Lucy's sister. I—" His eyes dropped and he wrung his hands. "I've already broken that covenant by showing it to others. I must not do so again."

"I understand." Benjamin set his glass down and pushed back. "I'd better be getting on, Martin. Thank you for the wine."

Martin stood to face him. "Think what you will, Ben, but I know Joseph has a sacred record and that he is translating it by the gift and power of God. I know it. As soon as it is finished, I'll get you a copy of the book and you will see for yourself."

Ben murmured something, again thanked him for the wine, and walked swiftly to his wagon. As he climbed up and drove back out to the road, he saw Martin watching him. He could almost feel his eyes on his back. He raised his arm and waved briefly, then the house came between them.

As he continued south toward Palmyra, Benjamin Steed's thoughts were no longer on the whereabouts of Joshua. His mind was filled with thoughts of Joseph Smith. But they were no less troubling and dark than the thoughts which had filled his mind before he turned into the yard of the Harris farm.

Chapter Sixteen

In the summer of 1828, Independence, Missouri, as an incorporated town was not much more than two years old. There had been settlers before—Lewis and Clark had passed by the site in 1804 on their way up the Missouri River. But once William Becknell took a pack train of supplies westward to the Cimarron crossing of the Arkansas River and then south into Mexican territory, the Santa Fe Trail entered the vocabulary of America. That was in 1821. Soon trappers, fur traders, explorers, and missionaries followed, opening up another great pathway to the West called the Oregon Trail. Both trails began at the main square of Independence, giving rise to its title of "Gateway of the West."

The first permanent settlers started arriving in 1825, and thereafter it became a steady stream. It was not surprising, therefore, that by 1828 Independence had become the newest and largest settlement in western Missouri. The raw newness showed at every glance. The main street was a long stretch of ankle-deep dust that boiled up into billowing clouds with every passing wagon and blinded and choked anyone standing nearby. When it rained—which was often—the streets turned into a quagmire of mud that clutched at man and beast with ferocious tenacity. Residences were a ragtag collection of sod huts, log hovels, and shanties patched together with rough-cut lumber, sheets of tin, or whatever else the owners had been able to steal, filch, or forage. Indian tepees with their packs of snarling dogs and filthy, naked children dotted the western edge of town. Here and there open campsites marked the habitations of the mountain men who disdained the finer comforts of "civilization."

The main business section of town was not noticeably better. A "hotel" next door to the stage lines office could only be identified as such from the crudely painted sign nailed over the door. The dry goods store was crammed into what had once been a two-room cabin. One could get a shave in the barbershop, which was made from nailed-together crates, but if a bath was also needed, it was given in the tent out back. At every turn, disorganization and clutter assaulted the eyes, but Joshua Steed, who had just finished supper at the town's only boardinghouse, found it to his liking. He stood for a moment, enjoying the hot sunshine against his shirt, letting his eyes run up and down the street.

The populace of Independence was as mixed and varied as were the buildings. Across from him, half a dozen Negro men with grizzled white stubble for beards wrestled with a load of freight. Missouri had largely been settled by slave-holding Southerners and had come into the Union as a slave state under the Missouri Compromise. Some settlers from the north were starting to balance that a little, but it was still heavily Southern, and Negroes were still in evidence everywhere.

A few feet from Joshua a man peered with curiosity into the window of the dry goods shop. His hair was long, jet black, filthy, and matted in hopeless snarls. A piece of cloth pulled it back away from the back of his neck. The buckskin he wore was likewise stained and soiled. His features were flat and broad, giving him a menacing look. He gave Joshua a long, surly stare, then moved away. Osage tribe, Joshua guessed, noting the man's height. The Osage were notably taller than the Missouri, the Fox, and the Sauk. They hunted the low hill country to the south and west, and it surprised Joshua a little to see one this far north.

Coming toward him were two heavily bearded men on horseback, stringing three loaded mules behind them. They were dressed very much like the Indian, with full-length buckskin breeches and shirts. They also wore hats made of possum and squirrel skins. Each carried a long-barreled rifle and had a huge hunting knife strapped to his waist. Joshua felt a quick twitch of envy. It was only mid-July. Experienced trappers knew an animal's fur was at its thickest and most luxurious in the winter months. Since it was only mid-July, this meant they had a long way to go to find good fur, perhaps even into the Snake and Columbia river basins of Oregon Country.

Joshua had arrived in Independence in late February. For a time he had been tempted to throw his lot in with the trappers and mountain men that were pouring in from the west to trade their furs. The romance of the vast regions to the west was enticing, and he found the quiet confidence of these men almost mesmerizing. John Jacob Astor had virtually cornered the entire fur market west of the Mississippi, and a man with some good business sense could make a small fortune in one season of trapping. Farming interested him not at all. The prairie sod was a tangle of roots so thick it took three yoke of oxen to plow it, and with the shortage of trees, the settlers lived in sod huts that leaked mud every time it rained.

Eventually though, Joshua was realistic enough to recognize that trapping was not the life for a novice. Tales told around camp fires and in the taverns spoke of snow ten and twelve feet deep, of hostile Indians that would skin a man alive and leave his flesh for the buzzards, of grizzly bears that could take a man's head off with one swipe of their paws, of wolf packs cutting a man's horse right out from underneath him. Besides, Joshua knew the freight business, and if there was one thing that was booming in Independence it was the moving of goods and people. He had plans for making his way in the world, and Independence figured heavily in those plans, not the wild, untamed stretches of the West.

Joshua paused for a moment on the plank sidewalk outside Roundy's saloon. The noise coming from the open doorway was boisterous and filled with energy. If freight was Independence's number one industry, then liquor had to be a close second. There were three taverns and four saloons along Main Street. This was due in large part to the nature of the town's inhabitants. This was the frontier in every sense of the word—the border of the United States and Indian Territory lay less than ten miles west of Independence. The West attracted the daring, the restless, and in many cases the lawless. If a sheriff or marshal came sniffing around, it was a simple thing to slip across the border into Indian Territory and out of any legal jurisdiction. Independence was a name well suited to most of the town's residents.

Taking a cigar from his vest pocket, Joshua cut off the end, carefully lit it, then turned and stepped inside. He stopped, squinting in the comparative gloom of the saloon. Then he smiled inside himself. The wagon master was at the table already and it was obvious that the poker game was just getting underway.

On the keelboats along the Ohio, Joshua had learned a valuable lesson about poker. He had saved over a hundred dollars before he fled from Palmyra. He lost all of it in one night of drunken poker playing. When he sobered up he realized that in cards there were two choices—you could be the fool or you could be the man who made fools out of others. Things changed dramatically for him when in Cincinnati he intervened in a barroom brawl and saved an older man's life. Though Joshua picked up a warrant for his arrest and a six-inch scar on his shoulder, he also learned the man he had saved was a professional gambler. They fled Ohio with the law in hot pursuit, but once they were clear, the man repaid his debt. Under his tutorship, Joshua learned the subtleties of the trade—picking the mark, recognizing the slicks and avoiding them, spotting a marked deck, how to string a sucker along, bluff and counterbluff. By the time he had won back more than triple his original stake, Joshua had tired of the game. There was too much Steed in him to make a living as a parasite, and he and the gambler had split company. But there were times when the old card skills could be used to advantage, and this was one of those times.

He stubbed out his third cigar, eyeing the man across the table through the heavy cloud of smoke in the tavern. The man was a teamster from Virginia, come to Missouri with three Conestoga wagons and nine teams of horses—six horses to a wagon—come west to make his fortune. Seven hundred eighty miles west of Jackson County lay Santa Fe, where wagonloads of manufactured goods could be lucratively traded for mules, gold, silver, and furs. The wagons were fully loaded, and the man had stopped in Independence just long enough to let his teams rest before plunging into the wilderness.

Joshua knew his kind well. After leaving his gambler-partner, Joshua stayed in Indiana, driving wagons along the National Road between Terre Haute and St. Louis. There he had learned the freight business. He had also learned the business of the men who moved freight. And this backwoodsman from Virginia was nothing more than a sharpshooter who had decided to go it on his own.

In teamster parlance, there were two kinds of wagoners—the regulars, who were continuously on the road with their horses and wagon, and the sharpshooters, farmers who put their farm teams on the road when rates shot up and there were quick profits to be made. Joshua had the natural disdain for sharpshooters felt by all the regulars. They provided unwelcome competition in a highly competitive market and did so in a way the regulars viewed as patently unfair.

This particular sharpshooter was trying to cross over. He had sold his farm in Virginia in order to get into the freight business and make it all back in one swoop. Leaving his wife and three little ones in the care of relatives, he had gone to Pennsylvania, bought three wagons and eighteen head of horses, then continued on to Pittsburgh, where he bought about forty thousand pounds of manufactured goods to sell out west.

Once Joshua had heard his tale, spilled out after a free whiskey or two, he had walked out west of town where the Virginian had left his rigs in care of the two hired men who drove with him. That's when Joshua's idea had first begun to incubate. The wagons were a sight to behold. These were the great Conestogas—named, like the teams that drew them, for the valley in eastern Pennsylvania whence they had originated. Now, there was a wagon! Every part was built of wood especially selected to stand whatever conditions it might encounter on the trail. The wagon box was four feet deep, fourteen feet along the bottom, and curved upwards to nineteen feet along the top, a feature which prevented spillage of the load when going up or down hills. It was also watertight, and with the wheels removed it could float across rivers or creeks like a barge, a feature which saved days of unloading the wagon at every crossing and then reloading it again on the other side.

And the teams! The Virginian had spared no expense there either. The Conestoga horse was a special breed, a powerful creature that stood sixteen hands high and weighed as much as fourteen hundred pounds. With six of those magnificent animals hitched to one of the Conestoga wagons, they could easily pull the twelve-thousand-pound loads—or the "hundred and twenty hundred pounds," as the teamsters liked to say—across a thousand miles of wilderness.

From that point on, Joshua had watched the man carefully.

A short man with a tremendous ego, he was brash, arrogant, and loud. And greedy! He was constantly at the tables seeking a game, and Joshua had noted he was a shrewd gambler. But his greed exceeded his wisdom, and that made him the perfect mark.

Joshua poured the man another glass of whiskey, then sipped at his own as he considered the cards in his hand. The game had started almost three hours ago now. Joshua had played carefully, lying back, taking enough losses to whet the man's appetite to the point at which the avarice shone in his eyes. Then Joshua had begun his move. Six had started the game. Two had dropped out after the first hour. The other two men were still in. One was about even with where he had started, the other, twenty or so dollars behind. But the teamster, a big winner for the first hour and a half, was now taking heavy losses. The man's earlier exhilaration had turned to obvious desperation.

As the stakes went up and the game became more intense, the scattered patrons of the tavern had gathered around one by one to watch. Joshua knew they would—in fact, counted on it. It was part of the strategy. The more people watching, the greater the pressure to save face. And now he finally had the hand he had been waiting for.

With barely a flicker, he glanced over at the slender girl behind the bar. Jessica Roundy was the only child of Clinton Roundy, the owner of the saloon. A pale woman whose face was somewhat scarred from a childhood bout with smallpox, she was three years older than Joshua. Quiet to the point of painfulness, shy as a fawn, she seemed a complete incongruity in a saloon on the western frontier.

She caught Joshua's glance and dropped her head quickly, but immediately grabbed a tray with a bottle of whiskey on it.

"I'll raise you five." The man next to Joshua had finally decided to stay in. He pushed a gold coin into the center of the table.

Out of the corner of his eye, Joshua saw Jessica move through the crowd toward him. She passed behind him, and though he had his cards close to his chest, he made sure she could see them. Coming around the table, she moved quietly up behind the teamster, leaned over, and took the nearly empty bottle off the table, putting a fresh one on. The man barely glanced up at her. He was glowering at Joshua. "You gonna play or not, Steed?"

Joshua scanned his cards again, brows knitting in concentration. As he leaned forward, he saw Jessica's little finger drop. He felt a quick stab of exultation. "Just hold your patience, friend," he growled. "Some things can't be rushed." With an effort, as though it cost him dearly, he picked up a twenty dollar gold piece and pushed it into the middle of the table. "I'll see that five and raise it fifteen more."

A sudden hush fell over the room. The teamster stared at the gold piece, then at his cards. The stack of paper and coins in front of him had dwindled to a small pile. Joshua calculated quickly. There was over a hundred in the pot already, almost half belonging to the wagon master, and the man now had only about forty dollars left in his pile.

The Virginian licked his lips, then counted quickly. He studied his cards, then counted again. The man on his left, the one who was already behind, finally shook his head in disgust and tossed his cards down. "I'm out." The other man fingered a gold double eagle, worth twenty dollars, picked it up, toyed with it, then suddenly made up his mind. "Me too." He laid down his cards.

The teamster smiled wickedly. "I think you're bluffing, Steed." He shoved the remainder of his pile into the center of the table. "I see your twenty and raise you twenty more."

Joshua studied the money for a moment, then smiled thinly. "Well, you've obviously got a good hand, but . . ." He looked at his cards, now holding them close to his chest protectively. "But I think my luck is still holding." He counted quickly, then pushed more paper and coins forward. "I'll see that and raise you fifty more."

There was an audible gasp from the surrounding onlookers. The man to Joshua's left whistled softly. The teamster blanched. "You know I don't have anything left."

Joshua shrugged and reached out and started to scoop in the money.

"Wait!"

Joshua stopped, feeling a quick stab of shame. The desperation in the man's eyes was like that of a starving man. Joshua wanted to look away, but forced himself to meet his gaze. The man was no child. A fool maybe, but then, poker was a game for fools.

"I've got some goods down in my wagon. I can cover it."

Joshua pulled at his lip thoughtfully. *Gently now!*

"What?" the man demanded.

But Joshua took his time. He poured another drink and sipped at it carefully. Finally, he set his cards down, face to the table. "Shall we really make this interesting, Mr. Farnsworth?"

Again there was a sudden gleam in the man's face, half desperate hope, half fear.

"You know I'm in the freight business too," Joshua continued. "Just getting a good start. I've got two wagons, six oxen, eight head of good horseflesh, plus a small barn and stable. The men here can vouch for me."

Several of those surrounding the table nodded vigorously or said, "Yeah, that's right. It's a good outfit. Worth a lot."

Joshua touched the pile of money in front of him. "I'd guess I've got close to five hundred dollars here. There's another two hundred or so in the middle there."

"Yes." It was a hoarse whisper.

"You've got what in your outfit?" He kept his voice bored, almost sleepy. It took real effort, for this was the moment on which all his careful planning hung.

"Three wagons, eighteen Conestagas to pull them, and about three thousand dollars' worth of freight on board."

Joshua took another drink, then shook his head, slowly, hesitantly.

The teamster leaned forward, his breath coming in short bursts now, reeking of whiskey even across the table. "What are you suggestin', Mr. Steed?"

Again Joshua shook his head. "This is crazy," he said, half to himself. "I put every dime I own into my company and it's just starting to pay off." He stopped and fingered the money, counting it slowly and deliberately. "And I've got enough here to buy me another full rig or more."

"Your company and everything on the table against my stock and wagons," the man cried, almost pathetic in his eagerness to get out of the hole he had dug for himself.

Joshua stared at the money before him, letting the moment draw out to the fullest. The other two men quickly slid their money off the table so as to make it clear they were out of the game. Finally, Joshua shook his head. "I don't think so."

The man shot halfway out of his chair. "Yes, Steed. That's my call. I see your fifty dollars and raise you with my outfit. Winner take all."

The crowd erupted, unable to bear the tension. "Do it, Joshua!" one man shouted from the back. "He's crazy," blurted another, not indicating whether he was speaking of the teamster or Joshua. Having moved back behind the bar, Jessica was watching Joshua, her eyes wide and frightened, hands deathly still on the counter.

Still Joshua hesitated.

"What will it be, mister?" Farnsworth shouted, sensing victory. "I've raised and called. Are you gonna play or fold?"

Joshua's mouth tightened. "All right," he said angrily, "I call. My outfit and what's on the table against your wagons and teams. Winner takes all."

A murmur of stunned shock swept through the room. Farnsworth leaped to his feet. Grinning widely, revealing uneven, discolored teeth, he spread his cards out on the table. "Full house, aces and queens." He stepped back. The breath went out of the crowd in a whoosh. It was better than they had thought. It was a powerful hand.

Joshua sighed, feigning a tremendous relief. Then, slowly, letting the drama work its magic, he laid his cards down. They were all spades, starting with a seven and going up from there. "Straight flush, jack high."

The tavern exploded with a roar. The teamster just stared, his jaw slack, bloodshot eyes unblinking in stupefaction. Then with a moan, he dropped back hard into his chair, slumped down, and threw his hands over his eyes.

Nine hundred miles to the east, at about the same time of day, Nathan Steed looked up from his plate of lamb stew. "Word in town is, Joseph is back."

His father looked up sharply, grunted something, then continued eating.

Mary Ann looked at her son. "Where did you hear that?"

"One of the Johnson boys was at the blacksmith shop. They live just a quarter mile up the road from the Smiths. He got back last night."

Melissa, Becca, and Matthew had also stopped eating now. Their heads swung back and forth between Nathan and their father, sensing the sudden tension.

Laying his fork down, Benjamin turned to his wife. "We have an agreement. There'll be no more talk of Joseph around this table."

Nathan took a deep breath, looking straight at his father. "Mr. Harris lost the manuscript."

There was a sharp intake of breath from his mother, but Nathan kept his eyes riveted on his father. He took some satisfaction in noting that at least the news had startled him. It had been two weeks earlier when his father had come home and recounted his conversation with Martin Harris.

"That's why Joseph came back. Mr. Harris was supposed to have brought the copy back to Harmony some time ago, but he never came. This morning Joseph sent word for Mr. Harris to bring it to the house. When Mr. Harris went to get the manuscript from where he had hidden it, it was gone."

Nathan's mother shook her head slowly. "How terrible!"

Benjamin was looking closely at his son. "How do you know all this?"

There was a moment's pause, then Nathan shrugged. "I saw Hyrum in town."

Before her husband could respond, Mary Ann asked quickly, "Is there another copy of the manuscript?"

His eyes dropped, reflecting the sick feeling inside him. "No. There was only the one Mr. Harris took."

"What's a manuscript, Nathan?" Matthew was following along intently, his seven-year-old face looking thoroughly puzzled.

"It's the paper Mr. Harris used to write Joseph's translation of the gold plates," Nathan said.

"*Supposed* translation," Benjamin muttered sarcastically.

Nathan felt a quick irritation. "You heard what Mr. Harris said, Pa. Joseph is translating. You think Mr. Harris would lie, Pa?"

His father glared at him for a moment. "Martin Harris is a fine man, but sometimes even a fine man can be a fool."

"But he was there, Benjamin," Mary Ann jumped in. "He actually was there while Joseph translated. And that experience with the professor, how can you just . . . ?"

The look he shot her was so wintry that she let the sentence trail off and looked away.

Melissa, filled with curiosity and uncowed by her father, turned to Nathan. "I'll bet it was Mrs. Harris who took it."

"Melissa!"

She turned to her mother. "Well, I bet it was. You heard her here the other day, Mama. She bragged about seeing the manuscript. And she is still angry that Joseph wouldn't show her the gold plates."

"Melissa, that's enough," her father said sharply.

"Her daughter told me that, Pa. She said her mother offered Joseph a big sum of money if he would show them to her. When he said no, she—"

The sharp crack of Benjamin's hand against the table made them all jump. "I will not have any more of this," he barked. "Is that clear?"

Nathan and Melissa nodded quickly. Matthew and Becca dropped their eyes and began to eat again hastily. Mary Ann sighed, winning another warning glance from her husband, and a heavy silence fell over the family.

Nathan ate slowly, watching his father out of the corner of his eye. He cursed himself for bringing up the subject of Joseph again now. The matter he had to discuss with his father would be tough enough, but he had been so upset with the news Hyrum had shared with him, it had burst out of him.

He let the silence run on for several minutes, then took a quick breath. He saw his mother was watching him. As he usually did, Nathan had taken this matter up with his mother first, to try it out. She nodded at him now, smiling her encouragement.

He pushed his plate aside. "Pa?"

The steady mopping of the gravy stopped, but his father did not look up. "I'll have no more talk of Joseph or the manuscript, Nathan."

"I know." He waited, then when nothing more was said, he went on. "Asael Carlson has put his land up for sale."

"Yes?" The bread was laid down slowly onto the plate.

"He's asking three hundred dollars for thirty acres."

"I know that." It snapped out, curt and impatient. "Not even half of it is cleared. And some of it is bottomland."

Nathan groaned inwardly. His father wasn't going to make this easy. "This farm's not big enough for two families, Pa."

For a moment his father just stared at him, then said, "What's that supposed to mean?"

His mother shook her head in exasperation. "It's supposed to mean Nathan's thinking about starting his own family."

Melissa's and Rebecca's heads swung around as though pulled by the same string. Matthew looked up too, but his face had a little of the confusion that now swept across his father's face.

"You're gonna marry Lydia?" Melissa shrieked.

Nathan grinned. "If she'll have me. I haven't asked her yet." He became instantly stern. "And don't none of you be going and saying anything to anyone."

"That's right," Mary Ann chided. "Not a word."

"Oh, Nathan," Becca crowed, with all the romance a ten-year-old girl was capable of, "I think Lydia is so pretty."

"And she's nice too," Matthew said soberly.

Nathan's father sat back, still a little dazed. "I didn't know it was that far along."

"Pa, I can't ask her to marry me until I have a way to care for her. I know our farm isn't big enough"—his words were tumbling out now—"but the Carlson land is just up the road. I could still help you farm this. Between the two of us we'd be all right, I think."

"Where you gonna get three hundred dollars?"

"Benjamin!" Mary Ann said sharply. "Can't you even congratulate him? This is an important day."

"You'll have your hands full trying to keep her happy," he half grumbled, "but she seems like a good woman. Be good to get her away from her mother," he added as an afterthought.

Nathan smiled, realizing that from his father that was about as good as he would get.

"There's still the matter of the three hundred dollars."

"I know, Pa. All he's asking is fifty dollars down, and the rest within two years."

"We've still got more than fifty in cash from the farm in Vermont and last year's harvest," Mary Ann said.

"I'd pay you back, Pa."

He brushed it aside. "That leaves two hundred fifty more."

And there it was. The moment had come. He straightened his shoulders. "Do you remember Mr. Knight, the farmer from down Colesville way? He was at the Smith home that night we were there?"

His father was suddenly wary. "Yes?"

"He's looking for some help to build some barns and clear some more land this fall. He said he'd pay top wages."

"How did you hear about that?"

"He wrote to Hyrum Smith. Hyrum recommended me."

"So you're just gonna up and leave me to do the harvest alone?"

"I'll help you, Pa?" Matthew cried.

Everyone turned and smiled at Matthew except his father. He was still watching Nathan, his jaw set.

"No, Pa. I told Mr. Knight I couldn't come before the end of September. I'd stay through the winter and be back in time to start clearing some of my land—" He stopped, struck by the feel of that. "I'd be back to help with spring planting."

There was a grunt, then Benjamin turned back to his plate, picking up the bread again. Every eye was on him. He mopped along the edge of his plate, then popped it into his mouth. He looked up, as though surprised at the attention he was getting. "Well," he growled, "I suppose every man's got to make his own way sometime."

Nathan felt relief shoot through him.

Mary Ann reached across the table and touched her husband's hand. Matthew clapped his hands. Becca was smiling as if she had just found a litter of kittens. Melissa was looking at Nathan, her eyes suddenly shiny. "I wish I could be there when you ask Lydia," she whispered.

If his father took note of those reactions, he didn't show it. "Does Lydia know you'll be leavin' her for six months?"

Nathan shook his head. "I'm going to tell her tonight."

His father nodded, stood up, and walked swiftly to the corner where the curtain divided off the sleeping area from the rest of the cabin. In a moment he returned, a small leather bag in his hand. "If you left right now, you could go by Mr. Carlson's and pay him the fifty dollars before someone else gets a mind to take that land."

Nathan stood slowly. For a moment he was tempted to reach out and embrace his father. But his father was counting the money. He dropped it into Nathan's hand, watching him closely. Nathan finally stuck out his other hand. His father looked at it for a moment, as if not sure what it meant. Then he grinned slowly and reached out and took it, gripping it hard. "Congratulations, son," he said softly.

"Thank you, Pa."

Chapter Seventeen

Lydia's not here." Mrs. McBride made little effort to hide the fact it gave her pleasure to be able to say that. "She didn't expect you until eight o'clock, you know."

"I know," Nathan said quickly, "but I had to come into town early and thought I'd see if she might be here."

Mr. McBride came up to stand behind his wife. "She hasn't forgotten you're coming, Nathan. You can come in and wait, if you'd like." He was hardly effusive with warmth, but at least there was some measure of cordiality—something that could not be said of Lydia's mother.

Nathan shook his head quickly. "Thank you, no. I've got some other things I can do." It was barely six o'clock. Mr. Carlson had not been at home and so Nathan had come straight into town, too elated to return home. He stepped back off the porch and waved. "I'll be back by eight."

As he moved away, a sudden thought came. If all went as planned, these two people would soon be his in-laws. He grinned ruefully. Over the past several months Lydia's mother had become civil with him, but barely. She still had great difficulty accepting the fact her only child had rejected far more eligible suitors and placed her affections on Nathan. In time, Nathan was sure he could win her over, but for now each visit always brought a marked coolness. On the other hand, the Steeds' reputation as hardworking, honest farmers was part of the softening he had seen on the part of her father. There were miles to go yet, but at least the signs were hopeful.

He stopped and looked around. He had said he had things to do, but that was just an excuse not to have to wait in the house for two hours, which would have been unbearable. For a moment he thought about going down to the docks to see if any of Joshua's old associates had heard anything more of him, but as he turned in that direction, he had another thought. Hyrum had confirmed that Joseph had indeed returned to Palmyra. Nathan had not seen him since last September, the night Joshua left. He had gotten one letter in the meantime, but he was anxious to hear how things were progressing. The Smith homestead was only a mile or so south of town. He turned on his heel and headed for Stafford Road.

"At first I thought my soul was lost." Joseph was playing with a two-foot length of stick, flexing it to the breaking point, then letting it snap back. He barely seemed aware it was in his hand.

Nathan simply waited. They had walked west from the house, out near the grove of trees beyond the cornfields. Now they sat in a patch of shade to escape the July heat. It would be another half hour before the evening began to cool the air a little.

"Twice the Lord told me no when I inquired if Martin could take the manuscript. Martin was heartbroken. He begged me, telling me how his wife and friends were making his life most miserable."

Joseph began to draw figure eights in the dirt in front of him, using the edge of the stick as a point. "You must remember, Nathan, Martin has been one of the few friends and supporters I have had through all this. You can't imagine what that has meant to me. He believed me. He even gave Emma and me fifty dollars to help us make the trip to Harmony." He sighed. "Maybe that was what set Mrs. Harris off. She became very hateful when I refused to show her the plates."

He fell silent for a time, the memories weighing heavily upon him. "Well, with Martin pressing me, I finally went to the Lord one more time." The stick had come up in both hands again. Suddenly, Joseph snapped it in two and flung the one half away. "Oh, why didn't I listen? Why did I insist on tempting the Lord God by not accepting his first answer?"

"But Joseph," Nathan protested, "how could you have known? Martin told my father he promised most solemnly not to show them to anyone except a selected few, and he admitted he had already broken that promise."

Joseph shook his head stubbornly. "No, the angel warned me wicked men would try to stop the work. I should have listened."

Nathan didn't know what to say. Joseph refused to be comforted and he was not about to shift the blame to Martin Harris to relieve his guilt.

"I should have gone after him immediately," Joseph continued, not looking up. "But shortly after Martin left, Emma went into labor." His voice caught and he quickly turned his head. "The baby was born shortly afterwards."

"Oh," Nathan said, brightening. "That's right. What did you have?"

"A boy." It was said so softly that Nathan barely heard.

"Wonderful. What have you named him?"

If there was anguish before, now it was open pain that Nathan saw when Joseph turned back to him. "We called him Alvin." He stopped, took a quick breath, let it out slowly. "He died a few hours after he was born."

Nathan's face dropped. "Oh no, Joseph, I hadn't heard that. I'm so sorry."

He smiled a brief, wan smile of thanks, then let out his breath slowly. "Emma nearly died too. She was emotionally and physically shattered. For a time I had to nurse her day and night. I had no time to worry about the manuscript or Martin or what he was doing. But finally, when Emma began to recover, I started to worry. There had been no word from Martin in almost three weeks. That's when I decided I had to come back."

He let the pain and weariness all come out in his voice. "When Martin told me he had searched everywhere and could not find the manuscript, I was sure I had lost my soul."

For several moments they sat there, Joseph lost in his sorrow, Nathan wanting desperately to comfort him but not knowing what to say.

"Maybe you could offer a reward." It seemed foolish the moment he said it, and he wasn't surprised when Joseph shook his head.

He tried again. "But the manuscript is of no real value. It's not like they have the gold plates. I know it's a lot of work, but can't you just translate them again?"

Joseph turned. The dappling of light through the leaves played across his face, highlighting the features as Nathan watched. His eyes, which characteristically caught and held anyone with whom he spoke, were now downcast. The lips, normally so quick to turn up in an engaging smile, were now pressed tightly together. The pain that lined Joseph's face was like a sudden shadow moving across the sun. "I fear I have lost my place as the one to do the work."

Nathan shot upright. "No, Joseph! It was not your fault."

"It *was* my fault! I should have listened. What can I say to Moroni? He trusted the work to my keeping."

Rocked deeply, Nathan sat back. "You must continue, Joseph."

Joseph stood slowly, as though pulling up a heavy weight with him. "I leave to return to Harmony in the morning. There

I shall humble myself in mighty prayer, and beseech the Lord for his forgiveness. But I do not know, Nathan. I just do not know."

"I can't believe the Lord has called you to this work to put you aside now."

For the first time, Joseph forced a hopeful smile. "I hope you're right. And I so need to hear you say that."

"I know it is true," Nathan said, realizing with abruptness that he really did feel that way. "All is not lost."

"Perhaps not. I have learned my lesson, Nathan. A great lesson. I will never forget it. From now on I will trust only in the Lord's counsel."

A voice echoed softly across the fields behind them. Joseph turned. Again the sound came. "Joseph!"

"It's Mother," Joseph said. "I'd better go." He stuck out his hand. "Thank you for coming, Nathan. I needed someone to talk to. Someone to tell me there is still hope."

Nathan shrugged, embarrassed by the emotion in Joseph's voice. "Mother sends her greetings. She is most anxious to hear about the work."

"I shall write to you both as soon as I know anything."

Nathan grabbed his arm. "You shall not have to. I have hired on with Mr. Joseph Knight of Colesville."

Joseph stopped dead, staring. "Do you speak truly?" he cried.

"Yes. I'll be coming to Colesville at the end of the harvest."

"But Harmony is just twenty-five miles from Colesville. Will you come and see us, Nathan?"

"I shall, work permitting."

"That's wonderful news, Nathan. Mr. Knight is a fine gentleman. He has already been most helpful to Emma and me." He suddenly sobered. "And what does this do to your courtship with Lydia McBride?"

Now it was Nathan who sighed. "I will be telling her tonight. How can we marry until I can make my own way in the world? But I don't know how she will take it. She hasn't even agreed to marry me as yet."

"Trust the Lord, Nathan," Joseph said. "All will work out for the good."

They started walking toward the house. Suddenly, Joseph put his arm around Nathan's shoulder and pulled him up against him, shoulder to shoulder. "You coming to Colesville. I can't believe it. Emma will also be pleased." He was grinning widely now. This was more like the old Joseph whom Nathan knew.

Nathan smiled back. "I am excited. And I will be most anxious to hear how the work is progressing, Joseph."

He instantly sobered again. "I hope it does progress, Nathan."

Nathan nodded. "It will. I know it will."

"Lydia, Nathan's here."

"Thank you, Papa, I'll be down in a moment." She turned back to the mirror, conscious of the excitement which had started her pulse quickening. But she also felt a sudden dread. Would Nathan understand? Could she make him see without hurting him too deeply? Since earlier that morning when her mother had sat her down and showed her the letter, Lydia had thought of little else. She had taken the afternoon and gone south of town to spend some time with her aunt. They had discussed every aspect of the question, explored every implication of deciding one way or the other. Aunt Bea's quiet gentleness had helped Lydia come to a decision, even though it would not be an easy one. She now knew where her heart was, but would Nathan understand?

She picked up the brush and pulled twice more through the rich darkness of her hair. It shone with luster in the light of the lamp above her, and with characteristic honesty she admitted to herself she was really very pretty tonight. She also admitted that tonight of all nights she wanted to be so, very much wanted to be so. Picking out a thin scarlet ribbon, she pulled her hair back away from her face and tied it there. Though he had never said so, she knew this was Nathan's favorite way for her to wear her hair.

A quick dab of cologne, one last turn in front of the glass to see that all was in perfect order, a quick silent prayer for help in finding the right words, and she started for the stairs.

Nathan was dressed in his best clothes. He rose immediately, watching her as she entered the room. The look in his eyes was all the compliment she needed. She ducked her head a little and smiled at him. "Hello, Nathan."

"Hello, Lydia."

"I'm sorry I wasn't home earlier."

"No reason you should have been," he replied. "As I told your mother, I had to come into the village early and just thought I'd see if you were home."

"Come sit over here, Lydia," her mother said, patting the place on the divan next to her.

"Now, Hannah," her father chided, reaching out to touch his wife's arm. "It's such a beautiful evening outside, why don't we let these young people go for a walk and be by themselves?"

Hannah McBride shot her husband a withering look which he fielded blandly. Lydia repressed a smile. Her mother knew she had scored a virtual triumph today. She wanted to watch Nathan's face when he heard the news. But Lydia was also grateful to her father for his understanding. Telling Nathan was going to be hard enough without having her mother hovering over them.

She looked up at Nathan. "Is that all right with you?"

"That's fine." This time Lydia nearly laughed outright. The look of relief on his face was so evident as to be almost comical.

Lydia got a white crocheted shawl from the wardrobe which sat in the hallway, and Nathan put it across her shoulders. As he opened the door, Lydia waved to her mother, then went up on tiptoes to kiss her father's cheek. "Thank you, Papa," she whispered.

He gave her hand a quick squeeze. "You two have a pleasant evening."

They stopped for a moment on the front step and Lydia slipped her arm through Nathan's and giggled softly. "For a moment I thought you were going to close your eyes and offer a prayer of thanks when Papa suggested we go for a walk."

Nathan grimaced. "Was I that obvious?"

She laughed again. "Let's just hope Mama can't read your face as well as I can."

Nathan's expression was rueful. "Do you think she'll ever consider me an acceptable suitor for you?"

"Mama has big dreams, but she likes you."

Nathan hooted.

"Well," Lydia said, laying her head against his shoulder, "at least she's getting used to the idea of you."

"Where would you like to walk?"

"Let's go up Vienna Street, past the cemetery. That's my favorite part of town."

They walked leisurely up the street, nodding to those they passed, stopping once to chat briefly with some of Lydia's friends. Mostly they both seemed content to retreat into their own thoughts. That surprised Lydia a little. Nathan was even more reticent than usual, almost pensive. Did he somehow sense what was coming?

"Do you mind if we walk through the cemetery?"

"Of course not."

Her friends thought it a little ghoulish that Lydia loved to be in Palmyra's cemetery, but it was one of her favorite spots. It was as though sounds could not penetrate past the wooden gate. The grass was a rich green, and though deep, it was neatly clipped. The numerous trees subdued the last rays of the sun, turning the area into soft patterns of light and shadow.

They passed the cottage of the sexton and waved to the children who played in front, then continued around a small hillock at the center of the cemetery to a spot where they were alone. Nathan stopped and turned to her, then bent down and kissed her softly. She went up on tiptoe, one hand coming up to touch his cheek, as she returned it fully.

"I missed you."

She smiled. "It's only been a week."

"I miss you every day."

"I know." She reached up and kissed him again.

He took her by the hand and led her to a spot beneath a spreading beech tree. He smoothed a place on the grass. "Can we sit for a while? I . . . we need to talk."

Surprised, Lydia nodded and sat down. Nathan sat so he was facing her. He fidgeted a little, trying to get comfortable, his eyes not quite meeting hers. When he finally looked up at her, she felt a sudden wrench in her heart. Could she really go through with this?

He cleared his throat, then coughed. One hand came up and his fingers began to fiddle at the buttons on his jacket.

"What is it, Nathan?"

He reached out and clasped her hand. "You know I love you, Lydia McBride."

Her eyes softened. "Yes, Nathan Steed. I do. And I can think of nothing that gives me more happiness."

"I . . ."

She watched, her heart warming to him. Oh, how she loved this gentle, good man!

He straightened, making up his mind to postpone it no longer. "I want to marry you, Lydia."

She squeezed his hand, her voice suddenly husky. "And I you, Nathan."

"But—"

She felt a sudden clutch. His eyes had dropped again and now she feared he would pull the button right off his coat. "But what, Nathan?"

He shook his head. "A man needs to be responsible if he's goin' to be startin' up his own family."

And then it all came out in a rush—the fact his father's farm wasn't big enough for two families, the Carlson farm coming up for sale, his conversation with his father, the offer from Joseph Knight in Colesville. Lydia sat back, nodding soberly at the appropriate time, murmuring an assent when required, but all the time feeling an immense sense of relief coursing through her.

Finally, he was finished. "It will mean I'll have to be gone for several months."

"But you're not trying to get out of marrying me?" she teased.

He blinked. "Of course not. It's just that—"

She clapped her hands. "This is wonderful news, Nathan."

"It is?" His bewilderment was delightful and she quickly moved over to sit next to him, pulling his arm up and around her.

"Nathan, I have something to tell you too. I've been worrying about it all day long. Now you have just solved my problem."

"I have?"

"Mother got a letter from my aunt today."

"Your Aunt Bea?"

"No. This is my father's sister. She lives in Boston. Her daughter is my favorite cousin. We were just like sisters until our family moved to New York."

He nodded, still puzzled.

"You know how my mother has been trying to ship me off to finishing school in New York City?"

Nathan's mouth tightened. "Yes, I think I also know why she wants to do it, too."

"Yes, she was hoping to break us apart. That's why I have refused to even consider it. But my aunt runs a girl's school. She wants me to come there for a year and stay with her."

"A year?" he said, his face falling.

"Yes. I love Boston and I've wanted to go back for so long. But I couldn't bear the thought of leaving you. But now, if you're going to be gone too . . ."

He was nodding, finally understanding. "When would you go?"

"In about a month."

He smiled. "But that's not much sooner than I have to leave."

"I know," she rushed on. "It's perfect. If I say no to this,

Mother will probably fight to send me to New York City again. Even Papa is pressuring me to accept."

She tipped her head back and kissed him quickly. "The thought of being away from you for that long makes me want to weep, but if you were gone and I were still here, I couldn't bear it. And I really would love to go."

Nathan was nodding now, his mind racing. "Mr. Knight said he needs help all through next year. If I could come home just long enough to help Pa with the spring planting, I could work all summer. By next fall I could earn enough to pay off the mortgage free and clear."

"I've always wanted a fall wedding," she murmured. "Or any other month you ask me."

He pulled her close. "A whole year."

Tears welled up unexpectedly in her eyes, as the reality of going that long without seeing him hit her. "I know. But when it's over, then . . ."

He kissed her, first with infinite gentleness, then suddenly with a fierceness that took her breath away.

"When it's over, then no more being separated ever again." He touched her nose. "And if your mother doesn't like that, she can just find herself a daughter who falls in love with the right person to begin with."

"She already did," Lydia murmured happily. "She already did."

The Susquehanna River has its headwaters in Otsego Lake near Cooperstown, New York, home of one of America's early novelists, James Fenimore Cooper. Fast-moving, shallow, and rocky, the river was not suitable for shipping, a significant loss considering it moved through the heartland of what would become one of America's most industrialized regions. From Otsego Lake the river moved southward, dipping briefly into Pennsylvania before making a giant loop back into New York, past Binghamton and almost to Elmira before dropping down again into Pennsylvania and on to Chesapeake Bay.

Nathan Steed sat on the wagon seat alongside his employer, Joseph Knight, Sr. They were moving steadily southward on the road that led from Colesville, New York, to Harmony, Pennsylvania. The road paralleled the Susquehanna River the entire distance, though for much of the way the river was hidden from view by the thick stand of trees and undergrowth that lined its banks.

It was a beautiful day in late May of 1829. The previous three days had been rainy and overcast, but this morning had dawned bright and clear, the air scrubbed perfectly clean by the previous day's showers. Now Nathan could feel the sun beating on the back of his shirt, and he reveled in the pleasant warmth.

"We're almost there." As Nathan came out of his thoughts, Mr. Knight raised an arm to point. About a quarter of a mile ahead of them, the road turned gently right, or to the west, forced to that course by the sweeping bend of the river. "Harmony Village is just around the corner. Joseph and Emma live less than half a mile west of there."

Nathan nodded, finding himself suddenly eager to see Joseph again. Twice Joseph had been to Colesville to see the Knights and Josiah Stowell, but one time Nathan had been on business for Mr. Knight, the other he had been back in Palmyra helping his father with the spring plowing and planting. So he had not seen Joseph since the previous summer.

From the Knights he had learned that after a period of repentance and humbling himself, Joseph had once again received the plates from the angel Moroni and the translation had resumed. He was eager to talk with Joseph and learn more of the details. A few days earlier, Mr. Knight had received word that Joseph was again in need of provisions if the work on the translation was not to cease while he was forced to find work. Immediately Knight purchased a wagonload of supplies—grain, potatoes, some writing paper—and packed it all into a wagon. Nathan was elated when Knight invited him to come with him to help unload the wagon.

Nathan glanced at the older gentleman sitting next to him on the wagon seat. There weren't many finer men than Joseph Knight, Sr. "It's a good thing you're doing, Mr. Knight," Nathan said. "A good thing."

Knight looked away, embarrassed. "Don't want Joseph to have to stop the work in order to keep his family in food."

Yes, thought Nathan. *It's that simple, isn't it?* And that was one of the things that made Joseph Knight the man he was.

"How did you come to first believe in Joseph?" Nathan asked. He had wondered that many times, but his natural tendency not to pry had held him back. Now it seemed an appropriate time.

Mr. Knight seemed surprised for a moment, but then smiled slowly, remembering. "Well, Joseph probably told you about his treasure hunting days with Josiah—Mr. Stowell."

"Yes, but he never gave much detail, only said he was involved."

"Well, Josiah often went north into the Finger Lakes area to buy wheat and flour, then sell it in New York City." He chuckled. "Made a handsome profit at it too. Anyway, Josiah had some map that supposedly showed the location of some treasure buried by the Spanish explorers. He got quite exercised about the notion of finding buried treasure."

"Spanish treasure up this far?" Nathan asked dubiously.

"Oh, the country was full of such tales," Knight said. "I never could get as excited about them as Josiah did. But anyway, on one of his trips to Palmyra he began hearing tales about this boy who had found some gold plates. People said he had magic powers. Josiah immediately sought him out for help."

"Joseph told me that he told Mr. Stowell he had no special powers."

"He did," Knight said, nodding. "That's exactly what he said. Said he had no magical powers at all. But Josiah was so impressed with his honesty, he offered him a job anyway. His pa too. This was in the fall of '25."

He stopped, and looked perplexed for a moment. "What was your question again?"

"I was wondering how you and Mrs. Knight came to believe in Joseph."

"Oh yes." He smiled sheepishly. "Polly says I'm starting to lose my memory. I say I just get concentrating too hard on other things."

Nathan smiled. "That's a good answer, if you ask me."

"Well, anyway, that's when I first met Joseph. Like Josiah, I was impressed with his honesty and his forthrightness. He was a good, hard worker. Minded his own business. Always cheerful."

Nathan was nodding.

"He finally prevailed on Josiah to stop searching for treasure. Said it was of no use. That impressed me too. He could have just kept taking Josiah's money. Heaven knows the Smiths needed it at that time. But Joseph wouldn't do such a thing."

He flicked the reins absently and clucked at the horses. "I hired Joseph in the fall of '26. By then he and Emma were courtin' quite serious like and he wanted to stay close." He looked suddenly pleased with himself. "In fact, I furnished him a horse and sleigh so he could go down to Harmony and see Emma."

"So when did you learn about Moroni and the gold plates?"

"Don't remember exactly. One night he told us all about it. I guess by then he trusted us." He nodded solemnly. "We trusted him too, Polly and me. It was just that simple. When he told us, we knew it was true. Never doubted it once."

"And you've been helping him ever since." It was not a question.

The older man shrugged, a little embarrassed. " 'Taint hard to help in the Lord's work," was all he would say.

Nathan nodded again, then fell silent, glad to be beside a man like this. And glad to be on his way to see Joseph again.

Emma saw them first. She was behind the small frame home, hanging clothes on the line. As the wagon pulled into the yard, she looked up, squinting a little into the noon sun. Once again Nathan was struck with what a handsome woman she was. Her features were clean and evenly sculptured, her dark hair and eyes giving her a sense of gravity which was quickly dispelled when she smiled. She did so now as she recognized them. She dropped back into the basket the shirt she was holding and came quickly toward them.

"Mr. Knight," she exclaimed, wiping her hands on her apron, "what a pleasant surprise! And Nathan, how good to see you again! Joseph said you were still in Palmyra."

He swung down and took her extended hand. "I was until just a week ago. But Pa and I finished the spring planting and so I'm back. I'll be with Mr. Knight most of the summer."

She turned, extending her hand to Mr. Knight, who had gotten down now as well. "And how is Mrs. Knight and the family?"

"Just fine. Polly sends her best to you and Joseph." He smiled. "And some of her blueberry muffins as well."

Emma laughed lightly, tossing her head so her hair bounced brightly in the sunshine. "She is a most wonderful lady. Please return our thanks."

A little embarrassed, Knight half turned to the wagon. "We brought a little something for you and Joseph."

Emma stepped to the wagon and instantly her eyes filled with tears. "Dear Mr. Knight," she cried softly. Her hand went out to touch a barrel. "You have done so much already."

He was suddenly gruff. "Wouldn't want you to be suffering, now, while Joseph continues the work."

For a moment they all three stood silently, as Emma fought back her emotions. Nathan had not seen her since that night in the Smith home. He thought now of what she had been through since then. As they had approached Joseph's home, Mr. Knight had silently pointed to the little cemetery which lay about sixty or seventy yards from the cabin. A fresh gravestone marked the site of Emma's firstborn. Joseph had told Nathan that Emma had nearly lost her life as well. As he looked at her now, he could see she had lost a little weight and her face was more drawn and pale than it had been when he last saw her, but somehow it made her seem all the more lovely. She and Joseph made a striking couple.

"And how is Lydia?" Emma asked, brightening again. "Joseph said you are engaged."

"Yes."

"That's wonderful. She is a fine young woman."

Nathan nodded and smiled, but with a touch of sadness. "I think so too. What I can remember of her."

"Go on with you, now," she chided, smiling warmly. "The time is nearly passed. A few more months and then you two will be together again."

The door behind them flew open and Joseph burst out. "Mr. Knight!" he cried, and in two strides he was to Knight and clasping his hand. He looked in the back of the wagon. "Once again you have driven the wolf from our door."

Joseph Knight simply shrugged. "It's little enough I can do."

"The Lord bless you for it. Thanks in part to you the work moves along swiftly now."

He swung around, his energy as boundless as that of the sea. "Nathan! What a pleasant surprise!" His grip as he took Nathan's hand was like that of the dockhands on the canal. "I thought you were still up with your father."

"Just returned a few days ago."

"Your family?"

"Well, thank you."

Emma turned to her husband. "I'll be putting some dinner on, Joseph. As soon as you have the wagon unloaded, it should be ready."

"All right. Tell Oliver and Samuel to come out."

A moment after she entered, two figures appeared at the door of the cabin. Nathan instantly recognized the nearer one. It was Samuel Smith, Joseph's brother. About two years younger than Joseph, Samuel was about a year older than Nathan. Though Nathan had not been around him much, what he had seen he liked. More garrulous than Joseph, Samuel seemed to take life with a grin. He liked people and people quickly liked him. It was also obvious there was a strong bond between Samuel and his older brother.

Nathan raised a hand and waved and Samuel waved back. Joseph turned to them and motioned them to come over.

"Oliver, you've already met Mr. Knight, but come and meet another of the fine men of the earth."

Nathan smiled. From someone else it might have sounded like fawning praise, but from Joseph it came out as guileless as if from a child. He truly meant it.

As they walked up, Nathan watched Oliver closely. He was close to Joseph's age, though he was dramatically shorter, no more than about five feet five inches, Nathan guessed. But he had a pleasant bearing. His forehead was high, and thick dark hair combed back and away from the forehead only emphasized the narrowness of his face. A full Roman nose, prominent chin, and thin lips gave an impression of sobriety, but that was instantly dispelled by his ready smile and the dark brown eyes which crinkled around the corners when he did so.

Joseph turned to Nathan. "This is a good friend from Palmyra, Oliver. Nathan Steed, meet Oliver Cowdery."

They shook hands. The grip was not as crushing as Joseph's, but it was firm and sure. "Nathan, I'm pleased to meet you."

"It's good to see you again, Nathan," Samuel said, reaching out to shake hands.

"And you as well," Nathan responded warmly. "I didn't realize you were down here. How are your parents?"

"Fine, thank you for asking."

"Samuel's been a blessing to us," Joseph said. "He's always quick to help." He turned to Cowdery. "And the Lord sent Oliver to me to serve as scribe," Joseph declared.

Nathan noted that Oliver seemed a little startled at Joseph's open reference to the translation work. Joseph evidently saw it too, for he laughed and clapped Oliver on the shoulder. "There is no worry with either of these two, Oliver. They are strong supporters."

He turned back to Nathan and Mr. Knight, sobering. "Oliver has learned very quickly that Satan is opposed to this work. The rumor makers are once again active and igniting the fires of hatred and persecution against me. A few nights ago we were visited by an 'official' delegation." He pronounced the word *official* with soft derision.

"Like the ones in Palmyra?" Nathan asked.

"The same. They threatened to mob us and take away the plates if I did not cease 'this work of the devil.' Fortunately, my father-in-law has become more friendly towards me now. He also has no tolerance for unlawful proceedings and was able to dissuade them from their intent."

"But it isn't finished," Oliver said quietly. "They'll be back."

"Yes," Joseph said, momentarily darkening. But then almost instantly he smiled again. "But the Lord has shown us the way to go. You'll be pleased to know we're coming back to New York."

"To Palmyra?" Nathan was taken aback. That was hardly a solution.

Joseph shook his head. "No. Oliver has made friends with a family in Fayette Township, about twenty miles south of Palmyra. We've written to see if they will take us in until we can complete the translation."

"That's wonderful, Joseph. Mother will be thrilled. She is anxiously awaiting any news of how the work progresses."

"Well, tell her it progresses well. Since Oliver has come we have finished nearly two-thirds of the record."

Both Nathan and Joseph Knight looked up quickly. "Two-thirds?" Knight echoed.

"Yes. We work most of the day, and often into the night. Oliver has been a godsend."

"So you have redone the pages which were lost by Mr. Harris?"

Joseph sobered almost instantly and shook his head.

"No?" Nathan was surprised.

"I forgot you didn't know. So much has happened since we last talked."

"Tell me."

Joseph leaned against the wagon wheel. "When I returned to Harmony and finally found favor again with the Lord, it was revealed to me that I was not to retranslate the portion I had already done."

"But why?"

"Because Satan had put it into the hearts of those who had the first pages to set a trap for me."

Even Knight seemed not to be aware of this, and Nathan saw he was listening intently.

"It was really very clever. They had the first copy of the manuscript. If I retranslated the same section, they had a perfect opportunity. They were hoping there would be differences, so they could show them to people and 'prove' I was a fraud. Even if I did produce a second copy exactly like the first . . ."

He left it unfinished, and Nathan started as he realized what Joseph was saying. "If it was the same, they would change the original."

Joseph nodded. "Either way, they would use it to discredit me. Or so they thought. The Lord simply told me not to retranslate it, but to go on from where I had left off."

"But . . ." Knight was troubled. "So we'll never have those original pages in the record."

Joseph frowned. "Not for now, Mr. Knight. But it is all right. The Lord knew of these things and prepared for them."

Nathan looked puzzled.

Oliver explained. "When Mormon—he is the ancient prophet who compiled and abridged the records—"

"That's why it's called the Book of Mormon," Samuel volunteered.

"Yes," Oliver continued. "Anyway, Mormon was abridging all of the records of this ancient people. The one hundred and sixteen pages Joseph had already translated was the first portion of the history. But at that point, Mormon found another set of plates among all the records. They covered the same period of time he had already abridged, but these plates were different. They focused on the more spiritual portion of the history. So Mormon inserted them into his record just as they were, without abridging them."

Joseph was nodding. "In other words, we had a double coverage of the first portion of the Book of Mormon. I had finished the first section when I left off the translating and gave the manuscript to Martin."

Now Nathan understood what Joseph was saying. "So when you started again, you just went on to the section that repeated the same history."

"Well, not exactly," Oliver said. "When I came down and became Joseph's scribe, we started in a different place in the translation. But we'll go back later and take in the period that the lost pages of manuscript covered, only we'll do that by translating the unabridged plates Mormon inserted. So eventually we'll have the same coverage but a better record than the first part that was lost."

"Yes," Joseph said, giving Nathan a rueful smile. "Do you realize what Oliver is saying? More than a thousand years before I was born the Lord knew I would be foolish and not heed his counsel. So he inspired Mormon to add the other plates so the work would not be harmed." He shook his head. "Can you imagine how that makes me feel?"

Oliver laid a hand on Joseph's shoulder. "But there were lessons to be learned, Joseph."

"Yes," Joseph agreed instantly. "And I have learned them. First, I have learned not to trust in the arm of flesh. I must be obedient to the Lord's counsel under all circumstances. Second, I have learned God's wisdom is greater than the cunning of the devil. This is God's work and it will not be stopped."

Behind them the door to the cabin opened again. "Joseph."

All four men turned to where Emma was standing in the doorway.

She smiled a little hesitantly. "There'll be food on the table in about five minutes. Perhaps you ought to get the wagon unloaded."

"Yes, of course." Joseph turned back, chuckling. "Emma always has to remind me. I get so carried away with conversation, I forget what it is I'm supposed to be doing."

As they walked around to the back of the wagon, Joseph

suddenly put an arm around Nathan's shoulder, pulling him in against his own. "Ah, Nathan, it is a boon to have you with us. Thank you for coming."

The moon was nearly to its fullest stage and the river diffused its rays into a thousand points of shimmering light. Nathan stood for a moment and looked across the water. Here, behind Joseph's home, the river was at least a hundred yards across. Nearby, a fox barked once sharply, then all was quiet. He sat down on the trunk of a huge river birch that years before had been undercut by the current and toppled into the water. He sat for a moment, breathing deeply, savoring the smell of the river and the spring flowers dotting the banks. Finally, he took out the letter from the inside of his jacket, holding the envelope for a moment, then extracting the two sheets and unfolding them carefully. Since it had arrived in Palmyra the week before he had returned to Harmony, the creases had been done and undone so many times that they were beginning to split open.

He moved a little so as to come out of the shadow of an overhanging branch, turning the sheets so as to catch the full light of the moon.

My dearest Nathan,

He stopped. Virtually every eligible young man in Palmyra and Manchester townships had vigorously sought Lydia's favors. It still left him a little awestruck to think she had rejected all of them in favor of Nathan Steed.

The months seem to drag by ever more slowly now that summer has come again. I have truly fallen in love with the city of Boston and my stay here has been glorious, but I find myself barely able to keep my mind on my duties now. My heart constantly betrays me and my thoughts race forward to September when I shall finally return to you.

Nathan let his fingers run across the paper, feeling the light tracing of ink, telling himself he could catch the faintest wisp of her perfume. Three months! When they had parted, a year seemed like an interminable amount of time. And while, in ret-rospect, the nine months had passed quickly, now that the end was in sight three more months seemed like an eternity.

Behind him a branch cracked, and Nathan turned. A dark figure was coming down the path which led from the small cabin down to the river. He hurriedly folded the letter and slipped it inside his coat again.

"Nathan, is that you?"

"Yes. I'm down by the riverbank."

Even if he had not called, Nathan would have recognized that it was Oliver Cowdery. The shortness of the figure and the narrowness of the shoulders clearly told it was not Joseph.

In a moment he was at Nathan's side. He smiled and then turned to survey the current and the moon's glowing path across the river. Finally, he sighed. "What a lovely evening!"

"Yes. I think summer has finally arrived."

"May I sit with you? Joseph and Emma have gone over to visit with her parents. Samuel has gone into the village."

Nathan slid down the log a little. "Of course. I was just en-joying the moonlight."

"And I thought to do the same."

Out of the corner of his eye, Nathan watched Oliver as he sat down, squirming for a moment to adjust the boniness of his frame to a comfortable position. He had a pleasant face, which only revealed the man inside, and Nathan had found himself liking Joseph's new scribe almost immediately.

After the dinner was over, Joseph Knight had started back, but he went alone, insisting Nathan stay another day so he could spend more time with Joseph. And so he had. After they had cleared the table, Nathan, Joseph, Samuel, and Oliver strolled out across the small homestead Joseph had purchased from Emma's brother. Nathan was enthralled as they spoke of the sacred record unfolding as the work of translation progressed. Samuel eagerly spoke of the few pages he had been allowed to read. Oliver, who as primary scribe had written the majority of what had been done thus far, was awed. Joseph spoke up too, but often seemed content to let the other two share their excitement with Nathan.

The Book of Mormon. Nathan was still getting used to the name. About four hundred years after Christ, Mormon, under the direction of the Lord, had gathered all the records of his people and abridged them, writing them on the gold plates so they could be preserved for future generations. He had given the plates to his son, Moroni, before he died. It was Moroni who had buried them in the hill where they would lie hidden as the centuries came and went until the Lord saw fit to bring them forth. It was that same Moroni, Joseph declared solemnly, who as a resurrected and glorified being had appeared and directed him to the plates.

Oliver and Samuel could barely contain themselves as they described what they had learned thus far. A prophet living in Jerusalem about six hundred years before Christ had been warned to flee the city with his family before it was destroyed. They had wandered in the wilderness for some years, then under the direction of the Lord, had built a ship and sailed to the Americas. They worshipped Jesus, were led by prophets, performed miracles. "It is much like the Bible," Oliver had exclaimed. "It is another record of God's dealings with his children."

Oliver cleared his throat. "You seem lost in thought," he said.

"Yes," Nathan agreed. "I was thinking of the Book of Mormon." He turned to look at Oliver directly, his natural reticence giving way to the driving curiosity within him. "What is it like?" he finally asked softly. "What is it like to translate?"

Oliver stood, suddenly filled with an eagerness that could not be contained. "Ah, Nathan, it is an experience the likes of which I have never known."

"Does he just read it to you?"

"In a way. He studies the writings carefully. Then he speaks slowly and distinctly, giving me the English one sentence at a time. When I am finished, I say, 'Written,' and read the sentence back to him. If it is correct, he then goes to the next. If I have missed something, he corrects me. But what is most amazing is that he does not correct himself. He never goes back and rewords a sentence. He does not hesitate or stammer. Some days we work for hours at a time in that manner. When we leave off the translation for meals or other things, he returns and picks up precisely where we left off. He does not ask to see the manuscript or have me read to him to help him find his place. It is as though there were no interruptions whatsoever."

Nathan felt a sudden rush of envy at Oliver's opportunity to be part of the actual process. "It must be wonderful."

Oliver returned to sit by Nathan, nodding solemnly. "These are days never to be forgotten—to sit day after day under the sound of a voice dictated by the inspiration of heaven. How can I ever adequately express the gratitude I feel that the Lord should give me such a privilege?"

"I can hardly wait until I can read it."

"I think if you asked, Joseph may let you look at some of the manuscript." He shook his head sadly. "But after Martin Harris lost those pages, he's very careful about letting it out of his hand."

Nathan nodded, and they both lapsed into silence. Finally he looked over at Oliver, hesitant again, but the desire to know driving him. "What do they look like?"

Oliver's head came up. "What? You mean the plates?"

"Yes."

Oliver shook his head firmly. "Moroni has forbidden Joseph to show them to anyone. Not even Emma has seen them. He keeps them under a cloth whenever he is not working on them. Joseph has allowed both Emma and me to feel them under the cloth. But I have not actually seen them."

Nathan was taken aback. "How can you not see them when you sit together as you work?"

Oliver leaned back a little, grasping one knee with his hands. "Joseph hangs a curtain between us. I sit on one side with pen and paper. Joseph sits on the other with the plates."

Nathan considered that for a moment, putting himself there in his imagination. "Aren't you ever tempted to peek?"

Oliver threw back his head and laughed. "More than you could ever imagine. But we've already learned the costs of disobedience, so I force myself to be patient."

His last word caught Nathan's attention. "Patient?"

He leaned forward eagerly. "Yes. Moroni has promised that when the time is right, the plates will be shown to a few faithful followers. I am determined I shall be obedient so I may be one of them."

Nathan stood now, feeling a sudden restlessness. He looked up at the fulness of the moon. "My mother is anxious to hear how things are coming. I will have to write to her tomorrow. When I was last with her, Joseph was frustrated because he had translated only a few pages. As Joseph said, your coming has been a godsend."

Oliver rose and came to stand by Nathan's side. "That is more true than you know."

"What do you mean?"

"Well, I was a schoolteacher in the Palmyra area. As is customary, I took room and board with the parents of those I teach."

"Mr. Knight said you had been staying with the Smiths."

"Yes. Their children were part of my class. I had only stayed with them a short time when I began to hear stories about their son Joseph. I pressed them for more information. At first they would not say anything. But finally they told me everything. I was stunned and yet moved deeply. I couldn't get it out of my mind. That night, I knelt by my bedside and prayed most earnestly to know if there was any truth to the matter."

He took a deep breath and let it out slowly. "I felt an overwhelming peace come over me, something like I've never felt before. So when I learned that Samuel, Joseph's younger brother, was coming to Harmony, I determined to come with him and meet Joseph for myself. I did, and two days after my arrival I was writing for him as he translated."

Oliver reached inside his jacket and pulled out a folded piece of paper. Nathan thought it was a letter, just as he had one in his pocket, but as Oliver unfolded it and waved it at him, he could see there was no envelope.

"After I arrived and Joseph and I had talked, I felt that Joseph was telling the truth, and I became his scribe. A few days later he inquired of the Lord and received a revelation in my behalf."

Nathan was staring at the paper. "You mean he wrote it down?"

"Yes. Through the Urim and Thummim, the sacred interpreters, he inquired of the Lord."

He turned so as to let the full light of the moon fall on the paper, then held it up close to his face, squinting to read it. His finger traced down the lines quickly. "Ah, here it is. I won't read it all, but listen to this, Nathan. 'Verily, verily, I say unto thee, blessed art thou for what thou hast done; for thou hast inquired of me, and behold, as often as thou hast inquired thou hast received instruction of my Spirit. If it had not been so, thou wouldst not have come to the place where thou are at this time.'"

He looked up. "That was true. I had come to Harmony because I had inquired of the Lord about Joseph." He looked back at the paper. "Now listen to this. 'Verily, verily, I say unto you, if you desire a further witness, cast your mind upon the night that you cried unto me in your heart, that you might know concerning the truth of these things.'" He paused for a moment, then went on, reading each word slowly and distinctly. "'Did I not speak peace to your mind concerning the matter? What greater witness can you have than from God?'"

Nathan was watching Oliver carefully. He could see his eyes were shining. When he finally spoke again, his voice was heavy with emotion. "What you have to remember, Nathan, is that I had told Joseph nothing of my experience in Palmyra. Nothing."

He folded the paper and slipped it back inside his jacket. "That's when I knew without any doubt that Joseph was a prophet of God. And I knew I was meant to serve as his scribe as he translated the Book of Mormon plates."

"So you really were brought by the hand of the Lord?"

"Yes. Don't ask me why. I am no different from other men."

"You believed," Nathan corrected him firmly. "That makes you quite different from most."

"Yes, but so did you. So have others. Why should I be the one chosen to sit at Joseph's feet and help in this work?"

"I don't know," Nathan answered gravely. "But you have been chosen, and now you must stand by Joseph's side. It will not be easy."

Oliver was nodding, but obviously was only half listening. Suddenly he seemed to come back, searching Nathan's face. "There is something else, Nathan."

Nathan looked up at him. "What?"

"I asked Joseph if I could tell you. He had no objection."

Nathan felt pinned by the intensity burning in Oliver's eyes and he felt a sudden tingle. "What?"

Oliver broke off a branch from a low-hanging limb and began to methodically strip off the new leaves, shredding them as he considered how to begin. "Let's sit down," he said, dropping to the grassy riverbank and patting a spot next to him.

Nathan sat beside him, almost immediately feeling the dampness through his trousers. But Oliver seemed oblivious to it.

"A short time ago, we were translating a most wonderful portion of the Book of Mormon. After his resurrection in the land of Palestine, the Savior came to this continent and ministered for a time among the people here."

Nathan leaned back, staring.

"That's right. The resurrected, glorified Christ appeared to his people here in the Americas." His hand shot out and he gripped Nathan's arm. "It is a marvelous account, Nathan. If Joseph will let you read parts of the manuscript, that's where I want you to read. But that's not what I want to tell you.

"While the Savior was here, he chose twelve disciples to help minister to the people, just as he did in Palestine. The record says he gave them the authority to baptize people into his church."

Nathan's mind was whirling, but he simply nodded, not wanting to interrupt Oliver's rush of words.

"When Joseph had translated that passage, it came to us with great forcefulness that we had a problem. The scriptures make it clear man must be baptized to be saved. But they also teach that the authority to baptize must come from Christ. What were we to do? Without question we had to be baptized if we were to receive salvation. But who could perform such baptisms? Neither Joseph nor I had the authority."

"But the ministers say the Bible is the only authority needed."

"I know, but the scriptures do not speak in that way. In ancient times, both in the Bible and in the Book of Mormon, men had to have authority from God to baptize. Joseph and I discussed it at some length. He also discussed it with his father, who visited with us for a time. It was he who suggested we go to a secluded spot and kneel in prayer. Joseph and I came down by the river." He turned, looking into the shadows of the surrounding trees. "We found a spot not far from here."

He leaned forward, his head down, his fingers toying with the leg of his trousers. It was almost as though suddenly Nathan were no longer there. He waited, but Oliver was lost deeply in his own thoughts. Finally, Nathan could bear it no longer. "And?" he pressed softly.

Oliver looked up, almost startled. Then he shook his head. "This was just a little more than a week ago, on the fifteenth of May, to be precise," he said, as if that explained the sudden awe that had come over him.

"What happened?"

"It was the middle of the day. The sky was clear and it was in the full blaze of the sunshine."

Nathan leaned forward and grabbed his shoulder. "What, Oliver?"

"Joseph and I knelt in prayer and supplication, asking the Lord what we should do concerning our own baptism for the remission of sins. On a sudden—" He stopped, turning to gaze deeply into Nathan's eyes. "On a sudden, the veil was parted, and an angel of God stood before us."

Nathan rocked back. When Joseph had first told him of heavenly visions, he had found it deeply disturbing. Once he had come to believe it, it was no longer troublesome. But he had assumed all of that was over now. The plates had been given, the translation had commenced. Now it was up to Joseph.

"That's right, Nathan," Oliver blurted out. "An angel from the presence of God. I saw him with my own eyes. His glory made the radiance of the sun pale in comparison. His raiment was white beyond any description. Can you imagine our feelings? Can you even begin to fathom the joy that pierced our hearts at that moment?"

Nathan just shook his head.

Oliver took a quick breath. "The messenger announced his name was John, the same who was called the Baptist in the New Testament."

"John the Baptist!" Nathan exclaimed.

Oliver nodded with great solemnity. "He said he was acting under the direction of Peter, James, and John, who held a higher order of priesthood. He then laid his hands on our heads. 'Upon you my fellow servants—'" Oliver's voice was suddenly husky. "Imagine that, Nathan. An angel from the presence of God and he called us his fellow servants." He shook his head, still finding it difficult to believe.

"'Upon you my fellow servants,' he said, 'in the name of

Messiah, I confer the Priesthood of Aaron, which holds the keys of the ministering of angels, and of the gospel of repentance, and of baptism by immersion for the remission of sins.' "

Oliver held out his hands, looking first at the back of them, then turning them over to stare at his palms. It was as though they had done something that was still amazing to him. "Do you understand what I'm saying, Nathan? If you had to choose one person who unquestionably had the power and authority to baptize, it would be John the Baptist, for it was to him the Savior himself went to be baptized. And now he stood before us, giving us the same power and authority, direct from heaven."

"Does that mean you can baptize?" The implications of what Oliver was saying were just now beginning to hit him.

Oliver nodded. "When the angel had finished, he instructed us to baptize each other. We were near the riverbank, and so accordingly we went into the water. Joseph baptized me. Then I baptized him. When we were finished, Joseph ordained me to the priesthood after the order of Aaron, and I turned and did the same to him.

"John told us the Aaronic Priesthood did not carry the authority to confer the gift of the Holy Ghost. That comes with the priesthood of Melchizedek. But he promised that that authority would shortly be restored as well."

Nathan got to his feet, his mind swirling like some of the eddies in the river before them. The rational side of him was shaking its head. Angels appearing forth in broad daylight? John the Baptist—beheaded after Salome cunningly manipulated Herod—coming back to earth, laying hands on mere mortals? It was enough to cause one to reel. But then Nathan focused inward, searching his heart. These were the same thoughts he had had when Joseph had first told him of his experiences. Only when he had turned to look inside himself had he come to feel an inward burning which told him it was true. He had learned to trust that feeling, and as he searched now, he felt it again.

Oliver seemed to sense what was happening, and was content to sit back now. He took the last of the branch, now completely stripped of leaves, and flipped it into the water. It turned slowly for a moment, then picked up speed in the current, crossed the path of the moon's reflection, and disappeared.

Nathan finally looked up.

"Well?" Oliver said quietly.

"I would like to be baptized for the remission of my sins," Nathan said slowly. "Will you baptize me?"

For a moment, Oliver was silent. Then a smile stole slowly across his face. "After Joseph and I told Samuel what I have told you, and after he became convinced it was of the Lord, he asked the same question you just did. I baptized Samuel the next day."

He reached out and laid a hand on Nathan's arm. "We'll talk to Joseph first thing in the morning."

Lydia McBride smiled as she walked along Tremont Street, the eastern boundary of Boston Common. It was one of those days in mid-June for which Boston was famous. For two weeks heavy overcast had left the days hot and sticky. But this morning had dawned bright and clear with a sharp breeze off the sea that kept the temperature cool and delightful.

She loved this part of Boston. Virtually every step carried her across history's doorstep. To her left was Boston Common, America's oldest public park. William Blackstone had built a house in the early 1600s not far from where she now walked. In 1634 the Bostonians had set aside nearly fifty of Blackstone's acres as "common ground" for the city, using it as public pasture and for drilling the military.

Ahead of her, clearly in sight now, was Beacon Hill, so named for the tallow pots set on its summit to warn the city of danger. The craggy summit had been leveled considerably to make way for the new State House which now dominated the hill. Designed by Charles Bulfinch, America's first important native architect, it had been completed in 1798, just before the turn of the century.

In a moment she would pass the white steepled Park Street Church, also known as "Brimstone Corner" because it had been used as a storage depot for munitions during the War of 1812. Just beyond she could already see the trees of the Granary Burying Ground, final resting place for such notables as Paul Revere and John Hancock and Benjamin Franklin's parents.

And so it was everywhere in Boston. A block or two from where she walked was the site of the Boston Massacre. Further east was the wharf where cases of English tea had been thrown into the water in Boston's own version of a "tea party."

She tipped her head back, drinking in deeply of the air. A thousand smells spilled out of the shops that lined the narrow streets and mingled in a potpourri of tantalizing fragrances. She stopped for a moment, trying to identify specific scents. There was the tang of lye from a soap maker; the tallowy aroma of candle wax; a quick, delicious scent of baking rolls, gone almost as quickly as it had come; leather from the cobbler shops; spices from India and China and a hundred other ports of call. And through it all, she could smell the salty air of the sea and the gamey aroma of the docks, a smell which some of the fastidious Bostonians found repelling, but which she loved.

A draft wagon with iron-tired wheels rattled past, the clatter reverberating off the buildings and echoing down the narrow passages. With a little shiver of regret, she clasped her parasol and started walking again. She would miss it. She would miss Boston when she returned home. It had been a long ten months and she had missed Nathan fiercely, but it had also been a wonderful time. It left her filled with sadness to realize it was soon coming to an end. Then a sudden thought popped into her head. Perhaps someday, once the farm was established and the children were older, Nathan would bring her back.

The thought cheered her considerably, and when she finally walked up the steps and entered the front door of her aunt's house, she was singing softly to herself.

"Lydia, is that you?"

"Yes, Aunt Althea. I'm back."

Her aunt appeared at the top of the stairs. She was holding two letters in her hand.

Lydia felt her heart leap. "Is the mail for me?"

"Yes. There's a letter from your father and . . ." She didn't bother to finish.

Lydia flung her parasol into the corner, not caring that it completely missed the ebony umbrella stand there, and raced up the stairs. It had been almost two months since she had heard from Nathan, and the look on her aunt's face confirmed that her wait was at last over.

She snatched the two envelopes from her aunt's hand. "Thank you."

"Dinner will be in half an hour," she said, smiling. "Don't be late."

"I won't, Aunt Althea," Lydia replied. She glanced at the handwriting quickly, then darted into her bedroom.

Fifteen minutes later, Lydia sat motionless on her bed, the last page of Nathan's letter still in her hand, staring at the wall with unseeing eyes. She was conscious of nothing except the sudden trembling she felt in her lower lip.

Finally she forced herself to focus on the words again. There were strange words and phrases—priesthood, immersion, Mormon, remission of sins—and she didn't fully understand all she had read. But she understood with brutal clarity one thing. She looked down, her eyes finding the place instantly.

There are no longer any questions, not in my mind, not in my heart, about Joseph or the work he has been called to do. My darling Lydia, when I realized the authority to baptize was restored again to earth, I asked Joseph to baptize me, which he did Saturday last. I cannot describe the joy which now fills my heart. I no longer stand on the outside of this great work of restoration and look on with curiosity. I am an active participant and feel a burning commitment to be part of God's great work. I long for the day when you return and I can share with you these feelings which have become as precious to me as fine gold.

She threw it aside, the anger starting to smoulder inside her. In ten months of correspondence, Nathan had not said so much as one word about Joseph, and she had assumed, with considerable relief, that he had put the whole thing behind him. After that night when they had gone looking for Joshua, both had seemed reluctant to bring up the subject of Joseph again, and little else had been said. But suddenly here were three solid pages of Joseph Smith—words of passion, words of commitment, words that left her feeling shocked, betrayed, and a little bit ill.

She rubbed her eyes, trying to ease the burning in them. Churning inside, she picked up the second letter. In the first letter, Nathan's handwriting was bold, scrawled across the page in firm lines which tended to be uneven in their haste. On the other hand, her father's writing was smaller, neat and precise, as though each word were one of the items in his store and put on the shelf in its appointed place. As she opened the envelope and slipped the letter out, she saw it was only one page. The message was as clipped and brusque as was his handwriting.

Our dearest Lydia,

An item of great concern has recently come to our attention. Nathan Steed has returned to Palmyra from Pennsylvania just a few days ago. He says he has returned to help his father on the farm, but reliable sources report it is really because Joseph Smith has returned to this area.

So much for your intended's commitment to work and pay off the mortgage on the farm he is supposedly purchasing. The Smith charlatan is living in Fayette Township, about twenty miles from here, still working on his so-called translation of the gold Bible. He still has no gainful employment and lives with a family who took pity on him and his poor wife.

Nathan came in the store yesterday. I confronted him and he openly admitted he has joined Smith and his followers. I need not tell you how your mother and I feel about this. Lydia, to this point I have largely stayed out of this decision you have made, feeling you are a responsible young woman. But I can remain silent no longer. This recent turn of events only confirms our deep concerns about your choice of Nathan Steed and I must forbid you from pursuing this relationship further.

It is time you faced reality. Your Aunt Althea has asked if you could stay in Boston for another year. We too feel it is the best place for you for now. Your mother and I miss you a great deal, but we both agree there are some fine families in Boston from which a suitable husband might be found. The situation here is intolerable.

We eagerly await your response to this letter.

Love,
Papa

Lydia let the page drop to her lap. What had been smouldering anger before now burst into open flame. Nathan in Palmyra? His letter had said nothing of that. Had he wanted to soften her up first, see how she would react to the "news" of his baptism before he also told her he was following after Joseph like a skunk after hen's eggs?

Slowly, Lydia gathered up the sheets of paper from her bed. She did not read them again. She folded her father's letter and put it away, then did the same with Nathan's. She rose, looked at herself briefly in the mirror, then left the bedroom.

As she came into the kitchen, her aunt was at the big stove in the corner, stirring a pot of soup. Her fourteen-year-old cousin, Dorthea, was setting the table. Both looked up in surprise. "Dinner's not quite ready yet, Lydia," her aunt said.

"Aunt Althea?"

Something in her voice made her aunt stop and turn around fully. "What is it, dear?" Dorthea was also staring at her.

"Something has come up. I'll be leaving for home as soon as I can make the necessary arrangements."

Jessica Roundy's father had beaten her soundly for the first eight years of her life. It was not frequent, but after every heavy drinking bout he would come home in a rage and take it out first on Jessica's mother and then on her. After Jessica's birth, her mother had conceived and then aborted three other children before the final miscarriage took her life as well. That had sobered Roundy sufficiently that thereafter he brought his drinking under control and turned what little affection he was capable of toward his only living offspring. Jessica Roundy became the woman of the house—or rather, the woman of the tavern, for Clinton Roundy was a saloon keeper.

She was small, almost frail, and her shoulders were rounded, as though perpetually cowering from another blow. It was this, along with her tendency to look at the floor when she spoke, that conveyed the feeling of a shy nocturnal animal, half-startled by the light and ready to flee at the slightest sound.

She was not unattractive in her facial features, but her hair was flat and straight, and this, along with her unfailing habit of wearing a dress of simple cut and drab color, made her seem plain. Her eyes were light brown, her mouth small but pleasant.

Newcomers to Roundy's saloon, located on the main street of Independence, Jackson County, Missouri, were taken aback by the presence of this silent, doe-eyed creature serving up drinks behind the bar. Some were so foolish as to equate barmaid with bawdiness. They learned quickly enough that the locals felt a strong, fatherly protectiveness for Jessie, as they all called her. A mountain man, fresh from the high country, liquored up and hungry for the touch of any white woman, was carried out with a broken jaw and glazed eyes. Two men who worked the boats coming up from New Orleans got no further than one lewd comment before they found themselves staring down the working end of a double-barreled shotgun. Word quickly spread. Jessie Roundy was to be treated with courtesy and respect.

It had surprised no one when Jessie fell for the newcomer from New York State called Joshua Steed. Though he tended to broodiness, he was young, and cut a handsome figure. He was also, after his stunning win of three Conestoga wagons and the teams to pull them, fast becoming one of Jackson County's leading businessmen. Several women—from both sides of town—had set about to win his favors. But to everyone's surprise, Joshua largely ignored them. Women seemed of little interest to him.

Except for Jessie. He seemed drawn to her quiet shyness and her unabashed admiration of him. Even the most hardened of the patrons of Roundy's saloon began to note the change in Jessie. First it was just a touch of rouge on her cheeks. Then it was a small red ribbon to tie her hair back, or a golden brooch pinned to her dress. She began to smile more, and even looked some customers straight in the eye.

When Joshua went into partnership with Jessie's father and opened a second saloon, tongues began to wag and wagers were made that a marriage was in the offing. But if Joshua was aware of such speculation, he gave no sign, and after several months the matchmakers lost interest. But Jessie hadn't. Every time Joshua came into the saloon a look of adoration lightened her eyes, and for as long as he was there they rarely left him.

But on this particular afternoon her thoughts were on other things. Joshua had left during the last part of April to take six wagonloads of freight west to Santa Fe. It was a round trip of nearly two thousand miles, and he would not be back for another week. She was in the back room of the original tavern, in what served as part storeroom, part office, and part living quarters for her and her father. A large book lay open on her lap, and she hummed softly as her finger traced the words out one by one.

To her father's amusement and then disdain, she had announced in the middle of the previous winter that she wanted to learn to read and write. He had brushed it aside as a woman's foolishness. But Joshua had not laughed, and her father had backed down almost immediately. Joshua had even offered to pay half the costs of having the new schoolteacher —a stern, preacherlike man with a pinched face but a gentle manner—give her private tutoring. Though deeply grateful for his support, she had not accepted Joshua's offer. She had saved most of the small earnings her father gave her and she didn't want any help, not from her father, not from Joshua. Somehow it was fundamental she do this herself. She still read slowly and with hesitation, but she read, and it was still new enough that she thrilled each time she did so.

A sudden noise at the door brought her head up. For a moment she stared in disbelief, then leaped to her feet, the book hurtling to the floor. "Joshua!"

"Hello, Jessie." His clothes were covered with dust, his boots caked with mud long since dried. Even the wrinkles around his eyes showed the dirt of the trail, and his heavy beard carried a light dusting of gray. His eyes were bloodshot and filled with weariness.

She smiled joyously. "But you aren't supposed to be back yet."

"I rode ahead. The wagons are still a couple of days back."

She took a step forward, then stopped, her natural shyness holding her back. "I'm . . . it's good to see you, Joshua."

He looked past her to the desk at which she had been sitting. "Your pa said I had some mail."

Her face fell and she turned slowly. "Yes."

He stepped up beside her as she opened a drawer and pulled out the small stack of letters.

She felt her earlier elation dropping rapidly. The smell of whiskey was heavy on his breath and he swayed a little. But it was not that which hurt her. If there was one thing she was used to, it was men with liquor on their breath. What hurt was that he had felt no urgency to seek her out, that he had gone to the saloon long enough to get comfortably drunk, and most especially, that he had come looking for the mail and not for her. It hurt bad. And what hurt the most was knowing what it was in the pile of letters he was looking for.

He thumbed through them quickly, dropping them onto the desk one at a time without opening them. Jessie stepped back, her eyes locked on the two battered brown envelopes. She had placed them on the very bottom of the pile, as if the placement might delay the pain, both for him and for her.

Joshua stopped. He looked at the last two envelopes slowly, first one and then the other, holding them up to the light from the window. "When did these come?" He didn't look at her.

"They came back together. About two weeks ago."

He swung around on her, making her step back, making her hate herself for being afraid of him. "I told you to mail these almost seven months ago and you're telling me they just came back?"

"They came two weeks ago," she repeated softly.

He jabbed the envelopes in her direction, as if they were a spear he could use to intimidate her. "You never mailed them."

"I mailed them, Joshua," she said wearily. "But there weren't no one to pay the postage when they got there. Look at the note on them. It says 'Unclaimed.' "

When a letter was sent through the new and still-growing postal service, postage was not paid for by the sender, but by the recipient before the letter could be claimed. Either the letters had not gotten to the right place or no one was willing to pay the postage.

"Then you've been hiding them from me for all this time so I wouldn't write again. You never wanted me to write to her."

Her head was down, and to the casual observer it may have looked as though she was cowering before him. But that was just her way. Actually, for Jessica, she was standing her ground quite firmly. There was a wounded look in her eyes, but she shook her head. "I never wanted you to write to her," she admitted, "but I did nothing with your letters."

"Liar!" he screamed. He stepped back, breathing heavily.

She knew it was the whiskey making him mean, and she hated it. She had always hated it. What it did to her father. What it did to all men. "Look at the envelopes," she cried. "She never opened them. She sent them back to you without reading them."

She was near tears now, and it made her angry, a rare thing for Jessica Roundy. "She doesn't want to hear from you." She flung it at him, desperation and hurt making her want to wound him back.

It struck a nerve, for he blinked twice, then sat down slowly, staring at the two letters. He looked at her, then at the envelopes. He put them on the desk and smoothed them with his hand. He leaned over and peered at the writing.

Suddenly his head came up. His eyes were triumphant. "See this?" One finger jabbed at the dark lettering scrawled across the bottom of one of the envelopes. "Lookee here. It says 'No longer in Palmyra.'" He stopped and peered at it again, to be sure. Then he nodded. "That's her mother's handwriting! I've seen her write in the ledger books in the store. It's her mother who sent these back."

Jessica turned and took a shawl from the door. "I've got to go. Pa's waiting for me to take over at the other place."

"Did you hear me, Jessie? Lydia didn't send them back. It's that old witch, her mother. She never did like me."

"Yes, I hear you, Joshua." She turned and went out, not bothering to close the door behind her.

It was almost ten o'clock that night before Joshua came to the bar. His eyes were still bloodshot, but he seemed to have sobered up. He had bathed and changed into clean clothes. He had also been to the barber, for his beard was trimmed and his hair combed and shortened by an inch or two.

Jessica saw him come in, but didn't give any sign she had. He stood for a moment, answering the called greetings from the men gathered at the tables. Then he moved to the bar, shouldering a man aside so he could face her directly. "I'll have some beer."

Jessica turned and reached for the stout pewter mug she kept in a special place beneath the bar. She filled it with beer, then placed it in front of him. She wanted to search his face, to see if the anger was still there, but she couldn't bring herself to do it. She just wiped with a rag at the wet spots she had made on the counter, waiting.

"I've got a load of window glass to pick up in St. Louis next week," he said gruffly. "Have to haul it to Fort Leavenworth. Then I've got to make another run to Sante Fe. It'll be late October or early November before I'm back."

"I understand." Freight hauling was his business, and Joshua personally supervised every load of any worth. Why was he telling her all this?

"It'll be too late for much else by then."

She turned away quickly, not wanting him to see the sudden pain that wrenched at her insides. "It's what you do, Joshua." It was a deliberate attempt to thrust aside what was coming. He didn't seem to notice.

"Come spring," he said flatly, "I'll be heading east for a time."

Her head came back around slowly. Her eyes were wide. Now there was no attempt to hide the hurt, the vulnerability.

He looked away. "It's time to see my family."

She dropped the rag on the counter. "You mean it's time to see Lydia."

"It's time to see my family," he said again. And with that he took his beer and moved away to join a poker game going on at one of the tables.

Chapter Twenty

The arm was starting to throb again, and Benjamin Steed took a swallow of the tangy, cool ale. That won him a quick glance from his wife, but Mary Ann didn't say anything. She just kept folding the dress and shawl and other things into their battered old valise. It was her best dress, the one she would wear tomorrow, Sunday, when they saw Joseph Smith and his dutiful little band of followers. The thought filled Benjamin with sudden anger.

He took another deep pull from the bottle, this time slowly and deliberately. She didn't look up again, but he could tell from the sudden set to her mouth that he had made his point.

Three weeks earlier, Benjamin had given a foot-thick hickory tree one last blow with the ax, then stepped back into the clear. Or so he thought. It had not snapped cleanly, and the tree twisted, pulling sharply to the left. Matthew, standing about twenty feet behind him, had shouted a warning and Benjamin leaped away. But not quickly enough. One of the upper branches caught him across the back and knocked him sprawling against a log. In addition to being bruised and battered, his left arm was fractured between the wrist and elbow.

Much to his good fortune, it had only been a simple fracture. Compound fractures almost invariably brought on infection, blood poisoning, and gangrene, and so most doctors simply amputated the broken limb immediately and avoided the complications that followed. One-armed or one-legged men were a common sight in most parts of the country, and Benjamin knew he was fortunate not to be one of them. As it was, the doctor had simply bound the arm tight with a heavy splint and told him to wear it for five or six weeks until it healed.

Yesterday, Benjamin had finally passed the point of patience and took the splint off. It galled him deeply to have to be dependent on anyone, even Nathan, who, on the day that word reached him, quit his job with Mr. Knight and returned to the farm. That irritation had only deepened in the ensuing days as he had to watch Nathan do all but the most humiliatingly simple tasks. He had brushed aside the protests of his family. The arm was healing nicely. He would be careful. He didn't need their mothering.

That had been yesterday. During the night, he had turned in his sleep and laid on it. Now it throbbed incessantly. But there was no way he was going to put the splint back on while Mary Ann was still here to point out the folly of pride.

The front door burst open and Matthew stuck his head in. From its earlier combing his blond hair had burst loose into disarray. Now nearly eight years of age, he looked like a young gentleman, except for that one stubborn lock of hair. "Mama," he said, "Nathan's got the wagon hitched."

"We'll be right there."

As the door slammed again with a sharp crack, she turned. "Melissa, Becca. It's time." She shut the valise carefully and fastened the straps. She took a bonnet from the bed and stepped to the mirror, placing it upon her head.

Begrudgingly, Benjamin watched. She was not an especially handsome woman, not in the way the world looked at things—not anywhere near as striking as that flighty Lydia McBride whom Nathan had chosen. And yet he found himself very much taken with her, even after twenty-three years of marriage. She had an inward beauty and serenity that had, over the years, permeated her outward countenance as well. He knew every line in her face—the ones that showed when she was tired; others, around the mouth, that showed some inner sorrow; and those, like now, which gave evidence of the stubborn determination deep inside her that made her so unbendable.

Quickly he took another drink, angry that he found himself softening toward her. She finished tying the ribbon around her chin and turned, catching him watching her.

"Are you sure you're going to be all right?"

Normally she allowed no liquor in the house, especially in front of the children, and he sensed her stern disapproval. But she also knew she had pushed him into a corner already and would not dare challenge his drinking, not now at any rate.

"I'll be fine."

"We'll be home before dark tomorrow. There's some soup in the pot. Just swing it over the fire. Nathan's cut plenty of wood. The bread's in the—"

"I said I'll be fine," he snapped. "Ain't no need for you to start worryin' 'bout me at this point."

Mary Ann sighed. "Ben, we've been over that. After yesterday's rain it's too wet to do much around here. And tomorrow's Sabbath, so we wouldn't be working anyway. Nathan can start cutting the barley on Monday."

"Nathan's got his own farm now. I'll be doing my own harvesting."

Before she could answer, Melissa came down the stairs from the upper bedrooms with Becca right behind her. Both were dressed in pinafore dresses made from the same bolt of material which Mary Ann had found in the village. Melissa, now eighteen, looked so much like her oldest brother, Joshua, that it sometimes hurt Benjamin to look at her. She had her mother's gentle temperament mixed with a generous helping of Joshua's impetuousness and her father's hardheaded practicality.

Eleven-year-old Rebecca was much more like her mother in outward appearance, and had Nathan's quiet strength of will. A deep dimple on her left cheek was always startling in its abruptness when she smiled, which she did now as she saw her father watching her. Her cheeks were aglow with excitement, and she fussed nervously at the bow in her dark hair.

Since their move to Palmyra Township almost three years ago, the younger children had traveled no farther than the village. So the prospect of the twenty-mile trip to Fayette Township was as exciting to her and Matthew as going to a place like New York City or Boston. Benjamin felt a sudden prick of guilt for stubbornly opposing the trip. For the children, it was a well-deserved outing.

"Nathan's got the wagon hitched," Mary Ann said. "Melissa, you take the bag out. Becca, make sure Matthew got his and Nathan's bag in."

"Yes, Mama." They both came over. "Good-bye, Papa," Melissa said. She leaned down and kissed him on the cheek. "I hope your arm doesn't bother you too much."

"I'll be fine. You have a good time."

"Good-bye, Papa." Becca's eyes studiously avoided the bottle on the table as she kissed him.

He swatted her affectionately across the bottom. "You keep Matthew out of trouble."

"I will, Papa." She moved quickly to the door, with Melissa and the valise right behind her. As they went out, he finally looked up to his wife, who was watching him steadily.

"You could still come, you know. Nathan can drive. You can't do anything with that arm, anyway."

"Someone's got to milk the cow and feed the stock."

She nodded, a quick, weary acceptance of his petulance. "You know Nathan's got Mr. Harris's hired man to come over both tonight and in the morning. You're just going to get your arm hurting all the worse."

"There ain't nothin' in Fayette Township that interests me."

She turned and walked slowly to the door, but stopped before she opened it. Finally, she turned around to face him. "You know this is real important to me, Ben. I don't ask for much. Why are you so dead set against it?"

"Joe Smith—"

"He prefers to be called Joseph," she cut in quickly. He knew that, and knew it galled both her and Nathan when he used the shorter form. The townspeople usually added a third word, making it "Ol' Joe Smith"—which was always said in open derision.

"Joe Smith has done nothing but bring trouble to this family. First Joshua and his madness, now Nathan, running after him like he was some kind of holy king or something."

"Ben—"

But he was not going to be stopped. "And now you, leaving off like this when there's work to be done. Taking the children. Filling their heads with all kinds of spiritual mumbo jumbo." He snorted his disgust. "I won't stop you. I believe in letting people make their own way in life. But you know how I feel. You're going against my direct wishes, so don't ask me to smile and pat your cheeks, because I ain't about to do that."

He picked up the bottle and, turning his back on her, took a deep swig, ignoring the stab of pain that shot through his arm. He heard the door open, then shut again softly. He didn't bother to turn around.

Fayette Township lay south and east of Palmyra Township about twenty miles, almost midway between Cayuga and Seneca lakes. In the township, but north and west of Fayette Village, was the farm of Peter Whitmer, Sr., and his family. It was to the Whitmer cabin, a solidly built two-story structure, that Mary Ann Steed and her children came late that Saturday afternoon.

As they drove into the yard, hot, tired, and hungry after a six-hour wagon ride, Mary Ann felt her heart sink. Joseph's request that Nathan bring his mother to see him had included an invitation to stay with the Whitmers overnight. But the Whitmers had seven children. The oldest daughter had recently married and moved out, but that still left eight people at home, counting the parents. Add to that number their permanent houseguests—Joseph, Emma, and Oliver—and the Whitmer cabin had to be bursting at the rafters.

"We should have stayed in Waterloo and just come tomorrow, Nathan," she said. "They must already have more people than they have room for." Waterloo was the village about three miles back. There had been an inn there that looked comfortable and respectable, and the rates were within the amount Mary Ann had brought with her.

But before Nathan could answer, the door opened and Joseph came bounding out. "There you are," he boomed, waving. In four strides he was at the wagon. "Mrs. Steed, how pleased I am you would come." He held out his hand to help her down.

"Hello, Joseph. It is good to see you again."

He turned as Nathan jumped out of the wagon and clasped his hand. "Welcome, Nathan. And how is your father?"

Nathan shook his head. "You know Pa. He took the splint off yesterday. The doctor said two more weeks, but Pa won't hear of it."

"That's no surprise. One thing to say for Benjamin Steed, he'll not easily be beholden to any man."

"That's the truth," Mary Ann said.

Joseph laughed, then turned back to the wagon. His face instantly registered surprise. "But Nathan," he cried, "I thought you were bringing your family. All I see here are strangers."

Matthew's face fell. "I'm Matthew, Joseph, remember?"

Joseph fell back a step. "No!" he breathed. "This can't be. The Matthew Steed I knew was only this high." He held up his hand at belt level.

"He's just teasin' you," Becca said, poking her brother in the back. Matthew looked startled for a moment, then his face split into a grin which nearly cracked his cheekbones.

Joseph swung around to face Rebecca. "And this must be Melissa," Joseph said, bowing low. Her mouth dropped and for a moment Becca was perplexed. Then realizing she too was being teased, she started to giggle, ducking her head and blushing furiously.

Melissa stood up. "Hello, Joseph."

Joseph looked up at her, shaking his head. "Just look at you." Melissa colored as she took his hand and hopped down from the wagon. "You have become a lovely young woman, Melissa."

"Thank you."

Joseph swung around, grabbed Matthew, and with a flip that left him squealing had him riding piggyback across his shoulders. He glanced again at Melissa, then turned to her mother. "I think I'd better go tell Father Whitmer to lock his boys in the barn," he said solemnly. "When they see this daughter of yours, they'll be smitten speechless as pillars of salt."

If Melissa had blushed before, now her face turned bright scarlet. Nathan laughed out loud. This was Joseph. How could anyone help but like him? His unbounded joy and enthusiasm was like a tonic that cleansed the soul. It had been a little over two years since he had been at the farm helping the Steeds clear their land. And yet in no more than a few moments, the time was brushed away and he was one with them again. Matthew hugged him tightly; Becca watched him with unabashed adoration.

"Have you heard from Lydia yet?" Joseph asked Nathan.

There was a quick shake of the head, accompanied with a soft sigh. "No. I told you I wrote to her about being baptized. But I haven't heard anything back yet."

"It will be all right," Joseph said with confidence. "She's a fine woman."

"I hope so." He paused for a moment. "Where's Oliver?"

"He and Martin went down to the village to get some things."

Mary Ann looked up. "Martin Harris?"

"Yes. He's been here for a few days. But he has to go back to Palmyra after supper."

Nathan smiled. *Martin too.* This was good. It would be an evening with much to listen to.

With Matthew hanging on to his neck, Joseph put out his arms and swept Melissa and Rebecca in front of him. Motioning with his head to Nathan and his mother, he said, "Come on, I want you to say hello to Emma and meet the Whitmers."

It had been almost four months now since Oliver Cowdery had gone to Pennsylvania to meet Joseph Smith for the first time. A day or two before leaving Palmyra, he had become acquainted with a young man come to Palmyra from Fayette to do some business. A quick friendship was struck, and Oliver had told David of his intent to go to Harmony and learn for himself whether there was any truth to the account of gold plates and angelic visitations.

Oliver, in company with Joseph's brother Samuel, stayed overnight at the Whitmers on the way south, and once again Oliver spoke of Joseph. David made Oliver promise that once he arrived there, he would write and tell David what his conclusions were. Oliver had written not once but twice, telling David about the sacred record and his new calling as scribe to Joseph. The Whitmers were impressed enough that they began to pray about the matter.

Meanwhile in Harmony, problems began to get worse. Emma's father, who had softened somewhat toward Joseph and had agreed to help them while Joseph translated, had cooled again as opposition from the locals began to increase.

Joseph suggested Oliver write to his friend and see if the Whitmers could provide a place for them to live until the translation was finished. The Whitmers had agreed immediately and sent David with a wagon. And so the Whitmer family had been increased by three more adults.

"How is the translation coming?" Nathan asked eagerly as they approached the cabin.

Joseph stopped, grinning almost as boyishly as Matthew. "It's done, Nathan."

Mary Ann stepped forward and touched his arm. "Really, Joseph?"

"Yes. Completely done. Finished three weeks ago. July first, to be exact. One month to the day from when we arrived here."

"That's wonderful, Joseph," Nathan exclaimed.

"It's more than wonderful," Joseph agreed happily. "Oliver has been making another copy of the manuscript—" A quick frown darkened his features. "I've learned the foolishness of having only one copy."

Mary Ann nodded soberly, remembering Joseph's devastation at the time Martin Harris lost the only copy of their work.

Joseph instantly brightened again. "Now the task is to find a printer, but I think we may even have that problem solved."

Mary Ann felt her heart soar. "That is good news, Joseph."

He nodded, sweeping them up again. "After supper we'll read some of it for you."

Mary Ann Steed had grown up with the Bible. Some of her earliest memories were of sitting in front of the fireplace and listening to the melodious voice of her mother reading from the pages of the Old and New Testaments. She had taught her own children to read from those same pages, tracing the lines with their stubby little fingers as she read aloud to them. She loved the word of the Lord and had come to recognize the power which flowed from the Bible into her life whenever she supped from its pages.

Because of her own experience in searching for the right church, Mary Ann had not had any problems believing the story of Joseph's visitation from God. Indeed, she had felt her spirit resonate in response to the story as Nathan had recounted it. After that, she had prayed mightily to know whether Joseph spoke the truth. She felt she had received confirmation of that thrice over.

But as events with Joseph continued to unfold, other feelings began to trouble her. It was not really doubt. She still continued to pray about Joseph, about the sacred record, about his calling from God, and she still found peace each time she did so. On the other hand, she knew what people were saying about Joseph. She had listened to their gibes, felt their scorn for him. No small part of that scorn came from her own husband. And that created a sense of turmoil within her. It was as though she were standing in the midst of a violent storm. She did not question whether the place where she stood was right or not, but the winds which howled around Joseph buffeted those who chose to stand with him. She was willing to stand with him; more than that, she wanted to stand with him. But if she was going to do so, she needed something more tangible, more substantial than just subtle feelings of peace.

She fully understood what had driven Martin Harris to go to New York City and seek out the professor of ancient languages. He didn't really doubt Joseph. But when everyone around you was incessantly battering at you, trying to cut the ground out from under you, you needed some kind of anchor point, something you could sink your roots into to help you weather the storm.

Over the past several months, Mary Ann had gradually determined what the test would be, what would provide a sufficient anchor point for her faith. She had not spoken of it to anyone, not even Nathan, but that was one of the reasons why she had not backed down in the face of Benjamin's anger that morning. She had to come. This was her chance to know. Standing with Joseph would not be without its costs. She was already paying some of them—Joshua was gone, Nathan and his father were experiencing increasing strain, and a coldness had crept into her marriage which left her with an ache in her heart. She was willing—more than that, determined—to pay those costs, but she needed additional confirmation.

She loved the scriptures. She knew how she felt inside when she read the Bible. She knew why the Lord had called his words the "bread of life." And this would be her test. If this record Joseph was translating was the word of God, as he claimed it was, she would know. She had no doubt of that. It would either produce the same feelings, give her the same power, nourish her spirit in the same way as the Bible, or she would put the whole thing aside and make her peace with Benjamin.

The supper had been pleasant. The Whitmers were gracious hosts and seemed not to even notice the fact that five additional mouths had sat at their table. After supper, dishes were quickly cleared and washed and the older children sent out to play and tend the Whitmer grandchildren. Now the adults sat in a semicircle around the great stone fireplace that half filled the south wall of the cabin. There were eighteen of them in all, spread around the main room of the cabin which served as kitchen and main living room.

In addition to Nathan, Melissa, and Mary Ann, Martin Harris sat near the west window. As usual, he was impeccably dressed and looking very distinguished. Next to him was Peter Whitmer, Sr.—or Father Whitmer, as all called him—and his wife, Mary. Hardworking, filled with integrity, expecting nothing from life but that which they earned by their own labor, they were of that stock found across the face and breadth of America. Come to New York State in 1809 from a colony of German immigrants in Pennsylvania, both still spoke with a pronounced German accent.

Elizabeth Ann—at fourteen the youngest of the Whitmer children—was out with Matthew and Becca, but the older ones had stayed, and now all, save one, sat together. Four sons— Jacob, John, Christian, and Peter, Jr.—sat in a row along the east wall. Jacob and Christian sat with their wives. John and Peter, Jr., not yet married, sat next to their oldest sister, Catherine, and her husband, Hiram Page.

Mary Ann noticed that Peter, Jr.—at nineteen the youngest of the four—had sat where he could catch Melissa's eye. And Melissa, blushing at almost every turn of his head, was like a flower burst forth in the spring sunshine. All of the boys had shown considerable interest in their winsome visitor, but it was Peter, closest to Melissa in age, who had pursued that interest with vigor, and she positively basked in his attention.

Next to Hiram Page sat Oliver Cowdery. He and Martin had returned from Fayette Village shortly after the Steeds' arrival. Almost immediately Mary Ann understood why Nathan had spoken so warmly of Oliver. He was, for that time, a particularly well-educated young man, and it showed in the polish of his speech and the graciousness of his manners. And his experience as a schoolteacher showed in his open love for the children. In moments after his return, he and Joseph had the younger children rollicking in the meadow behind the cabin.

Sitting shoulder to shoulder with Oliver was David Whitmer, the fifth of the Whitmer sons. Almost the same age as Oliver and Joseph, David was more serious in nature than either of the other two. Quiet and less given to idle conversation, he was nevertheless affable and pleasant to be around. He smiled easily, had a quiet sense of humor, and, of all the children, had made the greatest effort to make the Steeds feel welcome. Now, as he spoke quietly to Oliver, Mary Ann detected a slight German twang in his speech as well, though not nearly as pronounced as the accent in his parents' speech.

The last two in the room were, of course, Joseph and Emma. Mary Ann had met Emma only once before, and then only briefly in the village. Nathan had nothing but praise for Emma, and Mary Ann had looked forward to finally getting to know her better. She had not been disappointed. Emma was a woman of quiet dignity, culture, and good manners. She was a gracious lady in every sense of the word and provided a fitting and proper wife for Joseph.

And then there was Joseph. He had sat quietly for the past several minutes, content to let the group converse with one another, pleased with the company around him. Beside him on the table sat a thick sheaf of papers. This was the copy of the manuscript which Oliver had made. She could see the lines of neat and precise handwriting on the top page. She was ready for him to begin. This was what she had come for, and while she found the conversation and the company most pleasant, she willed Joseph to begin.

Finally he stood, picking up the manuscript, and the room quieted almost instantly. Mary Ann breathed a quick, inward prayer. "O Lord, if this be thy word, help me to know it without question. Open my heart to thy feelings, Heavenly Father, I pray in Jesus' name."

Joseph was clothed in an open-necked shirt and linen breeches. His hair was still slightly tousled from his wrestling with the children, which gave him a touch of boyishness. He smiled as his blue eyes scanned the faces of those present. Mary Ann saw Emma smile up at him and nod her encouragement.

Carefully, so as not to wrinkle the foolscap, he pulled off the top two-thirds of the stack and set it on the table. He turned more pages, now one at a time, searching for the place he wanted. After a moment he found what he was looking for and set a few more pages aside. He looked up, quite sober in his demeanor. "The part I would like to read this evening takes place in the Americas shortly after the time of the Savior's crucifixion and resurrection."

The blue eyes that could be so piercing, almost looking through a person, were suddenly filled with joy. He looked directly at Mary Ann. "Of all the Book of Mormon, I particularly love this part," he said simply. As he read, his voice was deep and sonorous, and it was obvious that he was familiar with the material, for he did not stumble. But within moments,

Mary Ann forgot about Joseph's voice. She focused on the words he spoke, letting her heart open to make its own judgment.

There was mention of prophets. They had foretold of the signs which would accompany the Savior's death. Now those signs were given. A terrible storm arose across the face of the land. Thunder cracked with terrifying power. Exceedingly sharp lightnings flashed downward, setting buildings on fire. A great tempest, the likes of which had never before been seen, swept across the land, carrying people away. A terrible earthquake shook the earth, wreaking terrible destruction.

After the earthquake a thick darkness settled across the land. For three days and three nights the darkness prevailed. The people were astonished. Their prophets had warned them of these things and called on them to repent of their evil ways, but many had not listened. Now, the survivors rent the air with their cries.

Joseph stopped for a moment, and Oliver spoke quietly. "Listen carefully," he said. "I wept when we were translating this part."

Nodding, Joseph went on, reading more slowly now. The darkness lifted, the earth was finally still. A group of disciples, those who had believed and looked forward to the promised signs, gathered at a temple in a land they called Bountiful. While they were conversing one with another about the great and marvelous things which had transpired, they suddenly heard a voice, coming from the heavens.

Mary Ann felt a sudden thrill course through her body. She leaned forward, her eyes fixed on Joseph's face as he read.

" 'And it came to pass that while they were thus conversing one with another, they heard a voice, as if it came out of Heaven; and they cast their eyes round about, for they understood not the voice which they heard; and it was not a harsh voice, neither was it a loud voice; nevertheless, and notwithstanding it being a small voice, it did pierce them that did hear, to the centre, insomuch that there was no part of their frame that it did not cause to quake; yea, it did pierce them to the very soul, and did cause their hearts to burn.' "

That brought Mary Ann up sharply. In Luke's Gospel, the two disciples on the road to Emmaus had used those same words. They had walked and talked with the resurrected Christ, though they did not recognize him. After he vanished from their sight, one said to the other, "Did not our heart burn within us?" She had always loved that phrase, for it best described how she felt when she read the Bible. She felt a leap of joy. It also described how she was feeling at this very moment.

Mary Ann pulled herself back as Joseph continued.

" 'And they did look steadfastly towards Heaven, from whence the sound came; and behold, the third time they did understand the voice which they heard; and it saith unto them, Behold, my beloved Son, in whom I am well pleased, in whom I have glorified my name, hear ye him.' "

Mary Ann felt a hand slip into hers and turned to see Nathan looking at her. She suddenly realized she was crying. She squeezed his hand back. "It's all right," she murmured. "It's all right."

Joseph paused, and Mary Ann realized he and the others were all looking at her too. She brushed quickly at the corners of her eyes with the back of her hand. "Please don't stop, Joseph."

Joseph's eyes softened as he nodded and found his place again. " 'And it came to pass as they understood, they cast their eyes up again towards Heaven, and behold, they saw a man descending out of Heaven; and he was clothed in a white robe, and he came down and stood in the midst of them, and the eyes of the whole multitude were turned upon him, and they durst not open their mouths, even one to another, and wist not what it meant: for they thought it was an angel that had appeared unto them.

" 'And it came to pass that he stretched forth his hand, and spake unto the people, saying: Behold I am Jesus Christ, of which the prophets testified that should come into the world; and behold I am the light and the life of the world.' "

Oh, Benjamin! Why aren't you here now to hear this, to hear these words which set my heart aflame? How could you then deny? How could you say there is no power in all this?

The sounds of the children playing outside could be heard faintly through the open windows, and somewhere further away a meadowlark was giving his last song of twilight. But within the cabin no one made a sound. Every eye was on Joseph.

Joseph's voice had dropped now but was still filled with a quiet power. " 'And it came to pass that the Lord spake unto them saying: Arise and come forth unto me, that ye may thrust your hands into my side, and also that ye may feel the prints of the nails in my hands, and in my feet, that ye may know that I am the God of Israel, and the God of the whole earth, and have been slain for the sins of the world.

" 'And it came to pass that the multitude went forth, and thrust their hands into his side, and did feel the prints of the nails in his hands and in his feet; and this they did do, going forth one by one, until they had all gone forth, and did see with their eyes, and did feel with their hands, and did know of a surety, and did bear record, that it was he, of whom it was written by the prophets that should come.

" 'And it came to pass that when they had all gone forth, and had witnessed for themselves, they did cry out with one accord, saying: Hosanna! Blessed be the name of the Most High God! And they did fall down at the feet of Jesus, and did worship him.' "

Joseph stopped, took the sheets in his hand, and put them back with the ones he had set on the table. He was gazing out of the window, his eyes seeing something far away. Finally he turned. "Martin has got to start back or it will be midnight before he gets to Palmyra. We'll read some more tomorrow."

There were murmurs of disappointment, but people began to stir themselves. As they began to talk or to go outside to check on the children, Mary Ann did not move, barely aware of what was going on around her. *Hosanna! Blessed be the name of the Most High God!* Thus had the people cried. So now did her own heart cry out. It was enough. This was the anchor she had been seeking.

She was jerked out of her thoughts when she realized that Joseph had come to stand before her and was looking down at her, smiling softly. "Well, Sister Steed," he said, "did you get it?"

Startled, both at the form of address and his question, she stood up, quickly smoothing at her apron.

"Well, did you?" he said, looking deep into her eyes.

"Did I get what?"

"The answer for which you were seeking."

She rocked back a little, stunned that he would know.

He laughed and held out his hands. She took both of them, tears suddenly welling up again. "Yes," she smiled through them. "Yes, Joseph, I did."

It had not been a good two days for Benjamin Steed. Even though he had replaced the splint on his arm right after his family left, it continued to ache abominably. He went to bed early, but slept little until he rose about midnight and downed a third of a bottle of whiskey. That had dulled the pain to the point of bearability, and he finally slept, though fitfully. But this morning he had awakened with a raging headache, and the throbbing in his arm was back.

An empty house and having to fix his own breakfast did little to improve his temper. By ten o'clock he was in the barn, puttering around awkwardly, his mood growing blacker each hour. In almost twenty-three years of marriage he and Mary Ann had had their disagreements—what man and wife didn't?—but there had always been a common bond, shared goals, unity of purpose. Now he felt that slipping away from them, and the harder he fought to halt the slide, the more it widened the gap.

From the time he was a small boy working alongside his father in the fields, he had enjoyed throwing himself against the land and wresting victory from its reluctant grasp. That he understood. When you had a problem, you lowered your shoulders, bowed your neck a little, and charged into the fray. Hard work, integrity, good old-fashioned common sense—these had always proven sufficient to win the day. But now he was up against something without form or substance. It frustrated him, and even though he knew he was driving a wedge between him and his wife, standing by and saying nothing chafed at his basic nature.

The sounds of a wagon in the yard brought his head up. For a moment he felt a quick surge of elation. Mary Ann felt bad. She had returned early. But almost immediately the irritation bubbled up again. It was time to put this thing down once and for all. He had been trying to patch a board the cow had kicked loose. He tossed the hammer aside angrily and stomped out into the yard, in a mood for battle.

He stopped, blinking in surprise. Martin Harris was just going onto the porch of the cabin.

Along with each successive wave of immigrants that came to America came the folk medicine of the Old World. Drawing liberally from the elaborate pharmacopeia of the native Indians and the secrets of African medicine men brought as slaves, the folk medicine of America was a blend of superstition, good old common sense, a touch of white magic, and, in some cases, blatant charlatanism. Butternut bark (effective only if peeled upward off the tree), slippery elm, bloodroot, jimsonweed, and pokeberry soon mixed with Old World favorites like saffron, pennyroyal, and tansy. Some of the formulas and recipes made at least marginal sense. Cholera morbus, which was rarely fatal, was treated with a combination of French brandy, lime juice, sugar, and a little hot water. Such a mixture was bound to improve one's attitude if not the sickness itself. But the shakes and typhoid fever were treated with soot from inside a chimney—

stovepipe soot was useless—mixed with sugar and cream. Juice from the woolly-headed thistle could cure even the most virulent forms of cancer, while a rival recipe prescribed white-oak ashes mixed with calomel, saltpeter, and pulverized centipede applied to the afflicted area with a piece of new, soft leather. Fried-mouse pie cured bed-wetting. Cow-dung poultices were for serious bruises. Amulets hung round the neck for at least twelve days prevented a host of general infections.

Benjamin had never put much stock in such shenanigans; in fact, he had never had to, because he was rarely ill. So when Martin brought out the bottle of herb tea prepared and sent by his wife, Benjamin looked at it suspiciously. "What's in it?" he asked.

Martin Harris shrugged. "Lucy never tells me. But it works. I had a toothache one night last year. Thought I'd go mad before morning came and I could get to the doctor. Lucy made me drink one cup of this tea and in twenty minutes the pain was all but gone. I've been a believer ever since." He laughed. "Though it takes me half a day to work up my courage to drink it."

He poured a generous measure into the cup he had gotten from the cupboard. "Come on. I know your arm must be hurtin' like the devil."

Still reluctant, Benjamin picked up the cup and sniffed at it, wincing almost instantly.

Martin laughed. "Don't think about it too long, or you'll not have the nerve to drink it. Just hold your breath and down it."

If it had been anyone else, Benjamin would have refused, but he didn't want to offend Martin. He sniffed again, then taking a quick breath, drained the cup in three great gulps. He gasped, his face contorting as the bitter liquid hit his throat, burning all the way down.

Martin laughed again. "Pretty awful, ain't it?"

Benjamin barely repressed a shudder and set the cup down. "Thank you." He managed a grin. "I think."

Martin chuckled easily. "You'll see. Won't be long and the arm will be back down to the point where you'll barely notice it."

He took the bottle of tea and the cup and carried them over to the table. "I'll leave the rest for you."

Benjamin swallowed twice, trying to clear the bitterness from his mouth. "Tell Mrs. Harris thanks for her consideration."

Martin nodded absently. He was gazing out of the window. One hand had come up, and the fingers were drumming on the tabletop. Benjamin watched him closely, sensing there was more to this visit than simply bringing medicine to an ailing neighbor. He was nervous. He had spoken too quickly, laughed a bit too loudly, and had pattered on like a woman at a corn-husking.

Turning, he came back and sat down at the table facing Benjamin. He took a quick breath, then leaned forward. "I was in Fayette yesterday, Benjamin."

Benjamin's head came up slowly.

"I had a good visit with Mrs. Steed and Nathan before I came back last night."

The heavy dark brows lowered as Benjamin stared at his neighbor. "Did Mary Ann send you?" he asked tightly.

Martin's hands shot up in protest. "No, no. She doesn't know I'm here. I did ask about your arm and she said it was bothering you some. I just thought some of Lucy's tea might help."

Benjamin sat back again, pushing down the anger that had fired almost instantly within him. Differences between a man and his wife were strictly their own affair. He would have taken it as a serious breach if Mary Ann had been talking things over with Martin. "That was right thoughtful of you," he finally said, forcing himself to relax again.

Martin nodded. Benjamin's reaction had done nothing to lessen his nervousness. His fingers picked at a thread on one of the buttons of his jacket. His eyes would meet Benjamin's momentarily, then flit away, only to dart back again to see if Benjamin was still watching him.

"Joseph's got the translation of the Book of Mormon done," he suddenly blurted.

So that was it. Benjamin winced inwardly. He was hardly in a mood for that this morning, but all he offered was a noncommittal, "Oh?"

Martin went on in a rush, obviously relieved to have finally started. "The problem now is to find a publisher." He took a breath. "At first he went to the E. B. Grandin shop here in Palmyra. Grandin prints the *Wayne Sentinel*. He's probably got the best print shop around. But Grandin refused to do it. He said Joseph had no money and no one was going to buy the book, so he wouldn't take the risk."

"Can't hardly blame him for that," Benjamin said carefully. He had no wish to offend Martin Harris, but neither was it his nature to hide what he felt. "Knowing the way people around here feel about Joseph it would be foolish to assume people will buy it."

"Oh, I think they will," Martin said eagerly. "Once they see it and find out what it is, I think everybody's going to want a copy." Then, not wanting to be sidetracked, he hurried on. "Grandin finally agreed to take the job if Joseph would put up some kind of security."

"What kind of security?" Benjamin asked slowly, finally sensing where this was leading and not liking it one bit.

"Three thousand dollars."

Benjamin stared. "Three thousand dollars!"

"Yes," Martin said glumly. "It's a lot, isn't it?"

"Look, Martin," Benjamin began, choosing his words carefully. "I've used all my savings getting this farm up and working. Even this year's crop will barely cover—"

He stopped. Now it was Martin who was staring at him. Then suddenly Martin threw back his head and laughed.

Benjamin waited, taken aback by his reaction.

Martin was shaking his head, still chuckling. Finally he

sobered. "Benjamin, did you think I was going to ask you for help?"

"Well, I—"

"I would never presume on our friendship like that. I know how you feel about Joseph."

Chagrined, but also very relieved, Benjamin shook his head. "I'm sorry, it was just the way you started. I . . ." He shrugged.

"I understand. No, Ben, what I'm going to do is take out a mortgage on my farms. I'll go to the lawyer tomorrow and draw up the papers."

The memory of Lucy Harris going from house to house asking people to hide her possessions so Martin wouldn't "steal" them from her flashed into Benjamin's mind.

Martin seemed to guess his thoughts. "I haven't told Lucy yet."

"Three thousand dollars. That's a lot of money, Martin."

He nodded soberly. "I know."

Benjamin leaned forward quickly. "Are you sure, Martin? Don't let Joseph talk you into this unless you're sure."

"I'm sure," he said evenly.

But Benjamin didn't accept that. All his frustration welled up again. "All this talk about angels!" he burst out. "It's crazy talk, Martin. And the gold plates. If he has them, why hasn't he shown them to anyone?"

The older man leaned back, absently rubbing his beard.

"I'm sorry, Martin. I know you like Joseph, but when you start talking about three thousand dollars, I've got to speak my mind."

Martin didn't seem the least upset by Benjamin's directness. "Ben, would you say I am an honest man?"

There was no hesitation. "Of course."

"A man of integrity?"

Benjamin nodded emphatically. "You know I have great respect for you, Martin. I'm just saying that giving Joseph three thousand dollars—"

Again his hand came up, cutting Benjamin off. "I understand, but it's important to me that you consider me an honest man."

"Of course I do."

He nodded thoughtfully, then stood up and began to pace back and forth in front of Benjamin, hands behind his back. "There's something I must tell you, Ben."

"What?" Benjamin was puzzled by the somberness on Martin's face.

He stopped, turning to look at Benjamin, debating. Then he nodded, half to himself, as though finally convinced by some inner voice he was hearing. "What would you say if I told you I have seen the plates?"

Benjamin leaned forward so quickly that he forgot about his arm and bumped it sharply against the table. He had to bite his lip quickly to stop from crying out.

Martin's voice lowered into an awed whisper. "What would you say if I told you *I* have seen the angel?"

"What?" Benjamin had come half up out of his chair.

Martin reached inside his jacket and withdrew a piece of foolscap, folded in thirds. He fingered it for a moment, watching Benjamin carefully. Only when Benjamin sat down again did he unfold it. He laid it on the table, smoothed it once with the palm of his hand, then turned it around and pushed it toward his friend. "This statement is going to be published in the front of the Book of Mormon."

Reeling, Benjamin continued to stare at Martin, feeling his flesh crawling a little. Then he reached for the paper and gingerly picked it up and began to read.

THE TESTIMONY OF THREE WITNESSES

Be it known unto all nations, kindreds, tongues, and people, unto whom this work shall come, that we, through the grace of God the Father, and our Lord Jesus Christ, have seen the plates which contain this record, which is a record of the people of Nephi, and also of the

Lamanites, his brethren, and also of the people of Jared, which came from the tower, of which hath been spoken; and we also know that they have been translated by the gift and power of God, for his voice hath declared it unto us; wherefore we know of a surety, that the work is true. And we also testify that we have seen the engravings which are upon the plates; and they have been shewn unto us by the power of God, and not of man. And we declare with words of soberness, that an Angel of God came down from heaven, and he brought and laid before our eyes, that we beheld and saw the plates, and the engravings thereon; and we know that it is by the grace of God the Father, and our Lord Jesus Christ, that we beheld and bear record that these things are true; and it is marvellous in our eyes: Nevertheless, the voice of the Lord commanded us that we should bear record of it; wherefore, to be obedient unto the commandments of God, we bear testimony of these things. And we know that if we are faithful in Christ, we shall rid our garments of the blood of all men, and be found spotless before the judgement seat of Christ, and shall dwell with him eternally in the heavens. And the honor be to the Father, and to the Son, and to the Holy Ghost, which is one God. Amen.

At the bottom were three signatures—Oliver Cowdery's, David Whitmer's and, in bold strokes, that of Martin Harris.

He looked up. Martin was nodding at him. Quickly he looked down and read it through again, this time more slowly.

"As Joseph neared completion of the Book of Mormon," Martin said softly when he finally finished, "he came across a passage of great interest. It said that three witnesses would be chosen and by the power of God they would see the plates and be asked to bear their testimony to the world."

His eyes were shining, and his voice was suddenly heavy with emotion. "I asked Joseph if I could be one of the witnesses.

At that point he said the Lord had not designated who they would be. I felt unworthy—after losing the manuscript—but I wanted it so badly."

He sighed deeply. "Then about a month ago now, I accompanied Father and Mother Smith to Fayette to see Joseph. The translation was nearly done, and again I asked Joseph if I could be one of the witnesses. Again Joseph said it was not his will which prevailed in these matters, but the Lord's. But then Joseph received a revelation for me, Oliver, and David Whitmer. It said that if we were faithful we could be the ones chosen to see the plates.

"A short time later, we had our usual morning worship service—we read from the scriptures, sang some hymns, and prayed. As we rose from our knees, Joseph reached out and took my hand. Speaking with a solemnity that even now sends chills up and down my back, he said, 'Martin Harris, you have got to humble yourself before God this day, that you may obtain a forgiveness of your sins. If you do, it is the will of God that you should look upon the plates, in company with Oliver Cowdery and David Whitmer.'"

Tears welled up in the older man's eyes, but he seemed unaware of them. "We went to a stand of trees not far from the cabin in which we were staying. There we knelt down and began to pray with much faith that the Lord would give us the realization of the promises he had made. We each prayed in turn, Joseph beginning, followed by the three of us in succession."

"What happened?" Benjamin asked, surprising even himself.

Martin's voice was a sound of deep pain. "Nothing."

Benjamin sat back, strangely disappointed, and yet at the same time immensely relieved. And yet—

"We began again, each praying in turn once more." Now the lines on Martin's face were etched with sorrow. "Again nothing happened. I knew what was wrong. It was me. The Lord was still displeased with me. I knew it! Deeply distressed, I stood and told the three of them to continue without me and I withdrew."

"And did they?"

"Yes."

"And?"

"I will tell you first of what happened to me."

Benjamin noted that Martin's nervousness was gone now. His hands were folded comfortably across his chest and he seemed in repose. "I went some distance away and began to importune the Lord, pleading for his forgiveness. Still nothing happened. Then on a sudden, Joseph came through the trees. He was very excited. He told me the angel had appeared to them, that he had shown the plates to Oliver and David."

"The angel?" Benjamin asked slowly.

Martin's eyes came up to meet Benjamin's. "Yes, the angel Moroni. The same that first delivered the plates to Joseph." He was shaking his head slowly. "As you can imagine, I was shattered. The thing I most longed for was to be denied me. I begged Joseph to join with me in prayer to see if we could not prevail."

Benjamin's eyes never left Martin's. His voice had dropped almost to a whisper, and Benjamin leaned forward slightly to better catch his words. "We began to pray together. I pleaded with the Lord as I have never asked for anything before. Suddenly I felt something."

Martin was looking at a spot directly above Benjamin's head, as though something were there which left him transfixed. It was like hearing an unknown noise in a dark barn. Suddenly there were chills coursing up Benjamin's back.

"I looked up. There above us in the air, a light had appeared. The light was more brilliant than the morning sun in the heavens, and in that moment, my heart was filled with an inexpressible joy, for I knew I was about to receive that for which I had been longing so much." He stopped, his eyes halfclosed, his face radiant. "In the midst of the light was a heavenly being. It was the angel Moroni."

"You actually saw him?" Benjamin breathed.

Martin nodded solemnly. "He was no further than five or six feet away from me. There was a table in front of him. On it were the gold plates and other sacred articles, including the Urim and Thummim. The angel took the plates and stepped forward. He showed them to me, turning the leaves over one by one so I could distinctly see the engravings on them. The characters were just like the ones Joseph had copied for me and which I took to New York City."

"Were the plates really gold?" Benjamin breathed.

"Yes. They were about six inches by nine inches." Martin held up his hands to demonstrate. "Each plate was about the thickness of heavy parchment, and there were many of them. They were bound together like the leaves of a book, with three metal rings which passed through the back edges. As I told you before, about two-thirds of the total plates were sealed with a metal band so they could not be opened.

"Suddenly from out of the light, above and behind the angel, a voice spoke. 'These plates,' the voice proclaimed, 'have been revealed by the power of God, and they have been translated by the power of God.' Then it said that Joseph's translation of the plates was correct. The voice then commanded us to bear record of what we saw and heard."

Silence filled the room, and Martin finally sat back, watching Benjamin calmly. "You said I shouldn't risk three thousand dollars unless I am sure." He smiled, and a beatific look crossed his face. "Well, Benjamin, I am sure. You have my most fervent testimony, Ben. *I am sure!*"

Half an hour later, Benjamin still sat at the table. As he stared at the sheet of paper on the table before him, it occurred to him that the pain in his arm had subsided. *So Lucy Harris's brew did work,* he mused briefly. He would have Mary Ann find out what was in it. That was a medicine worthy of having in the home.

But almost immediately his thoughts came back to Martin Harris. He pushed at the paper, staring at the signatures. Benjamin did not know this Oliver Cowdery or David Whitmer, but he knew Martin Harris. It shook him more deeply than he could have imagined to have a respected friend and neighbor sit across the table from him and speak of seeing an angel.

Before he left, Martin had told him there was another statement of testimony that would be published in the Book of Mormon, this time signed by eight men. Martin had recounted the circumstances behind this statement more matter-of-factly and with less emotion, but with no less conviction. Not long after Martin's experience with the plates, Joseph traveled to the Palmyra area to make arrangements for printing the Book of Mormon. He was accompanied by four of the Whitmer sons— Christian, Jacob, Peter, Jr., and John—as well as Hiram Page, brother-in-law to the others. While they were staying at the Smith home, Joseph announced that the Lord was going to show the plates to eight more men—the five who had accompanied him from Fayette, plus Joseph's father and his brothers Hyrum and Samuel. They retired to the woods near their home, this time with Joseph carrying the plates concealed in a knapsack. According to Martin, for this experience there was no angel, no miraculous appearing. Joseph simply uncovered the plates and there, in the light of day, allowed the witnesses to hold them, turn over the leaves, and examine them closely. They too had drafted a statement testifying to the experience and to the reality of the plates.

"If you count Joseph, there are twelve testimonies, Benjamin," Martin had intoned. "Put them in a jury box and you could convict or acquit any man in the land." And that had shaken Benjamin nearly as deeply as Martin's account of the angel. It was one thing to explain away Joseph, but eleven others? And yet—

There was a soft knock on the door and Benjamin was spared from his thoughts. He stood, holding his arm and the heavy splint so he didn't bump it. He moved to the door and opened it, wondering if Martin might have forgotten something. But as he saw who was standing there, his jaw dropped in surprise.

"Hello, Mr. Steed."

It took him a moment to recover, and she smiled at his surprise.

"Miss Lydia," he finally managed. "But I thought you were in Boston."

"I returned by stage last night. Is Nathan home? I have to talk with him."

Chapter Twenty-two

As Nathan stepped onto the porch of the McBride home, he stopped and took quick stock of himself. He smoothed his hair back, pushing at the errant lock on the crown of his head that would never quite stay down. He lifted the bouquet of wild flowers he had picked from behind the cabin. Carefully, so as not to bump the blooms, he undid the wet rag he had wrapped around the stems, wadded it into a ball, and tossed it into the bushes. Then, with one last check of his coat and trousers, he took a quick breath and stepped to the door. He knocked sharply, eagerness lending energy to his motions.

For a moment there was silence, then from somewhere inside the house he heard a door open and close and footsteps approaching. Nathan felt his heart drop a little. It was a woman's footsteps, but they were not Lydia's and that meant only one thing. The door opened and Lydia's mother stood framed in the light from the lamp on the wall behind her.

"Hello, Mrs. McBride."

Nathan had expected coolness, but the cold hostility in the woman's face struck him like an open-handed slap. Nathan involuntarily fell back a step. "Is Lydia here?" he asked quickly, trying to regain his composure.

Her eyes met his for a moment, then with a sniff of disdain she looked at the flowers he held in front of him.

Slowly he let his hand drop to his side, feeling cheap and tarnished. "My father said Lydia is back home. She came out earlier—"

"Wait here," she snapped. She stepped back and shut the door firmly in his face.

It was almost two full minutes before the door opened and Lydia was standing inside. She was just wrapping a shawl around her shoulders. With a leap of joy Nathan stepped forward, but she was looking over her shoulder and not at him. He stopped as he heard the sound of heavy boots on the hardwood floor. In a moment her father appeared. He glanced at Nathan coldly, then turned to Lydia. She had not yet looked at Nathan. Her father laid a hand on her arm firmly. "Ten o'clock," he said gruffly. "You've had a long journey."

"Yes, Papa."

He shot Nathan another glance, then stepped back. Finally Lydia turned. She smiled at him, but it was faint and so fleeting as to leave him uncertain whether she had or not. As she stepped onto the porch beside him, Josiah McBride stuck his head out, jaw thrust forward. "Did you hear that, young man? Ten o'clock! Not one minute later."

The door shut loudly, cutting off Nathan's mumbled "Yes, sir" even before it had begun. For a moment he stared at the door. He never expected bear hugs and shoulder thumping when he came to Lydia's, but this? What was happening?

"I'm sorry, Nathan," Lydia said softly beside him. "They're angry because I'm leaving them on my first night home."

In an instant her parents were forgotten. He stepped back for a moment, drinking in the sight of her, the pain suddenly making him wince. Ten months! How had they stood it? He swept her up in his arms, crushing her to him. "Lydia, Lydia," he whispered, "is it really you?"

"Yes, Nathan," she said softly. Her arms came up to encircle him, but it was slow, hesitant. In his joy he didn't notice. He stepped back, holding out the flowers toward her.

"Why, Nathan," she said, for the first time really smiling, "how sweet of you! Thank you."

"Why didn't you tell me you were coming?" he demanded. "I would have been waiting at the livery stable when the stage came."

She looked down at the flowers, one hand brushing at the petals. "There wasn't time to write. Even my folks didn't know I was coming."

He leaned forward and kissed her softly. "Well, it's wonderful. I still can't believe it. You're here. Right here."

She kissed him back, but again it was only a halfhearted effort, and her hesitancy finally registered with him. Nathan stepped back, peering at her closely.

"Let's go somewhere, Nathan," she said, not meeting his eyes. "We have to talk."

The moon, in its last quarter, hung low in the eastern sky. Its faint light made barely a glimmer across the muddy waters of the Erie Canal. The last of the barge traffic was now tied up at the docks for the night, and the waters were still. A bat darted downward, its dark shape momentarily silhouetted against the moon. They sat on a small, grassy knoll a quarter mile east of the village. The silence now lay heavy between them, both of them retreating into their own thoughts when the confrontation had become too intense to continue. Across the water a carriage moved along parallel to the canal. The soft clatter of its wheels and the clip-clopping of the horse's hooves were muted, as though far away and hidden in mists.

The flowers lay in Lydia's lap. Nathan gave an ironic smile. Even in the semi-darkness he could see they were already starting to wilt. How appropriate! Her fingers absently picked at the blossoms, letting the petals flutter to the ground. Nathan watched her hands, loving their graceful lines and the gentleness in them, and yet also sensing the tension there, in her hands, in her.

He reached out, putting his hand over hers. She sighed, and finally turned, and he could see her eyes glistening in the faint moonlight. "Lydia," he began slowly, trying to choose his way carefully, not wanting to drive the wedge between them any deeper. And yet at the same time he was fighting a low undercurrent of anger within himself. People could be so blind, so quick to condemn. "I know how your parents feel about me and about Joseph Smith. But I'm not marrying your mother and you're not marrying Joseph."

"Aren't I, Nathan?"

"What's that supposed to mean?" It came out snappish, more sharply than he had intended. He was instantly contrite. "Lydia, I've not asked you to accept Joseph. By the same token, we can't let how your parents feel about me change how we feel about each other."

She pulled her hand away slowly. "How do we feel about each other?" she asked, her voice low and husky with emotion.

Frustrated, he shook his head. "I love you, Lydia. I've said that over and over." He leaned forward and gripped her shoulders. "I love you!" he repeated in a fierce whisper.

"Then why didn't you say anything about this obsession you have with Joseph Smith?" she burst out.

"But I did. That's why I wrote you the letter."

"*After* you had already been baptized."

"I—"

"And why did I have to learn from my parents that you had returned home to Palmyra? You didn't say one word in your letter about that. Was it because you knew I would be angry with you for leaving your work with Mr. Knight?"

He took a breath, fighting to keep the exasperation out of his voice. "I already told you. I had no plans to quit work with

Mr. Knight. I was planning to stay in Colesville until September as you and I agreed. Then Pa broke his arm. You saw him today. He can't run a farm. What was I supposed to do?"

She looked away.

"I wrote you again once I got back here," he said, pleading for her understanding. "You must have left before my letter got to Boston."

"And the fact that Joseph had come back too had absolutely nothing to do with your coming home?"

He started to shake his head, then dropped his eyes. When Joseph had announced he and Emma and Oliver were moving to Fayette, Nathan was bitterly disappointed. He had thrilled to be close enough to Joseph to hear firsthand how the work was progressing. Then word came of his father's accident. He would have come home either way, but he was elated to know he would still be close enough to see Joseph from time to time.

She pounced on his hesitancy. "See, Nathan? That's just it. What is this insane obsession you have with Joseph? Does he take priority over everything we've planned, everything we've worked for?" Her chin came up, her lips quivering. "Over us?"

"That's not fair, Lydia. I came home to help Pa."

"Do I come first before Joseph?" she asked quietly.

"Why do you keep saying Joseph?" he exclaimed. "It's not just Joseph. He has been called of God. I've had that confirmed in my soul. I'm not following after Joseph. I'm doing what God wants me to do."

She brushed it aside with an impatient shake of her head. "Do I come first or don't I?"

Nathan threw up his hands. "Do I come first before your parents?" he demanded back at her. "Your parents don't like me. They never have. Joseph is only a small part of it. It's because I'm not the son of one of the *acceptable*"—he emphasized the word with heavy sarcasm—"families of the township."

Lydia looked away quickly, but not before he saw the tears suddenly well up and spill over onto her cheeks. He moved closer, drew her to him, stroking her hair with gentleness. "I'm sorry, Lydia, but you know that's true. I'm just a dirt farmer, and that will never be good enough for your mother."

She swung around, the sudden fierceness in her startling him. "You have no idea how deeply my parents feel about Joseph Smith and this madness he has started. If you continue this insanity with Joseph and I marry you, I will be totally rejected by my parents. I will not be welcome in their home. My name will not be spoken in their presence again."

Nathan's head rolled back as though he had been struck.

She nodded, her chest rising and falling with the intensity of her emotions. As he stared at her he suddenly realized that this was not just her imagination. She was repeating an ultimatum which had already been delivered to her, probably on this very night. He shook his head, stunned by the revelation. "They wouldn't—"

Her head jerked up, eyes flashing. "They would!" Instantly her voice dropped to an agonized whisper. "They would, Nathan. They mean every word."

The breath came out of him in a long, drawn-out sound of bitterness.

"Are you ready to ask that of me? Simply so you can continue to follow after Joseph?"

"It's just a bluff, Lydia," he said lamely. "It's the only thing they can think of to hold over you."

She gave an impatient shake of her head. "Answer me, Nathan. Are you ready to ask that of me?"

"I love you, Lydia. I want to marry you."

"And I love you," she said, brushing angrily at the tears. She pulled away from his grip and stood, turning half away, staring out across the murky waters of the canal. "Don't you know that? I love you." She whirled back to face him. "But that's not the answer. I am ready to tell my parents that if they can't accept you, then they will lose me."

She looked down at him, the challenge on her face almost fiery in the darkness. "But I will not do that for Joseph, Nathan. He is a fraud. He has been deceived by some terrible, evil power. And I can't believe you have allowed him to deceive you too."

Nathan stood slowly, the pain inside him as real as though he had been struck by a broadside from a cannon. "Lydia, I . . ." He didn't know how to finish it. He felt his stomach twisting at the alternatives she was jamming at him.

"That's what it comes down to, Nathan. I am willing to choose you over my parents. Are you willing to choose me over Joseph?"

"Lydia," he cried in anguish, "it's not just Joseph, it's—"

"No, Nathan!" she flared. "Don't. Is it me or Joseph Smith, Nathan? Just answer me."

He stared at her for a moment, his mind churning. The fires of love or the fires of conversion. Which burned the brighter in him? It wasn't fair to ask that kind of question, to demand that of him. The blindness, the bigotry—it left him wanting to strike out at people like her father. His mind flashed back to that morning when he had emerged from the waters of the Susquehanna, dripping water and filled with joy and peace. What was so evil that her parents should recoil in horror?

"Is that your answer?" she finally said, in a voice that seared his soul.

"Lydia, I—" The frustration welled up in him like bile. "Those are not fair choices. What if I said I wouldn't marry you unless you left the Presbyterian church? What has that got to do with our love?"

She stepped forward. Her lips brushed his briefly and he felt the wetness of her tears against his cheek. "Good-bye, Nathan," she whispered. She turned and walked away swiftly. He stood there, too stunned to move. The night was suddenly rent by one sharp, sobbing cry torn from Lydia's breast, then she broke into a run and disappeared into the darkness.

"Good night, Mother," Melissa whispered.

"Good night, Melissa," Mary Ann smiled into the darkness. "Good Sabbath."

"Thank you. It was a good Sabbath."

"I know." Mary Ann was sitting on the edge of Melissa's bed. There was only one small window in her bedroom, and the light from the quarter moon was so faint that she could barely make out the dark shape of the bed. Matthew and Rebecca were both exhausted from the day's activity and the six-hour wagon ride home from Fayette. They had fallen asleep before their mother had fully tucked them in. Mary Ann had then slipped into Melissa's room and they had begun to talk quietly of the day's events.

"And what of the Book of Mormon, Melissa?"

She heard her daughter's breath rise and fall wearily. "I don't know, Mama," she finally said. "In some ways I was deeply stirred. The story of Jesus coming to the people was wonderful."

"Yes, it was."

"But it still seems so . . ." Her voice trailed off.

"So impossible?" her mother furnished. She moved back and sat on the bed again.

"Yes." Melissa's hand stole across the bed and touched her mother's. "Does that make you feel bad, Mama?"

That surprised Mary Ann. "Not at all, Melissa. This is something each person must come to on his or her own."

She sensed Melissa's nod and the relief. "Are you praying about it?"

"Yes, Mama."

"Then that's enough for now."

There was a long pause, then a squeeze from the hand on hers. "Thank you, Mama."

She smiled. This was so like Melissa. Being the oldest daughter in the family was never an easy thing. With two older brothers and a father who could be gruff and filled with New England stubbornness, Melissa had learned to move carefully, walking all around an issue so as to examine its implications before deciding which way to go. If Joshua had only had a small part of her caution . . .

She patted her hand, then stood up. "I love you, Melissa. You're a daughter that makes a mother proud."

"Thank you, Mama. I love you too."

She groped her way carefully to the stairs and started down. She had removed her shoes so as to move as quietly as possible. Benjamin had been in the barn when they arrived just after sundown. He had grunted a muffled greeting, passed on the message to a stunned Nathan about Lydia's visit, brushed aside Mary Ann's inquiries about his arm, and stomped back into the barn. He had not come into the cabin until a half hour ago while she was upstairs with the children. To her relief, he had immediately gone to bed, and now, as she paused to listen, she could hear his heavy breathing.

She heaved a sigh of relief. Tomorrow they would have to talk, but for tonight she wanted to savor the experiences of the day without facing Ben's skeptical barbs.

She undressed slowly, slipped on her nightdress, then knelt at the large oak chest against the far wall. She stayed there for some time, her lips barely moving. First there was a great outpouring of gratitude. It had been a joyous two days and she had gotten the confirmation she sought. But it was much broader than that. God's work was unfolding, and astonishing things were happening. It left her humbled to think of the fortuitous set of circumstances that had brought them to Palmyra just as Joseph was being directed to begin the work of restoring God's truth to the earth.

Then her thanks turned to the children. Each in turn was mentioned—Matthew, the joy of her life; Becca, so sweet and filled with fun; Melissa, steady as a rock and now a lovely young woman; Nathan, dear Nathan, who saw and believed and felt as she did. And Joshua. As they did every night, tears welled up as she pleaded with the Lord to watch over her oldest offspring, to keep him from harm and evil, to soften his heart so he would someday return and be reconciled to his father.

And then her thoughts turned to the man in the bed just behind her, and her pleading became all the more earnest. As a young girl she had once come across a puzzling reference in the Old Testament. It said a man should not plow with an ox and an ass together. She had asked her father why such a small thing would matter to God. As he often did, instead of answering her directly he took her to where the men were working on a section of turnpike. A yoke of oxen was hooked to a scraper, clearing and smoothing right-of-way. He stopped the animals long enough for her to take a close look at the yoke. He pointed out how each yoke was shaped and fitted to the particular animals who wore it so the pulling weight of both animals was evenly distributed to the load. Then he brought over the mule they used for lighter work. He made it stand beside the oxen. It stood at least two hands higher at the shoulder. He had said no more, but Mary Ann had never forgotten the lesson.

Years later, after her marriage, she was reading in the Apostle Paul's second epistle to the Corinthians. The words had leaped out at her from the page. "Be ye not unequally yoked together with unbelievers: for what fellowship hath righteousness with unrighteousness?" The lesson of so many years earlier came flooding back and it had troubled her for some time. She had finally concluded that while she and Benjamin, spiritually speaking, were not a well-matched span, they still pulled well together.

Now, in the past few months, she was no longer sure but what she and Benjamin had not become ox and mule—or mule and ox, she thought, momentarily taken with the wry question of whether she was ox or mule. But instantly she sobered. Had it come to this now? The thought frightened her, and so, as in all things that troubled her, she took it to the Lord in prayer. "O God," she supplicated, "wilt thou touch the eyes of his understanding that he may see and know for himself. And if that be not possible, if he cannot accept thy servant Joseph and the work thou hast given him to do, then wilt thou at least touch his heart so it may be softened towards the work. He is a good and gentle man, O Lord, and I seek not to bring contention and difference between us. And yet, dear Father, thou hast shown unto me these things are true—"

She stopped, suddenly realizing there had been a change in the breathing behind her. She had not spoken aloud. She had cried only in her heart, but now she felt Benjamin's wakefulness and his awareness of her presence. She offered a quick amen and slipped into bed as quietly as possible. She did not look at him. It was too dark to see anyway, but she didn't have to. There was no movement, no change in the steady breathing, but after nearly a quarter of a century of sharing the same bed she knew full well he was wide awake.

For several moments the silence stretched on, then he stirred slightly. "Is Nathan back yet?" he asked. His voice was too soft to reveal if there was any kind of emotion behind it.

"I thought I heard him ride in about half an hour ago," she answered, "but he hasn't come in."

There was no answer, and after a moment she turned onto her side to face him. "How is your arm?"

She felt him shrug in the darkness. "Martin Harris brought some kind of tea from his wife. That helps."

"Oh?" she said in surprise. "That was nice of him."

"Did you tell him to come and see me?" His voice was suddenly blunt and confrontational.

She tensed. "No."

"You didn't tell him to come tell me that ridiculous story about the angel appearing to him?"

Mary Ann turned back over and stared up at the ceiling, fighting back a deep melancholy that swept over her. "No, Benjamin, I had no idea he was coming."

"Well, he did."

"And you don't believe it?"

He snorted in derision.

"It wasn't just him, Ben," she said slowly. "Oliver Cowdery and—"

"Don't!" he snapped. "I heard it all."

356

"You think he's lying?" she said incredulously. If there was one thing Benjamin felt about Martin Harris, it was that his integrity was rock solid.

"No, not lying. I think he's been deluded. I don't know how Joseph has done it, but it's an evil thing, Mary Ann, and I want no part of it."

She couldn't repress the sorrow which rose from the depths of her soul.

"Did you know he's going to mortgage his farm and give Joseph three thousand dollars?"

"He's not giving it to Joseph," she answered wearily. "He's giving it to the printer to print the Book of Mormon. Joseph won't get one bit of that money."

"Three thousand dollars!" he repeated, as though she hadn't spoken. "It's insane."

"If you would just come and listen to Joseph, Benjamin," she began, her voice soft with its pleading, "if you would read some of the things he has translated from the gold plates . . ."

He came up on one elbow with a sharp jerk, and she could feel him glaring at her in the darkness. "You just get that out of your head, woman," he cried in a hoarse whisper.

"But you won't even try to—"

He slammed his open palm against the bed. "It's gone too far, Mary Ann. I shoulda put an end to it before now. I'll not have you and Nathan bewitched by this man like Mr. Harris has been."

"Bewitched?" she cried. "Is that your explanation for all this?"

He ignored the question. "I've put up with it till now because I've always believed a person's religion was their business, but now you're bringing the children in on it as well. Well, I won't have it destroying my family. I won't!"

She felt her heart plummet. "What are you saying, Ben?"

"There'll be no more going to Fayette, no more talk of Joseph Smith and his gold plates in this house—whether I'm present or not—and there'll be no more chasing after this deviltry. Not from you. Not from Nathan."

"And if Nathan refuses to accept that?"

"He'd better not."

"Will you slap his face too?"

There was a sharp intake of breath, and she instantly regretted having said it.

Finally he spoke, his voice thin and trembling with anger. "Nathan has his own land now. If he doesn't want to live by the rules of this house, then let him go his own way. I can't speak for him anymore."

He lay back down on his pillow. "But so help me, you are my wife. I can and will speak for you. And if you don't like it, then maybe you'd better think about moving in with Nathan."

And with that he turned his back to her, leaving her to stare upward at nothing in the darkness.

"Bring this man another beer!" Joshua hollered over his shoulder at the young man behind the bar, then he turned back to face the ferret of a man sitting across the table from him. He had never particularly liked Caleb Jackson when they had worked the docks of Palmyra together. He had been shifty, always quick to select the lightest bale or crate, and Joshua more than once had suspected him of pilfering materials from the warehouse.

But all of that was brushed aside now. Here was someone from home. And recently so. In the twenty or so months since he had left, Joshua had talked with numerous people who had been in Palmyra, but they had merely been passing through, making no more than an overnight stop as they journeyed westward along the Erie Canal. Six months earlier a family from down Canandaigua way had come to Independence, but that was twenty-some miles south of Palmyra. They had never heard of his family, and the news was pretty thin.

He leaned forward eagerly. "So, Caleb, what brings you this far west?"

Caleb was a small man with a thin face dominated by a huge misshapen nose. Joshua had always wondered if someone had broken it for him, but had never felt it his business to ask. He had clear blue eyes, but they were always moving, never quite meeting one's direct gaze. It was this characteristic which made Joshua think of him as a ferret. In Palmyra he had worn a beard, an unkempt tangle of black, but now he was clean shaven, although a day's stubble darkened his chin.

The tavern boy brought two more beers, and Caleb grabbed the nearest one and downed the top quarter in one gulp. He wiped at the residue of foam with the back of his sleeve. "I heard there's money to be made out here."

The quick furtive glance around as he spoke told Joshua as much as the answer itself. Joshua guessed that, like many other residents of Independence, Caleb Jackson was in trouble with the law somewhere. Indian Territory was close enough to provide an attractive alternative for those looking over their shoulders. Well, that was all right. There was a constable in Cincinnati whom Joshua Steed would happily avoid, for that matter.

"Hear tell you haven't done so badly," Caleb went on, his eyes quickly surveying Joshua's clothes. The shirt was obviously a manufactured one from back east, the pants well tailored, the boots made of fine leather and hand tooled.

Joshua nodded, not trying to hide his pleasure. Let them know Joshua Steed could make his own way in the world. In a way, he wished Caleb was going back and could take the word with him. "I've done all right." He paused just long enough, then asked, "So, how are things back home?"

Caleb shrugged and took another deep drink from his mug. "Same as ever. Old man Benson is still bossing the crew at the warehouse like he was a general in some highfalutin army or something. I finally had enough of his mouth and just walked away."

Meaning you were fired, Joshua thought. *And probably for drinking.* But he merely smiled sympathetically. "Did you ever get to see any of my family?" he asked casually.

Caleb nodded. "Saw your pa at Phelps's tavern a month or so ago. He broke his arm cutting down trees."

Joshua didn't respond, just waited.

"Haven't been out there, but they say he and your brother are really making quite a farm out north of town." He grinned, an evil, leering expression. "I saw your sister at a town picnic—the one just younger than you. She's getting to be a real looker."

The look in Joshua's eye wiped the grin away instantly. He shrugged, turning his attention to the beer. "That's about it."

Joshua leaned back in his chair, watching him. "Ever see that storekeeper's daughter, Lydia McBride?" he asked evenly.

Caleb's eyes lit up. "Oh, yeah! Talk about a looker. I used to go into the store just to stand and gawk at her."

"How's she doing?"

Caleb was suddenly wary. "Fine, I guess," he hedged. "I never said nothin' to her. Besides, she was in Boston for nigh on a year."

"Boston?" He felt a surge of relief. No wonder there had been no answer to his letters.

"Heard she got back again just a day or two before I left, but can't say for sure. I didn't see her."

"She have a beau yet?"

A startled look flashed across his face, then Caleb looked down, staring into what was left of his beer.

"Well, does she?" Joshua pressed. Then he laughed, as though it didn't matter. "I was thinking of going back there next spring. To see the family," he added hastily. "Thought I'd call and pay my respects to Miss Lydia if she isn't hitched by then."

Caleb finally looked up. "You mean you haven't heard?"

Joshua kept his face expressionless. "Heard what?"

"She and your brother—" He stopped as Joshua came forward, the chair legs hitting the floor with a sharp crack.

"You mean Nathan?"

"Yeah, I guess that's his name." Caleb was squirming like a rat cornered by a tomcat.

"What about them?"

The ferret's head turned this way and that, trying to avoid the skewering hardness of Joshua's face. Joshua's hand shot out and grabbed his arm, pinning it to the table and causing him to wince with pain. "What about them?" he roared. A sudden silence swept the room as several men jerked around in surprise. The boy behind the bar was wide-eyed and staring.

Caleb swallowed hard, his Adam's apple bobbing once in fright. "They're engaged to be married."

Joshua released his grip, sagging backwards. "When?"

Caleb shrugged, licking his lips. "Everybody in town was talking 'bout it. She came home from Boston to get hitched. I reckon they're probably married by now."

"Mr. Steed, I ain't sure this is such a good idea."

Joshua whirled, swinging the bottle angrily at the man standing next to him. The man easily sidestepped the blow, then had to step forward quickly to stop Joshua from falling off the step.

"You're being paid, Parson," Joshua shouted, his voice slurring heavily. "Now stand there and shut up."

He turned back to the door and battered at it with his fist. "Roundy! Blast you! Open this door."

There was a muffled sound inside, and then lamplight glowed in the window. Joshua stepped back. Suddenly some sense of decorum gripped him, and he hastily tossed the whiskey bottle aside and tugged at the bottom of his jacket. Not that it mattered. Jessie Roundy was one woman that if there was manure on your boots, it wouldn't make no never mind with her.

The door opened and Jessica Roundy stood there, clutching at the shawl around the shoulders of her nightshirt, blinking at them in dazed bewilderment. "Joshua?"

"Who is it, Jessie?" It was a muffled call. There was the crash of a chair being overturned, then Clinton Roundy stumbled out, dressed in red long johns and clutching a shotgun. He stopped, likewise staring at the men at the door. "Steed! What—do you know what time it is?"

Joshua stepped back and bowed low. "I've come to ask you for the hand of your lovely daughter in marriage."

Jessica fell back a step, her eyes wide and suddenly dazed.

"You're drunk," Roundy said in disgust, coming to the door and opening it wider.

"I'm not that drunk," Joshua protested. He stepped inside, swayed dangerously for a moment, then remembered his companion. "Parson, get yourself in here."

The man removed his hat and came inside. He looked first at Jessica, then at her father. "I'm sorry, Mr. Roundy. He got me out of bed. I tried to tell him this ought to wait until morning, but—"

"Mornin' nothin! I want to get married, and I want to do it now." Joshua swung around and groped for Jessica's hand. She was still staring at him as though she had been struck by one of his wagons.

"Look, Joshua," Roundy said, forcing a smile, "I think you'd better go on home and sleep this off. Then we'll talk about it tomorrow."

Joshua ignored him. Suddenly he seemed cold sober as he leaned forward, peering into Jessica's eyes. "I came to marry you, woman. It's now or not at all. Will you have me to be your husband?"

For several moments, the soft doe eyes of Jessica Roundy searched Joshua's face. They were filled with an infinite sadness, but finally she nodded. "Yes, Joshua, I will."

She turned to the minister. "Just give me a few minutes to get dressed."

Chapter Twenty-three

Good wood always warms you thrice."

Nathan put down the drawknife and wiped at the sweat on his brow with the back of his sleeve. It was mid-March, and there was a strong chill in the air. The sky was slate gray and lowering, and there'd be rain, if not snow, for sure by nightfall. His breath came in little puffs of white, disappearing almost as quickly as they formed. Yet in spite of the cold, Nathan was sweating.

He was sitting on the shaving horse smoothing hand-split cedar shingles. His trouser legs were covered with cedar shavings and there was a pile growing around his feet. It was not back-breaking work, but it required considerable effort, and he had quickly shed his coat.

It was his Grandpa Steed who had said it. Nathan had found the work of splitting short lengths of hickory logs into firewood hard work for a slender ten-year-old. He complained loudly that he was sweating too hard to see clearly. His grandfather's old gray head had come up slowly, the eyes frowning their disapproval. "Wood warms you thrice, boy," he had said gravely. "Once when you cut it, once when you burn it, and then the embers warm your soul."

It was so like the old man, Nathan thought with fondness. He would sit quietly, the gnarled hands looking as knotted and grained as the wood they worked, the fingers moving with slow precision as he whittled out an apple-butter scoop from a piece of oak, or shaped a wooden pail from a hollow sycamore trunk. The acorn brown eyes would lift above the wire spectacles and peer briefly at his grandson. Then would come a sentence or two that would leave Nathan pondering for days. "Wood is like a good woman," he'd say. "Treat her with love and gentleness and she'll show you her best qualities." Or once, when Nathan kept dawdling over the task of cleaning the chicken house, a task which he hated with all the passion a young boy could muster, his grandfather simply said, with the utmost gravity: "Son, if you've got to eat a toad, don't look at it too long. And if you've got to eat two toads, you'd be smart not to eat the smallest one first."

Nathan found himself chuckling at the memory of that day. It had taken him almost a week and a little help from his mother before he figured out what toads and chicken houses had in common. Still smiling, he picked up the drawknife again and reached for another shingle. Wood warms thrice. Actually this wood would warm him in another way. Once the shingles were in place, they would warm him every time the winter snows came. He shook his head, marveling at the simple but profound wisdom of his grandfather.

He looked around at the work he had accomplished in the last five or six months. The small two-room cabin now stood framed and complete except for the roof and the inside finishing work. A barn was enclosed enough to shelter stock. The well was dug and rocked in. A smokehouse also lacked only the shingles on the roof. Now that it was his cabin, his barn, his smokehouse that he was working on, he knew the deep satisfaction that came from meeting nature and shaping it to serve your needs.

"The preachers," Grandpa had once snorted in disgust, "they say God cursed Adam by making him earn his bread by the sweat of his brow. I say it was the best thing the good Lord ever did for man. To conquer and subdue the earth is the joy of man."

Now Nathan understood what he meant. To subdue meant watching the point of a plow turn over virgin earth for the first time. It meant seeing corn and squash and melons growing where only elderberry and birch had grown before. To conquer was to drive a spout into the heart of a sugar maple when the snow covered the forest floor, then boil the sap down into one of God's sweetest gifts to mankind.

But those words had more subtle meanings too. Under his grandfather's tutelage—teachings reinforced by his own father—Nathan learned that one subdued through little things as well. For example, he knew the cedar shingles he was making would not completely tolerate the square-headed nails Nathan had bought at the blacksmith's shop. As the shingles cured in the hot suns of summer, they would begin to squeeze out the nails—not all the way, just enough so each head would show about a thumbnail's width. But Nathan would not go up and hammer them down again, for come winter the roof's porcupine surface would stop the snow from slipping down the pitched shingles, thus holding nature's insulation in place and cutting down significantly on the amount of wood it would take to heat the cabin.

There were a hundred other examples. Hickory twigs tied in a bundle around a stick made a simple but efficient broom. Strips of birch bark could be woven around willows to make a fish trap. Cedar bark went into his mother's big oak chest to ward off moths and other pests. Pitch pine, or "candlewood," as it was called, made a dangerous fuel for the fireplace because it left a flammable resin in the chimney. But split the pine into thin strips and light it and one had a wonderful "candle" for moving around outside at night.

Nathan stopped, suddenly angry with himself. He knew what he was doing. He had done it many times before. He was deliberately forcing his mind to concentrate on the ordinary, on the humdrum, so it would not turn to Lydia McBride. It was a battle he had fought many times before in the last eight months. Eight months! They had spoken only three times since. Twice there had been accidental, painfully brief encounters in the village. The only satisfaction he had found in them was the pain in her eyes which told him she found no more joy in the separation than he did. A third time he had gone to her home, determined to talk it through, to find some kind of resolution. Her father had left them alone in the parlor, but only to go into the kitchen where he kept the door open and sat within easy hearing, rigid as an ice sculpture.

Dismal and without hope, Nathan had made no further attempts to see her. Instead he threw himself into the work of turning virgin land into a working farm. There was joy in that—in the mind-numbing work of clearing trees, of cutting and curing lumber, of building rock walls and cabins and outbuildings. There was joy and there was also sadness. By now she could have been carrying their first child; she could have been directing the finishing work inside the cabin or spading the patch of ground he had cleared for a garden on the south side of the cabin.

He shook his head impatiently. He thought he had dulled the pain to the point of bearability, but just an hour ago Melissa had come to see him. She and Mama had been to the village. In a dress shop they overheard two young women talking. Lydia would be returning to Boston to live with her aunt. She would be leaving around the first of May. The sharpness of the pain surprised him. It lanced through him like a needle of fire. But he knew why. Boston dashed any hopes. Boston was finality. Boston meant it was truly over.

He began to pull the drawknife with savage intensity across the shingles, making the shavings fairly fly. He worked that way for almost ten minutes, bending his mind to the task as fiercely as he bent his back to the work.

Suddenly he stopped, staring at his hands, his breath filling the air in front of him with mist. He slammed the drawknife down, startled by the vehemence he was feeling. Lydia was going to Boston and here he sat, wallowing up to his withers in self-pity. Why didn't he just take out a white hanky and wave good-bye to her from the top of some far-off hill?

With sudden determination he gathered up his tools and carried them into the barn. He came back out, picked up his coat, jammed his hat on his head, and strode across the yard, headed for the road that led south to Palmyra Village.

Mary Ann stood at the small table pushed up against the kitchen window, humming softly as she peeled potatoes for the supper stew. Outside, the day was gloomy and darkening, but she didn't mind. This was now her favorite spot in the house. The kitchen had been her husband's winter project. It was a one-level addition to the main room of the cabin, and it had expanded their living space on the main floor by almost a third. Then, with a reckless surrender to luxury—they had had their second good year with the crops—Benjamin had ordered eight glass windowpanes and enough slate to build a large sink next to the window. Just two weeks earlier he had completed the sluice from the creek which brought water to the house. Now all she had to do to get water inside the kitchen was tug on a rope and lift the sluice gate. Within moments the sink was filled. Of all the things she had missed about their home in Vermont, the running water to the kitchen had been most dearly given up.

The view was to the east, toward the road that passed their farm on its way to the village. Once the foliage came on the trees, her view would be limited, but now she could catch an occasional glimpse of any traffic moving north or south. It made her feel as though she were in touch with the outside world, a feeling which was exhilarating after four months of winter lockup.

The door opened and Benjamin stood at the entrance. He stomped his feet a couple of times, then brushed at the straw on his pants.

"Did you get finished?"

He nodded, then came in. He had been out in the icehouse, helping the men from Canandaigua unload the huge slabs of ice cut earlier in the season from the lakes that dotted the region. They had left nearly an hour before, but Ben had then taken forkful after forkful of straw from the barn and layered it carefully over the ice so it would last them through the summer.

He came to the sink and washed his hands in the pail set aside for that purpose. He looked around, then reached out and picked up one of the potatoes she had peeled and bit into it. It crunched solidly. He chewed a couple of times, seemed satisfied, and turned to the cupboard where there was a small bowl of salt. He took a pinch and sprinkled it on the potato and took another bite.

Something out on the road caught Mary Ann's eye. She leaned forward, peering out of the window. A figure was walking south, a man. For a moment she thought it was Nathan, but before she could be sure, he disappeared behind a stand of trees. She frowned slightly. Had the news of Lydia shaken him as deeply as Mary Ann feared it would?

"Anything interesting in town?"

She whirled around, startled. But her husband was reaching for another pinch of salt and seemed to be making no more than idle conversation.

She felt herself relax a little. "I told you what Melissa heard in the dress shop about Lydia McBride."

"Yes." He finished the potato and licked absently at the salt on his fingers. "Probably just as well. As long as she's in town and unmarried, he's gonna find it hard to get her out of his head."

Mary Ann sighed. It was so like him. He was right, of course. But was he really so oblivious to the hurt his son was enduring? If he made comments like these to Nathan it would not help their relationship, which since Nathan's baptism had already become strained.

He came back to her side and picked up another potato, this time a smaller one. As he bit into it he looked around. "Where are the children?"

"Remember? Mrs. Harris asked them to help her empty the mattresses and restraw them today."

"That's right." He looked around again. "Matthew and Becca go too?"

"Yes. They were excited, and Melissa said she could use their help in holding the mattress covers."

"Hmmm."

She gave him a quick look, then continued with her peeling. He finished his potato, wiped his hands on his trousers. "If I'm going to help Nathan with his planking, I've got to have a new broad ax. Maybe I'll go into town."

"Oh. You should have said something. Melissa and I could have got it for you."

He hesitated for a moment. "I might stop at the tavern for a while."

So that was it. She turned back to the potatoes, feeling a quick burst of resentment. Since his ultimatum eight months previously, Mary Ann's relationship with her husband had stabilized. She never spoke of Joseph or his work of translation. She also honored his request—demand!—that the subject never be spoken about in the house. The only time she and Nathan talked now of Joseph and the Book of Mormon was when they were at Nathan's home. She felt a quick stab of irritation. The relationship had stabilized, but only because she had given in to his wishes and sacrificed her own personal feelings. In his mind, everything was back to normal between them. But the bitterness in her was growing a little with each day. The fact that he sensed none of it, that he could go off to

drink with his friends at the tavern and boast about the good-
ness of his marriage, really galled her. And today, of all days,
her emotions were close to the surface.

As he turned to walk away, she spoke. "I saw Joseph Smith
in town today." He stopped in midstride and she could sense
him stiffen. "He said the Book of Mormon should be finished in
about a week."

He turned around slowly, his brows lowering. Suddenly her
eyes were moist and filled with pleading. "Ben, I know how you
feel. And I've honored those feelings."

He looked away, his mouth tight.

"Ben, please." She took his hand. "I'm not asking you to believe. I'm not asking that you do anything. But you always said
if I chose to join myself to one of the churches, you wouldn't be
stopping me."

"You want to join a church, I won't be stopping you," he
said evenly. "But I won't be having you part of no devil's
work."

"Ben, all I'm asking is that you let me buy a copy of the
Book of Mormon. It's—"

"No."

"Ben, I'll use what little I've been saving from—"

"I said no!" It was flat, brutal in its finality.

She stared at him for several seconds, trying to penetrate the
coldness of his eyes. But there was nothing, just an implacable
hardness that left her empty inside. She turned away. "Then I'll
not be holding supper for you." It was not a question but a flat
statement, her way of striking back.

For a long moment there was silence, then his feet scraped
on the planks of the flooring. "You have it your way," she
heard him mutter under his breath as he moved away from her,
"but I ain't bending on this."

For a moment Nathan was afraid Lydia was not in the store.
Then he saw her in the back, helping a man near the rack of
tools. At the same time, Lydia's father, behind the main coun-

ter, saw Nathan. His jaw instantly tightened and he shot Nathan a wintry look. Nathan simply smiled briefly at him, then turned away and ignored him.

As though sensing a new tension in the store, Lydia turned around. There was a quick widening of the eyes, a sudden tautness in her posture. For several seconds their eyes locked, then she murmured something to the man. He looked at her in surprise, but she was already moving toward Nathan.

"Hello, Lydia."

"Hello, Nathan. How are you?"

"I'm fine, thank you." He took a quick breath. "Is it true what I hear? About Boston?"

She looked away quickly.

"We have to talk."

"I . . . I'm working. How long will you be in town?"

If he waited, the determination driving him might melt away. He shook his head. "We've got to talk now."

Her father had come from behind the counter and was wiping his hands on his apron. "Is there something you wish to purchase, Mr. Steed? If not, my daughter is busy at the moment."

"I'll be taking your daughter out for a while, Mr. McBride." He didn't look at her father, just kept his eyes holding hers. Her mouth opened and there was a quick murmur of shock from her father.

"Lydia is working, Mr. Steed. She has a customer and I'll be thanking you to leave us alone."

"You'll be thanking me for nothing, Mr. McBride," he said evenly. He reached out and took her hand. "I'll have her back within the hour."

It was as though Nathan had slugged him in the stomach. He was staring at Nathan, his mouth working, but nothing came out. Without waiting for further confirmation, Nathan started for the door, gently pulling Lydia with him. She looked once at her father, then fell into step beside him. They paused only long enough for her to get a shawl and a hat, then they left.

A soft drizzle was starting, and Nathan moved toward an overhanging porch, but Lydia shook her head. "I don't want to stop. I don't mind the rain."

He nodded. They were walking along Canal Street, near the eastern edge of town. Nathan had left Main Street specifically to avoid meeting too many people Lydia knew. There were people moving along Canal Street, but most were not the kind of people Lydia associated with, and while they garnered more than one curious glance, they were left alone.

She smiled faintly. "I think you shocked Papa back there."

He snickered a little, without mirth. "I was trying to make a good impression."

She laughed, this time with genuine amusement, and squeezed his hand. "It's not very often I see my father totally speechless."

He squeezed her hand back, the momentary glimpse of the old Lydia cutting into him with tangible hurt. They walked on for almost another block, not speaking, neither one ready yet to face the painful questions which hung between them like a curtain, both wanting for a moment to simply bask in the joy of each other's presence.

But they couldn't walk forever, and finally Nathan cleared his throat. "So, is it true? Are you going back to Boston?"

She looked up at him, the dark brown eyes now nearly jet black in their sorrow. "I can't stand it here anymore, Nathan. I . . ." She shrugged, looking down at her feet.

"I understand."

"Do you?" she said.

He looked at her. There was no challenge in his expression, only pleading. "Yes, I do. Coming to town is agony anymore. First I'm afraid I'll see you. Then I'm afraid I won't."

"Yes. Exactly. Every day I find myself staring out of the store window, jerking up every time a man walks by." Her voice caught. "I can't. I can't take it anymore, Nathan. At least in Boston I won't be looking for you on every street corner."

"And in Boston there'll be other young men to help you forget."

Her steps slowed and she let his hand drop.

"I'm sorry, Lydia. But it's true. That's what's torturing me. You won't last a year there. Every eligible young man in Boston will be after you."

There was a fleeting, pain-filled smile. "You have a way of complimenting a girl in a most hurtful way, Nathan Steed."

He took a breath, then just shook his head.

She stopped, turning him to face her. The rain had left wet spots on her cheeks, and they looked like tears. "Nathan, I . . ." She exhaled slowly, then started again. "If it isn't going to work between us, Nathan, then the sooner we move on, the less painful it will be."

For a moment he just stared at her, not liking to hear it spoken so baldly, but finally he nodded. She was right, of course. That was why he had come.

"Lydia, I know that. I"—he took her hand and began to walk again—"I know it seems hopeless, but I've been thinking and thinking about this."

"As have I."

He nodded. "It's been eight months. I should have been over you by now, and here I am, mooning around like a bloated calf."

She smiled up at him, and now there were tears. "I don't think many girls have been told they are loved in quite that way."

"Well, I do," he burst out. "I love you like I never thought it was possible, Lydia."

"And I love you, Nathan. But that doesn't change things."

"I know that." He let out his breath in a burst of frustration. "I know that. But I can't let you go without making one last try."

"Has anything changed?" she asked, her voice soft and now tinged with an edge of bitterness.

"Yes."

She spun around.

He searched her face, trying to collect his thoughts, trying to choose his words carefully. "I understand how you feel about Joseph. I understand how your parents feel about the whole situation. I think it's tragic when people judge him without even listening to him, without even giving him a chance—"

Her mouth had tightened and she looked away. "Nathan—"

"No, let me finish. I said I understand how you feel, and I do. I'll honor and respect that. I'll not ask you to believe. I'll not ask that you change your feelings. I'll not suggest you read the Book of Mormon or listen to what Joseph's saying or attend any meetings where he is."

The pain of his own words stopped him for a moment, then he pushed on doggedly. "Ma and Pa are miles apart on this issue too, but they have agreed to not talk about it for the sake of the marriage."

"That's not an ideal situation, Nathan."

"It's better than losing you!" he exploded.

She put a hand on his arm, her eyes filled with softness. "Are you saying you would give up Joseph?"

"It's not Joseph I'm following. But if by that you mean will I stop seeing him, will I stop going to the meetings he holds"—he paused, his mouth falling—"yes, I guess that's what I'm saying."

She threw her arms around him. "Really, Nathan?"

He nodded, fighting to hide the gloom settling over him. This was costing him dearly.

"That's wonderful, Nathan." She reached up and kissed him firmly, then blushed as she saw a woman stop to stare. But she continued to hold him, her arms around his neck. "And you'll renounce your baptism?"

He had started to tip his head down to kiss her back. He stiffened. "My baptism?"

"Yes. If you renounce that, then Papa will be convinced you really have rejected Joseph."

"I'm not *rejecting* Joseph," he said slowly. "I'm just . . ."

Her hands came down from around his neck and she stepped back, the joy fading from her eyes. "You're just what?"

"You said my association with Joseph was what made your parents angry. All right, I'm willing to stop that association. But that doesn't mean I no longer believe in what he's doing."

"But, I thought—"

"Why would I renounce my baptism?"

"Nathan, it's not just your association with Joseph. It's believing in him. It's . . . it's . . ." She was groping for the right word. "It's being baptized by him. That means you're one of his followers."

"No, Lydia," he said, the anger rising. "I'm not one of *his* followers. I am following God. I am following what my heart tells me is true. When I was baptized, I didn't make any promises to Joseph. I made them with the Lord. Are you asking me to give those promises up?"

"You're just playing with words," she exclaimed.

"No, Lydia! These are not just words. What would you say if I asked you to renounce your faith?"

"My faith is not based on a charlatan!"

He turned away, shaking his head. "You're all the same. You won't listen. You won't investigate. You won't find out for yourself. Just blind rejection."

"Don't talk to me about being blind," she snapped. "I was there that night, remember? I heard Joseph. I saw the way you all looked at him, listened to every word that fell from his lips. It's sick, Nathan. How can you ask me to accept that?"

He swung around, his eyes flashing. "I'm not asking you to accept it, Lydia. That's the point. I'm not asking you to believe. I'm not asking you to accept Joseph. I'm not asking you to give up one thing you believe." Suddenly his voice dropped and he was pleading. "So why are you asking me to?"

"If you won't renounce your baptism, then you're asking me to give up my parents," she said, the anguish twisting her voice into a half whisper. "How can you say you're not asking me to give up anything?"

"I *am* willing to compromise, Lydia. I'll stop my association with Joseph so your parents won't have their reputations sullied." In spite of himself the bitterness had crept back into his voice. "But they have no right to ask more than that of me. *You* have no right to ask more than that of me."

She bit her lip, staring at her hands. "Then it comes to this again, doesn't it?" she finally whispered.

He looked away, unable to believe there was no bending in her. Finally he turned back. Her eyes were brimming with tears, her hands clenched together. He nodded slowly, his eyes flat and lifeless. "I guess it does."

Chapter Twenty-four

Jessica Roundy Steed—Mrs. Joshua Steed—let her hands run across the smoothness of her belly, feeling the roundness there. It was March twenty-sixth. If her calculations were correct, she was now five and a half months from the time of conception. She lay perfectly still, willing the life within her to move, to give some sign that everything was all right.

Jessica had never associated much with other women. Her mother had died in the midst of her third miscarriage when Jessie was eight years old. Jessie had not gone to school. She had never been inside a church. And growing up in a saloon did not make for many associations with other females, of her own age or any other. Now, for the first time, she wished it were not so. She had so many questions. When did a woman feel the first stirrings of life? How big would a baby be at this point? Was she big enough? She had heard talk of the sickness that accompanied the first months of pregnancy. She had had none of that. Was that normal? Since she had first realized she might be with child, she had watched other pregnant women with great interest. But she could only watch and guess. They seemed to be larger than she was, but maybe they were further along in the birth process. The only thing she knew for sure was there was a growing fear that something was amiss. And that left a sickness all of its own.

Joshua stepped away from the sink, razor in hand, his face still half-lathered with soap. He had been watching her in the mirror. "You all right?"

She forced a quick smile. "Yes. I was just wondering how big he is by now."

He grinned. "Probably not big enough to handle a wagon yet, but give him another three or four months."

They never spoke about it being a girl. It was part of their game, and she didn't mind playing it with him. She knew if it did turn out to be a girl, the disappointment would only be momentary, for Joshua was in love with the idea of being a father. First choice was a boy, but a girl would be loved as well.

As marriages go, Jessica was aware hers did not stand out in any particular way, but it was more than she had ever hoped for, and she was content. Joshua had not gone back east during the winter, and that meant a great deal to her. He was gone frequently with the loads heading east or west, and he still drank a lot, but it was no longer the desperation drinking which frightened her so much. He was rarely tender with her, but Jessie Roundy had not been raised on tenderness. He was not abusive, even when drunk, and that was more than many women in Independence could say about their husbands. Occasionally he treated her with a gentleness of spirit that surprised her and made her hope he might even be coming to love her.

He finished shaving, took a shirt from the wardrobe, and pulled it on over his head. He buttoned his pants, then stuffed the shirt into his trousers. Her father always did it the other way around—stuffed the shirt in his pants, then buttoned them. That was certainly the easier way. But one of the things she found peculiarly endearing about Joshua was that he was not like other men, not in big things, not in little things.

He went to the door, then turned around. "Anything you need?"

"No. I'm fine. I'll be coming over later to help count the new shipment from Kentucky."

"All right." He opened the door and was gone. She sat up, pushing the pillow back against the bed's headboard enough to look out of the window and watch him stride up the street for a few moments. Then she lay back. Without being aware of it, her hand stole up to her belly once more and began to trace the contours of the roundness there.

There was a sharp knock on the door and Nathan looked up from where he was nailing board planks down in the main floor of his cabin.

He set the hammer aside and went to the door. He opened it to find Martin Harris standing there, clutching a newspaper.

"Look at this!" He thrust the newspaper in front of Nathan's nose. No preliminaries, no handshakes, no "Hello, Nathan, how are you?" His hands were trembling slightly as he held the paper out in one hand.

Nathan took it from him, glancing at the masthead. It was the *Wayne Sentinel*. Martin's hand shot out to jab at a spot on the page. Then Nathan felt his own heart leap. There it was, in bold letters: "THE BOOK OF MORMON." He started to read.

THE BOOK OF MORMON

An account written by the hand of Mormon, upon plates, taken from the plates of Nephi. Wherefore it is an abridgment of the Record of the People of Nephi, and also of the Lamanites; written to the Lamanites,

which are a remnant of the House of
Israel; and also to Jew and Gentile;
written by way of commandment, and
also by the spirit of Prophecy and of
Revelation.

"That part's taken from the title page of the Book of Mormon," Martin said. He dropped his finger a little further down
the page. "Look here."

The bottom paragraph was short, only three lines long.

The above work, containing about
600 pages, large Duodecimo, is now
for sale, wholesale and retail, at the
Palmyra Bookstore, by
HOWARD & GRANDIN.
Palmyra, March 26, 1830.

It was yesterday's date. Nathan looked into the older man's
eyes, which were shining with excitement. "So it's finished!"

"Yes." Martin reached inside his coat and pulled out a book
he had tucked up under his arm. It was rather small, only about
five inches by seven inches, and an inch and a half thick. The
cover was of fine leather and a soft, golden brown. There was
nothing on the front or back covers, but the spine had a small
square of black near the top with gold lettering stamped into it.
It read simply, "BOOK OF MORMON."

"This is one of the very first copies."

Reverently, almost disbelieving it could really be what it was
purported to be, Nathan took it from him. Martin took the
newspaper back, watching as Nathan caressed the lettering
with his finger and rubbed the leather. He opened it slowly,
almost in awe. The first page was the title page, laid out a little
differently but containing the very words he had just been reading in the advertisement. He let his eyes skip down to where he
had left off.

Written, and sealed up, and hid up unto the LORD, that they might not be destroyed; to come forth by the gift and power of GOD, unto the interpretation thereof; sealed by the hand of Moroni, and hid up unto the LORD, to come forth in due time by the way of Gentile; the interpretation thereof by the gift of GOD.

"I can't believe it, Martin," he breathed. "I just can't believe it."

"Nor can I," the older man agreed.

Nathan's eyes dropped further on the title page.

. . . which is to shew unto the remnant of the House of Israel how great things the LORD hath done for their fathers; and that they may know the covenants of the LORD, that they are not cast off forever; and also to the convincing of the Jew and Gentile that JESUS is the CHRIST, the ETERNAL GOD, manifesting Himself unto all nations. And now if there be fault, it be the mistake of men; wherefore condemn not the things of GOD, that ye may be found spotless at the judgment seat of CHRIST.

Nathan read one phrase again, marveling. "To convince both Jew and Gentile that Jesus is the Christ." He shook his head. "I can hardly wait to read it."

"I'll bet Joseph is beside himself," Martin went on. "After all these years, it's finally completed." He laughed. "I can't wait to see him."

Nathan was thumbing through the book, pausing to note the headings. Here were words he recognized from his conversations with Joseph and the nights Joseph had read to them from the manuscript. Nephi, Jacob, Alma. He could not put aside the sense of wondrous awe that lay upon him. This was scripture. The first scripture given to man in almost two thousand years. And here it lay before him, waiting to be read, waiting to be digested.

"I'm going down there now."

Nathan finally pulled out of his thoughts. "What?"

"I'm going down to see Joseph now. He's at his parents' home. This is a great day and I wish to be with him."

There was a quick stab of pain. A week ago he had promised Lydia he would break off his association with Joseph Smith. But the offer had been flatly rejected. The void it had left in his life still gaped before him like some immense, bottomless chasm. But his compromise had been spurned. There was no longer any such commitment. He felt a leap of relief even in the midst of the pain. He untied the carpenter's apron he wore and tossed it onto a bench. "I'm coming with you, Martin."

The older man clapped him on the shoulders. "Good."

"And we'll stop in the village at the Palmyra Bookstore. I must purchase my own copy." His eyes lit up. "No!" he exclaimed. "I shall purchase three. Mother must have one too."

Martin looked puzzled. "But that's only two."

"Yes, I know. But I think I know what to do with the third copy."

"It has been a monumental work." Oliver Cowdery sat on the sofa next to Joseph, looking at Nathan. "Seven months just for the printing."

Joseph nodded soberly. "And Satan's hand has not slackened for one moment as we sought to bring it forth."

"But it is finished," Martin said fervently. "It is finished."

Martin and Nathan had arrived at the Smith home about two that afternoon and had, for a time, worked with Oliver, Joseph, Samuel, Hyrum, and Father Smith in getting some old dead wood culled from the woodlot. After a warm supper prepared by Emma and Mother Smith, they retired to the Smiths' parlor to talk. The other Smith children—Sophronia, William, Catherine, Don Carlos, and little Lucy—had also joined them. The younger ones sat on the floor to watch and listen as the adults talked. It was a warm gathering, filled with excitement and exhilaration.

Samuel Smith chuckled a little. "It was a big job for old Egbert B. Grandin. Even the big book printers in New York City usually only do one or two thousand copies."

"What do you mean old Egbert B. Grandin?" Emma chided. "He's younger than Joseph."

"I know, I know," Samuel continued. "But when Joseph wanted five thousand copies . . ." He laughed. "And him barely hung his shingle out for book printing!"

"It was a massive amount of work," Oliver said soberly. "He was right in feeling a little overwhelmed." He turned to Nathan. "Have you ever watched a printer at work, Nathan?"

"No."

"Well, of course, every letter has to be set in place by hand. One at a time."

Joseph laughed easily. "Oliver ought to know. He set some of the type himself. In fact, he was at Grandin's shop enough that he could be a printer himself now."

"Yes," Oliver agreed, "I was beginning to feel as if printer's ink was the milk on which I had been nursed. But when you think that each sheet has to be printed by hand, even with sixteen book pages on a sheet, with five thousand copies that's over a hundred and eighty thousand sheets Grandin had to print."

There were low whistles and some oohs and aahs.

"And that doesn't count the folding, trimming, stitching, and binding," Joseph added.

"No wonder it took him seven months!" Sophronia said.

"It was certainly not without it's challenges," Father Smith said.

Joseph was nodding vigorously. "That's what I said, Satan did not slack his hand."

"What do you mean?" Nathan asked.

"You haven't heard about Abner Cole?" Emma said with faint bitterness.

"No."

Joseph looked weary. "Well, after we lost the first manu-script"—several glanced quickly at Martin Harris, who dropped his head slightly, but Joseph had not looked at him, nor did he notice the reaction—"I was not willing to take any more chances. I had to return with Emma to Harmony, so I left Hyrum and Oliver in charge of the project. I instructed them to take every precaution."

"First we wrote a complete copy of the manuscript for the printer," Hyrum said. "Then each day I would take only a por-tion of the manuscript to Grandin's shop. At night I would return and pick it up again."

Mother Smith, who was in the rocking chair, leaned for-ward. Nathan had come to admire this plucky woman, barely five feet tall. She was a fierce defender of her son. "We had a chest under the bed where we kept it," she said. "The chest was just high enough that when we placed it under the bed, the whole weight of the bed rested upon it. Once we had returned the manuscript to the chest, we could sleep in peace."

Little Lucy, nine years old and named for her mother, piped up. "But remember, Peter Whitmer would stand guard too."

"Yes," Hyrum said. "We didn't take any chances."

"And still we almost had the work stopped." Joseph turned to Nathan again. "This Abner Cole publishes a small paper called the *Reflector* under the fictitious name of Obediah Dogberry."

"Oh yes," Nathan said. "I've seen it."

"Yes. Well, unbeknownst to us, Cole comes in on eve-nings and the weekend and uses Grandin's equipment. When he learned that Grandin was printing the Book of Mormon, he promised his subscribers that he would print excerpts of it in his paper and save them the cost of buying the book from us."

"One Sunday," Hyrum went on, speaking quietly now, "this was in December, both Oliver and I felt very uneasy about the project. We went into town and found Cole working like a madman on his next issue. It was not just the Book of Mormon though. Mingled with the scriptural passages, he had thrown together a parcel of the most vulgar, disgusting collection of prose you have ever laid your eyes on. It was a tremendous shock to us."

"So what did you do?"

"I told him we held a legal copyright on the book and that he was violating that copyright. We demanded that he cease."

"He absolutely refused," Oliver broke in. "He was arrogant and haughty. He believed the Book of Mormon was rubbish and planned to discredit it in this manner. He said he had permission from Grandin to use the press and that gave him right to the Book of Mormon too."

Father Smith stirred in his chair. "When Cole went right ahead and started to publish the excerpts, Hyrum and Oliver asked me what ought to be done. I thought Joseph needed to know about it, so I went to Harmony to fetch him."

Joseph smiled ruefully. "We got back on a Sunday. Father and I nearly froze to death. The weather was bitter cold. But as soon as I had recovered a little, I went to Palmyra. There was Cole working on his paper, just as on the previous Sunday when Hyrum and Oliver found him. When I saw what he was doing, I told him the book belonged to me and I forbade him from meddling with it further."

"What did he say?" Nathan asked.

Joseph seemed amused. "He threw off his coat, rolled up his sleeves, and came towards me, smacking his fists together. 'Do you want to fight, sir?' he bellowed. 'Do you want to fight? I will publish whatever I please. So if you want to fight, just come on.' "

Nathan smiled, remembering when Joseph had nearly yanked his arms out of their sockets in a stick pull.

"I told him to put his coat back on. It was cold and I told him I would not fight with him. But I told him I knew my rights and he would certainly stop printing my book or I would exercise them. 'Sir,' he bawled, 'if you think you are the best man, take off your coat and try it.' "

Joseph laughed. "He really looked quite ridiculous. I told him again I would not fight him, but I reminded him of the law, and told him I would invoke it. He finally cooled down a little and agreed to take the matter to arbitration. Of course, it was settled in my favor, and that was the end of it."

"Well, only the end of Cole's dishonesty," Oliver corrected him. "But harm had been done."

"That's right," Martin Harris broke in, speaking for the first time in several minutes. "When word spread there'd be no getting the book in the *Reflector*, a group of the townspeople got together and made a resolution that they would not purchase the book when it was completed, and also that they would try to influence all they knew to stay away from it too."

Nathan gave a weary sigh. "Yes, I heard about that. Lydia's father was one of the primary forces behind the meeting."

Mother Smith stirred. "He was also the one who influenced the Presbyterian church to bring charges against us."

"Really?" Nathan asked in surprise.

"Yes. Back before Joseph had his first vision, I, along with three of my children, had joined the Presbyterian church. We haven't been involved with them of late, of course, but we were notified this month that they were charging us with neglect of public worship."

"Yes," Martin said. "That would be Josiah McBride, all right. Well, anyway, after the town meeting, Egbert began to worry. Here he was with five thousand copies of a book nearly done and the whole town saying they were not going to buy one copy of it."

Joseph looked at Martin and smiled warmly. "By then I had returned to Harmony, so I had to come back again and try to assure Grandin he would not lose his money."

Martin was shaking his head. "Joseph also had to convince Martin Harris, faithless Martin Harris, that he wasn't going to lose his farm over this either." He looked pained. "When suddenly it looked like no one would buy the books I got worried. Remember, it was my mortgage that convinced Egbert to take the job in the first place."

"I inquired of the Lord," Joseph said softly. "He gave a special revelation to Martin."

This came as a surprise, not only to Nathan, but to some of Joseph's family as well.

Martin was obviously chagrined and yet too honest to spare himself. "The Lord told me I was not to covet my own property, that I was to be concerned about the needs of my family, but otherwise I was to impart of my property and pay the debt which I had contracted with Egbert so the work could continue."

"There were also some other wonderful things the Lord told Martin," Joseph said, pleased with Martin's obvious contrition. "Some night when there is more time, we shall read it together."

"There was one beautiful line," Martin said softly. "I have committed it to memory, for it is exactly the counsel needed most in my life."

"What does it say?" Mother Smith asked.

Martin took a quick breath, glancing around the room at them. "It says, 'Learn of me, and listen to my words; walk in the meekness of my Spirit, and you shall have peace in me.'"

There were quiet murmurs as the others considered that.

"So I talked with Egbert," Martin went on, with more assurance now. "I told him I would stand behind the project. He had no need to fear that he would lose his money. So he finally agreed to continue."

"And the Lord is pleased, Martin," Joseph said. "Very pleased."

The group lapsed into a comfortable silence for several moments, each lost in his own thoughts, then suddenly Joseph slapped his leg. "But Nathan, I have forgotten the most important thing."

"What?"

"What are you doing Tuesday next? Not this coming Tuesday, but a week from. April sixth to be precise."

Nathan shrugged. "I'll be starting into spring plowing if the weather holds. Why?"

Joseph's eyes were shining, and there was a radiant sense of excitement about him. "The Lord has made it known that we are to organize his kingdom again upon the earth."

Again he had caught several in the room completely by surprise. Samuel leaned forward eagerly. "You mean a church?"

"Yes, Samuel. The *Lord's* church."

"But—" Nathan stopped, overwhelmed. "And it's to be done on that day?"

"Yes. The Lord has specified it."

"The exact day is to be April sixth," Oliver said.

"A church," Samuel said again in awe. "We'll have a church."

Joseph smiled. "Now the Book of Mormon is finished, the Lord wants us to move on. There is a great work yet to do."

"Will it be done here, Joseph?" Nathan asked.

"No. It will be at the Whitmers' in Fayette. We have much less opposition there. Can you come? Will you come?"

Nathan looked into the blue eyes that seemed as deep as eternity. "Even as strong as you are, Joseph, I don't think you could keep me away. May I bring Mother?"

"Of course. Melissa too." He paused. "How will your father feel about it? Will he let them come?"

Nathan frowned, and once again his thoughts leaped backwards to his last meeting with Lydia. "He'd better," he finally said in a low voice. "I'm getting a little tired of people telling others what they can or cannot believe."

Chapter Twenty-five

Nathan finished shaving in the icy water of the watering trough, without benefit of mirror, then toweled himself dry and walked back inside the barn. Since the interior of the cabin was yet to be finished, Nathan had been sleeping in a pile of meadow hay he had cut, dried, and put in the barn last fall. Above his bed he had tacked a rough set of shelves where he kept most of his personal belongings. He set the straight razor and the shaving mug on one end, then turned to the other. There sat two of the books he had purchased the previous day in Palmyra. The top one had a bookmark at page 54, the spot where Nathan had stopped reading the previous night. The second one lay new and unopened as yet.

He set the top one aside and picked up the other. For a long moment he held it, staring at it vacantly, his thoughts on what he was about to do. Then, chiding himself for vacillating, he thrust it under his arm. Moving quickly now, he gathered up the other items he needed and put them into a small wooden box. There was the crow-quill pen, a small inkwell hollowed from soft stone, the bottle of butternut ink he had made three days before, a small jar of fine sand, a carefully folded sheet of wrapping paper saved from one of his mother's purchases in town, a small roll of string, and, finally, four or five sheets of writing paper.

He took a small detour as he came out of the yard and walked to the area behind the barn which served as his small lumberyard. There he found a discarded cedar shingle. It was not serviceable for the cabin, but it was smooth enough to make a good lapboard.

Since there were no furnishings inside the house, he carried his things to the front step of the cabin. The morning had dawned bright and cold. The overcast, rainy skies that had hung over the eastern United States for the past two weeks had finally moved out over the Atlantic. By afternoon the temperature would probably reach into the high forties. Now, just an hour after sunup, the air temperature was still hovering around the freezing point, but the first rays of the sun bathed the south-facing porch of the cabin with warmth, and he walked there, moving swiftly now that his mind was set.

He put his things down, poured a small quantity of ink from the bottle into the inkwell, then sat himself down. Taking the lapboard and a sheet of paper, he leaned back against the supporting post, then reached for the pen.

My dearest Lydia,

He stared at the words, momentarily stumbling at his own boldness. Did he yet dare refer to her in such endearing terms? His lips pressed into a tight line. That was how he felt. If she did not, then she would have to deal with it. Writing slowly, carefully trying the words out in his mind before he committed them to paper, he began.

I write to you with the heaviest of hearts, for I know the distance which separates us and the depths of pain I have caused you. Would to God I could somehow reach out and heal the breach that lies between us.

In a few weeks you shall leave for Boston. Though it tears at the roots of my very being to think of that day, I understand now what it is that drives you to do so. This place, this little homestead over which I labor, once filled me with joyous anticipation because I saw in my mind's eye the day when you and I would share it together as man and wife. Now, the labor is drudgery. I drive myself with ever-increasing intensity to complete the tasks, but it is only so I can keep you from my thoughts. But it is to no avail. I am filled with a dark and heavy gloominess when I realize you shall never brighten these walls with your smile.

More and more of late I am possessed of the idea I shall sell the land, perhaps to my father, and head west. It would be a great boon to mother to learn of Joshua's whereabouts and if he is safe. We have long since given up hope he will write, so perhaps it is my mission to locate him and put my mother's heart at rest.

He leaned back, letting his eyes sweep across his little domain—the barn, the smokehouse, the split-rail fences. He felt a sharp pang. It was the work of his own hands, and it was good. But . . . He dipped the pen into the inkwell. Not without Lydia. Not here.

But my purpose in writing is not to dwell further on the pain we both share. What stands between us is centered around the person of Joseph Smith. I believe Joseph is a man called of God to bring about a great work in our time. You believe he is a charlatan and fraud, the devil's own servant.

I suggest there is a way to determine which of us is correct. It was given by the Savior himself in his great Sermon on the Mount. He said, "By their fruits ye shall know them." Oh, Lydia, that is the key! The Master said a good tree brings forth good fruit, and an evil tree, evil fruit. Well, there it is. If you would truly judge Joseph, you must examine his fruits.

With this letter, I am sending you a copy of the Book of Mormon. It is the fruit of Joseph's labors. It is a way to judge for yourself whether he is what you and your parents see him to be, or what I and my mother have come to believe he is.

Near the very last of the book, on page 586, I have marked a passage for you. It was written by Moroni, the last scribe of the Book of Mormon and the man who Joseph claims came as an angel and told him of the sacred record. Moroni gives each reader of the book a personal test and promise. Here are his words:

Nathan stopped and picked up the book. He opened it to the back, found the testimonies of the three and the eight witnesses, backed up three pages, and let his eyes run down the page till he found the place which Oliver Cowdery had pointed out to him the night before. Carefully he drew a bracket in the margin. Then he began to copy the words to his paper.

"And when ye shall receive these things, I would ex-hort you that ye would ask God, the Eternal Father, in the name of Christ, if these things are not true; and if ye shall ask with a sincere heart, with real intent, having faith in Christ, and he will manifest the truth of it unto you, by the power of the Holy Ghost."

My dearest Lydia, I ask no more of you than that. Read the book and take the matter to God. Trust in his will and wisdom. I pray daily—nay, a dozen or more times each day—that he will somehow intervene in our behalf and heal the breach between us. But with faith, I shall leave all in his hands.

The other day, as I was reading in the Bible, I found a verse that expresses the deepest feelings of my heart. If you would know how I truly feel, read the words of John as found in his second epistle, first chapter, fifth verse.

> Yours, with a love beyond measure,
> Nathan Steed

He read it over again slowly, finding his loftiness of language a little surprising, even to himself. It was another evidence of the power of the emotions that drove him.

Taking the small jar of sand, Nathan sprinkled it carefully over the page. He let it sit for a moment, blotting up the ink, then tipped the paper and blew the sand away. He read through the whole thing once more. Satisfied, he folded the paper carefully, placed it inside the front cover of the book, then reached for the wrapping paper and string.

Nathan didn't want his pa to think he was sneaking behind his back, so he did not go straight to the house. He turned into the barn. It was empty. The milk cow was still tied in her stall, her tail switching lazily as she chewed her cud in a slow, contented rhythm. One look at her udder, now shriveled and half its normal size, told Nathan his father had already finished the milking. He walked through the barn and around to the toolshed. He checked the icehouse and the smokehouse, then the small chicken coop. The hens were pecking at the wheat scattered on the floor, but there was no one there.

Puzzled, Nathan stopped and turned around. Once his father came out for chores, he rarely went back in the house before he was called in to eat breakfast. And that would likely not be ready for another half hour. He lifted his eyes to scan across the fields. About a quarter of a mile away there was a movement down by the trees that lined the creek. He shaded his eyes against the rising sun. The figure of a man with a rifle under his arm was just entering the woods. *After a squirrel or maybe a raccoon*, Nathan decided. For a moment he considered going after him, then shrugged and turned and headed for the house.

"Nathan!" Matthew was at the table working arithmetic problems on a small slate board. He was up like a shot and threw himself at his brother. Nathan caught him and swung him around, nearly losing his balance. Come July, Matthew would have his ninth birthday, and he was starting to fill out rapidly now.

At the head of the stairs, Becca's head appeared. "Hi, Nathan," she called. She was still in her nightshirt, brushing at her hair.

"Hello, beautiful."

She giggled and disappeared. Mary Ann stepped out from behind the sheet that curtained off the parent's bedroom from the rest of the house. She had a stack of folded trousers and shirts. "Hello, son."

"Good mornin', Ma."

"Had breakfast yet?"

He grinned a little sheepishly. "Not yet."

"Good."

"Pa go huntin'?"

"Yes. He saw three or four pheasants down in Mr. Harris's cornfield last night." She walked to the wardrobe and began to put the clothes away. Nathan reached inside his coat and brought out the book he had hidden there. When she turned around, he was holding it out toward her.

She stopped, squinting a little, then her eyebrows shot up and her mouth opened in a silent "Oh!"

He nodded and stepped toward her. "Yes, Ma. It's done."

She took it from him and, as though she were blind, let her fingers run over the title and the fine leather work of the cover.

"What is it, Nathan?" Matthew said, arching his head to better see the front cover.

"Yes, Nathan, what is it?" Melissa was coming down the stairs, her hands behind her, tying the belt of her dress.

"It's the Book of Mormon."

"Really?" She came to stand beside her mother, who opened the book to the title page. They read it together.

Matthew eyed it suspiciously. "Does it have any pictures?"

Nathan laughed. "Nope. No pictures."

"But oh, Matthew," his mother said softly, "a book doesn't have to have pictures to be a wonderful book."

"Where did you get it?" Melissa asked.

"Mr. Harris came to the house day before yesterday to show me his. I went right into town that very day and bought it from the Grandins' bookstore."

Mary Ann opened to the middle of the book and let her eyes read quickly. She turned to another place at random and did the same. Then slowly, almost as though it were an effort, she closed the book and held it out to him.

Nathan shook his head. "This copy is yours, Ma. I bought it for you."

Her eyes softened. "How thoughtful of you!"

As she took it, Nathan drew a wrapped package from his jacket and handed it to Melissa. "Will you do me a great favor, Melissa?"

"What?"

"Will you go into the village today?" He paused, his brows pulling downward.

"For Lydia?" she asked softly.

He nodded. "If I so much as go in the store, her father will come running like a horse with a nest of hornets on its tail."

"Of course. What if she doesn't take it?"

"She'll take it." His frown deepened. "The question is, will she read it?"

His mother looked up slowly, a shadow darkening her face as well. "I can't even take mine, Nathan."

He was startled for a moment, then his jaw set. "Ma," he

said firmly, "this is my gift. Pa can't be holdin' that against you if it's a present."

She shook her head. "The night we came home from Fayette—" She looked down, noting Matthew's wide eyes following every word. She let the book drop to her side. "Matthew, we're going to need some eggs for breakfast. Go check the henhouse and the barn and gather up enough for the family."

"Ma!" he cried.

"Go on with you now," she said firmly.

"But I'm doing my 'rithmetic."

Melissa put both hands on his shoulders and turned him toward the door. "Since when are you excited about doing your arithmetic?"

With the exasperated sigh that only a child can give full justice to, he dropped his shoulders and walked to the door.

"I saw one of the hens behind the toolshed," his mother called as he pulled it open and stepped out. "Start there."

Once the door was shut she turned back to Nathan, her eyes filled with sadness. "Your father and I had a talk the night after we came back from the Whitmers. He was very angry. Mr. Harris had come earlier and told him about his experience as one of the three witnesses."

"And he didn't believe him?" Nathan burst out incredulously.

She shook her head. "He doesn't think Martin is lying. But he's convinced he's been deceived. *Deluded* is the word he used. He calls it devil's work."

"But that's crazy. He's always been so respectful of Mr. Harris," Melissa said.

"I know. When Martin told him he had seen the angel himself, it's like it snapped something in your father." She looked up at Nathan. There was no hope in her voice. "He's absolutely set against it, Nathan. He's forbidden me to talk about it. With him. With you. Last week, I . . . I specifically asked him about the Book of Mormon. He absolutely forbids it." She held out the book again toward him.

"He has no right to do that!" Nathan said hotly. "No right."

She pushed the book gently against him until he took it. "I won't sneak behind his back, Nathan. I can't keep this."

"Well, I can," Melissa said, snatching it from Nathan.

"Melissa," her mother warned, "your father will be furious."

"He hasn't told *me* I can't have it," she retorted, tossing her head. "This is what I've been waiting for. You both believe in Joseph, and I think I do too, but I want to read the book first."

"I don't think this is wise," his mother started, but Nathan raised his hand.

"He can make that decision for himself," he said, "but he has no right to make the choice for you or Melissa."

She looked away, staring out of the window. "Well, maybe the Lord will soften his heart. But until then, I am still married to him."

Nathan's jaw set and he started to say something, but Melissa gave him a quick shake of her head. In an instant, Nathan's anger left him. He stepped to his mother and took her by the shoulders. When he turned her around, her eyes were shining.

"It'll be all right, Ma, you'll see." *Yeah! Just like with Lydia.* The bitterness was like a cocklebur in his throat. He put his arms around her and pulled her to him.

They stood like that for several moments, then Nathan cleared his throat. He didn't want to add to her sorrow, but she had to know. "Ma?"

"What, son?"

"There's something else."

She stepped back. "What?"

"Joseph has been instructed to organize a church."

She stared at him for a moment, not comprehending.

"A church?" Melissa blurted.

"Yes, he's to organize the Church of Christ on the earth once again."

"Oh, Nathan," his mother breathed, "I knew it. I just felt it would come to this. That's wonderful news."

"Is it?" he blurted. "You think Pa is going to let us join it?"

She took a deep breath, then let it out slowly. She reached up and touched his cheek. "You're on your own now. You do what your heart tells you to do."

He whirled away from her, biting his lip. Finally he turned back. "It will be a week from this Tuesday, down at the Whitmers'." He looked at Melissa, then gave a short, bitter laugh. "Joseph said you and Ma are invited to come."

Melissa had missed the irony. She was thinking only of the implications. "But I'm not sure I'm ready to join his church yet," she said, troubled now.

"He's not asking you to. He just said we were invited if we wanted to be there when he organized it."

"Think of it, Nathan," his mother said softly. "The Church of Christ once again on the earth."

"Mother, you've got to be there," he said, nearly choking as a sudden pain twisted inside his chest. "You believed before I did. You've always known."

"Yes." It came out simply and without any pride. "Yes, I have. I would . . ." Her head dropped, and Nathan saw that her lower lip was suddenly trembling. "I would give anything to be there."

"Then I'm taking you," he said with determination. "Pa will just have to learn to live with it."

She shook her head slowly. "No, Nathan."

"Yes, Mama!" Melissa broke in, grabbing one of her hands. "Nathan's right. If it means that much to you, you have to go. I'll talk to Papa. I can make him understand."

She patted Melissa's hand gently. "Not on this one, you can't. Not even you, Melissa." She managed a smile. "But I want you to go, Nathan. Be there so you can tell me everything."

He started to shake his head, but she grabbed his arm, suddenly fierce. "Yes, Nathan. It's my only chance to hear of it."

Then her shoulders straightened and she smiled warmly at

the both of them. "Come on. Your father will be home from hunting and there'll be no breakfast on. That won't do. Especially not this morning."

Nathan stood stock still, watching the pain being pushed aside, watching this woman that he loved and admired so much bite down on her frustration so she didn't cry out. He stepped to her and kissed her quickly on the cheek. "Ma, I'll not be staying for breakfast."

Her head came up quickly. "Why not?"

He shook his head grimly. "I've got the flooring to put down." His eyes narrowed. "And it's best I not see Pa right now, I reckon." He reached out, touched Melissa's arm. "Thanks for taking my package in, Melissa." He spun on his heel and walked out of the door.

Benjamin Steed arrived at Nathan's cabin shortly after nine o'clock, the leather pouch which carried his carpenter tools slung over one shoulder, the broad ax over the other. As he walked into the yard, he heard the sound of hammering coming from inside the house, and nodded to himself. Martin Harris had been right. As Benjamin had gone hunting that morning for pheasants, he'd found Martin down by the creek fishing. They visited for a few moments, though there was an obvious strain between them now. But Martin had mentioned that he'd been to see Nathan the day before yesterday and found him just starting to put the planks down in the cabin. It had irked Benjamin a little to have to find that out from his neighbor instead of from his son. Planking a floor could be done by one man, but it was heavy work and two could make it go more than twice as fast as a man working alone. He understood a man's taking pride in doing his own work, but there was no shame in asking family for help.

He stepped onto the porch, stopping a moment to notice the front door. It was of fine chestnut, and Benjamin noted with satisfaction that Nathan had used shiplap joints, which meant that the vertical and horizontal boards both had a notch cut out so they fit together like a tight puzzle. Mitered joints might look all fancy, but as soon as the wood cured, they pulled apart and the door began to jam. It pleased him that Nathan had listened and learned.

The hammering had stopped now, and Benjamin suspected his son had heard his footsteps on the porch. He set the ax down, opened the door, and stepped in. Nathan was on his knees, laying down the next row of "cellar strips" to which the planks would be nailed. When he saw who it was, he straightened slowly, laying the hammer down.

"Mornin', Nathan."

"Mornin', Pa." There was a definite coolness in the air which Benjamin sensed almost immediately. Nathan could not afford glass at this early stage of being on his own and had put up oiled paper across the two front windows. The back door was open, letting in a little more light, but the cabin was half in gloom and Benjamin could not see Nathan's face clearly.

"Heard you were putting in your floor. Thought maybe you could use some help."

"Who told you that?"

"Saw Martin Harris down doing some early-morning fishing. Said he'd been here day before yesterday."

Nathan's head came up. "He tell you why he was here?"

"No." Benjamin noted the sudden tightness around his son's mouth. "Why?"

Nathan shrugged and picked up his hammer again.

Benjamin was puzzled by what seemed to be some undercurrent of resentment, but brushed it aside. "Where you got the planks? Looks like you're about ready for some more."

Nathan stood, letting the hammer hang down at his side. "Ma tell you I was over to the house this morning?"

That caught Benjamin off guard. "No. This morning?"

He nodded.

"What for?" Then a thought struck him. "You come to ask for help?"

"No." It snapped out, like a blacksmith's tongs clipping a nail head.

Benjamin unslung the tool pouch, perplexed. Something

was definitely eating at Nathan, but he had not the slightest clue what it might be.

Nathan's chin came up. "I brought Ma a Book of Mormon."

He lowered the tools carefully to the floor. "You what?"

"I brought Ma a Book of Mormon. I went into town day before yesterday and bought her one." His lip curled in disgust. "Oh, don't worry, Pa. She wouldn't take it. Said you'd already threatened her if she did."

In one moment his perplexity turned to cold anger. "It's a good thing."

Nathan stepped forward, his jaw working, his fingers clenching and unclenching. "No, Pa. It is not a good thing. It's wrong. Real wrong, Pa."

"Now, look—"

Nathan's voice had risen a step. "No, *you* look! What right do you have to tell us what we will or won't believe?"

"You believe what you want, just stay away from Joseph Smith and his devil ways."

Nathan threw up his hands, then whirled away, too angry to speak.

"You and your ma want to join some normal church, thump the Bible a little, say your prayers, that's your business. But when you start taking on with evil, then I draw the line."

Nathan spun back around, eyes blazing. "That's right. Call it evil. That makes bigotry all right, then. That's what the Christians said about the Jews before they slaughtered them by the thousands. They were Christ killers, so wipe the whole lot of them out."

Benjamin rocked back.

"And so it goes. One religion persecuting another. After all, if they're different they've got to be evil."

"I don't—"

But Nathan bored in, overriding him. "That's what I thought America was all about. No more kings telling people what to believe. No more churches persecuting other churches." He stopped, breathing hard. "Is that what Grandpa Steed gave his leg fighting for? Freedom to believe in whatever you want as long as Benjamin Steed or Josiah McBride happens to approve of it first?"

"You know that's not what I'm—"

Nathan's voice dropped to a bare whisper. "Grandpa must be real proud about now."

For one moment, Benjamin felt the same blinding rage that had exploded in him the night in the saloon when Joshua had laughed at him. The very memory hit him like a blow alongside the head, nearly taking his breath away. He stepped back, his eyes burning, his chest heaving. Nathan's eyes held his, full of condemnation, full of shame.

"I came here to help," he said in a hoarse whisper. "I don't need to stand here and take this." In one movement he reached down and grabbed his tool bag, then spun on his heel and started for the door. As he grabbed the latch, he heard a strangled sob. He stopped, his flight arrested.

"No, Pa," came the hoarse whisper from behind him. "Go. I don't want your help." There was an agonized silence for a moment, then, "I'm not proud to be your son anymore."

The tinkling of the bell echoed through the store as Melissa shut the door, stopping to peer around the room. After the brightness of the sunshine, it took a minute for her eyes to adjust. When they did, she felt her hopes fall, for there was no one in the store except Josiah McBride. He was behind the counter, his account books spread before him, a quill pen in one hand. He looked up and smiled pleasantly. "Good morning, miss."

Dropping the package to her side and moving it slightly behind her, Melissa moved slowly forward. "Good morning, Mr. McBride."

"How may we help you?" He was still smiling, and it was obvious he had not yet recognized her. She decided she would capitalize on the advantage quickly.

"Is Miss Lydia here?"

He shook his head. "No. Lydia has gone with her mother and her aunt to Canandaigua to shop."

"Oh." There was no hiding her disappointment.

"She won't be back until tomorrow night. Is there something I could help you with?"

Melissa bit her lip, considering the options quickly. She knew the importance of putting this into Lydia's hand directly, but she also knew she had been lucky to get away and come to town without a major confrontation with her father. He had come back from Nathan's, silent and withdrawn, and gone straight to the barn to work. When Melissa had approached him to ask permission to go to the village, quaking at the thought of what she would say if he asked her purpose, he had merely shrugged, brushing her away as if he hadn't heard. Another day and she might not be so fortunate.

Then Josiah McBride took the decision out of her hands. His eyes had dropped and was looking at the package she had half-hidden behind her. "Is that something for Lydia?" he asked.

Slowly she brought it around, nodding. He reached out for it. She could only withhold it from him by making a lot of explanations. Reluctantly she handed it across to him. "Yes. I was asked to deliver this directly to Miss Lydia. Could you see she gets it?"

"Of course." He smiled again. "Any message to go with it?"

Greatly relieved at his pleasant demeanor, Melissa shook her head. "No, thank you. If you will just see she gets it."

"That I will."

"Thank you."

He nodded absently, set the package down, and was back to looking at the books even as she turned around and headed for the door, pausing once to look over her shoulder.

Josiah McBride realized his eyes had strayed once again to the package sitting on the counter beside him. Something was nagging at him and he finally set the pen aside and picked it up again. It was wrapped in plain brown paper tied neatly with a string. One word—*Lydia*—was written boldly on the front. He picked it up, looking more closely at the handwriting, knowing it looked vaguely familiar. It was definitely a book. He could feel its shape, and the weight of the package confirmed it.

Suddenly he started. The girl was a Steed. That was why she had looked familiar. He peered at Lydia's name, a sick feeling coming over him. It was Nathan's handwriting. That could mean only one thing. Looking quickly around the store and seeing he was still alone, he carefully untied the string and let the wrapping paper fall away. There was a sharp intake of breath when he saw the title of the book that now lay exposed before him.

Five minutes later he refolded the letter and put it back inside the book. He had read and reread it three times, each time his lips becoming more compressed, each time his eyes growing colder. As he shut the book there was no hesitation in him. He swept up the wrapping paper and string, along with the book, and strode to the back of the store where they kept the large trash barrel. He had just emptied it that morning. With great satisfaction he slammed the book into it. Then he moved to where he had been unpacking some bolts of material from the mills of New England. He gathered up the paper wrappings which had protected them, wadded them into balls, and stepped again to the trash bin. When he was finished, he leaned over and looked inside. The book and its wrapping were now completely covered with several more inches of paper.

Satisfied, he went back to the counter and turned to his account books.

"Are you sure you told Pa supper's ready?"

Matthew looked at his older sister as though she were daft. "Yes, Melissa, I told him twice."

Mary Ann looked up. "What did he say, Matthew?"

"Nothin'. He just moved his head up and down and kept staring out the door."

Becca looked worried. "That's what he was doing when I went out to feed the chickens too, Mama."

Melissa turned to her mother. "And this afternoon, when I asked him if I could go to the village. It was like he barely heard me."

Mary Ann stood up. "You children go on and eat. I'll go talk with your father."

She took off her apron and took down a shawl from the pegs near the door. "Melissa, there's more lamb in the pot."

"Yes, Mama."

It was nearly full dark, and with the sun gone the air had turned crisp and chill. She pulled the shawl more tightly around her, dreading what was about to come. When her husband had announced after breakfast that he was going over to Nathan's to help with the flooring, she had nearly dropped the dish she was washing. But as she had grappled with how to say there might be a better day, he had got his hat and was gone. Then, no more than twenty minutes later he had come back. She had watched him from the window, stiff as an ax handle, not looking to either side, striding forward with eyes grim and mouth taut. With a sinking heart she knew her fears had been realized.

She stopped at the barn door, took a deep breath, exhaled slowly, then stepped inside. He had lit no lamp, and the interior of the barn was getting quite dark now. She stood there for a moment, letting her eyes adjust, finally making out his dark shape sitting on the workbench he used to fix the harnessing equipment. She moved slowly to his side, feeling more than seeing his eyes upon her. For several moments, she stood beside him, neither one speaking, then she reached out and put a hand on his shoulder. He did not move.

"Ben, what happened between you and Nathan?"

He stirred but said nothing.

"You've got to remember, Ben, he's still very upset over Lydia."

"He said he brought you a Book of Mormon."

His voice was empty, hollow sounding, and she felt herself tense. "Yes, but I told him I couldn't take it, not without your blessing."

"He said that."

She squeezed his shoulder a little, suddenly realizing that in spite of all the frustrations, she loved this man deeply. "I'll not be going against your will, Ben. I told you that."

He nodded in the darkness, then again the silence stretched out. Finally he straightened. "Does it mean that much to you?"

"What?"

"Joseph and the Book of Mormon?"

She felt her breath catch in her throat. "Yes," she finally whispered. "It means more to me than anything besides you and the children."

She could feel the disappointment in him, but his next words hit her like the weighted end of a hayrack in full swing.

"Then I'll not be saying anything more about it."

She stared at him, not comprehending.

"You want to read the Book of Mormon, you have my permission."

Dropping to her knees in front of him, she clasped his hands. "Do you mean that, Ben?" she cried, hot tears springing to her eyes. "Do you really mean it?"

He nodded slowly. "My feelings about Joseph haven't changed . . ." He finally turned to look at her, though his face was nothing but deep shadows in the barn's gloom. "But I'll not be making you try to accept my feelings anymore."

Mary Ann sat back on her heels, her heart soaring. Then a thought struck her, and she felt it plummet again. She took a quick breath. "Ben?"

She felt his eyes on her.

"Joseph is going to organize a church."

There was a sudden stiffness, but again he only nodded.

"A week from Tuesday, down in Fayette. He invited Nathan and Melissa and me."

"Melissa too?" It came out almost as a cry of pain.

"Melissa's not sure if she accepts it yet. And I'll not be pushing her to it. I promise you that. But Peter Whitmer will be there and I think she'd like to go." She paused, waiting for a response. When there was none, she took the final plunge. "If I were to be baptized . . . ?"

He stood, moving slowly, as though weighed down with an infinite tiredness. But he took her hand and brought her up to face him. Then, taking her by the shoulders and holding her gently, he said, "I told you, I'll not be telling you what you can and can't believe. If that's what you want, I'll not be stopping you."

With a cry of joy she threw her arms around him and buried her face against his chest. "Thank you, Ben! Oh, thank you!"

Matthew scurried out of the house on a dead run, flying off the front porch in a great leap. "Nathan, Nathan!" he shouted.

"Hello, Matthew." He stuck out his hand and pulled his little brother up onto the wagon seat beside him. Grinning from ear to ear, Matthew settled in beside him.

Nathan looked at him solemnly. "Think you can hold the team while I help Ma and the girls get their stuff loaded?"

Matthew whooped. "You bet!" He took the reins, chest puffed up, hands held high. Neither of the two animals was stirring, but Matthew cinched up on the reins a little and called, in his deepest voice, "Ho, mules!" One of the mules turned around, its ears flopping back lazily, and gave him a baleful stare.

Laughing, Nathan swung down and started for the house. As he stepped onto the porch, the door opened and his father came out, carrying his mother's case. Both stopped short. They had not seen each other for a week now, not since the morning when Ben had come to help with the flooring.

"Hello, Pa."

"Good morning, Nathan."

"I . . ." His shoulders raised and fell again. "Pa, about the other day. I'm sorry for what I said."

"It needed to be said," he said gruffly. Then quickly changing the subject, he straightened a little. "Get the floor done?"

A twinge of shame shot through Nathan. "Yes. The planks are already starting to cure. By the time they shrink up, I think it will take another board or two."

"Probably. Our floor here finally took four more boards."

Nathan dropped his eyes. "If it's all right, I thought maybe we could work together on the spring plowin'. Get yours done first, then mine."

There was a brief smile and a quick nod. Nathan felt a flood of relief. It was his father's way of saying the apology was accepted.

Melissa came out, followed by Rebecca and their mother. Both girls were dressed in new spring dresses Mary Ann had made just for this occasion, and they looked as cheerful and bright as a hillside filled with honeysuckle. Nathan gave Melissa an admiring look and a low whistle. "I think we'd better build a fence round you, keep the wolves from prowling in too close."

"Go on with you," she said, slapping at his shoulder and blushing down about three layers deep.

"And look at you, Becca," Nathan went on, still speaking with mock sobriety. "We could paint a picture of you and sell it in the stores for a double eagle or two."

Rebecca took the compliment more as her just due, smiling quickly and giving him a quick curtsy.

"And you, Ma. You sure look pretty!" Her dress wasn't new, but it was one of her two Sunday dresses. Nathan suspected the other was in her valise to wear at tomorrow's meeting. It was clear she was infused with some inner joy, and she was positively radiant this morning.

"My, my," Melissa teased. "Aren't you in the complimentary mood this morning."

They moved to the wagon. Nathan put their things at the back, then moved forward to straighten the small benches which would provide seating for them on their journey. Satisfied, he swung around in one swift move and grabbed Becca. She squealed as he swung her up.

Suddenly the mood of gaiety quieted as Mary Ann stepped up to face her husband. She started to smile, but in an instant her emotions overwhelmed her and tears sprang to her eyes. It embarrassed Benjamin and he looked away. Going up on tiptoes, she kissed him on the cheek. "Thank you, Ben," she whispered.

He nodded, then awkwardly put his arms around her as she hugged him fiercely.

"Joseph didn't say what time the meeting would be held," Nathan said, finding his own voice suddenly husky. "If it's early enough, we'll come home tomorrow night. If not, we'll leave first thing Wednesday morning."

Benjamin nodded and stepped back, letting his wife go. Nathan helped Melissa, then his mother, up into the wagon, then climbed up alongside Matthew. He took the reins. "Good-bye, Pa."

"Good-bye, son. Don't forget to rest the mules every five miles or so."

"I will." He snapped the reins sharply. "Giddyap, mules."

"Good-bye, Papa," the younger children yelled, waving vigorously.

Melissa suddenly stood, holding on to Nathan's shoulder to steady herself. "Thank you, Papa," she called. There was a moment's pause, then louder, "I love you."

Nathan's head snapped around and he looked up at his sister. His mother was also staring at her. If Melissa noted their surprise, she did not give any sign of it. Though the Steed family had strong bonds of affection, they were rarely expressed openly. Now, tears were streaming down Melissa's face as she looked back at her father. Her hand came up and she waved to him, now as eagerly as the children. "I love you, Papa!" she shouted again.

Nathan glanced backwards. His father had frozen in midstride, and he was staring at his daughter. Then one hand came up slowly. His reply was nearly lost in the creaking and rattling of the wagon, but they all heard it. "I love you too, Melissa," he called.

The first thing she noticed was the emptiness inside her belly. It puzzled her, and for several moments she tried to force her mind through the haze that clouded it. She was aware of a vague sense of alarm but could not define it clearly. Next came the awareness of the pain. It was not terrible, but it was there, steady and evenly spread across the lower part of her abdomen.

"Jessie?"

It came to her as though from a far distance. She turned her head, or thought she did. Nothing moved. She had to begin again and consciously will the neck muscles to obey her mind. Only then did her eyes bring Joshua into focus.

"She's still under heavy sedative, Mr. Steed."

The voice had a vague familiarity to it. She had heard it recently, but try as she might she couldn't quite recollect who it was or where she had heard it. But the face hovering over her was no problem to her. She had spent too many hours studying the clean features, the dark eyes and heavy brows, the full mouth that could turn down so quickly or just as easily break into a smile that softened his whole face.

"Jessie, it's me, Joshua." Then his head turned. "She's awake."

"Joshua?"

"Yes, it's me. I'm here."

"Where . . ." Her mouth felt like she had been chewing on a mouthful of milkweed pods. "What happened?"

His eyes closed momentarily, then she felt him take her hand. "It's all right, Jessie. The doctor has given you something to help ease the pain."

"Pain?" She felt a sudden panic. There *was* pain, she remembered now. And blood. She had hunched over a chair. Joshua's eyes had been wide and frightened as he had helped her to the bed, then plunged out of the door to find the doctor.

Suddenly her hand shot to her stomach. The roundness was gone. It was flat, the skin strangely flaccid. Her eyes flew open. "The baby?"

Joshua took her other hand in his. "You're all right, Jess. That's what matters." The pain in his eyes was more unbearable than that in her body. "It will be all right," he repeated dully.

As they crossed the Erie Canal, wheels rattling hollowly across the wooden slats, Melissa sat straight up, startling herself with the idea that had come into her mind. It took her aback for a moment, but almost as quickly as it came she knew it was right. She stood up. "Nathan, I just remembered. There's something I have to do in town."

He turned around. "You what?"

Her mother was equally surprised, but Melissa pretended she didn't see it. Afraid they would press her for details she couldn't give, she rushed on. "This will only take a minute. If you drive slow, I can catch up."

"It isn't something that can wait?" her mother asked. "We want to be to Fayette before dark."

"No." She had one hand on the side board and hopped lightly over it and began walking alongside the wagon. They were close to the Old Cemetery, where John Swift, one of Palmyra's first settlers, was buried. It was only a few rods to Main Street from there. "Really, Mama," she urged, "this won't take long."

"Can I go too?" Becca cried.

"No, Becca," her mother said firmly.

Nathan reined up. "Where do you need to go?" he asked wearily.

"No!" she blurted. Then quickly, trying to recover her nonchalance, she went on. "I'll walk. It's not far." She was drawing more and more quizzical looks from both her mother and Nathan now. "It's, it's"—there was a quick flash of inspiration—"it's a surprise."

"All right," Nathan said. "We'll just wait here for you."

Stop being so helpful, Nathan! She smiled up at him. "No, really. Mama's right. We don't want to be late."

"All right," her mother finally agreed.

"If you haven't caught up to us by the time we've reached the first crossroads," Nathan suggested, "we'll wait for you there."

"Oh, I'll catch you way before then."

Nathan gave her one last look of exasperation, then clucked at the mules. She stood where she was, watching as they pulled away. She gave Matthew a quick wave, then started for Main Street, walking sedately until she turned the corner and moved out of the line of sight of her family. Immediately she changed direction slightly, angling across the street towards McBride's dry goods store, moving very briskly now.

She stepped inside, holding her breath. If only Lydia's father was here again, all of this would be for nothing. She felt a wave of relief as she saw Lydia behind the counter waiting on a woman and a young girl. Lydia looked up, recognized her, and smiled. "Hello, Melissa. I'll be right with you."

Normally a few minutes to herself in a dry goods store was Melissa's idea of time wonderfully spent, but now she could do nothing but stand in place, shifting her weight from one foot to the other, wanting to shout at the lady and her daughter to stop dawdling over their purchase of some needles and four or five spools of thread. She was quickly losing her nerve, and with each minute the wagon was moving further south. She couldn't wait much longer.

But finally the woman took the package Lydia handed her and called out her good-byes. Lydia came immediately over to her. "Melissa, it's so good to see you again." She stepped back, eyeing her dress. "Don't you look pretty?"

"Thank you. How are you?"

"I'm fine." The thick lashes dropped a little and there was suddenly two spots of color high on her cheeks. "How is Nathan?"

Melissa took a quick breath. "Actually that's why I'm here."

"Oh?"

"It's been over a week now, you know."

She looked up. "I beg your pardon."

"I know how you feel, Lydia, but I think Nathan deserves an answer of some kind. Is that too much to expect?"

"An answer?"

Melissa's breath exploded in a little burst of exasperation. "Yes. Even if you refuse to read the book, the least you could do is tell him so."

She was genuinely perplexed. "Melissa, what are you talking about?"

Melissa searched her face, then her hand flew to her mouth. "Your father!" she cried.

"My father?"

"Yes. I gave it to your father. He said you had gone to Canandaigua with your mother."

"Yes, I did, but—I don't understand."

Melissa felt a sharp pang of guilt for her snappishness. She liked Lydia. She liked her a lot, but the thoughts of her spurning Nathan had really cut into her. Now she was instantly contrite. "Nathan sent you a package," she explained, "a gift. He asked me to bring it to you. When you weren't here, I left it with your father. He told me he would give it to you."

Lydia was very still and the color in her cheeks had spread. "A package for me?"

"Yes."

"You said it was a book?"

Fear that she might be messing things up terribly now struck

Melissa with great force. "I . . . I'd better go," she said in a rush. "My family is going to Fayette. I've got to hurry to catch them." She turned.

Lydia caught her arm. "No, wait."

Melissa reached out and put her hand over Lydia's, looking deep into the eyes of this woman, just two years older than she was, who she had so hoped would become her sister-in-law. "Nathan doesn't know I'm here. Please don't tell him." She turned and moved swiftly to the door, leaving Lydia standing where she was. She stopped at the door's entrance, looking back. "He loves you so much, Lydia. It isn't right that your pa wouldn't give it to you."

It took Lydia almost an hour to find it. She made the mistake of assuming her father had simply hidden it from her. Only after she had searched behind every item on the shelves, through both storerooms, and up in her parent's bedroom had she returned to the store, frustrated and angry. Then her eyes fell on the trash barrel. With a week gone by, it was nearly full. Twice she had to break off her search when customers came in. When they saw her going through the pile of garbage, they gave her very strange looks. But she did not answer their quizzical looks, nor did she wait until they were out of the store before she returned to her unpleasant task.

She knew what she was looking for. Melissa's slip of the tongue about a book was the first clue. And Lydia had seen the advertisement the previous week, announcing the publication of the Book of Mormon. It angered her, almost as much as her father's subterfuge. They had gone over and over this issue. If he wasn't willing to change, why couldn't he let it go, leave her alone? All this did was keep the wounds from healing.

The book was at the very bottom of the barrel. Some coffee grounds had settled through the paper and other clutter and stained one corner of the brown leather cover. She rubbed at it with a corner of her skirt, but the damage was permanent. Something about the ugly discoloration on the new cover stirred a different anger in her. Perhaps she too would have taken the book and thrown it into the trash barrel, but that was her choice. Not his.

She opened the inside cover and withdrew the letter. Slowly, she unfolded it and began to read. She read it again, then once more. The last paragraph again caught her eye. "If you would know how I truly feel, read the words of John. . . ."

She walked around behind the counter where her father kept a supply of Bibles for sale. Setting the Book of Mormon and the letter aside, she thumbed through the book, finally locating the Second Epistle of John near the end of the New Testament. She glanced again at the letter. Second John, chapter one, fifth verse. Her finger ran down the page. Suddenly the words in front of her blurred as she read them. She brushed at the tears, then read them again.

Now I beseech thee, lady, not as though I wrote a new commandment unto thee, but that which we had from the beginning, that we love one another.

When the door opened and her parents walked in five minutes later, she was still standing there, Nathan's letter in one hand, her eyes staring at the open Bible, seeing nothing.

"Lydia, we're back—" Her father's words were cut off in midsentence as he saw the pile in the corner.

Her mother had turned to the door to hang up her shawl, but when she turned, she gave a little cry of dismay. "Lydia, my word, what have you been doing?"

"I was looking for the package Nathan sent me," she said evenly.

Her father's eyes darted to the book on the counter and the letter. His Adam's apple bobbed twice as he swallowed quickly.

"Well?" she asked, still keeping her voice level.

He stepped forward, his jaw suddenly thrusting out. "Well, what?" he demanded. "The minute I felt the weight of it and saw who it was from, I knew what it was. And I was right."

"So you threw out *my* package?"

Her mother came forward quickly to stand next to her husband. "We'll not have that evil thing in our house, Lydia," she said, her chin held high. "And we don't appreciate Nathan sending it to us, all wrapped up and hidden so we wouldn't know what it was."

Lydia whirled. "He didn't send it to *us*, Mama! He sent it to *me*." She turned back to her father. "Did you read the letter too, Papa?"

He wouldn't meet her eyes, but his mouth was set in a stubborn line. "When I saw it was the Book of Mormon, I threw it in the trash. Where it belongs."

"I want to know, Papa. Did you read my letter too?"

He still wouldn't meet her eyes, and she had her answer. She shook her head, her face registering the bitterness of her disappointment.

"Give me the book, Lydia. It's going back in the trash."

She folded the letter, slipped it back inside the Book of Mormon and tucked it under her arm.

"Lydia." His voice rose sharply.

She came out from behind the counter and walked past the two of them, not looking at either.

"Lydia! Give me the book. I'll not have you reading it."

"Lydia!" Her mother's voice was shrill.

She reached behind the door and got her own shawl down and slipped it over her shoulders. "I'll be going for a walk, Mama. I don't know if I'll be home before supper."

Jessica Roundy Steed had not cried since her mother died. When she was a little girl her father's drunken rages had terrified her, and when he had slapped her around she had cried pitiably. But she quickly learned that it only infuriated him further. "If you were a boy," he would yell at her, "you wouldn't bawl like a baby every time you get hurt." By the time she was five or six, she had learned it was easier not to cry. She would duck her head and tremble before him, but there would be no tears.

Then, when Jessica was eight her mother had died in a miscarriage, her third since Jessica's birth. Jessica could still remember the hot burning behind her eyes that welled up until she could hold it back no longer. She had thrown herself against her mother's body, which even then was turning cold, and burst into huge, racking sobs. Somehow it had strangely touched her father and he had not ever beaten her again. But it had been the last time the tears had gotten away from her.

Now she felt that same burning, that same feeling of having a wall of water pushing to burst out of its confinement. She squeezed her eyes shut tightly, feeling one tear trickle out of the corner of her eye and start down her cheek. She turned her head quickly away.

Clinton Roundy reached out and laid the back of his hand against her face. "Jess, Jess," he said softly. "It's all right. Everything will be all right."

She turned her head even further, until the pillow touched her face and blotted the tear away. Then she turned back. Outside the window it was dark. "Where's Joshua?"

Her father dropped his eyes. "He'll be back in a bit, Jess."

"Where is he, Pa?"

There was a deep sigh. "At one of the tables. With a bottle of whiskey."

"He's been there this whole time?"

"Yes. Since the doctor left."

She turned away, her mouth tight.

"He'll be back, Jess. It's . . . well, this hit him kinda hard."

Her head jerked around and she looked at him incredulously.

His eyes darted away, unable to meet hers. "He really wanted this baby," he finished lamely.

"This hit *him* kinda hard?" she asked contemptuously.

Clinton Roundy, a hard man used to dealing with hard men, looked away. His face was stricken, his hands fluttered around hers, not sure whether to touch or withdraw. She made no move to lessen his discomfort. Finally he stood up. "The doctor says you need to rest. I'll check on you in a while."

She turned her face to the wall as he stood and bent over to give her a quick, awkward kiss on the cheek. She did not turn back as she heard the door open and shut and his footsteps fade. Then, from deep within her, a cry welled up, a cry of anguish and of anger. *Oh, Joshua! And to what bottle do I go to find my comfort?*

And for the first time in nearly eighteen years, Jessica Roundy cried, the sobs shaking her body as she buried her face in the pillow, no longer trying to hold back the sorrow that tore at her soul.

Peter Whitmer Cabin, Fayette Township

The Peter Whitmer cabin was not much more than an oblong box, twenty feet wide and thirty long. It was basically only one story, though the pitched roof was high enough to provide three bedrooms above the main floor in what was called the "chambers." The main room that served as primary living area as well as kitchen and dining room was dominated by a large stone fireplace which rose all the way to the ceiling, its mass broken only by the heavy oak beam that served as mantel.

One small painting of a winter scene in New England above the fireplace and some oilcloth curtains painted with an intricate floral design were the only concession to aesthetics. Everything else showed that this was a room designed for people and not for fashion. There were two stand-alone cupboards for the dishes and cooking utensils, a large table with leaves that folded down when not needed, eight spindle chairs, and two backless stools. A wooden bench near the west doorway had boots lined up neatly beneath it and pegs above it for coats. A small cupboard hung from the wall was reserved for Mary Whitmer's fine china. A beautifully crafted mahogany trunk, almost a yard tall and a full five feet long, held the family's extra bedding and linens.

A sudden thought struck Mary Ann as she looked around. Was it in a home such as this that the first church was organized? She couldn't remember if the Bible said exactly where Jesus had first begun his church, but it certainly wasn't done in a palace or a castle. It must have been in a fisherman's hut, or a farmer's cottage, maybe even out under a grove of olive trees. Somehow it thrilled her to sense the common bond of simplicity this group shared with those first disciples in Palestine.

She looked around. There were between fifty and sixty present. She let her eyes move from face to face. Like the home, these were not the show people of the world. There were no kings here, no nobility, no aristocracy of social class or wealth. They were workers for the most part—men of the soil, men who made things with their hands, women who toiled alongside their husbands as they took nature as they found her and made a good life from her.

They had come from basically three areas. Near the west window sat the Knights and the Stowells from Colesville and South Bainbridge. Some of Joseph's earliest and most consistent supporters, they had led a group of about twenty on the hundred-mile trek from the southernmost part of the state to Fayette.

The Steeds had come with those from Palmyra and Manchester townships. The Smiths were the largest part of that group—which included Father and Mother Smith, Samuel, Hyrum and his wife, Jerusha, Joseph and Emma, Don Carlos, and William. Martin Harris was also there, sitting comfortably next to Nathan and Melissa. Orrin Porter Rockwell and his mother and sister, neighbors to the Smiths, had also come.

Finally, there was the Fayette group itself. Most conspicuous, of course, were the Whitmers, with father, mother, five sons (two with wives), and their daughter Catherine and her husband, Hiram Page. But there were others as well—the rest of the Pages, the Jolleys, and others—those who had become associated with Joseph since the previous June when the Whitmers had taken Joseph and Emma and Oliver into their home.

They came from diverse backgrounds and places, but all were knit together by their love of God and their conviction that he was working once more among the children of men. No wonder an almost reverential feeling gripped those present, leaving the air charged with great expectancy.

In one corner, Joseph Smith was conferring quietly with Oliver Cowdery. Next to them, on a small sideboard, was a round loaf of bread set on a plate next to a large pewter mug filled with wine. Joseph checked them quickly. Then, satisfied, he straightened and turned around. Almost instantly the room fell quiet. He smiled and moved over to stand in front of the fireplace where he could see the full group better.

"Brothers and sisters, my dear friends. It is time we call this meeting to order. We are met this day to officially organize a new church. According to the laws of the state of New York, we must have from three to nine trustees in order to form a legally recognized religious organization."

Several people were nodding.

"Therefore, I designate myself, Joseph Smith, Junior, and the following men as trustees of the new Church of Jesus Christ—Oliver Cowdery, Hyrum Smith, Peter Whitmer, Junior, Samuel H. Smith, and David Whitmer."

Mary Ann looked at each in turn as Joseph said their names. Young men, each one. At thirty, Hyrum was the eldest. Joseph would not be twenty-five until December. Peter Whitmer, not long past twenty, was the youngest, though Joseph's brother Samuel was only just twenty-two. David and Oliver were nearer to Joseph's age.

Joseph then suggested that all present kneel together in solemn prayer to invoke the Lord's blessings on the procedures.

The quarters were a little crowded, but in a moment all were on their knees. It was a prayer as simple and unpretentious as the place in which they met, a prayer filled with both thanksgiving and supplication. Mary Ann found herself echoing the words in her own heart, making it a personal offering of rejoicing and prayer as well as one for the group.

As the group stood and found their seats again, Joseph cleared his throat. "My brothers and sisters." It seemed as though his eye caught and held everyone present. Mary Ann felt a quick thrill as the solemnity of the occasion settled upon her. "We are met for the express purpose of organizing the Church of Jesus Christ again upon the earth. Oliver Cowdery and I have been called and chosen under the hands of angels to act as presiding elders. Those present who can accept Oliver and me as your teachers and who are in favor of organizing a church, please indicate so now."

Mary Ann raised her hand, glancing around quickly. Every hand was up, every eye riveted on this tall young man with the cheerful demeanor.

"Thank you. I propose, then, that I now ordain Oliver Cowdery as an elder in the Church, and that he do the same for me."

Oliver came forward with his chair and sat down. Joseph laid his hands on his head and ordained him as an elder in the Church, empowered to act in the name of God and perform his ordinances with power and authority. He finished and they changed places, and Oliver performed the same ordination for Joseph. Then together they moved to the small sideboard where the bread and wine were set.

"It is fitting and proper that the sacrament of the Lord's Supper be administered to those present who have already been baptized."

A sharp pang of disappointment shot through Mary Ann. She fully planned to request baptism before this day was over, but as yet she had not done so. Surprised when someone took her hand, she looked up to see Melissa smiling at her. Melissa would not have the privilege of partaking either, but she was smiling, her eyes telling her mother it would be all right.

Joseph picked up two or three sheets of paper as Oliver began to break the bread into small chunks. "In preparation for this day, the Lord has given a revelation." He held the sheets up. "It contains the articles and covenants by which the Church shall be governed. As part of that revelation, the Lord has given us the prayers which are to be used to bless the Lord's Supper."

He stepped back, looking through the sheets for a particular place. Then, as Oliver finished breaking the bread, Joseph knelt before the small sideboard, sliding the papers in front of him. He bowed his head, and all followed suit.

"O God, the Eternal Father," he began, "we ask thee in the name of thy Son, Jesus Christ, to bless and sanctify this bread to the souls of all those who partake of it, that they may eat in remembrance of the body of thy Son, and witness unto thee, O God, the Eternal Father, that they are willing to take upon them the name of thy Son, and always remember him and keep his commandments which he has given them; that they may always have his Spirit to be with them. Amen."

Bless and sanctify. And to the souls of those who partake. Not just the body, but the soul. Mary Ann felt the simple power of those words sink into her heart. *That they may always have his Spirit!* A promise of inestimable worth. The blessing had already been partially realized. Her soul was soaring!

Joseph got up from his knees and stood back as Oliver took the plate and moved slowly through the group. Mary Ann was surprised when she saw she was not in the minority. While several partook, many did not, for they had not yet been baptized. Martin Harris did not partake, which surprised her. She had assumed he had been baptized months before. Joseph's parents also let the plate pass them by. She felt a little burst of envy as she watched Nathan reach out and reverently put the bread in his mouth.

Oliver returned and set the plate on the table, then he

kneeled at the sideboard. Again all the heads in the room bowed. "O God, the Eternal Father," Oliver read, "we ask thee in the name of thy Son, Jesus Christ, to bless and sanctify this wine to the souls of all those who drink of it, that they may do it in remembrance of the blood of thy Son, which was shed for them; that they may witness unto thee, O God, the Eternal Father, that they do always remember him, that they may have his Spirit to be with them. Amen."

As the mug filled with the fruit of the grape passed from person to person and each of those who had been baptized sipped from it, Mary Ann felt the tears well up inside her. They were not tears of sorrow that she could not join in, but tears of joyful anticipation. The next time the sacrament of the Lord's Supper was administered, she would be ready to partake. Of that she was absolutely sure.

When the wine had gone around the room and returned to the table, Joseph stepped over to the fireplace again. "Brothers and sisters, when Peter and John went to Samaria, as is recorded in the Acts of the Apostles, they met with those who had been previously baptized by Philip. It then says Peter and John laid hands on them, and they received the Holy Ghost."

He stopped, letting the import of that sink in for a moment. Then he continued: "Simon, the sorcerer, was so impressed by this remarkable gift, he offered Peter money so he might do the same. Peter rebuked him, for this power cannot be sold. The gift of the Holy Ghost can only be given by those who have been given authority from God to do so."

His mouth softened into a happy smile. "As part of the priesthood power restored to the earth through angelic ministration, Oliver and I can now bestow that gift upon you who have been baptized. We will also confirm you members of the Church of Jesus Christ."

Those wonderfully alive blue eyes swung around until they rested on Mary Ann Morgan Steed and held her as though in a vice. "And those of you who have not as yet been baptized, rest assured that if it be your desire, before this day is through we shall find a place with sufficient water to bring you into the kingdom as well."

It was early evening. The air was cool and the first of the spring mosquitoes were starting to come out and annoy man and beast. The group was gathered at the bank of a small stream, now dammed up enough to make the water nearly waist deep. Some present earlier had returned to their homes or the places where they were staying for the night, but there was still a goodly group who had come to witness the baptisms.

It was simply a capstone on the day's activities, in Mary Ann's mind. The meeting in the cabin had continued almost for another hour. She still felt a sense of wonder at being there, at being a part of it. It had been a time of rich spiritual out-pourings. All those previously baptized had been confirmed. Several of those were filled with the Spirit immediately upon confirmation and rose from the chair praising God and, in some cases, prophesying.

Mary Ann turned and smiled at her son, her heart brim with joy. The moment Joseph and Oliver had completed the ordinance of confirmation for him, Nathan had stood and walked to face his mother. He took her hands, looking deep into her eyes, his own face aflame with joy. "Mother, by the power of the Holy Spirit within me, I testify that what has happened here this day is in accordance with God's mind and will. And I say to you, the Lord is pleased with the purity of your heart. You shall live to become a great woman in the cause of truth and for the restored gospel. Your posterity, which shall be numerous upon the earth, shall rise up and call you blessed."

Then suddenly he had stopped, and tears sprang to his eyes. "And through your example of love and faith and patience, your good husband—our father—shall someday be led to exclaim that Joseph Smith is the Lord's servant and did naught but God's will."

With tears streaming down his face, he then turned to his sister. "And you, dear Melissa, your heart is troubled. Let it be at peace. It is our Father's will that you put aside your doubts and embrace his gospel. You have been reading in the Book of Mormon and you have felt the quiet power of the Spirit. That is the answer for which you seek. Be baptized by those holding authority, so you can also receive this most precious of gifts, given through the grace and power of God."

Even now the memory of his words, and the expression on his face, sent chills running up and down Mary Ann's spine.

"Father, if you would come down in the water."

Joseph's words pulled Mary Ann out of her reverie. He was standing in the midst of the creek. His father and mother stood before him on the bank, determined to be baptized at the hand of their son. Hyrum also stood nearby.

Joseph Smith, Sr., took Hyrum's hand and stepped into the water. There was a quiet intake of breath as the cold water hit his flesh. Born five years before the Declaration of Independence, Father Smith was approaching his sixtieth year. To Mary Ann he seemed suddenly frail and vulnerable, but his face was calm and in repose. Joseph came to him and led him to the deepest portion of the creek. He smiled at him, then raised his right arm and bowed his head. "Joseph Smith, Senior," he said solemnly, "having been commissioned of Jesus Christ, I baptize you in the name of the Father, and of the Son, and of the Holy Ghost. Amen." Then the son put his hand behind the father's back and lowered him gently into the water until he was completely submerged.

As Father Smith came out of the water, Joseph exclaimed, "Praise be to God! I have lived to see my own father baptized into the true Church of Jesus Christ!"

Mother Smith went next. She was barely five feet tall, if that, and the water came nearly to her chest. Emma stood near the water's edge, smiling her encouragement, holding a large towel for when she came out. Joseph baptized her and then swept her up in his arms hugging her tightly. Martin Harris followed Mother Smith, smiling and talking animatedly as he completed the ordinance. Then Orrin Rockwell and his mother and sister were baptized. When they were done, Joseph climbed out of the creek and joined them on the bank.

Mary Ann's face fell. "Joseph, Melissa and I also desire to be baptized."

"Aye?" he said, his eyes teasing. "Is that true, Melissa? Would you indeed choose to be baptized?"

"Yes, Joseph," she said happily. "I have made up my mind."

"Good." He bent over and began to squeeze the water from his trouser legs.

Mary Ann was dismayed. "Well?" she prompted.

Joseph was enjoying himself. He straightened slowly. "Sister Steed, do you not recollect that Nathan Steed, who I believe is your son, was not only confirmed a member of the Church this day but was also given the priesthood of Aaron and was ordained to the office of priest in that priesthood?"

She was puzzled. "Yes."

"And did you know that in the articles and covenants of the Church which I have before mentioned, we learn that a priest has the power to baptize?"

Nathan's head came up sharply.

"Do you mean . . . ?" She stopped, overwhelmed.

"Yes, Sister Steed. I think it fitting that you and Melissa be brought into the kingdom of God by your own flesh and blood."

He turned to Nathan. "You'd best be getting into the water, young man." He clapped him on the shoulders. "The prayer must be properly done, but I'll help you."

It was a little past noon by the time Nathan had unloaded his family and their belongings at the house, unhitched and fed the team, and then walked to his own homestead. He was still fired with the events of the previous day, and even his father's grumpy welcome had not dampened his spirit.

As he came around the barn, he stopped. A slight fluttering

movement at the cabin caught his eye. There was a sheet of paper there, tacked to the front door. Puzzled, he moved across the yard.

As he stepped onto the porch and leaned forward, he felt his heart leap. There was only a single line of writing, but he recognized it instantly. It was Lydia's handwriting! He peered at it more closely. "Book of Ruth, chapter one, verses sixteen and seventeen."

He dropped his valise with a heavy clunk, snatched the paper from the door, and turned and strode quickly to the barn. He went to his shelf and took down the small Bible he kept there, fumbling in his haste. When he finally found the place, he read slowly, the words leaving him a little dazed.

And Ruth said, Intreat me not to leave thee, or to return from following after thee: for whither thou goest, I will go; and where thou lodgest, I will lodge: thy people shall be my people, and thy God my God.

The words suddenly blurred and Nathan felt his eyes burning. Could this really mean . . . ?

Feeling his pulse racing, he turned back to the book.

Where thou diest, will I die, and there will I be buried: the Lord do so to me, and more also, if ought but death part thee and me.

Slowly he read over the passage again, his mind reeling, not daring to hope it meant what it seemed unmistakably to mean.

There was a soft noise behind him and Nathan whirled. Lydia stepped out from one of the livestock stalls. She stood motionless, hands clasped together in front of her, her dark eyes watching him solemnly.

"Lydia?" he cried softly.

"Hello, Nathan."

He took a step toward her and stopped. His eyes registered several things at once. Her dark hair was slightly tousled. There were small pieces of meadow hay on the skirt of her dress. Her eyes were large and filled with a curious mixture of joy and weariness. In her hands she clasped a book.

Nathan stared. It was a small book with a light brown leather cover. He couldn't believe his eyes. It was the Book of Mormon! The book he had sent her. He nearly threw himself across the space toward her, but something in her eyes held him.

He held up the Bible. "Does this—" He stopped, wanting to choose the words very carefully. He still held the sheet of paper from the door. He thrust it out. "You wrote this?"

She nodded.

"Does that mean . . . ?" He shook his head. "Are you saying . . . ?" He couldn't bring himself to say it. There had been so much pain between them previously. If this was some cruel joke, or if he was misinterpreting what was happening, he could not bear it.

Her lips softened and her eyes were suddenly glistening. "Yes, Nathan, that's what I'm saying."

He fell back a step, too stunned to believe his ears. She laughed through her tears. "Does the thought of marriage so terrify you?"

"Marriage?" he echoed.

She took a step forward, her eyes filled with tears, but teasing him. "You're not going to withdraw your offer now, are you?"

He finally came out of his shock. In two great strides he was to her and swept her up in his arms, nearly crushing her. "Lydia, Lydia, Lydia," was all he could say as she laughed and cried with him all at once.

When he set her down finally, he reached out and took her face in his hands. He kissed her gently. "Oh, my darling Lydia, can this truly be happening?" he whispered.

In answer she kissed him back, then threw her arms around his neck and hugged him fiercely. Suddenly he felt her body begin to tremble, then start to shake with sobs. Surprised, he stepped back. As he looked at her, she fought back her tears, fighting for control.

"Lydia, what's the matter?"

She started to shake her head, then her lip started to tremble and she looked away quickly.

"Tell me. What is it?"

"Do you think there would be a place at your parents' home where I could stay until we are married?"

Was that all? He felt such a rush of relief, his knees felt suddenly weak. Then almost immediately he realized what she was saying. His eyebrows shot upward. "Have your parents . . . ?" He let it trail off, already knowing the answer.

She nodded.

"Because of me?" he started, feeling the anger starting to rise.

She sighed. "Can we talk, Nathan?" She walked to the corner where his things were and set the Book of Mormon on the shelf. He noted with surprise that one corner of it had a dark stain. Then he noticed a piece of hay stuck in the back of her hair. There were a few more flecks of it on the back of her dress.

He stepped to her, understanding finally dawning. "You slept here last night?" He gently pulled the hay from her hair and held it around in front of her.

Her head bobbed up and down once.

He turned her around to face him. "How long have you been here?"

"I came yesterday morning."

"Yesterday morning?" he echoed dumbly. "If I had known I would have come home."

"I knew you were gone, but I needed someplace to—"

"Have you had anything to eat since then?"

She shook her head.

Shocked, he took her by the shoulders. "We're going right over to my parents'," he said. "You must be starving."

"Please, Nathan," she said, "first, let's talk." She took his hand. "Bring the Bible. There's something else I want to read to you."

They sat on the porch of the cabin in the hazy sunshine of spring. Lydia leaned against him, holding his hand. She seemed lost in her thoughts, but Nathan was content to wait, still reveling in the joy of having her there beside him. Finally, she straightened and began to speak in a low voice. "When Melissa came and told me about your package, I was very upset."

"Melissa?"

"Oh, that's right. She said you didn't know." She smiled. "Dear Melissa. If she hadn't come . . ." She told him quickly of Melissa's appearance at the store, of her own search for the package, and of the confrontation with her father.

"I was so angry. I was angry with him." She squeezed his hand. "I was angry at you. Why couldn't you leave me alone? All you were doing was raking up the pain all over again."

He started to say something, but she shook her head and went on quickly. "When I left the store, I was in turmoil. I have never felt so betrayed. My parents are not that way."

Some pain deep inside her stopped her, and for a moment she was fighting her emotions again. But then she went on, talking more slowly now. "I went to the cemetery. You know how I love that place. It's so peaceful. And the trees are just starting to come into leaf now. Anyway, I spent all afternoon there. At first I read your letter over and over. It really touched me. Knowing you couldn't bear to stay around Palmyra, either, made me want to cry. Then, that scripture from John. What a lovely way to tell me that you still cared, that you had not given up on us! At that moment, I just wanted to hold you."

"But?" he said, sensing something more coming.

"But your suggestion that I read the Book of Mormon irritated me. All that talk about judging Joseph Smith by his fruits. It was just more words. It was the same old thing. There was Joseph, looming between us again, keeping us apart."

She poked at him, the very memory of the irritation bringing back a little of the frustration all over again. "Sometimes you can be so stubborn."

He just laughed.

She smiled, then sobered again immediately. "I was even tempted to go home and tell Papa to throw the Book of Mormon away again. And yet . . ." She grew thoughtful. "But finally, I opened the book. My father had absolutely forbidden me to read it." She looked at him with a sudden mischievousness. "I'm afraid I started to read it more to spite him than to please you."

"As long as you started," he said happily, putting an arm around her and pulling her in tight against him again.

She laid her head against his shoulder, her eyes half closing as she remembered. "I read for several hours. At first I was filled with resentment. I was looking only for proof that Joseph was a fraud. I'm afraid I didn't get much out of it." She paused, her face turning thoughtful. "Except this—I didn't find it to be the evil thing my father said it was."

Now suddenly her voice choked. Nathan just held her, letting her take it at her own pace. She sniffed, brushing at the tears angrily. "I returned home just after dark. My parents were frantic. I had stormed away and they had no idea where I was. I know now that was part of it. They were upset. I was still upset."

"What happened?"

"My father asked if I had started to read the Book of Mormon. I told him yes. He was furious. He demanded I give it to him so he could burn it with the trash." She shook her head. "It was the wrong thing to say. I was still fuming over his attempts to control my life. I told him I would do what I wanted, and I turned around and stomped off to bed."

Nathan laughed softly. "It's a good thing I'm the only stubborn one around here."

That made her laugh too. "Oh, our poor children."

Nathan sat up straight, staring at her.

"What?" she said, puzzled by the look on his face.

"Our children," he murmured. "Our children. Do you know how many times I've used those words in my mind, and how many times I've thought it would never be." He kissed her cheek quickly. "I'm sorry, go on. You stomped off to bed."

"Yes. Well, I couldn't sleep, of course. I lay there and lay there. But I kept coming back to what you said. You didn't ask me to believe you. You didn't ask me to believe Joseph. You asked me to ask God."

"Yes. Did you read the place I marked for you?"

She nodded. "After lying there for almost an hour, I got up again and lit the lamp. I went to that place and read it again and again. *That's it*, I thought. *This is how I can know once and for all.* And I decided right then that if I didn't get an answer, I was going to leave for Boston immediately. I couldn't bear to be around you any longer."

"And if you did get an answer?"

"I didn't want to think about that yet." Her voice dropped now. "I began to read, this time with a different attitude. I kept asking God to let me know if it was true. I didn't want to be deceived."

Nathan felt his heart soaring. "And you got your answer?" He nearly shouted it.

"I read most of the night," she said, her voice barely a whisper. "By morning, I knew." She was gripping his hand with a sudden fierceness. "I've never felt anything like it. There was nothing blinding or miraculous. I just knew." Her voice caught. "I just knew."

She straightened now, moving away from Nathan, her eyes filled with pain. "I also knew what I had to do. I went down to face my parents first thing yesterday morning. It was terrible. I told them I knew the Book of Mormon was true and that I was going to marry you. I tried to explain to them what had happened. I was even foolish enough to try and get Papa to read the book too."

She shook her head slowly. "I've never seen him in such a rage." Though her face was calm as she spoke, a tear had welled up at the corner of one eye and now spilled over the lid and trickled down her cheek.

"So your father held true to his threat?" he asked softly.

She swallowed quickly, but could only nod.

"Lydia, they'll soften in time. Once we're married, they'll get used to the idea. Things will change. You'll see."

She shook her head quickly, the tears streaming openly down her face now. "My father turned to Mama and forbid her to ever speak of me again. I am no longer a part of the family. It is as though I had died."

She turned and buried herself against his chest. "Oh, Nathan," she sobbed. "I love my parents. How can I live without them?"

"They'll change," he said lamely, trying to comfort her, feeling the emptiness of the words he himself did not believe.

She pulled away from him and turned to where he had set the Bible. "I came here. I knew you were gone, but I wanted to be alone anyway. Then I remembered something a preacher used once as a text for a sermon. I was a young girl then and thought it was a terrible thing to say. But I searched in the Bible until I found it. It was the final answer I needed."

She opened the Bible and turned to the New Testament. When she found the place, her eyes read over it silently. Only then did she look up. "It is the Savior speaking." She took a quick breath, then let it out slowly. Only then did she begin to read aloud.

" 'Think not that I am come to send peace on earth: I came not to send peace, but a sword. For I am come to set a man at variance against his father—' "

Her voice caught, and for a moment she could not continue. But finally, she bit her lip and began again. " 'For I am come to set a man at variance against his father, and the daughter against her mother. . . .' " Her voice was stricken now, barely audible. " 'And a man's foes shall be they of his own household.' "

It was too much for her and she dropped the book in her lap. Gently, Nathan reached across and took it from her. His eyes found the place where she had left off. With his own voice filled with emotion, he finished it for her.

" 'He that loveth father or mother more than me is not worthy of me: and he that loveth son or daughter more than me is not worthy of me. And he that taketh not his cross, and followeth after me, is not worthy of me.' "

He stopped, then with strength and power, he read the next verse. " 'He that findeth his life shall lose it: and he that loseth his life for my sake shall find it.' "

He closed the book and set it aside. For a long time they sat there, silent, lost in their respective thoughts. Then slowly Nathan stood up. He reached down and took Lydia's hands and pulled her up to face him.

He touched her cheek, so filled with love for her that he thought he would burst. "It will be all right, Lydia," he promised. Then he suddenly grinned. It spread across his face rapidly, crinkling his eyes at the corners.

She sniffed back the tears. "What?"

"Do you know what my mother is going to say when we walk in together?"

Lydia laughed then too. "Do you think she'll be pleased?"

"Pleased?" he cried. "You don't know the half of it." Then he laughed right out loud. "And Melissa? She's gonna let out a yell that will be heard from here to Buffalo."

ABOUT THE AUTHOR

Gerald N. Lund received his B.A. and M.S. degrees in sociology from Brigham Young University. He also did extensive graduate work in New Testament studies at Pepperdine University in Los Angeles, California, and studied Hebrew at the University of Judaism in Hollywood, California.

During his thirty-five years in the Church Educational System, the author served as a seminary teacher, an institute teacher and director, a curriculum writer, director of college curriculum, and zone administrator. His Church callings have included those of bishop, stake missionary, and teacher.

Gerald Lund has written nineteen books, including such novels as *Fire of the Covenant*, *The Alliance*, *The Freedom Factor*, *Leverage Point*, *One in Thine Hand*, and *The Kingdom and the Crown, volume 1: Fishers of Men*. He has also written several books on gospel studies, including *The Coming of the Lord* and *Jesus Christ, Key to the Plan of Salvation*. He has twice won the Independent Booksellers "Book of the Year" Award and has received many other honors for his works.

He and his wife, Lynn, are the parents of seven children and live in Alpine, Utah.

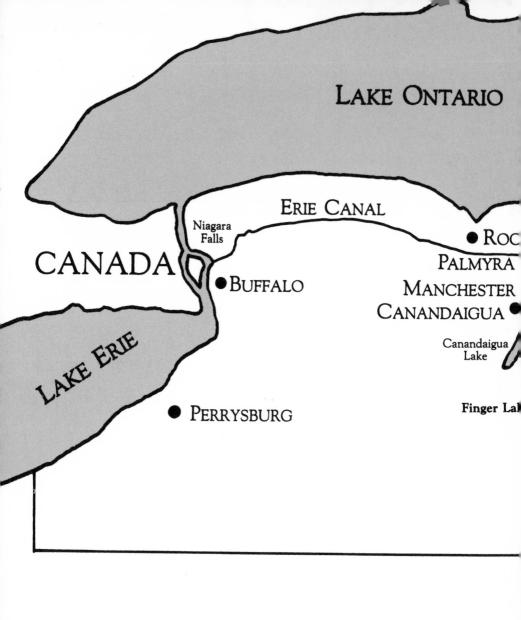

LAKE ONTARIO

CANADA

ERIE CANAL

Niagara
Falls

ROC

PALMYRA

MANCHESTER

CANANDAIGUA

Canandaigua
Lake

Finger Lal

●Buffalo

LAKE ERIE

● PERRYSBURG

PENNSYLVANIA

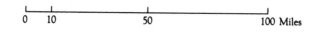

0   10   50   100 Miles